Peter Biddlecombe is a ... much-acclaimed first bo... described his travels throu... been followed by four m... global business trips: *Trav...* *World – On Expenses*; *I Came, I Saw, I Lost My Luggage* and *Very Funny – Now Change Me Back Again*, all of which are available from Abacus Travel.

Also by Peter Biddlecombe

FRENCH LESSONS IN AFRICA

TRAVELS WITH MY BRIEFCASE

AROUND THE WORLD — ON EXPENSES

I CAME, I SAW, I LOST MY LUGGAGE

Very Funny –
Now Change Me
Back Again

PETER BIDDLECOMBE

An *Abacus* Book

First published in Great Britain in 1997
by Little, Brown and Company
This edition published by Abacus in 1998

Copyright © 1997 by Peter Biddlecombe

A CIP catalogue record for this book
is available from the British Library.

ISBN: 0 349 10969 9

Typeset by Solidus (Bristol) Limited
Printed and bound in Great Britain
by Clays Ltd, St Ives plc

Abacus
A Division of
Little, Brown and Company (UK)
Brettenham House
Lancaster Place
London WC2E 7EN

Contents

Very Funny –
Now Change Me Back Again

Introduction

Round about the cauldron go
In the poison'd entrails throw
BA snack and sausage roll
Saudi juice and leather sole
Rubber duck and airline fag
Beaujolais and vomit bag
Double, double, toil and trouble
Fire burn and . . .

Heaven help me, witchcraft, black magic, voodoo, ju-ju, call it what you will, are more common than thought in the travel business. Not, of course, that there is much thought in the travel business.

I mean, how come, in the time it takes to say 'Your flight has been delayed. There will be no further announcements until next Thursday afternoon,' these witchdoctors and voodoo men and women can either – zap – make you disappear into thin air or – zap – change you into something completely different?

I go to check in. I'm my usual self: relaxed, smooth, charming, impeccably groomed. The very model of a boring run-down, middle-aged businessman with a wife, a house, a car, six cats and the whole catastrophe, desperately trying to conceal the fact that he is just dying for another three-week export tour of all the luxury up-market bars, restaurants and fun-spots of the world.

What happens? Within three seconds some secret, black and midnight hag has turned me into a screaming lunatic.

1

'What d'ya mean the flight's closed? I've got a valid ticket, haven't I?'

'Yes, sir.'

'For this flight?'

'Yes, sir.'

'It's confirmed, isn't it?'

'Yes, sir.'

'I'm here on time, aren't I?'

'Yes, sir.'

'So why the hell are you telling me . . .'

'Because you . . .'

'. . . I can't . . .'

'. . . haven't got a seat assignment.'

'. . . get – since when do I need a seat assignment? I've got a valid ticket, haven't I? It's for this flight, isn't it? I'm here . . .'

You know the story, probably better than I do. They deliberately overbook the flights. They check everybody in. Then they hope to hell they can bribe some poor innocent schmuck with a promise of a milkshake with the airline manager's granny to give up his seat. Which is plane crazy. Except this time there were no schmucks. Nobody even wanted a night out with the airline manager's wife. So who got bounced? You got it.

Then there's security. How many times have you been taken apart by security men?

My last time was at Heathrow. I check in, and what's more I actually get on the flight I *am* booked on, seat assignment or no seat assignment. I'm about to head for the departure lounge when—

'Hey.'

I turn round to the woman who checked me in. A choppy finger is lying upon her skinny lip. 'You can't leave it there. Take it to security.'

'I beg your—'

'There.' Her choppy finger is now waving to somewhere vaguely in the distance. 'There. Take it there.'

'But I've just checked it in. I can't—'

'You've got to take it there. Yourself. You've got to check it in again. For security.'

'But how can it be security when—'

'Next.' She now waves her choppy finger at the guy behind me and that's me – zap – gone, disappeared, wiped off the face of the earth. For ever. As if I had never existed.

I drag my suitcase off the conveyor belt and head down the length of the terminal to the edge of this riot which is threatening to engulf some cardboard shack. Inside, three tired old men are laboriously, with a stub of a pencil, writing down on a single piece of dirty screwed-up paper the name of each passenger, a description of their suitcase, their destination and the flight number. This done, each suitcase has to chug its way through the x-ray machine. Once out the other end exactly the same details have to be recorded again. With another stub of a pencil. On another sheet of dirty screwed-up paper.

That done, I go to grab my suitcase and drag it all the way back to—

'Hey! You can't do that,' one of the security men barks at me. 'You got to leave it with us. Here. Security. You understand?'.

I tell you, if he hadn't already got a bone up his nose, I'd have given him one there and then.

My suitcase was now thrown on top of a million other suitcases destined for all points west of Hatton Cross, piled in a great heap in the middle of the terminal where anybody but anybody could pick it up and hobble away with it. Or worse still, stick something inside it attached to a clock.

By the end of all this, I can assure you I had turned quite ugly. But as if that was not enough, then came the body check.

I cannot for the life of me understand the other reason for going through a body check. The x-ray machine is invariably out of action. The archway can't tell the difference between two pounds of Semtex and a digestive biscuit. And they never ever check any books or files or newspapers you're carrying.

You mean you haven't noticed? Whenever I go through the arch I pile my papers on the rickety old table alongside it. I go through the arch. I then turn and pick up my papers. I could have God knows what hidden inside them. But nobody ever bothers to check.

The other thing that turns me into a shivering wreck is the way, wherever you are in the world, little old ladies are allowed to trundle through security arches with a string of trolleys piled high with enormous trunks and suitcases. I mean, anything could be inside them. Empty tubes for Saddam Hussein. Another nerve-gas plant for Colonel Gaddafi. A couple of tons of plutonium from the back door of the Sverdlovsk 44 Research Centre in the Urals. It terrifies the life out of me just to think about it.

You think I'm exaggerating? Let me tell you, once in the depths of Peru I met a little old lady from Birmingham. She told me that she was so scared of being mugged that twice a year she went to South Africa to buy a stack of CS gas canisters; twice a year when she flew back she told the airline she was carrying CS gas canisters, and twice a year they told her not to worry, she could take them in the cabin as hand luggage.

Now don't tell me that's not as dangerous as hell; why else would it be completely contrary to every air safety regulation you can think of?

Once – I know I was wrong, I should have kept my mouth shut – I actually said to a security guard who was pummelling his great fists in and out of my briefcase, smashing everything to smithereens and scattering my files and papers all over the airport floor, 'What about that little old lady? She could have anything inside that—'

My God, was that the last thing to say to a security guard or was that the last thing to say to a security guard! He went even more ape than he was already. He took me apart. I went black. I went blue. I went every colour of the rainbow.

But in spite of that, not to mention the cost of a new briefcase, I still maintain I'm right. Just because they're little old ladies, it doesn't mean they're really little old ladies. And anything *could* be inside those trunks and suitcases. Come to think of it, anything could be inside the trolley as well. I mean, if you've discovered a guaranteed way of getting through airport security, what's to stop you from building your own trolley with secret compartments? And another thing; how come little old ladies don't have to check in their luggage like I have to? Not, of course, that I'm ever going to mention this to anyone anywhere in the world. You understand, don't you?

The other thing that turns me into a raving lunatic is the length of time you have to queue up at emigration and immigration. Nigeria, Burkina Faso, Havana – they're all the pits. But the absolute pits has to be the States. Only once have I been to the States and got through immigration in less than 42 minutes. It's a nonsense; the greatest power on earth, the land with more computers and computer power than any other in the history of the world, and I have to wait 41 minutes 57 seconds to get some guy to ask me a few stupid questions to which he already knows the answers and stamp a stamp on my passport. It's crazy.

Once, flying into Atlanta, we were greeted by a bunch of weirdo sisters on immigration all, as they say, so withered and so wild in their attire that they looked not like th' inhabitants o' the earth. They took a million years to process just one passport. By the time I got there I was a quivering wreck.

'Yes, sir, you here for business or for pleasure?' this way-out sister drawled at me.

'Does anyone ever come here for pleasure?' I drawled back.

Boy, did she and the sisterhood go bananas. That trip I think I spent more time in some interview room buried in the depths of Atlanta airport, trying to explain the difference between business and pleasure, than I did doing my rounds.

Funnily enough, the only place I've never had problems with witches and witchdoctors and black magic is in Haiti, the land of voodoo. In fact, I'd go so far as to say there are fewer witches and witchdoctors and less voodoo in the whole of Haiti than there are at Heathrow. Terminal 2. Ground floor.

Not that you don't come across them in Haiti. On my first trip, I was way up in the mountains looking for somebody who could do me a nice line in little wax models of check-in hags, security bonzos and customs and immigration officers. Not to mention fat ladies, kids and Frenchwomen who insist on taking their little poodles in their own little doggy bags on planes with them. I was in this tiny shack in the middle of less than nowhere. Four men suddenly burst in. They had shorts and bits of cloth tied around them. They had bands around their heads. And they were smeared in feathers and what looked like blood. They said they had just had a night out together.

'Rotary?' I wondered. 'Ladies' night, maybe?'

But it was nothing as exciting as that. Instead, they told me, they'd been out killing werewolves.

'Werewolves? You have werewolves in Haiti?'

They nodded. 'If we don't kill werewolves, werewolves kill us. They enter our bodies. They take over our hearts. We become like werewolves,' the leader of the pack explained.

He took out what looked like a dirty beer bottle with a cork in it. It was called, he said, Grr, Grr, GRR. He pulled the cork out. 'Here,' he said, thrusting the bottle at me, 'drink this. This stop you becoming werewolf.'

What could I do? I took the slightest sip. But even that was too much. My eyes spun round. My head roared with thunder. My stomach churned. I felt as sick as a dog. The nearest thing I can compare it to is the effect you get after taking that first sip of Beaujolais Nouveau in an off year. What am I saying, in an off year; in *any* year.

'Now,' he said, 'You will not become werewolf.'

Peter Grr, Grr, Biddlecombe, on his hands and knees, Grr, Grr, in a wooden shack, Grr, Grr, somewhere high in the mountains above Kenscoff, Haiti.

Port-au-Prince

To me, Haiti is more Greeneland than anywhere else in the world. And I'm not trying to be a comedian – if anything, the opposite. Because somehow or other his 'shabby land of terror', his 'evil slum floating a few miles from Florida' seems to have taken the Greene mantle unto itself far more than, say, Mexico or Havana or Sierra Leone or even, I suppose, Brighton. Well, maybe not Brighton. Judging by how it's changed over the last few years, no self-respecting Kolley Kibber would dream of going there nowadays and flashing around copies of the *Daily Messenger* without a string of bodyguards. They would strip him of all his ten-bob notes before he turned the first corner.

Mention in passing that you happen to be going to Haiti, and immediately everybody goes on about the book, Burton, Taylor, the film, and you did know, didn't you, it wasn't filmed in Haiti? It was filmed in the South of France and Dahomey, West Africa (which is now called Benin). Because of the political situation in Haiti at the time. And in any case, Dahomey was much cheaper. Besides, the people in Haiti originally came from there. Blah blah blah.

I wouldn't call *The Comedians* Greene's best, mind you. Don't get me wrong – I'm not saying it's Jeffrey Archer. Jeffrey Archer books are in a class entirely of their own. But let's be honest, *The Comedians* is all a bit Greene, isn't it? A bit like a grown-up's *Three Men in a Boat*: Brown, some kind of Catholic hotelkeeper drop-out; Smith, your typical innocent American abroad, and Jones, your regular pretend-military con man. An island. Secret police. Dead bodies in – surprise, surprise – the bottom of swimming pools. A kindly upper-class doctor who is really a closet communist. The usual comings and goings, although with Brown, it strikes me, it's more coming than going. In fact I reckon if he had spent less time coming and more time going around his hotel and drumming up business he wouldn't have ended up in Santo Domingo trying to get a job as a canteen manager on, of all things, a banana plantation. Which always struck me as having some kind of special Greene significance. But I'm probably wrong.

It's hardly the real world, is it? How many men do you know who will hang around statues all night waiting to pick up some Venezuelan mother with a handicapped kid, or who are looking for any chance to dress up as a woman? And as for the American, how many of them do you know who are such total innocents, who have no idea what's going on around them, who think they can solve any problem by throwing money at . . . Oh, I don't know; maybe it's not so far off after all.

Anyway, as soon as you step off the plane in Port-au-Prince – or Pee-Pee as it is known locally, a fact which our Graham conveniently forgot to mention – like it or not you're in Greeneland. It's still shabby. It's still evil. It's still a complete slum. And you're still surrounded by strange men in dark glasses who make a note of your every movement, your every contact. Except they're no longer Ton-Ton Macoute. They're consultants with the World Bank who are blowing over US$17 million dollars on, of all things, a tourist development study, when what's obvious to anyone who does not spend their life travelling the world first-class and barricading themselves inside luxury hotels is that what the place needs is decent food, decent housing and a decent chance of not being found dead in an open sewer the following morning.

But that's probably too simple for them. In any case I'm forgetting. The World Bank was created, like the Royal Opera House, Covent Garden, to transfer money from poor people to rich people and not the other way round.

To me, Haiti is not a country. It's a crazy cocktail of

grotesque, unbelievable violence, unrelenting poverty and wild, irreligious fanaticism. I mean, can you believe it, they actually worship Shirley Temple as the goddess of fertility.

But simply calling it 'a shabby land of terror', as Greene did, is only half the story; Haiti started off with lots of pluses. The first independent black nation of all times, it was born out of a slave revolt against Napoleon Bonaparte led by, among others, the gloriously named Toussaint L'Ouverture. It had a model constitution, which they almost immediately threw out of the *fenêtre*. Freedom from want; freedom from fear; freedom of speech – out they all went. In came the heavy guys. In came misery, poverty, corruption, exploitation, the whole catastrophe. And as if that was not enough, in came the Americans interfering in their affairs and firing embargoes at them from all directions. Thomas Jefferson, who was president at the time, was apparently scared as hell that enormous, dominant, rich, militaristic Haiti was going to invade the tiny, insignificant United States, rampage through the country, free all the slaves and make off home with them.

Haiti, as a result, was isolated. The super-rich tried to maintain their links with Paris; the occasional son was sent off to the Sorbonne to learn about wine, women, food and how to milk state enterprises and banks without getting caught. The rest stayed at home, tried to survive as best they could and got in some practice with pins and little wax dolls.

Then came 1915, when that great democracy and respecter of human rights and national sovereignty, that international scourge of colonial brutality and racist degradation, sent the Marines storming into little old Haiti shooting at anything that blinked. The reason: National City Bank in New York was scared a loan was not going to be repaid. Not that it had not been repaid. It was not even up for payment. They were just scared it was not going to be paid. What's more the Marines the US sent in were all from the deep South, because the State Department believed they knew how to deal with 'darkies'. And deal with them they did in their time-honoured fashion. Charlemagne Peralté, who put together a tiny band of guerrillas to fight the illegal invasion and the gross infringement of their national sovereignty, was crucified on a door for his troubles.

After the Marines left, the US flooded the island with CIA agents, FBI spies and your ordinary, average, typical all-American businessmen from the deep South who could just about tell the difference between an inventory and a long white cloak with a big pointed hood on top. To make matters worse the Americans did their usual double and triple somersaults to explain away what they had done. The result: another of their good-neighbour policies. They went storming in, they said, wounding and killing people and destroying everything in their way, because they wanted to help the poor Haitians.

The Haitians did, however, eventually manage to pull one over the Americans. Following the Japanese attack on Pearl Harbor, they immediately declared war on Germany. The Americans didn't. The Americans, in spite of what they had suffered, dithered. It was only when Haiti announced their decision that the States followed the lead set by the country they had invaded in order to help them and teach them how to behave.

Then, of course, came the guys who stamped their person-alities and left their imprint on the country for ever: Papa Doc, Baby Doc and Graham Greene. Haitians haven't looked back since. Except to check they're not being followed by a guy in a smart suit with a pair of shades and a machete.

And of the three, the one whose imprint will last forever is without doubt Graham Greene. What famous landmarks they have, were created by him.

Take the huge stone statue of Christopher Columbus, behind whose back Brown and Martha kept leaping in and out of each other's cars. For years it stood on the edge of the water by the port, staring intently at the complete mess he went on to discover in 1492. But in an uncontrollable rage, I was told, the French-speaking Haitian people rose up as one and in 1992, the 500th anniversary of the biggest mistake he ever made, toppled it into the sea. Some people said it was because if Spanish-speaking Spain was giving Spanish-speaking Santo Domingo, next door, all the glory as the great man's first landing place in the Caribbean, what was the point of having the damn thing there? Whether it was yet another project sponsored by the Institut Français d'Haiti, I couldn't find out. The officials who were present at the time had been long ago promoted to New Zealand or somewhere in the South Pacific where they could exercise their cultural talents on a wider stage. Others say it was just another dreadful mistake. The Haitians got confused. They thought Columbus was the first American (or MRE, Most Repugnant Elite, as they are known locally) and decided to show their appreciation for everything they had done for them over the years.

My theory is that Columbus was so fed up with Brown going on about whether Martha was sleeping with Jones or not that he threw himself in the water rather than face any more of it. And who could blame him? I mean, if Brown was *married* to Martha you might understand it. But this was, let's be honest, just another late-night casino pick-up. Whether she was sleeping with Jones, her damned dog, or Papa Doc himself had nothing whatever to do with Brown. What is far more interesting is how good old Martha, in all the comings and goings, didn't damage her back. Obviously something else Greene knows about better than me.

As for the Peugeot, it's still there. At least I'm sure the rusty pile of junk heaped up by the roadside was at one time some kind of car.

In the little public park nearby, Greene said, there was a musical fountain which had stood for years, 'black, waterless, unplaying', as well as electric globes which winked out their nocturnal Bourbon pronouncement, 'Je suit le drapeau Haitien, uni et indivisible. François Duvalier.' Well, not only is the 'black, waterless, unplaying' fountain not there, neither are his electric globes. As for the little park itself, if he meant a dirty patch of dust covered in what could be the remains of a musical fountain not to mention a couple of million smashed electric globes, then that could still be there. In fact, instead of leaping in and out of each other's cars, why didn't they use a little bit of common – or rather the park – instead? It would have saved the seat covers, if not all those scratches on Martha's legs. But maybe, again, Greene knew more about these things than I do.

Neither Brown nor Martha probably ever noticed, but the new buildings near the port, he said, had been built for an international exhibition in 'so-called modern style'. All I can say is, if two breeze-blocks buried under a pile of rubbish overflowing with raw sewage is the 'so-called modern style' then give me old-fashioned Gothic any day. In fact it's difficult to imagine how the whole area . . . what am I talking about, the whole area? It's difficult to imagine how the whole town could be worse than it is. There are no real streets. What streets there are are full of pot-holes, abandoned cars and overturned trucks. Greene said he once saw a breakdown van with its crane lying sideways in a ditch, like a lifeboat broken on the rocks. Believe me, it's still there.

There are no real houses either, just shacks and corrugated iron and bits of cardboard boxes. The old French colonial buildings with their fancy latticework and iron railings are long since gone. Some say it was because the government or the army or the police or whoever needed the bricks to use as ballast in coffins. But I wouldn't know.

There are hardly any shops and even fewer offices, which is probably not surprising bearing in mind that out of 60,000 telephone lines in the country about six are working. And they're always engaged.

The Rex Theatre on the Champ de Mars is, however, still there. But it's now a broken-down, filthy-looking cinema showing all the latest films. When I was there, it was *The Ten Commandments*, which I must admit surprised me. I'd have thought that anywhere that had anything to do with Graham Greene would have dropped the Sixth and be running with just nine of them.

The café next door is gone. If Greene meant the one on the left, it's now the Big Star Market. If he meant the one on the right, it's now un Market et Boucherie, although there is a café alongside that. The park has disappeared into a pile of gravel, a lump of dirt and my God, what's that smell? Outside, all along the wall, are piles of even filthier French paperbacks with titles which strain not just your vocabulary but your imagination. Or at least they did mine. Well all right then, with one exception. For some reason they were also selling old copies of *Popular Mechanics*; maybe the French think such a title fits in with the other books they were selling. One book I did pick up was an old Haitian schoolbook. It began, 'Nos ancêtres, les gaulois, avaient lex yeux bleus et les cheveux blonds.' Our ancestors, the Gauls, had blue eyes and blond hair.

Something Greene didn't mention is all over the place: rubbish. Vast, smouldering, rotting, rat-infested mountains of the stuff. Except, surprisingly enough, in front of the gleaming white presidential palace which, in the days of Papa Doc, people used to think was full of Ton-Ton Macoutes, the bogeymen or stealers of men's souls, in their jeans, T-shirts, shades, gold chains and clubs or guns. Today they're all gone. Officially, that is. Unofficially they're still all over the place, except now they're all taxi drivers. Just like in Eastern Europe, where all the old KGB guys, or at least all the poor old KGB guys who couldn't get their hands on the secret bank accounts, are now taxi drivers. Today Haiti is full of a different kind of zombie: representatives of, once again, the World Bank, the International Monetary Fund and every other aid organisation trotting out the usual arguments for privatisation. Today, of course, because it is so white and so pure it wouldn't rate a mention in any Graham Greene book.

Behind the palace, the army headquarters are covered in rubbish. Opposite that, the old army hospital looks like a pile of rubbish. It's the same story wherever you go: along the side of roads, piled up against shacks and buildings. Along by the port I actually saw a family huddled together on one enormous heap under a filthy sheet, held down by bits of string tied to four car tyres.

You think that's bad. It's a million times worse. There's no sanitation. What open sewers there are seized up years ago. Not that it makes any difference to the enormous black pigs wallowing in the stuff. There are trickles and streams and great floods of, well, stuff flowing all over the place. Although I must admit I didn't see any dead bodies. Which I suppose is some kind of progress.

The whole place, as a result, is riddled with disease. Not just malaria, which seems to throw off a kind of yellow glow in this part of the world, but also diseases that have been virtually eradicated elsewhere, such as yaws, which is a bit like leprosy – once you get it, you just rot away – and kwashiorkor, a severe form of protein deficiency. Infant mortality rates are almost the world's highest, at 100 babies dying for every 1,000 born. In fact they are so riddled with disease and so poor and so desperate they practically fall off the bottom of any set of health statistics you care to name.

How they survive, God only knows. On rice, on beans, on whatever fruit they can get; maybe on high days and holidays some scraps of chicken. Like the head or the feet.

Two-thirds of the population are officially listed as unemployed. Can you imagine that? Two-thirds. Which means 99.9 per cent of the population are unemployed. I mean, how can a country which has nothing produce accurate unemployment statistics? It also means they are not just temporarily unemployed. They are wholly and for ever unemployed. The rest work for the government.

Three consequences: first, you hardly ever see beggars. When everybody is as badly off as you, what's the point of begging? Second, at night the place is as empty and silent as a cemetery. Some people say if the wind is in the right or rather the wrong direction the non-stop reggae music from Jamaica almost drowns out not only the noise of children crying with hunger but also the dying gasps of the middle-aged. Middle-aged, because few people live to be old in Haiti. In the old days, of course, the screams from the presidential palace and the army barracks drowned out the noise of the children crying with hunger and the dying gasps of the less than middle-aged. So I suppose progress has not entirely passed Haiti by.

Third, the place is as corrupt and as violent as hell. Or Lagos. Whichever is the worse. Lying, swindling, cheating – the Haitians have turned them into art forms. Partly because there is no way anyone can exist without lying and swindling and cheating; partly because they've been doing it for so long it's in whatever blood they have left in their veins. All praise to President Préval, therefore, for being the first politician in Haiti's history to come out into the open and admit he needs the dough. The fact that he is also a local baker might, of course, have something to do with it.

As for the 'fear and frustration' that Greene goes on about, it's still there, in bucketfuls. Murder; torture; rape; castration; looting; extortion; house burning; dog burning. Yes, dog burning. They think nothing of setting light to a dog and standing around watching it burn slowly to death. Alternatively, they'll suddenly for no reason race through the middle of town, smashing what few shop windows are left, setting fire to what few buildings are left, burning tyres, kidnapping anyone and anything that moves and burying their machetes in anything they like: trees, hotel lobbies, people's backs.

In Cité Soleil alone, a collection of shacks on the edge of the town, there are supposed to be a dozen different gangs: Base Bo Rigol, Base Bo Ray, Base Soleil 17, Base Little Haiti, Base Drouillard, Base Manyak, Base Explosion, Base Soleil 4, Base Big Up, and so on, all far more heavily armed, far more efficient and far more ruthless than the Ton-Tons. The only difference is they've ditched their sunglasses. Way back in September 1988, for example, a gang of heavily armed thugs burst into St John Bosco church, near the port, where Jean-Bertrand Aristide, the old president who was once a priest, and René Préval, the current president, were hiding, and tried to kill them. But they escaped through the side door. You can still see the results of their handiwork, which is not, I admit, as impressive as Canterbury Cathedral, but is in its own way equally interesting.

From my own point of view, however, I will admit that at no time during my trip, *pace* Graham Greene, did the police burst in upon me at four o'clock in the morning. Nor did they smash everything I had to pieces, point guns at me or hit me in the mouth. Nor, I have to admit, did I hear one single shot from the cemetery, let alone hear about a single execution. I also admit I didn't see any hotel owners driving around town in the middle of the night with a dead body propped up in the back seat of their car. It makes you wonder what on earth the place is coming to.

The week before I got there, however, the whole place was shot up in the middle of the night. Houses were broken into, shacks were levelled to the ground. At least eleven people were shot at point-blank range.

'But how could such a thing happen?' I asked some guy I met wandering around what was left of the Church of St John Bosco. 'Didn't anybody call the police?'

'They were the police,' I was firmly told.

Apparently one of the thousands of local gangs had killed a police officer, and in spite of all their intensive training, his colleagues just went on the rampage. I didn't dare ask which police force had been training them. I mean, for all we know they might not have been on the rampage. They might simply have been reacting the way they had been trained to: first, get the video cameras; then, go in and do your duty.

But don't despair. In spite of all this there are still some people who believe in law and order: the poor, distressed widows of Haiti. They not only sue for the illegal commissions owed to their dead husbands but win their cases again and again and again. Commissions, even on corrupt business deals, are a legitimate source of income, the judges have ruled, and must be paid whether the guy is alive or dead. Why they should have decided that I cannot imagine.

Even commission on illegal deals is an improvement on some of the sources of income they used to believe in. Like throwing their children under the wheels of a car to get the insurance or compensation, or both.

16

'So what did you do?' I asked an old French ex-pat who's been in Haiti for years. 'Get a local driver?'

'No way,' he said. 'You couldn't trust them.'

'So what *did* you do?'

'I used to back up and run over them again. It was cheaper to pay for a funeral than pay the compensation.'

The only thing that's real in this totally unreal world is the all-consuming, overwhelming, stomach-churning, practically over-powering stench. Two hours wandering around the back streets of St Martin, or around the back of the cathedral, or even, if you dare, Cité Soleil, and you feel like showering for a month non-stop. Except, of course, you can't. The 'erratic' electricity plant which Greene said was run by Luigi, the Italian engineer who spent all his time hanging around the casinos, is as erratic as ever, so there's no way the pumps are working. I'd no sooner checked in to my hotel for instance, way up in Pétionville, than I was warned the lights were about to go out 'between 24 to 40 hours'. Which turned out to mean between midnight and four in the morning. So maybe Luigi is getting a touch more reliable in his old age, or maybe he ran out of money and doesn't spend as much time in the casinos.

The only good thing about Port-au-Prince is that drinking water is practically unheard of. Which means that in order to survive one has to drink rum or whisky or even Pernod. Eating, however, is out of the question. The UN is in town. Which means you can't get near any halfway decent restaurant or hotel for all their fancy white four-wheel-drive vehicles blocking the way. There are so many of them parked all over the place, I swear UN stands for Unlimited Nourishment. The El Rancho Hotel where Brown's mother, Madame la Comtesse of wherever she said, held court in a shameless bed with a gilt curlicued footboard built for one purpose only, is probably their number one favourite.

Greene ridiculed it as a 'luxurious Americanised hotel' with bedraggled palm trees, bougainvillea which needed cutting back and a gravel driveway overgrown with grass. No longer. It is now an immaculate, beautifully decorated, beautifully whitewashed truly luxurious international hotel with long, sweeping driveways, manicured lawns and perfectly clipped hedges. Just the place for international peacekeepers and civil servants.

The complete opposite, a scruffy, dusty old hotel badly in need of repair with an overgrown garden, a rough old swimming pool, uneven steps, creaky wooden floors, doors that don't close properly and no air-conditioning is, however, the best place of all.

To Greene, it was the Trianon Hotel, with its towers and balconies and wooden fretwork decorations which were neither classical in the eighteenth-century manner nor luxurious in the twentieth-century fashion, nestling at the end of a steep driveway lined with palm trees and bougainvillea. To everybody else, it's the Oluffson, which is exactly the same today as it was then. Except I couldn't see any bodies in the pool. In fact, I couldn't see anything in the pool. Which is one of the reasons, I was told, why it is being replaced. The steep drive is still there lined with palm trees and bougainvillea. My first view of them, however, was in reverse. The place is so overgrown we had to reverse in, otherwise, I was told, we stood no chance of getting out again. The towers and balconies and wooden fretwork are still there. The John Barrymore suite from where you could see all over Port-au-Prince, the harbour, the palace, the cathedral, is still there.

I climbed the broken steps that looked as though they had been designed by Miss Havisham. On the balcony, where people came at lunchtime to have over-cooked steaks and ice cream, and at night to dip into soufflés and watch the grotesque Baron Samedi in his top hat doing his voodoo bit under the lighted palms, the odd couple were politely sipping coffee.

I looked back to the 'bathing-pool' as Greene called it. I could hardly see it, let alone a pretty girl making love to anyone. And, as I say, no dead body.

Inside, the Oluffson is one of the world's great originals. Everywhere there are broken white wicker chairs, extravagant paintings, loose electric wires and a glorious feeling of seediness and decay. In other words, a hotel of character.

There on the left was the long open bar where poor old Joseph, who not only had a limp but was chaste as well, as a result of being kicked around by the Ton-Ton Macoute, concentrated on making his world-famous rum punches. Today a young girl was making gallons of fruit juice out of the weirdest looking fruits using the strangest looking mixer which, whenever she turned it on, made the lights flash.

Instead of being run by a failed Catholic has-been like Brown, the hotel is now run by the Woody Allen of the hotel business, a young Haitian-American drop-out who went to college in the United States, writes songs for Bruce Springsteen, sells his own CDs and every Thursday night turns the place into the biggest jam session in town.

But I wanted to talk about Graham Greene.

Petit Pierre, the tiny, hilarious journalist with the pointed toecaps and the sharp, ambiguous features who used to 'swing from wall to wall on ropes of laughter', still drops by every day for a drink, except Sundays when he plays cards with friends. In real life he's Aubelin Jolicoeur, a tiny, dapper man with a gold-topped walking stick. Graham Greene calls him gay. Which is definitely not my impression. A friend of Papa Doc, a friend of Baby Doc and a friend of practically everyone who's been anyone on the island for over fifty years, he's lively and gossipy and obviously a great charmer. But gay, never. How come he has managed to survive so long in spite of having friends like the Duvaliers? Not to mention Graham Greene.

'I was born in a cemetery,' he always says. 'I began my life where everybody else ends theirs.'

How about Jackson, the military wannabe? He is based on an arms dealer who used to stay regularly at the hotel. Joseph was Cesar, the old barman at the hotel. The limp? Greene made that up. The flaky guy I saw in the bar one evening disporting himself in a tight pair of shorts was, I swear, the question mark on page 82.

Mère Catherine's compound where, Greene said, the girls

behaved with such decorum you'd have thought they were at some end-of-term celebration at a convent school, until they hit the stalls, was supposed to be, depending on whom you talk to, either Le Lambi, where they apparently were famous for stuffing their animals and sticking them on the wall; the Flamingo down by the port which was run by a Madame Georgette, or the third door on the right past the Norwegian seamen's mission. The green one, of course.

Most people I spoke to seemed to go for the Flamingo, which has now been flattened to make way for another rubbish dump. As for Madame Georgette, the story went that she had emigrated to Canada, where she became a pillar of the local community, waging war on everything she had previously fought to uphold. If you favour the green door option, I was told the best thing on the menu is what they call a black-and-white sandwich; far more satisfying, they assured me, than a *croque monsieur*, and unlike anything you'll get at home.

As for the casino, where only one roulette table 'functioned' – an odd word, I always thought, for Greene the master stylist to use – and where they tried to economise on the lighting by drinking whisky, played in a 'cavernous obscurity' and put all their tokens on the first column and kept winning, everybody seemed to think it was the Royal Haitian. When I tried to take a look at it I got stuck in this enormous traffic jam that stretched virtually all the way back to the US Aid compound, which, I swear, is bigger than the presidence itself. So I gave up and went for another drink at the Oluffson instead.

Something else I couldn't find was Doctor Magiot's three-storey house in Pétionville even though, Greene said, it had a dry, spiky Norfolk pine in the garden, heavy scarlet curtains, woollen tablecloths with bobbles at each corner and china objects all over the mantelpiece. My bet is it's been turned into some fancy restaurant and seized by the UN in order to maintain the peace.

But I did explore Pétionville, which is up in the hills overlooking Port-au-Prince and full of expensive restaurants and luxury hotels, the kind of area any doctor would expect to live in nowadays.

Oh yes, that reminds me: the body in the swimming pool, which started the whole thing off. That was Antoine Hérard, the old mayor of Port-au-Prince. He apparently used to go around introducing himself: 'Hi, I'm the body found in the swimming pool.' Whether it's the kind of electoral slogan that would work in a democratic society, I don't know.

And the body found dead in a ditch? Issa El Saieh swears it is him. How does he know? Because, he says, Greene told him. Four hours a day. Week after week after week. That's how. Which is crazy. Because to me Saieh is worth a book, if not an entire library, in his own right, not a passing reference in a ditch.

The second most famous person to be born in Bethlehem, he travelled the world, ended up in Haiti, was sent to an orphanage in America even though his parents were still alive, left, paid to be taken back, taught himself to play the tenor saxophone, worked with bands all over the place, can read people's fortunes by seeing them on television – 'It must be on television. If I see them for real I am affected by their personality' – and is today the man behind the worldwide success of Haitian naive art. You know, the stuff with the zebras and tigers in the vivid green jungles.

I met him in one of a string of enormous houses he has all over Port-au-Prince, which are full from floor to ceiling with thousands upon thousands upon thousands of Haitian paintings.

'Graham Greene,' he said. 'He used to come in here.' He pointed to a spot alongside a stack of paintings worth, I don't know, between £50,000 and £100,000. 'He used to sit there, hour after hour, just listening to what was going on.' Which obviously sheds fascinating light on the way a great writer researches his subject in depth before coming up with all those penetrating insights into the human condition.

What was he like?

'He was a heavy drinker. But he never mixed his drinks. If

he started the day on beer, he stuck to beer all day. If he started with whisky, he stuck to whisky all day.'

Was he at Mère Catherine's every night chasing, well maybe not so much chasing as catching, little Tin Tin?

Greene, of course, made out he was the world's most experienced brothel-creeper. Some people who maintained they knew him well said yes. You couldn't keep a good man down, and he was impossible to keep down. Others, who maintained they knew him equally well, said no. The only bed he ever boasted of sharing was John Gielgud's. He slept in the bedroom in the Oluffson which Gielgud used to have whenever he visited Port-au-Prince: the one on the first floor on the right-hand side with the balcony around it. Not the Graham Greene room downstairs. That's Mickey Mouse.

I did meet one guy, however, who told me that Greene came to him on the last night of his stay and told him he would like to visit a brothel, just to gather local colour. The guy said Greene didn't even have a suit with him, so he had to fix him up with a suit as well. Which at least tells you that if he was not the world's most experienced brothel-creeper, he was certainly the most civilised.

Oh yes, and one other thing. Apparently the whole time Greene was in Haiti he kept a huge two-foot-long crucifix resting on top of his bed. Why? Nobody could tell me.

But if it was to protect him from voodoo, it's not surprising. Even today there is this sense of voodoo pervading everything in Haiti.

When I first mentioned to people back at the office that much against my will and better judgement I was being forced to go to Haiti, I was immediately besieged. Everybody wanted me to bring them back wax models of somebody or other and a couple of million pins. Wives, mothers-in-law, fathers-in-law, brothers-in-law, every kind of in-law you can think of. As well as Directors of Human Resources, the boyfriend of that girl in accounts and what's-her-name who looks after the switchboard at lunchtime. But funnily enough, not one person asked for a wax model of their loving devoted husband. Strange, that.

Papa Doc apparently scored the biggest wax doll hit of all times. He had a wax model made of JFK, his arch-enemy, and whenever he got the chance he stuck pins in it. November 22nd 1963 was the happiest day of his life. That's when Kennedy was assassinated. Admittedly it took 2,222 pins, but who's going to argue about details? Especially in Haiti. To celebrate his triumph, he had all of Port-au-Prince blacked out apart from the palace. Judging by the way the electricity went on and off in my room, the celebrations are still going on.

I'm no expert on voodoo, but I've been to plenty of countries where they believe in it: good as well as evil voodoo. I could take you, for example, on tours not only of voodoo temples but of voodoo convents and even hospitals in Lomé, Togo, which many people claim is the voodoo capital of the world. We could go to the Snake Temple in Ouidah, next door in Benin, which was perhaps the slave capital of West Africa, which has its own voodoo pope and special voodoo day of the year. We could go to Ireland the week before the Cheltenham Gold Cup, when everybody is filling their pockets with rabbits' feet and drenching everything with tankerloads of holy water.

In South Africa, they not only believe in *tokoloshe*, tiny little hairy bad-luck fairies, but they still go around stoning and beating and burning to death women they suspect of being witches. Up near the border with Zimbabwe there is even a secret hideaway for witches who have fled their homes and families for fear of a *sangoma*, a witch hunter, pointing his magic bone at them and giving them the thumbs down. You think I'm kidding? Even serious, sensible businessmen will consult their local *sangoma* – on their health, on family affairs, even on how to run their company.

In Johannesburg, I once met a guy who ran a big company who told me that a *sangoma* had advised him that in order to boost his confidence and give him the courage to go on developing his company he should kill his biggest competitor, cut off his genitals, roast his penis, eat it, then grill his testicles until they were well done and rub the ashes all over his own body. Which I guess is what most businessmen would like to do to their biggest competitor, and far more positive than the wishy-washy stuff you get from Henley Management College. Whether he did it I didn't dare ask. All I know is next time I went there he had moved into a bigger office, he'd bought a string of other companies and was driving around in a Mercedes the size of a voodoo temple.

It's the same in the Far East. In Kuala Lumpur, for example, serious, sensible people think nothing of consulting their local *bomoh*, a traditional Malay fortune-teller or good-luck man who claims to be guided by *datuks*, good spirits. He gives them a single betel nut wrapped in a leaf. They have to eat half and throw the other half in the river. So long as the two halves never meet, they're safe.

The wife of a businessman over there told me she consulted a *bomoh* to see if he could stop her from growing old. He recommended gold needles inserted under her skin, which sounded a brilliant idea to me. You pay for twenty. The *bomoh* inserts only three. And sells the rest. Everybody's happy.

'So was it worth the money?' I asked her. Did she feel good she was no longer growing old?

'It is twenty past four,' she replied. 'Time to go to another *bomoh*.' Since the first *bomoh* had slipped a couple of hundred gold needles under her skin she had gone deaf.

What is amazing about Haiti, however, which is 70 per cent Catholic, 30 per cent Protestant and 100 per cent voodoo, is that voodoo is everywhere. And it's usually evil. Apparently, when the slaves were shipped out of West Africa they believed in good voodoo. When they were landed in Haiti, surprise, surprise, they believed in bad voodoo. Nor can anyone blame them. What it means is, whatever you do or don't do in Haiti has some kind of significance, and it's usually bad.

Go into a restaurant. Somebody offers you a plate of bits and pieces. Anywhere else you would immediately waggle your little finger in the air and grab the nearest one. Not in Haiti. Not if you want to see the end of the day. Instead you take the slice furthest from you.

If you get a headache, forget the aspirins. They give you great handfuls of leaves to chew, then they pound away on the drums until the middle of the night. If you have a nightmare, before you know what's happening they are rubbing you with leaves and muttering incantations all over you. Sneeze once and they're rushing you off to the nearest voodoo temple loaded down with lumps of cake and bottles of rum – not for you, for the gods – and plucking chickens and painting them blue.

I'm only glad I didn't get hiccoughs, otherwise I would no doubt have been smeared in the warm blood of a bull on the point of death and offered up as a victim to the Grande Erzulie, the goddess of fertility and lust. On the other hand I suppose I could drink a can of Coke without stopping and hope to goodness that makes me catch, hic catch them, hic catch them . . .

They seem to have voodoo gods for everything. Papa Legba is the spirit of the crossroads. He guards them and keeps all the bakas, loupgarous, zombies and other evil spirits at bay including, I'm told, traffic wardens and policemen sitting in stationary cars waiting for innocent, unsuspecting motorists to bomb past at 121mph. He tells people which way to go. Most of them he sends in the right direction; others he sends to their almost certain doom or Chislehurst. Then there is Gu, the god of whatever it is. Good old Damballa will protect you from something or other. And Hevioso. Nobody gets on the wrong side of Hevioso. I think.

On the other hand they will have nothing whatsoever to do with the idea of werewolves roaming the hills and wild open spaces and howling their heads off every full moon. That's Hollywood. Instead they believe in weremen, werewomen and even werechildren.

Take a trip out of Port-au-Prince into the villages high in the mountains above Kenscoff, where Brown's mother was, Greene wrote, 'dug in with due Catholic rites among the small tombs', with poor old Marcel weeping unashamedly at the graveside, although thirteen lines later he is admitting that because of the storm which broke on them with 'a clash and a fury' she would not actually be buried until that following morning. Now and then you will see, especially in the early evening, people wearing red headbands and male catskin shoes carrying bags of lemons, scurrying down dirty little alleyways, leaping across ditches and disappearing into the middle of nowhere like a bunch of masons heading for the monthly meeting of their local lodge.

No, they are not sweatbands. No, they are not trying to hide the grey ends of their hair which they say you get from eating cat meat. No, they are not going to some huge cement circle where they hold cockfights. No, they are not heading for the local squash club. This is Haiti, remember. These are the professional voodoo guys, off for a pleasant evening with the boys where they'll all have a couple of drinks, some laughs, and roast alive a couple of loupgarous or weremen; maybe even a werewoman or, if they hit lucky, a werechild.

You think I'm kidding? Listen, in Haiti this is for real and the headbands are part of their ceremonial costume. The lemons? They hold them up to their noses to protect them from the weresmell. Afterwards they throw cock feathers and bits of goat on the remains as a sacrifice to their gods.

To most people, apparently, it's just like any other evening out. You wish you hadn't stayed so late or spent so much money, and wonder why the hell nobody else bought their round of drinks. Others, however, can be changed for ever. Good people can become bad. Bad people can become good. Shy people can become bold and outrageous. Bold and outrageous people can become like Americans. During some ceremonies, my dear, I was told people can even change their sex.

Wandering around the tiny cemetery, which is now almost engulfed by tin shacks and tiny fields of onions, I met a withered little old man who I thought at first was standing next to a pile of bones. On closer inspection it turned out to be a donkey. He thought I was odd, because I was looking for a real-life grave of a fictitious person. He, on the other hand, was convinced the world was about to be overrun by loupgarous; so much so he told me he kept a necklace of human heads at home to protect him from them.

If you don't believe me, there's no way I can get them to take the spell off. You'll just have to stay the way you are for the rest of your life.

But that wasn't the big question on my mind right then. What I wanted to know was why Brown buried his mother high in the mountains in Kenscoff, which at the time must have been pretty near impossible to reach (for me, in a four-wheel drive, it wasn't much easier) and not in the big cemetery in the middle of Port-au-Prince. It couldn't have been because he wanted to avoid inviting everybody back to the house afterwards for drinks. Or could it? Admittedly the cemetery in Port-au-Prince is today a tiny cramped island with hardly enough room to bury a death certificate let alone a body, completely surrounded by open sewers, but in its day it must have been a pleasant enough spot. Like the one in Aquin, which Greene said was like 'a city built by dwarfs, street after street of tiny houses, some nearly big enough to hold ourselves, some too small for a newborn child, all of the same grey stone, from which the plaster had long flaked'. Besides, it would have been easier for poor old Marcel to visit, with that bad leg of his.

All in all, however, I reckon if Greene could go back today for another look around Port-au-Prince the way I did, and not spend all his time sitting chatting with Issa El Saieh, he would be thrilled to bits with the way things have turned out.

I don't mean Baby Doc. I don't mean the even worse mess the country has got itself into. *Plus ça change, plus c'est la même chose – ou pire* (the more things change, the more they stay the same – or get worse). An old – I mean, a middle-aged – Haiti saying. I don't even mean the way the ugly Americans, the leaders of the free world, the great protectors of liberty and freedom invaded Haiti, an independent sovereign state in order to protect it from disintegrating into the kind of social, economic and criminal mess you find in cities all over the

States. I mean the fact the place was run by an ex-priest who then swapped the power and the glory for some American lawyer and highballed it to Washington for the good life.

And if Greene did come back to Haiti, and if I did ever see him propped up at the bar of the Oluffson or buried under a pile of paintings at Issa El Saieh's, there is one question I would ask him – purely in the interests of literature, you understand. How the hell did Martha scratch her leg on what he called the radio in the car? Because, not that I have anywhere near the experience Greene had, I cannot for the life of me see how it's possible.

Unless . . . wait a minute . . . of course. He wasn't the great expert he made out he was. He just made the whole thing up. Like all great writers.

Berlin

Berlin, the once and future capital of Europe – oops, I mean Germany – is truly unique. And I mean unique as in, There is nobody else in the world like Mrs Thatcher. It has more history under a Zungenblutwurst than most cities have under a whole pile of throwaway Pizza Hut boxes. The Prussians. Sally Bowles. The Nazis. It's seen and survived them all.

For nearly thirty years, until the night of 9 November 1989, it was the *grosser Brüder* of divided cities. Beirut, Belfast, Nicosia, they were junior league. This was the real thing. A huge concrete wall which stretched for over 1,500 kilometres; watchtowers; gun emplacements; tank traps; God knows how many kilometres of barbed wire; over 600 people gunned down trying to cross it.

Today, of course, it's a capital that isn't a capital. The two halves are being put together so that, come the year 2000, or very shortly before, knowing the Germans, it will assume its rightful place as the capital of whatever.

But a word of advice. If you want to experience the real Berlin, don't go there on a sunny day. Go when it's raining. In the middle of the night. With a trenchcoat and a trilby. And wander along the cobblestone streets and squares, preferably with a single, solitary policeman staring at you from a doorway or from under a bank of floodlights. Call me impressionable, but as far as I'm concerned that's how to see the real Berlin and, maybe, try to experience it as well. Because when you think about it, apart from the occasional Olympic Games, practically everything that has happened in Berlin happened at night. The Reichstag fire. The burning of the books. The parties in Kurt Vollmoller's apartment in the Pariserplatz, where the women wandered around stark naked and Josephine Baker pranced about wearing nothing but a tiny pink muslin apron. The discovery of quantum theory, the general theory of relativity and the splitting of the atom. The meeting which came up with the final solution to the 'Jewish problem'. The bombings by first the British, then the Americans, then the Russians. The business in the bunker. The building of the Wall – or at least the start of it. The escape attempts. The spy swaps on Glienicke bridge which made Berliners call the place Agentensumpf, the city of agent swaps. The coming down of the Wall. My own first trip. A bit like the Allies, it took me a long time to get to Berlin, but when I finally got there, though, I got there at night. Without, I hasten to add, a trenchcoat and a trilby.

I'd been doing a Ride of the Valkyries in and around Magdeburg, a pretty nondescript town in the old East Germany, visiting companies and factories or what was left of them and generally experiencing the thrills and excitement of forty years of Soviet planning. The Wall had just come down. There was still that feeling of excitement in the air – and apprehension. In one company backing on to a railway line we were practically greeted like liberators. Everybody turned out to shake us by the hand. They thought we were coming to solve all their problems overnight and give them everything they wanted: more money, bigger houses, more money, new cars, more money, world travel, more money. Other companies were nervous. They wondered if they were going to be allowed to continue; if they could go on selling to Russia or if from now on they only had to sell to America; if they were going to have to change all their systems and in future do things the Western way or if they were just going to be taken over by a huge German combine and disappear.

Overall, three things struck me (apart from Tempo processed peas, which tasted like ball bearings; Vatol car shampoo, which actually burnt off what little paint was left on the

car; and Red Riding Hood demi sekt, which had me crying out
for my granny).

First, the absolute contrast between the propaganda and
publicity and what life was like on the ground. Like everybody, I'd seen the brochures, I'd read the reports, I'd heard the
speeches, I'd seen the films. East Germany, I thought, was a
modern, hi-tech country, a world leader across a wide range
of technologies with a string of world-famous companies to
back it up. But here I was driving along roads that were hardly
roads at barely 13kph, instead of the normal 130kph in West
Germany. In the villages people were living in shacks existing
almost exclusively on potatoes, corn and turnips. There was
no sewage system. Practically no electricity. In the towns
everything was run-down, drab, falling apart. I went into
factories more ancient than the ones I used to work in a
million years ago in Leeds. What machines were working were
leaking oil and pumping out thick black fumes. The air reeked
of sulphur. The offices were almost as bad. Telephones didn't
work. Telex – remember telex machines? – didn't work. The
workers didn't work. They couldn't. There was nothing for
them to do. There were no goods to be delivered. Because no
goods were being manufactured, there were no invoices to
issue. Because no goods were being delivered. It was unbelievable. One businessman told me his factory was taken over
by the communists in 1972. Between then and when he came
back to reclaim it the year after the Wall came down, nothing
had been spent on it – not on machines, not on the factory
itself, not even on painting the front door.

Second, the absolute lack of any sign of the Russians. In
other parts of Eastern Europe, all over the Baltics, you saw
them and signs of them everywhere. Not so here. In Magdeburg I was told there had been a barracks with over 10,000
Soviet troops. But nobody ever saw them, or had any contact
with them. Which somehow made things worse; more sinister,
scarier.

Third, the people. Why, I don't know, but I expected them
to be like us. They weren't. They didn't know anything of the

rest of the world. They had never visited anywhere west of Hotensleben, and didn't want to. A few, the occasional manager or factory director, had been to Moscow. Some of them had even been to Prague or Budapest. A few admitted to speaking Russian. And, of course, there was no reason why they shouldn't, but that had never occurred to me.

By the time I got to Berlin, therefore, I was ready for more of the same, but larger. What I was not ready for was what I got: two distinctly different cities, two distinctly different styles and cultures, two distinctly different peoples. And what's more, the following morning the sun was shining.

Other people, as soon as they got there, especially late at night, were picked up by Sally Bowles and whisked off to a wild no-holds-barred bohemian life of non-stop partying, booze, drugs and glorious dissipation. Failing that they would at least pop into the Romanisches Café in the Tauenzien-strasse, where Brecht and company used to hang out. Me, I was met by a driver in one of those enormous metallic blue Mercedes. I'd no sooner clambered in than he told me that before he came to the West he had been an East German border guard. Well, welcome to Berlin, I thought. I'm about sixty years too late. Again.

'The most boring job in the world,' he said as we swung out of Tegel airport and headed into town. 'There was nothing to do. All we did was walk up and down guarding it. It was a complete waste of time.'

Did he ever shoot at, well, anything?

'Never fired my gun once. Not even at the animals that kept wandering behind the fence around the Wall. Not once.'

Don't they all say that?

'No. It is true,' he said. 'Honest. I have no reason to make up story.'

So what was his first impression of the West?

'Poor people,' he told me. 'I just couldn't believe it. I still can't believe it when I see poor people in the West.' The traffic began to snarl up and we got closer into town. 'I remember the first time I came to the West after the Wall came down. I saw this man sitting on a bench. He had a bottle of beer in his hand. He was just sitting there, drinking. He wasn't doing anything. That kind of thing wasn't possible in the East. I just couldn't believe it.'

He swung out and overtook this broken down old Trabbie. 'In the old days, in the East it just wasn't possible. Everybody had a job. Everybody knew what they were doing. The State did everything. If you went to prison, when you came out the State gave you a flat to stop you from going to prison again. That doesn't happen now. Everybody has to work for themselves and look after themselves. There is uncertainty everywhere.'

Which did he prefer?

'If you like clothes and cars, if you like to travel, you have to like it as it is today. But there are more problems. Before we had no problems. Everything was organised for us. We had no problems.'

But in spite of all his reservations, since the Wall had come down he had spent a year in London learning English, he had married, he had made enough money as a taxi driver to get a flat, admittedly in East Berlin which is still much cheaper, and his wife was expecting a baby.

As soon as I'd checked in, I went walkabout. There was no way I was going to sit in a hotel room in Berlin writing up reports and memos. In two seconds I was in the flashy, gaudy Kurfürstendamm or Ku'damm, as it is known to the locals, which is said to be the most fashionable street in town. At one end is the Schöneberg town hall where Kennedy made his famous 'Ich bin ein Berliner' speech, which everybody told me actually means 'I am a big jam doughnut'. At the other end is Tiergarten, one of a million parks and commons and stretches of woodland you find in the city and, of course, the Brandenburg Gate. In between are 6,527 upmarket, luxury, wildly expensive stores, shops, bars, hotels and restaurants including a Chinese restaurant up an alleyway which I particularly liked called, would you believe, Ho Lin Wahl, and a mass of way-out psychedelic street sculptures and murals.

I had no sooner turned the corner than I was engulfed by a mixed group of men and women offering me what they called a Berlin quicky. Hey, maybe I'll see Sally Bowles after all, I thought, especially as the women looked as though they were dressed as men and the men looked as though they were dressed as women. But no. It turned out to be a visit to the Brandenburg Gate for DM19.

Resisting the temptation, I walked the length of Ku'damm. Past, please note, all the bars and cafés. Past Kempinski's, said to be one of the best hotels in town. Past a million restaurants. Past the apparently famous Kranzler Café which, compared to some of the fantastic cafés you see in places like Vienna, can only be famous for being so ordinary.

Turn left and past Zoo station, the famous railway station. Famous because it has had a book named after it, a film made about it and a pop song written about it. Not because it's full of tramps, drug addicts in green glossy leather boots, dope pedlars, ferocious police dogs and trains which run on time. It all proves my theory about why Germany is so hard-working, so efficient, so dedicated. Their superabundant energy comes from all the sugar in their wine. The more German wine they drink, the more sugar they get, the more energetic they are. Why are we so slow? We don't drink enough of their wine. True or untrue?

On Breitscheidplatz I saw the famous ruined Kaiser Wilhelm Memorial church, known to Berliners as the Gedächtniskirche, the powder box, which is being preserved as a memorial to all those who died in the fighting. Practically bearing down on top of it is the Europa-Centre, a huge office and shopping complex which, for some reason, is known as the lipstick. Funny sense of humour these Berliners. Maybe they've never got over the thought of Josephine Baker dancing around in a tiny little muslin apron. Things like that could easily affect the rest of your life.

A little bit further on, on the other side of the road on Wittenbergerplatz, is KaDeWe, the queen of Berlin's department stores and the biggest in the country. It is supposed to sell something like 5,000 different sauces, 10,000 different cheeses, 2.5 million different wines and over 8 million different loaves of bread. As if that's not enough they even have shoals of fish swimming around in giant tanks just waiting for the chop. It makes Harrods look like a two-bit Egyptian grocery shop. Which I suppose it is when you think about it.

Then it struck me. In many ways Berlin is, I reckon, the most American city I know outside America. Well, all right then, the most old-fashioned, New-York-Boston-Chicago-Champagne-Illinois American city I know outside America. It's fast-moving, non-stop, 24-hours a day. It's bright lights, Gucci, Versace, punk, wear whatever the hell you want to wear: suits, slacks, socks, no suits, no slacks, no socks, green and blue, what difference does it make? It's also food, food and still more food wherever you look. Bratwurst. Bierwurst. Curry-wurst. Meltwurst. Schlackwurst. Zervelatwurst. Zungenwurst. Do your worst. Besides McDonald's, it's Kentucky Fried Chicken and every other fast food operation you can think of. And do they eat? All the time. Everywhere. Everything. And enormous portions. An ordinary Berliner – it's true, it is a jam doughnut – is practically the size of the Brandenburg Gate.

As if that's not enough, the traffic is American, apart from the fact that nobody, but nobody, crosses the road until the light says go. The buildings, the run-of-the-mill buildings, are American. The backstreets and alleyways are American. The way people amble along the road is American. The way young kids rollerblade along the pavement is American. The way the police ignore them is American. The old men sitting on benches, just drinking, nothing else, that's American. Not to mention the fat old women with supermarket trolleys loaded with rubbish, the groups of punks actually camped out on street corners and a well-dressed man talking to himself all the way down Fasanenstrasse in Charlottenburg. Now that is all American. And, of course, the way every single thing is of enormous historic importance. Except, of course, in this case it is.

As it began to get really dark, I decided to try a Berlin quickie of my own. I got a cab.

First, I went to Checkpoint Charlie on Friedrichstrasse which is still all spotlights and barriers and barbed wire and wooden huts and men ambling backwards and forwards. Except the old Checkpoint Charlie was no more. It is now an enormous building site. Where years before people would wait for hours on end to be processed in order to enter another world, now they are building a huge American business centre where in future people will wait hours on end to be processed in order to enter another world of gum-chewing, Coke-swilling – and no doubt sniffing as well – super-keen, high-powered, all-American business executives convinced they know more about Germany and the needs of German industry than any German businessman.

Nearby was just about all that is left of the Wall; a great chunk of concrete and bricks and slabs about 100 feet long and 20 feet high. Most of it is covered in graffiti, although here and there you can see crosses people have scrawled to commemorate those who were killed trying to get across. Not, I hasten to add, by my old taxi driver, my present taxi driver or any other taxi driver in the whole of Germany. All that kind of thing was done by somebody else.

After the Wall came down the authorities agonised for weeks about whether they should destroy it altogether, preserve whole sections, paint it white, red or rosé, cover it in tinfoil, or just keep a single length as a memorial. By the time they had made up their minds, the decision had been taken for them. The Wall, for thirty years a symbol of unbelievable domination, had disappeared. An estimated one million tons of concrete, not to mention 214 watchtowers. As souvenirs. As keepsakes. As a nice line for tourists. As foundations for new greenhouses. As whatever. All that is left is this single lump and a 350-metre stretch out in Hotensleben.

I got out and walked around. It was dark, though not raining. And I couldn't see any military. But the place was full of shadows.

By now it was getting late and I had meetings early the following morning. Having seen Checkpoint Charlie, however, there was no way I was going to miss the Brandenburg Gate. Again, when I got there it was dark, though not raining. And I couldn't see any military. But it is as moving and as impressive as hell. This enormous gate, originally built in 1789, the year of the French Revolution, is slap bang in the middle of the Pariserplatz. The statue of victory on top, complete with chariot, has her eye firmly fixed on the kaiser's palace. This was added two years later in 1791, which was obviously the last time the Germans were late with deliveries.

I walked across the square to the Gate. You could imagine everything it has seen and witnessed: the Prussians, the Nazis, the bombing, the occupation. The building of the Wall. The night the Wall came down. Like the day Kennedy was killed, everybody remembers what they were doing the night the Wall came down. I was supposed to be flying to Cameroon. When I went to check in at Gatwick they told me the flight had been delayed. They didn't know how long, but it was going to be 12–15 hours. Instead of stretching out on a bench I went home. As I got home, I can remember seeing the scenes on television. It was unbelievable. We had a German girl staying with us at the time. She was sitting on the edge of her chair, her eyes popping out of her head.

As I walked back to the car I noticed on the edge of the square, on a wooden fence, somebody had scrawled, 'Past Tense. Future Perfect.'

On the way back to the hotel we drove slowly past a car park. There was what looked like a heap of sand by the side of the road. 'That,' the driver told me, 'is all that's left of Hitler's bunker. There's no sign, deliberately. They don't want to draw attention to it. But everybody knows.'

Whether it was true or not, I couldn't find out. But the idea of an Unknown Bunker for probably the most infamous soldier in history is well, interesting.

The following morning at seven o'clock – who says overseas travel is a piece of Torte – I was in a meeting with four Russians who had come all the way from Rybinsk, a decrepit industrial dump, sorry, town, about four hours' drive east of Moscow. Four hours by Mercedes; about two weeks by Trabant.

Three of them looked like ancient Heroes of the Revolution and seemed a touch disappointed they were not being hailed as such in the city they were convinced they saved. Berlin, that is, not Rybinsk. Nobody can save Rybinsk, the state it is in now. The youngest looked as though he had just got back from the Battle of Stalingrad. He must have been in his early twenties. He had on an old fairisle sweater, jeans and dirty great filthy boots. His hair was all over the place. He looked as though he hadn't shaved for a month. But he was selected by the others to lead the discussions.

We were in an office somewhere behind the new Berlin Rathaus or town hall in the old East Berlin which was in fact the old East Berlin Rathaus or town hall which was quickly converted into the new Berlin Rathaus or town hall when the Wall came down. If you follow me. Also with them was their German minder, who was born in the old West Berlin but who now lived in the old East Berlin.

The German officials we met seemed pleased to see us. Whether this was genuine, whether it helped them to meet some unspecified political objectives, whether they had been hitting the old liquid sugar the night before, or whether they were just very good officials I couldn't tell. All I know is they were 'sehr gut' this and 'vielen dank' that and polishing their rimless glasses in no time at all.

The German minder explained why we were there. The Russians were from a tiny engineering company which made heating and ventilating equipment. They no longer had the support of the government. They had been cut off without a rouble. They were on their own. They were determined to survive. They were visiting potential customers. They were eager to do business.

The officials nodded quietly. To each other. To the Russians. To their minder. Even to me. And polished their glasses again. The introduction over, the minder turned to the young man, who froze. He didn't say a word. He didn't even try to. He just stared straight ahead. So did the others. It was as if they had all been struck dumb by an invisible bolt from the Kremlin for their daring even to think of doing business in the West. The minder coughed gently. Still no reaction. He leant across the table and put his hand on the young leader's arm as if to bring him out of his trance. Still no reaction. He then practically shook him to bring him round. Which he did immediately. Except that he was now suddenly talking 27.5 to the dozen. In Russian.

The minder tried to switch him into German, but no way, the kid would only talk Russian. The Germans looked at each other with an understanding I am sure they would never deploy for a visiting British delegation. Their leader, the one with the most-polished glasses, suggested coffee. Which was immediately seized on by the minder as an opportunity to bring the young leader back down to earth.

During coffee, one of the German officials kept complaining about the amount of English creeping into German. A meeting was no longer a Treffung, it was a meeting. A fax was no longer a Bericht, it was a fax. He showed me a copy of *Bunte*, the big German news magazine. There was an article about Fergie which said, 'Herzogin von York, Prinzessin "bit on the side" . . .'

Now it was back to the meeting. In spite of two cups of coffee our Russian hero was still out of this world. The meeting, however, proceeded. The minder and our young hero mumbled backwards and forwards to each other in a mixture of Russian, German and plain mumbo-jumbo. The other Russians said nothing, just kept staring straight ahead. But it worked well enough. The two of them described the equipment they could supply, the quality and the delivery dates. Then came prices.

'So how much would you charge?' the top German asked through his gleaming rimless glasses.

The minder looked at the once and future leader. The once

and future leader looked at his three colleagues. They all looked straight back at him. This time he did the opposite of freeze. He went bananas. He dived into his briefcase and brought out an enormous out-of-date Russian diary about the size of a family bible. Page after page he flipped through, of tiny handwriting and figures. Then he stopped.

Into his briefcase again he plunged. Out came what looked like an old school exercise book. For the next hour and a half he sat muttering to himself, first flicking through his diary then scribbling furiously all over his exercise book. The minder tried to interrupt, tried the hand-on-the-arm routine, even tried the heavy shake. But to no avail. He looked at the three Germans in that special kind of German way. They looked back at him in that special kind of German way and started polishing their rimless glasses again. He looked at the other Russians who all managed to be looking somewhere else. He began to turn towards me. I hastily looked away. There was no way I could have looked at him and not reacted. Then it occurred to me; this kid was actually working out there and then the cost of supplying heating and ventilating equipment direct to Berlin, down to the last nut and bolt. This was what he was born for. This was what the workers, the factory, the whole town of Rybinsk expected of him. There was no way he was going to disappoint them. Little did he care for the Western way of doing business: obtaining estimates, preparing estimates, taking potential clients out to lunch, dinner and wherever they wanted to be persuaded to go afterwards. Not that anyone would ever mention it to anyone.

Two days later – or that's what it seemed like to me – he was finished. He took a dirty piece of paper from the back of the exercise book. On it, he scribbled a single figure. I couldn't see what it was, but it was his price, down to the final nut and bolt. This was obviously the new-style Russian way of doing business. But however intense, dramatic and, compared to many companies, supersonic it may be when it comes to submitting estimates, I cannot see it beating the German way of doing business in Eastern Europe: arrive in a brand new

Mercedes, have a quick chat with the managing director, leave the keys of the Mercedes by accident on the managing director's desk, leave by taxi.

The meeting was over. The rimless glasses smiled, the minder smiled, the other Russians smiled. The young leader gathered his books together. We all shook hands, said our farewells and were gone. The others had a meeting around the corner in Karl Marx Allee, a never-ending street running practically to the Polish border, and which many people say contains all the worst examples of Stalinist architecture. I made for the Brandenburg Gate to carry on where I left off.

The previous evening the Brandenburg Gate had been startling, mysterious, impressive. In broad daylight it was a giant flea market. Almost directly under the Gate itself stood a strange-looking woman with a non-stop silly grin wearing a top hat, fancy waistcoat and tights, with one hand playing a hurdy-gurdy organ strapped to the wheels of a pram and with the other waving a glove puppet of a monkey. All around her were stalls and wooden boxes and cake tins piled high with the last things you would expect to see at the Brandenburg Gate. Or at least, the last things I expected to see at the Brandenburg Gate: bits of German military uniforms; the odd French medal; a pair of Mickey Mouse binoculars; a couple of Russian dolls; T-shirts saying in French, German, Russian and American, 'You are leaving the American Sector'; chunks of any old brick wall from anywhere between the Atlantic and the Urals; a whole pile of souvenir gasmasks; battered East German soldiers' boots; cheap leather boots; amber necklaces and faded imitation Russian fur hats. Made in Taiwan.

I mean, honestly, is that what it's all about? Surely there must be some other way of commemorating the Brandenburg Gate, all that it stood for, all the people who died on both sides of it.

For the rest of the day, I explored the old East Berlin, which in spite of everything has not changed much at all. Still walls were being built. Still streets were being blocked off. Still there were vast no-go areas. Still there were cameras everywhere.

Still personnel carriers trundled through the streets all day long. But the walls being built were for offices, hotels, for vast shopping complexes; the streets were being blocked off for bulldozers and dumper trucks; the no-go areas were full of cranes and giant cement mixers; the cameras were tourist cameras and the personnel carriers were buses loaded with visitors. Why they made all that fuss about wrapping up the Reichstag I don't know. Every other building is covered in tarpaulin or something like it. Everything you could see, or rather couldn't see, was being refurbished, rebuilt or deconstructed. Partly because so many of the old modern buildings, if you see what I mean, are falling apart. Partly because so many of them are choc-a-bloc with asbestos and the government in Bonn is determined to get rid of the stuff before the first civil servant drinks his first schnapps on his first day in his new office. And partly because, let's face it, they're just going to need more offices if they're going to run the whole of Europe, I mean Germany, from there.

You think I'm kidding. One evening a German civil servant who looked as though he put the nein into canine told me that among themselves they now refer to Berlin as New Teutonia. He also told me a joke. Which in itself is unusual. Usually the German idea of a joke is to read Nietzsche in blank verse.

'The British prime minister, he says to British minister of finance, "We want to win election in year 2000. Find out what the economy will be then." Minister, he go away, he play with computer. Two days later he come back with big print-out. Prime minister, he say, "OK, we going to win election?" British finance minister, he say, "I don't know. I don't speak German." Very good, ja?'

'Yes,' I said. 'I mean, ja.'

The Reichstag, the old German parliament, burnt down by Hitler in 1934, used as target practice during the battle for Berlin, rebuilt in the 1960s, rebuilt again in the 70s, is being re-rebuilt yet again as the new United German parliament by our very own arch-modernist, Sir Norman Foster of millennium tower, Stansted Airport and Hong Kong Shanghai Bank fame. Like all his other buildings, surprise, surprise, it's going to be all glass and steel and walkways. Already Berliners have started calling it the Petrol Station. Parked outside, I couldn't help noticing, was a Rentokil van.

For over 100 years this was one of the most important and powerful places in the world, rivalling the Kremlin, Whitehall and the Quai d'Orsay. Yet it was also one of the most horrifying and wicked as well. Take Wilhelmstrasse. I mean can you imagine a worse bunch of neighbours. At 63 were Hess and Bormann. At 73 was von Ribbentrop. At 77 was Hitler himself. At 81–85 was Goering and his air force ministry. At 102 was Adolf Eichmann. Their Neighbourhood Watch meetings must have been, well, interesting to say the least.

I wandered down Unter den Linden, the famous avenue of lime trees, which is like a Prussian Champs Elysées. Instead of fashion stores and cinemas and shoe shops and car showrooms there was one ancient historic institution after another.

There's the 250-year-old opera house which is packed out night after night unlike its equivalent in the West, the Deutsche Opera, which is struggling to make ends meet. When I was there, of course, it was closed. Naturally. There's the Royal Library, known as the Kommode, where on the night of 10 May 1933 the Nazis burnt the books including notes by Freud, Einstein, Thomas Mann and one of my favourites, Heinrich Heine, and there's Humboldt University, where Hegel, Kant, Einstein and Grimm of fairy tale fame were all at one time teachers or professors – not to mention Max Planck, Werner Heisenberg, Hertz, Schrodinger, and practically everybody who won the Nobel Peace Price for physics or chemistry before the war.

There's the famous statue of Frederick the Great on top of his charger. I've always had a soft spot for Frederick. Not only did he like horses, he liked dogs as well. So much so that shortly after the Wall came down he was officially reburied by the new German state, in a special ceremony attended by Chancellor Kohl, next to his dogs in the grounds of Sans Souci, his old palace at Potsdam.

There's the Dom, the kaiser's cathedral, which as far as I'm concerned wins the prize for the most non-Lutheran-looking Lutheran church ever built. To me, Lutheran churches usually have the barest of minimum. This one blows the mind or, rather, the soul. It is almost Italian renaissance, pure and highly elaborate. There is an enormous organ which could have been designed for Johann Sebastian himself. There are lamps and gilt everywhere. All around the inside of the dome, looking down from a great height, are statues of Zwingli, Calvin, Luther and the rest of the purists. The prize I will nail on the front door during my next trip. Outside, as I came out, a brass band was playing. Bach, of course.

Across the way is this huge, long, low, neo-classical box, the Pergamon Museum, the largest and oldest museum in Berlin, which contains not just the occasional lump of rock or broken statue but whole cities of the stuff, including the actual altar from Pergamon itself with its beautifully carved frieze of the gods battling for the control of Olympus. What struck me more than anything was not the building itself, which was built not as an inspiration to Robert Maxwell but as a rival to the British Museum, but the statues of the two horses fighting lions either side of the entrance steps. The one on the left had the lion under control. The one on the right was having problems. Big problems. The lion was actually on its neck. It couldn't have much longer to go.

This, you could see, was the city the Prussians built to rule Europe. If not the world. Everything is big, permanent, impressive. Everything talks Prussian pride, Prussian confidence, the Prussian belief that they were Nummer ein.

I then wandered along some of the back streets, where everything was not exactly Prussian glory and magnificence. Behind the grand buildings, up dark alleyways, was the Schlock of what the real East Berlin was like. Buildings bombed by the Allies in the winter of 1944–45 are still there. Street after street of houses are just crumbling to dust. Where new houses, or rather vast concrete blocks of flats, have been built they are also crumbling to dust. Where they are not crumbling, or at least not too quickly, they are being turned into enormous sleazy bars and nightclubs. The best – or rather the worst – were in Prenzlaner Berg, I was told. But I didn't have time to go there. The story of my life.

I came out on Alexanderplatz which, in a city that is being torn down and rebuilt, deserves preserving because to me it's a beautiful example of the worst style of communist architectural kitsch you're ever likely to see. On the other side I could see East Germany's famous pin-up, the star of a million state-produced brochures, magazines, films, stamps and even postcards: the television tower, 365 metres high, the first, second or third highest building in the world depending on which state-produced East German guidebook you read in a government waiting room.

The CNN Tower in Toronto; the Space Needle in Seattle; the Eiffel Tower; the Empire State; the Sears Tower; the one in Sydney. The other one in where was it? I've been and done them all. Not that I've got a thing about towers or even about getting the T-shirt. It's just that they are ... what I mean is ... on the other hand, they are ... well, all right then. Wherever I am I just can't resist the opportunity to look down on people and places. But just my luck. I'm heading towards it and this American guy resembling a lumberjack who believes Superman is Nietzsche for grown-ups and Batman is a crazy mixed-up Kantian, suddenly latches on to me.

'Excuse me,' he says as I try to wander past him, 'can you tell me what berries these are on this tree?' He points to some tree in the distance.

What can I do? I can't ignore him or pretend I'm Chinese and don't know what on earth he's going on about. 'Well, I'm afraid . . .' I begin, the way you do when you're stopped short by Americans looking up at berries on trees in the middle of Berlin.

'Hi.' He shoots out his hand. 'I'm Bill Dobson. From Oregon. D-O-B-S-O-N. I once met an English gentleman who said to me, Dobson, Dobson. I knew a man once called Dobson. He was a dashed good cricketeer.' He laughs at his attempt at an English accent. 'What's your name? You can call me Bill.'

I was tempted to say Adolf Hitler. But I thought they might not have heard of Adolf Hitler in Oregon. And I didn't quite fancy the idea of anyone following me around calling me Adolf Hitler. Especially in Berlin.

'John Major,' I say. Why John Major, I don't know. Probably because he was the next most decisive leader I could think of. Well, would *you* give your real name to somebody called Bill Dobson from Oregon, who's hooked on trees, thinks he can do an English accent and practically hijacks you in broad daylight in the middle of Berlin?

After that it was gee John this, hey John that, and boy John the other. John my old buddy, do you know what that building is over there? John, you're a great guy, what date was it they built the Randomburger Gate? John, buddy boy, when was it, whatdyacallit, the war started? John, partner, have you ever had a real hamburger anywhere outside the US of A? John, you son-of-a-gun, do you know it costs DM40 a square meter a month to rent a flat in the Under the Lyden street? With no heating? Can you imagine that? No heating. John, baby, tell me, maybe you know this English gentleman who said to me, Dobson, Dobson. I knew a ... When did you say the war started?

I can tell you, he was the wurst possible kind of American to meet in Berlin. What do I mean, in Berlin? He was the worst kind of American to meet anywhere. He didn't stop talking. He didn't know nuttin. Not even who John Major was. Unless of course, God help me, he actually thought I looked like John Major. What's more, I couldn't get rid of him. Until, that is, I mentioned the Rathaus. I told him it was the tax office, and did he want to come in with me to a meeting. He went bananas.

'Tax,' he bellowed. 'You'll not find Bill Dobson from Oregon having anything to do with taxes. No, sir. Ain't never started yet. Ain't goin' start now neither. No, sir, not Bill Dobson from Oregon.' He shook my hand. 'John.' He sounded as if he was going to burst into tears. 'John. On your own from now on.' For a second I thought he was going to collapse. 'This is the end.' He shook my hand again. 'I won't say goodbye.' He turned round. I dashed into the Rathaus. Finally I had come in from the cold. I was free from foreign domination.

Two minutes later, with Bill Dobson from Oregon out of the way, I was back on the prowl.

With Bonn scheduled to be in Berlin by the year 2000, building after building is being turned into one ministry or another. The elegant eighteenth-century Schloss Bellevue is going to be the presidential palace, the Palace of the Republic, some glass and concrete pile, will be the federal chancellory, and so on.

'Nein, nein. Zee ministry of foreign affairs can have zat one.' You can imagine them dividing up the spoils. 'Zee ministry of transport can have zee royal horse stables. Zat is transport, ja?'

Many Germans are apparently against the idea, especially the civil servants with pleasant little houses in Bonn. But to me, it makes sense. No way is Bonn a capital city. In fact, as far as I'm concerned, it is still the safe, boring classic Small Town in Germany with embassies squeezed next door to hairdressers, cultural attachés on top of dance schools and an international trade delegation which can only be reached by going through a chemist's shop. Admittedly, it's so small everybody knows everybody, everybody knows what everybody is doing and, more important, everybody knows who everybody is eating Bratwurst with. But Berlin is much, much, much more of a capital city.

There's the Brandenburg Gate, the Reichstag, Unter den Linden, the two cathedrals, all those fantastic Prussian buildings. There's Potsdamerplatz, virtually the heart of the city, where in the main courthouse, more than 5,000 people were sentenced to death between 1934 and 1945. Destroyed originally by the British on a bombing raid on the night of 7 September 1941, it is now being completely rebuilt by Daimler Benz, Sony and half a dozen other multinationals. It simply cannot fail to live up to expectations, unless Richard Rogers gets his hands on it and dangles tubes and staircases all over the place. There's the old Esplanade Hotel. Built in the days of the kaiser, it was so snobby even dukes and duchesses had problems getting in. There's the Congress Hall, which looks like a cross between a pregnant oyster and a collapsed Sydney Opera House. There's the strange oval-shaped Olympic stadium of unhappy memory, now used for important, earth-shattering events like Rolling Stones concerts.

Berlin is also much greener than I expected. There are trees everywhere. Practically every few metres there is a small park. Practically every few kilometres there is a patch of woodland. At a guess I'd say there were more trees in Berlin than there are in the Black Forest. What am I saying? There are definitely more trees in Berlin than there are in the Black Forest.

As for Berliners, most people will tell you the Ossis, the easterners, are more subdued, stolid, serious, slower, quieter. I kept being told, admittedly by Wessis, that Ossis were reluctant to take business decisions, always preferring to be told what to do rather than decide for themselves. The Wessis on the other hand, are said to be flashy, hearty, self-confident, trendy, bright, brash, tough. And what's more they have a sense of humour. Which, I suppose, is what kept them going all those years they were practically cut-off from the rest of the world.

The only thing they seem to lack are smart, shiny uniforms. I can't swear by it, but I would say there is almost a total lack of uniforms, apart from the occasional scruffy-looking police uniform. There are no hotel uniforms, no commissionaires' uniforms. I don't suppose anybody is going to complain about that, although according to a secretary I met in an office along Unter den Linden who would have all the buttons popping and all the straps flying off anyone's Lederhosen, not just uniform but clothing generally is a big issue in Berlin. Especially the lack of it. For some reason I can barely understand, she told me that in the old days she and all other Ossis felt that the only way they could show their abhorrence of the naked aggression of the Soviets was to strip off naked whenever they got the chance. Which I found I could not disagree with although I thought it was a bit like saying the only way to show your horror of the dangers of alcoholism is to go out and get drunk. Which is something else I probably couldn't disagree with. Anyway the whole place, apparently, used to be littered with naked bodies unafraid to hide behind any kind of pretence whatsoever when it came to revealing their true feelings.

The problem came when the Wall came down, because to the Ossis it meant everything else came down as well. The result was that the Wessi nudies welcomed the Ossi nudies. But the Wessi prudies did not. The Wall coming down was one thing. But everything else, they decided, was going to stay firmly in place.

After one or two skirmishes when the gloves came off, not to mention everything else as well, both sides reached a compromise. The city that was famous for a single Wall is now, she told me, famous for a million walls. Walls on beaches. Walls beside lakes. Walls in parks. And on one side are the Wessi prudies and the Ossi prudies. On the other side are the Wessi nudies and the Ossi nudies.

Which struck me as a bit odd for a once divided city. And I've got nothing to hide either way.

Oslo

There's an awful lot of blubber talked about Norway.

An American I met in Minneapolis insisted that it was the capital of Sweden even though there are more Norwegians living in Minneapolis than in the whole of Norway. I mean, Sweden.

An Italian steel man once told me the Norwegians were the Belgians of Scandinavia and that Oslo was like Helsinki but without the vodka.

A guy I met in a bar in Mbabwe – I think he was from Uganda – said it was Horlicks country: one sip and you're fast asleep.

And he was quite right. To know Oslo is to experience that sudden thrill of boredom, give or take a triple axle with a double toe loop. And that's not Norse code. It's calm, quiet, pleasant, well-behaved. Nobody pushes in front of anyone in a queue. Nobody picks flowers in the park. Nobody sneaks in anywhere without paying. Nobody smokes – admittedly probably because it's debatable whether it's cheaper to buy a heart-and-lung machine or a packet of twenty.

Nobody drinks or, rather, drinks too much. In Finland they say alcohol-free beer was invented so that the Norwegians could have a good night out. Nobody ever misses the last ferry home. Partly because they have to spend too much time and energy queuing up at the state-controlled booze shops, Vinmonopolet, where it is literally kept under lock and key, to have any strength left to drink the stuff when they get it home. On the other hand they are the world's largest consumers of sugar and yeast, which as I recall are used for making either bread or the other. If it was bread, on my calculation every man, woman and child in the country would have to eat five loaves every day to account for the consumption of the stuff. So I assume it must be for the other. Especially as they are also the world's largest consumers of plastic tubes and tanks and those tiny perfume-size bottles of whisky, gin and ouzo essences.

Caviar is banned. Unpasteurised cheese is frowned on. And it is absolutely forbidden under pain of Norwegian law and a fine of over US$400 to give your child a perfectly sensible name like Iggy or Led or even Auberon. Call him Skagi, Dits, Fridvall or Odd, or even Bent, and that's perfectly acceptable. On the other hand they think nothing about clubbing seals, catching whales, or wolfing down the green and black eggs of the common gull, not to mention the eggs of the more exotic kittiwake or even the ptarmigan, a tiny mountain bird which changes colour from white in winter to brown in summer in a desperate effort to avoid ending up on a plate.

They give prizes to all kinds of peaceful people (entries close on February 1). They refuse to gossip about the Swedes and the Danes and the Finns, the way the Swedes and the Danes and the Finns gossip about them. They refuse to call Volvos, Lego or Bang and Olufsen Swedish or Danish. They call them Scandinavian. They are also responsible for one of the greatest contributions made to mankind, without which life today would not be possible. They invented the paperclip.

There's hardly any crime, probably because nobody can stay awake long enough, unless you think calling a policeman an 'onion' is a crime, in which case you're fined NKr4,000, sentenced to four weeks in a luxury holiday apartment and forced to accept NKr8,000 to cover your expenses.

Drugs are virtually non-existent. Everybody goes home every evening to his wife. Corruption is unheard of. Government ministers don't even use the air miles they clock up on official business for private trips. Not even to see their mothers.

There is no violence on television. It's censored by the government and nobody says a word about it. The only violence you see is in the street when artists, sculptors and craftsmen destroy their own work in protest at government plans to start taxing them, not only on the odd two or three cheap paintings or sculptures they sell in their lives but on all the high-priced junk cluttering up their garrets as well. As far as I was concerned, most of the stuff looked a darned sight better after it was destroyed than before. But then I don't know anything about art.

On land, everything is expensive pinewood and expensive stainless steel. Hotels are just expensive. Even bed and breakfast costs around £70 a night. That's without the tiny mountain birds. The seas are full of oil and gas and sea kelp.

This is the only country in the world where state assets exceed private-sector assets which, for the economically challenged, means they have so much money in the bank they couldn't care less what anyone says. If they want to do their own thing, they can, and the money is there to pay for it. Which is probably why they can't stop themselves from saying thank you.

When there is such a thing as a crime, even the criminals say thank you. Like the ones who stole that painting of the guy on the bridge. 'Thanks for the poor security,' they said in the thank-you note they left behind.

In fact whichever Norwegian you speak – one is Norwegian Danish, the other Norwegian Norwegian – I'm told it is not only pretty well impossible not to say thank you, but there are a million different ways and words for saying thank you.

Please – now that's another matter. Would you believe it, there's no way of saying please in Norwegian. The word just doesn't exist. Which is obviously why they've still got Oslo.

Now, I'm not saying Oslo is like the rest of the country, thank you, although it's a million times better than getting a massage from the Norwegian prime minister. It's just that it makes me feel as if I'm slowly dying on the inside; I suppose

52

if you'd had Ibsen rammed down your throat since you were a troll, you'd feel the same.

Remember that painting by Münch before it was stolen? I'm no Sister Wendy, but I reckon it's got nothing to do with man's eternal cry for understanding in a world trying to bridge the evils of whatever she was going on about. To me it's a picture of a poor guy enjoying fishing for herring who's just been told by his wife that she's got two tickets for yet another revival of *The Wild Duck*. And who can blame him? The one I saw had Hayley Mills in it doing her I'm-a-little-innocent-who'll-believe-any-strange-man-I-bump-into-in-a-garden-shed-is-God routine, so I know exactly how he feels. And what about Hedda Gabler, who I reckon is nothing but a loser, and a bored and boring one at that; Mrs Elvsted, another bundle of laughs; Nora and all those macaroons; Torvald ... My God, I'm beginning to feel depressed just thinking about them. Imagine how much misery the world would have been saved if, when Ibsen was wandering up and down the Sognefjell road, presumably with ragged trousers, talking to a bunch of trolls, elves and goblins, looking for inspiration for *Peer Gynt*, he'd been hit by a stray boulder, or maybe an avalanche.

The wonder is the poor guy on the bridge was content with screaming his head off. I'm amazed he didn't throw himself over the edge and be one with Ibsen once and for all.

The first time I went to Oslo, thank you, I wanted to visit all the interesting, exciting places. After five minutes I was finished. And that included watching some guy in his Doc Martens and Benetton jumper playing a penny whistle outside the railway station.

The royal palace, thank you, at the end of Karl Johansgate, is very nice, thank you. Just in front of it is the National Theatre, with its two statues outside, Ibsen on the left and some exciting guy called Bjornstjerne Bjornson on the right. Trouble is it's so expensive to get in nobody bothers. As a result, the place has become nothing but a big traffic intersection. For westbound trains take the right-hand tunnel, for eastbound, the left. Buses stop right outside.

There's the sculpture, thank you, outside the Konserthus which captures the spirit of . . . I mean, it embodies Norway's . . . what I'm trying to say is, without it, the city would be . . . Well, it was so interesting I can't even remember what on earth it looked like.

And museums, thank you. I've never known a city to have so many museums. Thank you. Thank you. Thank you. There are probably as many museums in Oslo as there are rope sandals, woolly sweaters and beards. And they always seem to be worn by women. At least, I think they are. Stand still long enough and, so desperate are they for anything of interest, they'll probably turn you into an instant museum as well: Desperate Tourist Bored Out of his Tiny Mind Museum.

I once asked a Norwegian engineer working for Shell Oil which was the most impressive and exciting building in Norway. Without even thinking he said the enormous 121-metre high Holmenkollen ski jump, which is stuck half-way up a mountain outside Oslo. To him, it was the Eiffel Tower, the Statue of Liberty and the Taj Mahal rolled into one.

I was in Oslo once, thank you. I was at a loose end. I'd been there all of two and a half minutes, and was wandering around looking for a restaurant that was open after nine in the evening. I asked a troll of an old man if he could help me. He threw his hands up in the air.

'Hey listen,' I said, 'does anything exciting happen round here?'

'I don't know,' he said. 'I'm only eighty-five.'

You think I'm kidding. Let me tell you, Oslo is the only place I've ever been where when young soldiers hit town they head for the nearest ice-cream parlour; where the local chapter of Hell's Angels drives around at 30mph in the street, as opposed to on the pavement, with smart leather jackets, clean boots, and even slows down for old ladies; where the only illegal posters are for lost cats and where people keep their raincoats on when they go into a restaurant, talk endlessly about triple lutzes, three-and-a-half-turn loops and triple jumps, and wonder why they've all got twisted hernias.

Bergen, out on the west coast – a big sigh of relief from Manchester – is the wettest place on earth. Thank you. It's so wet, they say babies are born with raincoats on and horses shy at anyone not carrying an umbrella. But it's still slow, dull and jammed with umbrellas, most of which are given away free by the locals in order to bribe you to stay more than an hour and a half. But so desperate are they to avoid being labelled the wettest and second most boring city in the country, they claim they are Grieg's home town, although he actually lived about fifty kilometres away in a tiny white wooden house above Lake Nordas. In spite of this their new concert hall, which is shaped like a grand piano, is called the Grieghalle. Which is a bit like Ealing Broadway claiming to be the birthplace of Shakespeare and building the town hall in the shape of a quill pen.

If Bergen is famous for its rain, Stavanger is famous for the sun. Thank you. Trouble is, whenever it's hot and bright there you don't know whether it's the sun or just another oil or gas flare.

As for the rest of the country, thank you, it's not bad providing you like under-skate temperatures in the minus 30s, massive glaciers with white boulders the size of houses, dangerous crevasses, towering mountain peaks, merciless hairpin bends and timid little valleys dotted with silent houses where they still wear fishskin shoes, train dogs to catch puffins and even penguins on the ice, and catch eagles with their bare hands, rip the wings off and sell them as feather dusters. As far as I'm concerned, however, it leaves me cold. One bleak, pine-covered, granite island is pretty much like any other bleak, pine-covered, granite island. One spectacular, frozen, steel-grey, glassy-watered fjord with practically vertical slopes and plunging waterfalls that don't even touch the sides is pretty much like any other spectacular, frozen, steel-grey, glassy-watered fjord, with practically vertical slopes and so on. That includes even the Seijordvannet which boasts its own Loch Ness monster, Selma; which, like our Nessie, has never been seen.

I'm sorry, and I hate myself for saying this, since the Norwegians buy railway lines from us and every year give us a Christmas tree, which is more than the French have ever given us for saving, well, half of them from the Nazis, but you've got about as much chance of enjoying yourself in Norway as chatting up a troll hiding under a bridge, thank you, because somehow they seem to have a glorious knack of putting a damper on everything.

In bars, restaurants, offices, halfway up an oilrig, even in a tiny wooden hut in a pine forest, buried in snow, in sub-zero temperatures just inside the Arctic Circle, they simply don't seem able to enjoy themselves. Not even, I'm told, the occasional Norwegian au pair. Which might, of course, have something to do with only being able to say thank you all the time. Thank you. In fact, I reckon the only reason the Israelis and Palestinians agreed their peace deal was to avoid having to go to Norway again for another meeting.

All the usual things just seem to leave them cold. Politics, thank you, they're not interested in. They just want to be left alone with their oil, their gas, their fish and all that money in the bank. The day after they voted nej and smashed a big wooden stick with an extra large nail through the middle of it into the European Union, *Verdens Gang*, one of their daily papers, published a cartoon showing the big European steamer ploughing towards the horizon. Behind it, a rope had snapped, leaving Norway, a tiny little dinghy, behind. 'Hurrah, Hurrah,' said the caption.

Food and wine, the good life, thank you. Elk, roast moose, reindeer, fresh minke whale steaks, even smoked reindeer and elk sausages – all they want to do, would you believe, is eat the stuff, not talk about it. If they do talk about food and drink it is to tell you how, without electricity, they cooked a delicious dinner for eight in a chalet halfway up a mountain using only a tin of meatballs. I ask you, is that the most important thing in my life?

The cinema, thank you. The last time I was in Oslo, the most exciting film of the year was some boring, shaky, appallingly edited, home-produced, amateurish thing called *Fog*. A love story shot on 35mm film on a budget of less than $55,000. But it was packing them in. Talk about *Forrest Gump*, it was all about this young Norwegian couple on a trip around the world. Well, actually, to Paris, Normandy, Cairo and New York. There was no dialogue, only the characters talking direct to camera.

'If you think back in time now, about how you thought the future would be, and if you compare it with what it became, it turns out differently.' That, I was told, was one of the more memorable, if that's the right word, lines in the whole thing. The critics panned it. 'Vapid, hamstrung and embarrassing,' was one of the kinder comments. But the more it was damned, the more successful it became.

Skiing, ice skating, bobsleighing, thank you. When it comes to winter sports I'm a rink outsider. You wouldn't catch me wearing a multi-coloured reindeer-and-snowflake-patterned thick wool sweater, a thick woollen hat with a bobble on top, a fur coat, fur boots and real wool mittens, even if Torvill and Dean got up off the ice and begged me. And no way would you ever catch me indulging in what is, I was told, the latest craze: naked skiing. I mean, I know how your tongue sticks to metal when it's cold. Not the Norwegians. It's in their blood. Kids learn to ski before they can walk. As soon as they can put on a bobble hat they're whizzing about, breaking European land-speed records with their plastic toboggans, doing triple axles and three-and-a-half-turn loops, running up and down mountains for exercise, waiting for ferries, drinking alkohol-fritt beer and reminiscing yet again about Lillehammer and what did you do during the ski jump, Daddy. Give any of them a million pounds, I reckon they'd head straight for the nearest mountains, pitch their tent, light fires, cook their favourite kjottaker – it's best not to ask what it is – boil steaming hot coffee and worry about how to stop the neighbours from finding out. Whereas the French would buy a whole new wardrobe, a home in the South of France and take another mistress. Norway is the only country I've been to where parents ring up their children on Sunday mornings and ask them whether they've been skiing yet. Which always strikes me as odd. I'd have thought the kids would be safer playing in the traffic in the middle of Oslo. But then maybe the Norwegians are not interested in the cheaper ways of breaking a leg.

Ramming a harpoon through the middle of a minke whale, thank you. Norway, I thought, would at least be full of weeping and whaling and death-defying stories of adventure on the high seas. Like trying to get away from Greenpeace. No way. They didn't even want to talk about their death-defying adventures on dry land – trying to get away from some Californian group so concerned about the environment they go around having a minke of a time sinking whaling boats. All they utter is the occasional grunt and groan, not even as musical or as rhythmical as the sounds made by the whales – which, according to half the world, is evidence of whales' abstract, syntactic, sophisticated mental and communicative skills and to the other half is evidence that, magnificent though they look, they have the brain of a hedgehog, the intelligence of a dog and the communication skills of a bunch of canaries. And that's the males only. And for just six months of the year.

Call me suspicious, but I can't go along with people who go along with sinking other people's property based on the theories of a physician who in the late 1970s was trying to convince the US government that the Galactic Coincidence Control Center was planning to send agents to Planet Earth; whose only practical research on whales was carried out on dolphins in the Virgin Islands and who believes 'in the eyes of whalekind, there is little difference between the behaviour of the monsters of the Reich and the monsters behind the harpoon'.

My theory is that the Norwegians don't want to say anything in case they let the cat out of the bag, or rather the whales out of the off-shore rigs. Think about it for a moment. How come such a tiny insignificant whale-eating country as Norway has so many so-called enormous oil and gas rigs? Because they are really giant hideaways for their fishing fleets. As soon as a Greenpeace ship is spotted on the horizon – zap – they're all inside, out of sight, until the coast is clear. And why are the platforms so high? Because that's where they stock the fish until they get a chance to take it ashore.

Smashing baby seals over the head with a lump of wood with a nail through the middle of it, thank you. Try to raise the subject with a Norwegian and they look as though they themselves have been hit over the head with a heavy club with a nail through the middle of it. It's for scientific reasons, they whimper. Like, the seal hunters need the work. There's too many of them anyhow: seals and seal hunters. And they only kill baby seals – blub, blub – that have been abandoned by their mums.

Yes, but what's the scientific reason?

'Oh. We want to find out whether the most humane way of killing seals is with a lump of wood with a nail through the middle of it or with a rifle.'

Why do they try to slalom round the problem? Because if anybody knows anything about conservation and have demonstrated it to the world, it's the Norwegians. Way back in the early 1980s they saw their fish stocks in the Barents Sea, which they call simply the Ocean, being seriously depleted. They slapped on it some of the tightest fishing restrictions ever imposed, and today it's choc-a-bloc.

Even the usual, they don't seem to be interested, thank you. Which is obviously why, not being able to say please, there are only four million of them left in a country almost the size of France. Maybe it's what happens if you spend your time skiing naked down mountains. Maybe it's all this Ibsen stuff. After all, Hedda Gabler would put anybody off.

Maybe it's because they don't drink. Go out with a Norwegian to celebrate winning some big order and it's a struggle to finish the bottle of beer. Alcohol-free, of course. In fact the only case they've had of drunken driving in the last 250 years was in Haugesund. The vehicle in question being a lawnmower. But after the driver was charged, taken to court and convicted, the case was thrown out, because he was only doing 6mph, too slow to be covered by any legislation.

Maybe it's the lack of whale steaks, whale meatballs and even whaleburgers in their diet. Even though minke whales are no more in danger of extinction than law-breaking Greenpeace activists who think nothing of breaking into whaling boats, opening the sea-locks, padlocking engine rooms and sinking the whole thing, or even boarding whalers in mid-hunt and deliberately sabotaging the harpoon cannon, the Norwegians are getting such a complex about it all they are turning to yoghurt.

Maybe it's something to do with all this slaloming. Going suddenly one way. Then going suddenly the other. Then suddenly back again. As if they can't make up their minds. They don't just do it going downhill, they do it all the time. So much so I reckon they should call the place Neither/Norway. Take *Sophie's World*, the unreadable runaway bestseller by Jostein Gaarder, which is supposed to be whoosh, a swing to the left, a beginner's guide to philosophy which he reckons is the new rock 'n' roll, then whoosh, a swing to the right, it's some kind of mushy story about a teenage girl and a middle-aged philosophy nut, who keeps pushing letters through the kid's mailbox, telling her what the Great Thinkers thought. Am I being clear? No. Good. Neither is the book. Like Stephen Hawking's *A Brief History of Time*, I got through the title page and the first page, then I gave up. But then I couldn't understand what 'A wop bop a loo bop, a wop bam boom' meant either.

Maybe it's because for all these years we've been making them feel guilty (and obviously limp as well) for the raping and pillaging they did all over Europe – even, according to experts, as far as America – when it wasn't really their fault, because they couldn't say please. Thank you. In fact the real reason I reckon they said nej and smashed the European Union over the head with a lump of wood with an extra large nail through the middle was that they knew once they were in they would have to open their borders up to people from other parts of the world who would obviously enjoy it far more than they do and would very quickly fill in those empty spaces.

The only thing that seems to turn them on is – football. English football, thank you very much. Which is probably the nearest thing they can get to raping and pillaging nowadays. Liverpool, Queen's Park Rangers, Tranmere Rovers, Stoke City, Woking, even Accrington Stanley, they go on and on about them. The minister of finance, I was told, supports Manchester United. The leader of the Socialist party is a Tottenham Hotspur fan. The leader of one of the minority parties backs Barnet. The man I met halfway up an oilrig in a fjord near Stavanger supports Port Vale.

I once met a guy in a shipyard in Ankers Stord who told me he was an official in the Scandinavian branch of the Liverpool Supporters Club. He went to all their matches, knew everybody's name, who scored, who didn't score. But he'd never seen anything of England. Only the football stadiums. 'Big Ben. I see Big Ben on television. Why do I want to see Big Ben?'

The biggest disappointment in his life was when Norway actually beat England in some World Cup qualifier. He was shattered. England. His heroes. The one team in the world he looked up to. Beaten by his own national team. I can still see him wiping the tears from the corner of his eye.

And so, if the judges would be so kind, could we have your vote please on Norway?

For presentation:	6.7	6.6	6.5	7.0
For content:	1.0	1.2	1.2	1.2
For chill factor:	7.0	7.0	7.0	7.0

Please mind the ice on the ground on your way out.

Stockholm

Press button. Switch on computer. Flick on screen. Just listen to that hum. Try to avoid watching all the Microsoft and Word Perfect junk for the millionth time. Slot in floppy. Click. Click. Click. Get that sizzle. Up come all the file headings. Click. Ask to open. Engage A-drive. Click. That's the file I want. Go to OK. Here comes the text . . .

Welcome, Cybersurfers, to S-W-E-D-E-N which, I reckon, has gone just about as far as it is possible to go towards creating the most advanced, sophisticated, computer-controlled, xytp.wwxy.k9p.uk. kewl, interpersonal digital multimedia nightmare in the world. In other words, Cyberia.

The home computer, the two-computer family, the computer village, the paperless office: forget it. That was the age of the geek dude. The country that pandered to all our fantasies by giving us the unbelievable, unforgettable, fantastic Swedish model: the combination of the most famous, the most generous, the most all-embracing and most expensive social welfare system in the world – they fired people if they worked too hard or too long even if they were trying to save their company from going bust – is now turning itself into the new Bjorn-again most technically advanced computer society in the world. In other words, in Sweden today, nothing is mightier than the mouse.

First – click – and this is entirely natural for any country with an everlasting supply of trees (half the place is covered with them) – they gave us the paperless office. No memos, no letters, none of those enormous proposals that nobody ever reads. Not even those silly little yellow stickers that seem to be taking over the world. 'From every room in the office it is our determination paper to abolish,' I was told by a Swedish director of a big bank who had obviously learnt his English in Germany.

'From every room?' I hesitated. 'Even from the . . .'

'From every room.'

I admired his confidence. But part of me felt nervous.

Click. Now they're giving us the office-less office. In Sweden they don't just talk out-working, they live it as well. Like religion. Or, rather, like religion ought to be. Gone are all those vast offices. Companies now seem to have tiny head offices with huge computers and, hooked up to each, a million laptops. In fact, as far as I can tell the whole place is buried in micros, macros, laptops, modems, video-conferencing cameras, TV monitors and the rest of the electronic catastrophe. Everywhere you look, wherever you go, whoever you see, they're e-mailing, dialling up, failing-over, terminal interfacing, database checkpointing, rollback/recovering, hoteling, orphaning, hot-desking or going on about document scanners, electronic boxes and things called band widths, fork-lift upgrades, latency routers and whether the British will ever be IT-literate. That's the simple bit. The difficult bit is getting into or, better still, getting out of conversations about 100 megabytes of hard drive, two megabytes of memory, the relative merits of 1,200, 14,000 and 28,800 bits of information per second, something called minitowers which is something to do with storing whatever it is you want to store and God only knows what an algorithm is.

It's nothing like the Sweden we used to know and love and try to get stuck in years ago because of bad weather on the way back from meetings in the Isle of Wight. Especially on Friday nights. In those days interactive meant something more than computers talking to computers, and we all knew what gave the Swedes the idea for inventing the zip fastener. Today it's all computer work and no foreplay. For example, click, there is a special hi-tech electronics ministry-less ministry, which is virtually run by computers with little television cameras on top. The ministry, or what there is of it, is a bunch of terminals in Stockholm. The minister is 300 kilometres away in Karlstad taking the kids to day-care centres, washing nappies and shopping. Inevitably, it's the ministry of culture and the minister is a she. There, I bet that surprised you! There's an IT Commission for Youth, an IT Committee for Business, an IT Working Party for Digital Data, an IT Committee on Mail Enabling and Affordable Messaging Solutions, and two guys I met over a smorgasbord who were going on about the dangers from infection.

Visiting some bits of the States is also, I admit, like visiting tomorrow. But in the States tomorrow is artificial trees, plastic dogs and cats and Mickey Mouse robots. In Sweden, tomorrow is serious techno-élite stuff.

Click. What offices remain are not like the offices you and I used to know and sweat our guts out in when we were young. Gone are the huge black holes, the endless corridors, the staircases which stank of urine. Gone are the air-conditioned boxes full of UV rays, static electricity, fluorescent lights, photocopy fluids and every bug in the *Handbook of Tropical Diseases*. Gone also are the rows and arguments with the boss, the gossiping around the photocopier and the working late with two secretaries and a receptionist followed by a light champagne supper at the Savoy Grill followed by, well we won't go into that here. These offices are far more luxurious than the Savoy Grill. They have huge lobby areas with plants and paintings and sculptures and funny-looking lights. There are even shops, coffee bars, restaurants and all the sports facilities you can think of. Not just hidden away in the basement, but all over the place.

These offices are full of mobile telephones, bleepers and artificial trees with peaches and mangoes all over them. Peaches and mangoes on the same tree! That's how I knew they were artificial. And I didn't have to spend six days surfing the Net to discover that. Everybody, of course, looks blond, beautiful and rich.

Computer terminals drop from the ceiling to whatever height you want. Standing-up height for first thing in the morning, sitting-down height for the afternoon, and for the evening, presumably any way you want it. In one fancy office I spotted a sign flashing up on a screen: 'Please each candidate must answer each question by touching the appropriate area on the screen with his/her figure only'. Which, I must say, brought back memories of old, pre-computer Sweden.

As for desks, they're not. They're mobile workstations. Trolleys, to you and me. You want to do some work? You pick up a trolley, push it under a tree or between the two blondes from personnel who, I was told, have been known to keep their clothes on for longer than five minutes. For a bet. The personnel manager, however, insisted he hired them for their brains. 'At least that's what I keep telling them in bed,' he whispered to me under the peach and mango tree.

You want a computer, you pull it down from the ceiling; a chair – ergonomically designed, of course – you get from a special chair garage along the corridor. Now you're in business. After that, unless you fancy a workout in the gym or a smorgasbord from one of the restaurants, you can actually do some work.

For meetings there are glassed-in areas with café-style chairs and huge sofas. At least, I think they're for holding meetings. I spent nearly a whole day in one in a big company in Stockholm and the last thing we did was business.

Go into your typical Swedish boardroom and all you see is a large bank of Sony TV screens, a red light on top and a tiny camera which whirrs backwards and forwards at you all the time. No long table, no array of trays, not even a collection of indifferent oil paintings on loan from the National Gallery. Although, I must admit, I did once go into a Swedish company's boardroom where, usual fashion, everybody and their illegitimate third child were working on the text for their annual report. I was given a draft. At the top it said *Massage to Shareholders*.

It's not just offices that are going techno, though; so is

everything else. Take banks. Click. Gone is all the nonsense about namby-pamby relationship banking, now it's all inter-active voice recognition, personal identification numbers, social security codes and account numbers and computers that never make a mistake. It's enough to make you long for the days when Nat West kept mucking up your bank account and sending statements all over the world instead of to you.

Click. Even hospitals, I was told, are not like hospitals any more. There are no queues, no waiting for staff either too tired or too inexperienced to know what's wrong with you, or both. No nasty smells, no bags of dirty washing. Instead they're like computerised production lines. In you go one end, a poor pathetic heap of nothing. A nurse processor shunts you through forty-five different checks. Pow! Out you come the other end a brand-new shining model. What more could you want? But like ordinary hospitals, apparently they've been forced to close down wards and shut operating theatres. In their case, however, it's because they are too efficient. Patient flow (note the computer jargon) is now down to such a fine art they can cure people before they get anything wrong with them. And with fewer resources as well.

As for whether it's right or wrong, click, don't look at me. I've no idea. I suffer from what's known as a terminal illness. Ask me to do anything with computers and I'm a dead man. I can't even unpack a computer from its cardboard box without upsetting its compatibility. Not that I'm stupid, of course. I can just about tell the difference between a micro-wave oven and a video player, providing the wife's left the usual vegetarian pizza in it for me. Which is not as bad as some people. A Canadian economist on a World Bank project in Lomé, Togo, told me he once got back to his office and found all the floppies he'd been working on for years had holes neatly punched through their middles and were hanging on a piece of string inside his cupboard, with a note from the minister saying that in future all confidential records must be kept under lock and key.

In fact a few years ago I realised the age of technology was happening somewhere out there and I wasn't part of it. I'd heard something about an information highway. But to me a highway is for trucks. If the information highway is able to do only half of what people say it should do, they should call it an information jetway or rocketway instead. Either way, having spent a lifetime stuck in my own information lay-by I thought it was about time I joined in. But like most things I try to join, it wouldn't have me.

Click. I started looking at notebook computers. Everybody had one. Even our local parish priest had one. Half the parish said it was to keep our names, addresses and telephone numbers handy in case of emergency. Others said it was to help him remember which dates he'd preached which sermons so he wouldn't repeat them too often to the same people. I did try to get the hang of notebook computers, but however much I tried, I could still find names, addresses and phone numbers quicker by rummaging through my scruffy old-fashioned Stone Age diary than by pressing all those little buttons and hoping something would sooner or later pop up on the screen.

Similarly a PC for the office. Click. Everybody kept on at me to get one. My secretary because she was fed up trying to wash the black off her hands from grappling with carbon paper. My clients because they couldn't read what I had written and were nervous about what I said they had just agreed to. My accountant because he said it wasn't good for the taxman to have a company whose only capital asset was a seventeen-year-old clapped-out secondhand Volvo. In the end I gave in. As I always do. We got something called, I think, a Massey Ferguson 35X. But I've kept as far away from it as possible since the day it arrived. It just wasn't as easy PC as I was led to believe. I couldn't even understand the instruction book. Talk about complicated. I mean what on earth is image enablement functionality, let alone specification inter-operability? It's easier to read the bible in Klingon. After a great deal of time and effort, I did finally learn to operate the mouse. All these years, I never realised that moving the thing around and around on the desk actually had something to do with what was happening on the screen. I thought they were just fiddling about with it. Had it been called a rat, I'm sure I'd have got on with it straightaway, the experience I've had working with rats.

Then there's the laptop. Click. I don't know whether I've mentioned this before, but I do quite a bit of travelling and everybody keeps telling me I should get a laptop. Get a laptop! And spend the rest of my life lugging a huge metal suitcase around containing all the bits and pieces to make it work! Not to mention all the problems about parity settings, CCITT standards and grovelling on hotel floors trying to cut into the telephone wire to make an illegal connection without the maid finding out. Believe me, whatever country you try to get into, the customs officers always attempt to confiscate it. Not because it's against any regulation to bring it in, but because they know it will have an enormous resale value on the local market. I was with an American businessman once going into Zaire. He had the Compaq 386 laptop. The customs men told him that even though it had a plate on it saying Made in US, it had in fact been made in Zaire for export only. He couldn't therefore re-import it. He had to surrender it.

'Not true,' he said, as politely as he could in the circumstances. 'It was made in the US.' And to prove it, a stroke of genius I thought, he showed them the details of the sale, which he had stamped and signed in his passport.

The customs men looked at each other. He flashed me that 'That'll teach 'em to monkey avec moi' smile that Americans save for such occasions.

'OK,' the customs men said, 'a false passport as well. We're arresting you on charges of illegally importing a Zairian made computer and travelling on a false American passport.'

There was no way I wanted that kind of problem. Let alone the problem of lugging high-performance acoustic couplers, line testers, a sharp knife, a screwdriver, several phone leads, a cigarette lighter power adapter and a bag of thirty-six assorted adapters wherever I went. And that's just to plug it in.

But on a recent trip to Sweden I discovered the man who knows all there is to know about computers – click. That's Sven, even though at first sight he looks as if he is suffering from exhaustion after a life spent acting in one kind of Swedish movie or the other. The one kind you don't need me to tell you about. The other kind is *The Seventh Seal, Wild Strawberries*, aren't-we-all-having-a-wonderful-miserable-gloomy-time-of-it Swedish movie kind. Or, to put it in Cyberspeak, he was :-I.

He lived in Papersbrucket, deep in the middle of southern Sweden, your typical, copybook Swedish nightmare, oops, I mean dream town. Everything was clean, very modern, very up-to-date. If anyone ever tried to teach them to be untidy they'd have one hell of a job. There was no dust or dirt anywhere. Not even any dustbins. No traffic. No people. Everything looked as though it had come out of *Homes and Gardens*, or the Swedish equivalent, *Computers and Gardens*.

When I first met him, on a plane to Helsingborg, Sven told me he was into the more extreme forms of bondage. Which, to be honest, is not exactly an unusual opener in Sweden. Except in his case, he said bondage meant being bound hand and foot to his wife, his kid, his mortgage and the payments for all his computer equipment. He kept on about ISDN 2 lines and how VC 800 cards were the equivalent to four 80486 computer processor boards and how he did all his translations with a Windows 3.1, an 80386 processor with 6MB of disk space, a 4MB memory, 20MB of hard disk space and a VGA display screen. Me? I didn't even know that 2 Mbps stood for two million binary digits per second. And I still don't.

He invited me back for dinner, and because I didn't have a laptop to work on – see, another advantage of not having one! – I did the usual: I refused; I hesitated; then I accepted. Providing, of course, I wasn't putting him out and all the usual stuff.

He lived not far from the airport, in a tiny, single-storey, modern, cream bungalow in a row of five or six on the edge of a field. Click. Outside it was normal. Well, normal for

Sweden. Firewood was stacked up ready for winter. The grass was cut. The trees and flowers were in straight lines. In a kind of shed/lean-to were a couple of barrels of glogg, the Swedish equivalent of mulled wine with a couple of tons of raisins, cardamoms and cinnamon sticks thrown in.

Talk about a two-car family. Click. Inside there was nothing but computers, computers and still more computers. And all he did was talk computers, computers and computers. He knew everything there was to know, and a bit more, about Atari 8-bit computers, TIs (Texas Instrument computers. Come on. You don't mean to say you forgot they made them), Apple IIs, Apple Powerbook portables, and Commodore 64 and their 320 megabyte hard drives which he said were practically antiques compared to what was on the market today.

He waxed lyrical, positively Strindbergian, about subnote-books, palmtops, personal digital assistants, portable work-stations, three-dimensional sound, five-inch videodisks, digital broadcast television, stereo-imaging technology and the games he used to play on his old Atari compared to all the Segas and Nintendos you get nowadays. He then waxed about low-end monochrome inkjets, which operate at around 600 dots per inch compared to 100 a couple of years ago. By the year 2000, they'll be capable of producing 1,200 dots per inch, as if we didn't know. And he bored the pants off me going on about how motherboards which can contain the main bits and pieces of a PC are now one-quarter, in some cases one-fifth, the size they were five weeks or five years ago, I can't remember which.

Anything you wanted to know pre, during or post the launch of the super modern PC he knew: the difference between a 486 and a Pentium microprocessor; how laptop computers can be beamed up from the top of Mount Everest to a satellite and then flashed all over the world; and how one day computers, God help us, will include television cameras that can analyse exactly how hard we have to work enjoying all that extra leisure.

His life he measured out, not in coffee spoons, but in floppy disks. When he was a student at the Royal Institute of Technology in Stockholm, he learnt to program in Basic on his first Atari, now a dinosaur – according to him, not me. Five years ago when he got married, he bought his first dot-matrix printer. About the time they cut the start-up time on Windows 3.1 from 50 seconds down to around 10 seconds by using a 66 megahertz chip instead of a 16 megahertz 386 chip, they had their first baby; some computer-made cyberfreak.

'You want a beer?' he suddenly asked, in the middle of all this technobabble.

'Well, if you are.' The usual British response.

'In five years time,' he gabbled on, 'your sofa will know when you want beer. It will tell your home computer. The computer will tell the fridge. You will have beer.'

That might be OK for tomorrow, but did I get a beer today? Nuthin. He didn't move. So much for my chances of getting, as we cyberfreaks say, :∗).

So how did this cyber-happy family spend their fun-packed evenings? Click. Sven told me he loved nothing better after slaving all day over a computer than to pull up his 486 chip cyberhog, which runs at an amazing 66 megahertz, hit the cyberspace and surf the Net, or as he called it, the Infobahn.

Come in URL: http:/www.sura.net/matsci.html – some Materials Science Research Database. Then it's a quick spin across to URL: http:/www.syp.toppan.co.jp: 8082/besju-tart.html, the Chemical Society of Japan. After that, it's anything that takes his fancy. Perhaps a hack into some company's secret inner cyber room filled with personal tax returns. Sometimes he tries to unscramble computer messages between one country's secret police force and another country's secret police force; especially messages written in something called PGP, which is supposed to be the latest in mathematically sophisticated encryption technology and about as uncrackable as the lock on my brother-in-law's purse.

'Why secret police forces? Why not terrorist groups?' I asked.

'I will,' he said. 'Next year. This year my target is secret police forces.'

Then he has a couple of gos at getting the password and log-in on a couple of other secret computer programmers so that he can bust them another time.

If Sven would make you shiver in a sauna, his wife – click, click, click – would make you never want to leave a sauna. She was, as they say in cyberspeak, C:-1 !!!! Although on reflection, it probably wasn't his wife. Wives don't usually look like that, even in Sweden. Either way she too was curled up with a portable computer on some awful IKEA-type sofa.

'I hear from my friend on Internet,' she said. 'The other day in London an old lady sees something on Barclay Square shopping service and she goes to Berkeley Square in London to have a look and she can't find it anywhere. Don't you think that's funny?'

Very cyberfunny, I thought. Especially if she had told me the story in hypertext transport protocol. Or maybe not.

The son – click – a real little cybergeek or :-& K:P:->%-, to put it politely, was in another room with another computer, this one had a built-in facsimile modem as well as a CD-ROM player with speakers for playing games. He was sending electronic messages to friends all over the next street whom he hadn't seen since they left school two hours ago; typing up his homework; checking out Cupid's Love, Love Link and what Miss DiNora is up to; tuning into alt.rave: to get the latest on Severed Heads, Snog and Black Lung and watching God knows what when his parents, or rather the others, were not around.

They asked if I would like to join them for an evening of virtual reality. I said no, thank you. My own personal mental PC had just crashed and I couldn't take any more in. Instead, click, I wanted to go and get drunk in some boring virtual bar in the middle of virtual nowhere. At least it was my kind of reality. Why I should be picked up by a computer freak in Sweden of all places and not by one in, say, Santa Ana, or further up in Silicon Valley or in Seattle, or better still in

Grenoble in the South of France – Silicon Valley dans le soleil – I don't know.

To me, click, Sweden always seemed to be not just pre-computer but practically pre-abacus; the most beautifully engineered socialist paradise anyone could imagine: full employment, peaceful industrial relations, some of the most successful companies in the world, cars whose lights never go out, shops which refuse to sell war toys, Action Men or Power Rangers; the world's most inefficient police force – ten years later and they still haven't found the guy who killed Olof Palme in broad daylight, nor even the murder weapon – and gaols which are not just more luxurious than their hotels, the prisoners, oops, I mean guests, are actually paid to pursue what is known as environmental conservation exercises.

'What are environmental conservation exercises?' I once asked a Swedish social worker. It's not difficult to find one. They're all over the place.

'Shooting,' he told me. 'We teach them how to hunt and conserve nature. It helps them re-establish their identity with the real world.'

I had also thought of Sweden, which is the same size as Spain but with only 8.5 million people, as – click – stark, unyielding Lutheranism: pale faces, long silences, deep stillnesses, sin, confession, punishment, forgiveness, and people sitting on trains openly reading books like *The Lesbian Sado-Masochism Safety Manual* or, worse still, *Oral Sadism and the Vegetarian Personality*. But that's probably what comes of watching too many Bergman films when you're young. Or were they Scottish Widows TV commercials? I get so confused.

The Swedes – click – seem to do nothing but worry: about what they're doing; what they're not doing; what people think of them if they do or do not do something; whether they should have done this or that; what would the rest of the world say if they had or hadn't and why don't they have more small companies in the economy. They also seem to worry that there are too many giant companies in Sweden: Saab, Tetra-pak, Perstorp, Volvo. Talking of which, everybody thinks

Volvo came up with a great road safety idea by building their cars with the lights already switched on. No way. Sweden, the Land of the Midnight Sun, is dark for most of the day. They designed the cars for the Swedish market. When they came to export them they'd forgotten how to turn the lights off. And they couldn't find the formula because it was so dark they couldn't see what they were doing. They made up the road safety idea because do you know a Swede who admits he made a mistake?

Then, of course, they also worry about such things as where the new jobs are going to come from; whether the King of Morocco will order more Volvos – he's already got 158 of them; why America beat them 111–0 in women's rugby and why they don't have more small companies in the economy.

I thought the Norwegians had the big inferiority complex. Not so, it's the Swedes. And that was even before they got buried up to their necks in the snow by the Norwegians at the winter Olympics in Lillehammer.

Whenever I go there they want to know whether I've heard of Sweden, which immediately shows you how switched on they are; what I think of the country; did I know how big it was. 'Do you know we're the largest country in Europe?' I'm always being asked. Which I must admit surprises me. I always thought France was the largest country in Europe. Not according to the Swedes.

'Do you know, if you take Sweden and swing it round so it runs to south of Europe, it will reach the centre of Italy?' Which, again, I admit surprises me. I knew it was big. Stockholm's only halfway up the country. The rest of the place is full of trees.

Other questions I've been asked? You'll never believe it so I'll only tell you some of them. How long will the Stomatal sign at Slussen remain the oldest neon sign in the country? For ever, or until the police arrest whoever killed Mr Palme, whichever is the sooner.

Is the Levi Strauss poster which covers no less than 480 square metres of the front of the upmarket NK department store the largest advertisement in the world? No. There's a bigger one in Norway. (There isn't really. It's just that it makes them hopping mad if they think Norway can do more than beat them mittens down at winter sports.)

Is the poster for the newspaper *Folkbladet Ostgoten*, showing a man's hand groping under a woman's skirt under the slogan 'Folkbladet makes a point of prying into what others try to hide', a sophisticated attempt at English humour or plain disgusting? It depends if you're a liberal or a dyed-in-the-wool reactionary. Liberals will hate it and dyed-in-the-wool reactionaries will love it.

Do the Swedes really eat more baked beans than the Germans eat instant curries? If you'll stand still a minute and stop jumping about all over the place I'll tell you.

What's the difference between a Russian submarine lurking off the Baltic coast and a bunch of minkes out for a swim? Whatever it is don't ask the Swedish Navy. They always get it wrong.

Is it right for Swedish courts to sell child sex videos to the general public, which apparently they do under some kind of freedom of information law which says that the public has the right to any public documents? Zygt!!!?*,%!!zz!

What can we do about the lack of small companies in the economy? Zzzzzzzzzzzzzzz.

During one visit I met a woman from the Swedish Union of Commercial Employees who told me that, as people were worrying too much, they had decided to run a special series of courses to teach people to laugh. 'We should all wake up with a smile and go to bed with a laugh,' she said. 'Do you agree?'

Honest. I couldn't think of what to say.

Joking apart, click, even though it's more like Paradise Lost now than anything else – the welfare state is crumbling, unemployment is rising, there is a huge public sector deficit and their once mighty, global companies seem to be falling apart – everything is still well-ordered, systematised, well kept, beautiful, clean. Just like a Swedish prison, in fact.

Click. Jump in your car. Wherever you want to go it's one and a half hours away driving at a steady 110kph. Whichever road you take, it's empty. There is no such thing as a traffic jam. Whenever you arrive you know waiting for you is not only a parking space but an electric socket so you can plug your car in and keep it safe and warm and happy until you come back. And whenever you come back, you know it will still be there.

Click. In the countryside, which includes some of the best farmland in Europe, everything is very clean, very earnest, very puritan, as if they feel they are locked in a continual life-or-death struggle against the elements. The fields go on forever. There's a clump of trees here and there. Everything is flat. No hedges or ditches. The villages are smart and clean. Sometimes there is only a cluster of houses. The country lanes they line with capsules of wolves' urine to stop passing deer, hare or rabbit from being run over. Farmers are considered poor if they have only two Volvos and spend less than eight weeks a year holidaying in the South of France. Or Spain. Or Italy. Or anywhere the sun shines.

Click. The rest of the country, of course, closes down completely for the month of July, when government ministers refuse to do anything, even attend emergency meetings of the European Union in Brussels. Offices, shops, factories all hang up their 'Closed till August 1' signs. In addition, there's all the other kinds of holidays. Like maternity leave, paternity leave and can I have a week off I've got a headache leave? There are even proposals that paternity leave should not be simply paternity leave but a special, exciting 'Daddy Month' off work to help with all the gruesome details involved in the birth of a baby. I don't have any children myself – it runs in the family – but I can't imagine anything more likely to push up the emigration figures than that.

As for the Swedes themselves – click – before my first visit, I was convinced half of them would be wearing long black cloaks and moping around waiting for death or the Scottish Widow, whichever is worse. The other half I thought would be skipping around stark naked. And of course they were. Except when I got there it was the women who were wearing long black capes and the men who were skipping around stark naked, especially on Midsummer's Eve when they all head off for the woods to collect wild flowers and dance around enormous midsummer poles which, knowing the Swedes, might signify something or other.

But the only compatibility they seem interested in nowadays, I quickly discovered, is whether your modem can relate to their printer. As for all the old, much-loved Swedish traditions like licking marmalade off naked bodies, the only one still into it seems to be the 15-year-old son of King Carl and Queen Silvia who was caught in the act – and this is what I don't understand – during a religious class at a private school. At a private school, I can understand. But at a religious class? Things have changed since I went to Sunday school. King Carl and Queen Silvia were apparently shocked. Not because of what he was up to, but because it was marmalade – and marmalade in Sweden carries heavy overtones of everything English. Maybe they should be done with it and send the lad to an English public school. He's obviously developed the right kind of taste for it. All the same there's no way I'm having marmalade for breakfast in Sweden ever again. At least not on toast. Not even if I could afford it.

Speaking of which, click, Sweden is no longer the land where everything comes free. A glass of champagne in a plastic cup in a bar just off Biblioteksgatan, Stockholm's Bond Street, cost me roughly half my air fare. Which was bad enough. A pretty ordinary fish soup in Ostermalmshallen, one of the big indoor markets, cost me around £10. As for a Toast Laplandia, smoked reindeer in sour cream covered with Swedish caviar; all I can say is I emptied one wallet and a pocketful of change and still it wasn't enough. A couple of telephone calls back to the office from the hotel cost me as much as a two-week trip to Vietnam. And I wasn't staying in the Grand Hotel, the wonderful stately old pile on the waterfront, where I used to go to read the *Financial Times*, which was stuck up on the wall in the gents. Trouble was it meant you had to spend a fortune in the bar in order to go enough times to finish reading the damn thing.

Stockholm itself, click, when you can stop worrying about the cost of everything, is like Venice. It's built either on water, or on anything between 14 and 24,000 islands, depending on how much akavit you've drunk and whether you've yet realised you've got to take out a second mortgage to pay for it. But where Venice is Venice, Stockholm, with its stately architecture, its dignified seventeenth- and eighteenth-century merchant houses, is more formal and straight down the line. Except, perhaps, during something called a Glad Festival, when everybody eats crayfish, runs three-legged marathon races through the streets holding up the traffic, and goes around smashing plastic woodpeckers with a mallet, presumably because of the damage they are doing to their beloved trees.

There are other things you can do in Stockholm you can't do in Venice. You can swim, no problem; even slap bang in the city centre. You can fish, no problem. You can sit down outside the parliament building and fish for wild salmon to your heart's content. You can take the boat out and pop across town to other islands, no problem. One in ten of the population owns a boat. If you want to play something called water golf, however it is played, no problem. You can play it any time, anywhere you like. If you want a drink, heap big problems. For the real stuff you're going to have to find yourself a System bolaget store, get a ticket, then queue for hours, like some kind of criminal, for your weekly ration. Failing that you could drag yourself, like I do, from bar to bar to bar in the old town trying to find a decent Swedish beer for under the price of a bottle of Dom Perignon at Le Crillon in Paris.

Göteborg, however, click, is completely different. It's built on canals rather than on the sea. Apart from that, it's exactly the same. The architecture is quite pleasant, with heavy Dutch overtones. If you want to do whatever you want to do, no problems. Unless, of course, you want a drink. Apart from the fact that nobody can pronounce Göteborg correctly – they go on and on about it – their other problem isn't pollution, but the opposite: it's too clean. Apparently the clever, clever, oh so environmentally conscientious Swedes have cleaned up Lake Vanern, the country's biggest lake, so well that the fish can't survive in its ultra-ultra-clean water. Now, laugh, the first country to be awarded the European Union's coveted blue flag for clean water and beaches is having to make it deliberately filthy again. Serves them right, that's what I say.

Malmö, by comparison, click, is positively riotous. Over the last 10 years a lot has happened to the place. They now have three bars in town. And chances are if you go to at least one of them you won't be alone. You think I'm kidding. The centre of most towns is a public square surrounded by bars and clubs and restaurants. In Malmö, it's a cemetery. Either they all died waiting for a drink or else they were so worried about losing their jobs they died at their desks and their families were too busy working themselves to afford the time to bring them home. But what's going to happen in the next ten years could change all that dramatically if THE BRIDGE, click, goes ahead. For the plan is to link Copenhagen and Malmö direct and create Copmalm, a big new Euro regional development area. Further along the coast – click – is Halsingborg, which I think is my favourite Swedish city. Not because of the town itself, which is pretty boring. Last time I was there there was an outbreak of smash-and-grab raids, which surprised me, because I thought everybody in Sweden had everything they wanted. All I can think is that some of them just wanted to spend time in prison trying to improve their conservation skills. No, I like Halsingborg because the Grand Hotel is the only hotel I know in the world which puts the mini-bar not on the floor but at eye level. Which is where it should be. Just think. If, like me, you make straight for the mini-bar as soon as you get into the room, you're probably already suffering from gout, a throbbing liver, poor eyesight and backache, to name only the least embarrassing problems. The last thing you want to do is grovel around on the floor for a handful of miniatures. Put it at eye level and you can empty the thing before dinner without any inconvenience or suffering. Five stars to the Grand, I say. Hic.

As for the bits of Sweden in between – click – it's full of nothing but wide open spaces, empty roads, empty villages, even emptier towns. I'm not saying it's exactly deserted – I've driven and flown all over the place – but in most places you don't even have to look before you cross the road. It's almost eerie.

I used to think it was deserted because, for a while, I was travelling with a Swedish venture capitalist who had two secret ambitions: to play the mouth organ and to sing soppy Swedish love songs. Before we hit any town anywhere, I used to think, people must have got wind of what he wanted to do and evacuated the place. But no. They were like that all the—

DISK FULL. DISK FULL. DISK FULL.

Click. Back to file. Click. Ask it to close. Click. All those damn pictures again. Now – click – the business in the top left-hand corner. Click. Close. Wonderful. A clear screen. Now wait for the flipping C-prompt to come up at the top of the screen. One. Two. Three. Four. Five. Six. Seven. Eight. Flick off screen. Flick off computer. Peace. Again. At last.

Sofia

I blame Robert Maxwell.

As if playing host to Carlos the Jackal, the man who tried to kill the Pope, and Anastasia, sole survivor of the Romanovs, was not enough, the poor Bulgarians also had to contend with Robert Maxwell, the so-called 'King of Bulgaria', who not only ran the local football team and all kinds of shady currency deals with the government, but also wheeled and dealed on their behalf throughout the world. One morning he even stormed into Sofia and announced to a waiting world that in Bistrica, a tiny village in the mountains high above the capital, he was going to establish the most prestigious seat of learning in the whole universe, the Robert Maxwell Business School complete with swimming pool, library and solarium, through whose stately portals the cream of East European managers would in future stream, to earn the much coveted red, black and turquoise Robert Maxwell Business School Certificate.

Which was obviously, not to put too fine a point on it, a shock from which they have never recovered. For even though it was only a half-day visit, it clearly put the Bulgarians off foreigners for ever. As a result, I reckon the whole country is still suffering from one of the most insidious and deadly maladies known to man: post-Robert Maxwell trauma. They are in a state of complete bewilderment; distressed, uncertain of what to do next and deeply distrustful of everyone and everything. Up until now this has been a condition known only to affect thousands of elderly, insecure people who are suddenly uncertain of where to turn or what to do next. As far as I know, Bulgaria is the first case where it has been known to affect a whole country, which is why today it is equally elderly in its ways, insecure as far as its future is concerned and completely uncertain about where to turn or what to do next.

If another country has suffered the same kind of long drawn-out, agonising shock, it has to be Israel. Remember the heartache, the questioning, the terrible anguish they suffered, and are probably still suffering, when they discovered what their leaders had done. Except they had one big advantage over the Bulgarians. When Robert Maxwell arrived in Israel to be buried in the holiest of holies, he was at least dead. Although even then there were bets being placed on how long that would last.

The result is that instead of welcoming foreigners, especially foreigners bearing huge sums of money to help them develop their industries, exploit their enormous natural resources and get their fair share of the growing Black Sea Economic Development Zone, the Bulgarians refuse to have anything to do with them. Which is crazy because, as far as foreign interests are concerned, the former sixteenth Socialist Republic has lots of aces up its sleeve. Unless Robert Maxwell managed to steal them when they weren't looking.

Just look at the facts. The Bulgarians are at the heart of the Balkans, squeezed between the Serbs and those great friends, the Greeks and the Turks. They've got a fantastic history. In addition to Robert Maxwell, they've been trampled on by Thracians, Romans, Ottoman Turks, not to mention Hitler and Stalin, all of whom have left their mark. Some more than others.

They have played host to every religion under the sun: Jews, Christians (all three and a half varieties), Romans, Orthodox Greek and a touch of Armenian, as well as Islam and that funny guy with the red hat and the book who stands outside the National Gallery in Bulevard Tsar Osvsbsditel opposite the mausoleum.

They have learnt to live with minority after minority after minority, a state of affairs which in other more excitable countries would have been a recipe for full-blown disaster. Not only do they not have minority problems, they don't have lots of minority problems either. They don't have problems with the ethnic Turks, nor with the Greeks; they don't have problems either with the Muslims themselves or a whole string of Muslim minorities, including Pomaks, or even ethnic Bulgarians who have switched to Islam. At least, not at the moment.

They don't have problems with any of their neighbours: Russia, Greece, Turkey, Serbia. Especially not Serbia. But maybe that's got something to do with the fact that every day 3,000 Bulgarians cross into the old Yugoslavia on their motorbikes and sell petrol at a profit of US$1 a litre. Although I may be wrong.

They've also avoided problems with the new Macedonia, even though they've fought three wars over the place in the last hundred years. Some say it's because Bulgarian ports are handling most of the trade with Macedonia as a result of the official Greek blockade against the struggling new republic, and they are not going to jeopardise the business. Others say it's because the Macedonians are really Bulgarians, so what's the problem. Either way, there could have been problems but there aren't.

The most orthodox and the most loyal of all the old Russian states, the place was run by Todor Zhivkov so strictly according to his master's wishes in Moscow that not once did the Russians have even to consider invading the country to set matters right. Since the Russians left, surprise, surprise, they've had big problems adjusting to the new set-up. In those five years, they've had six prime ministers, six governments, and about twenty-seven different government policies. But at least the changeovers have been peaceful, which in itself proves how far they have travelled, although today the communists are back in power, this time calling themselves the Bulgarian Socialist Party. To most people it's a modern European party of the left, but to some it is you-know-what under a different label. A red label.

Over I forget how many other Red Labels in a bar opposite the American Club in the centre of town, close to one of Carlos's hideaways, I was given the lowdown. All but two of the 110 members of the party's supreme council were on the once supreme and all powerful council of you-know-which party. The leader of the parliamentary group was still going around saying the word communism was sacred among their members. A major plank of their policy was experience. They were insisting that anybody appointed to a position of authority must have had at least five years' experience of government. Which means they must have held office while you-know-who was in power. What's more, the left-wing newspaper had started carrying cartoons showing capitalists as big fat men in pin-striped trousers, black jackets and bowler hats.

Which may well be the case. But as I see it, if there were free and fair elections and they were elected, there's not really much anyone can do about it. Until the next election. That after all is what democracy is all about.

As a result, either because the government are really Reds in disguise, or because they don't know what to do, or because they are just frightened to make decisions, they have started reforming themselves. But slowly. Many people say they are the slowest of all the old Soviet republics, but they have made a start. Which is a start.

So far they have put in place all the political, financial and economic institutions they need to run a Western-style operation. The only area where they seem to have been really dragging their feet is privatisation. Some say it's because they like things the way they are; it's a Bulgarian tradition, selling. I mean, selling raw materials at high prices to friends running state enterprises and then buying back the finished products extra-cheap to sell at the highest possible price on the open market. You make money on selling the raw materials. You make even more money re-selling the finished products. And the state enterprise? The money it loses is picked up by the state. The friend running the state enterprise? Well, maybe a mistake is made somewhere along the line and something is wrongly transferred to his Canadian bank account.

Canadian, note, not Swiss. The Bulgarians don't seem to trust the Swiss. They prefer the Canadians. Probably because they've got it into their heads that one day they're all going to end up as taxi drivers in Toronto, so they might as well start putting something by as soon as they can.

Another reason maybe for them dragging their heels is that the state enterprises are not yet ready for privatisation. They have to be properly packaged for future investors. In other words, the old trick, the big guys are appointing all their old comrades to every state enterprise they can find. They are then letting them sell off everything that moves on the old capitalist principle of 'two for you, one for me. And this is the number of my bank account,' which also happens to be – in Canada.

As if that's not enough Balkan intrigue to be getting on with – John Buchan, thou shouldst be living at this hour – there's an even more mysterious third theory surrounding a sinister group of thirteen former senior communist officials and secret policemen who in a secret backroom deal have got together so that when the time is right, they can snap up anything worthwhile through a string of off-shore subsidiaries based mainly in Cyprus.

'Why thirteen?' I asked the man in the dark suit with his hat pulled down over his eyes.

'Because there are two Judases in it,' he whispered.

Shh. Say no more. Swallow that piece of paper and forget we ever spoke.

Now I know the Bulgarians are not the most popular people on earth – the Poles can't stand them; you watch the next time you see a Bulgarian speaking and there is a Pole in the room. He will deliberately look away and yawn – but they are not capitalising on what they have done so far and getting the credit, not to mention the loans, leases, overdrafts, mortgages, securities, long-term investments and, oops, I nearly forgot, money they deserve.

Since the Wall came down and the Soviet empire crumbled, the Poles, the Hungarians, the Czechs have all received billions of dollars in aid. Bulgaria has received only US$750 million. Why? Because obviously having been burnt by Robert Maxwell – another of his projects, a massive Bulgarian newspaper complex, still stands unfinished on the outskirts of Sofia – they appear to have decided they don't want anything to do with foreigners or their money. Whatever they do, they're going to do on their own, in their own way and with whatever resources they or the mysterious group of thirteen can come up with. The result is the whole place is going the way of the Robert Maxwell Business School and the Robert Maxwell Bulgarian newspaper empire; it is crumbling into the dust.

Everybody who can is jumping ship. As soon as they opened up to the outside world, everybody who could leave the country did so. The very rich: senior party officials, police chiefs, businessmen and all the fixers and arrangers in between. The not so rich: professors, teachers, students and anybody who knew anybody anywhere in the outside world. Some people say it was half a million, others a million. So it has continued ever since, officially and unofficially, which is one of the reasons why the European Union is snooty about Bulgaria. They fear it could be the open back door into the Community.

The result is whenever I go there I get the impression that the place is empty. Not only first thing in the morning or late at night, but all day long. It's as if everyone is at home studying for their Robert Maxwell Business School degree in pension fund management (the degree certificate is red with a black border), or there's this fantastic party going on somewhere and I'm the only one who's not been invited. Which is not a new experience for me. The whole place is grinding to a standstill.

Sofia, I know, is not exactly the fun spot of the Balkans, or of anywhere. The centre is choc-a-bloc with huge Stalinist monstrosities; bars and restaurants are few and far between; the roads are full of pot holes; pavements are crumbling; hotels are pretty basic. How Carlos put up with them all those years, I don't know. It's enough to turn you off being a terrorist. As for Anastasia, I think it was touch and go which was worse: being shot with the rest of the family or being forced to spend twenty-four years stuck in Gabarevo, 140 miles east of Sofia.

In the centre of town there are plenty of obviously new, tiny, privately owned shops selling all the little luxuries that make life worth living, from leather-covered beanbag chairs to Italian-style hand-made toothbrush holders. The pavements are full of stall-holders, guys selling off the back of a lorry, and little old ladies in thick woolly cardigans selling fruit and vegetables they picked fresh that morning. Trouble is there are no buyers. Money is short. Most people have two, if not three jobs. I forget how many people I met, managers, engineers, teachers, who had second jobs in the evenings and at weekends as photographers, decorators, and teachers. Which obviously keeps people off the streets.

Transport is a problem. The trams, most of which seem to be driven by women, presumably on the basis that if they are on rails there is not much they can do wrong, look as though they came out of the Ark. The buses, the ones that concertina in the middle, look as though they were not far behind. And like everything in the Ark, when they do come, they tend to come in pairs. Cars either have no lights, no bumpers, no windows, three doors and three and a half tyres, or they're beautiful, immaculate and sparkling clean. Trouble is, all the beautiful, immaculate, sparkling ones are smuggling petrol to the Serbs. And the reason they are beautiful, immaculate and sparkling clean is that when the police spot them they are so dazzled by their brilliance they have to turn round and look the other way.

And there simply aren't many people around. Stroll from the university, with the two massive statues of its founders sitting either side of the main entrance, where they learn the theory, across the square to the parliament building, where they fail to put it into practice, you'll be lucky to see two old ladies loaded with bundles of nothing, or an old soldier with a row of medals and a wooden leg.

Wander from the huge Alexander Nevsky Memorial Church, the massive neo-Byzantine pile built in the late nineteenth-century to commemorate the Russian soldiers who died fighting to save Bulgaria from the Turks, to the National Art Gallery, which used to be the royal palace until that fateful day in 1943 when King Boris mysteriously collapsed and died just after having met Hitler. You might see a couple of artists trying to sell their paintings on the street, a group of policemen in their light blue uniforms and leather boots having a smoke, or an old soldier begging.

Pop into the large, solid Hotel Balkan Sheraton which looks as though it could withstand a nuclear explosion. You can get into the coffee shop no problem. I'm not saying it's the least popular place in the whole world. All I know is, there were more ancient Romans wandering around the ruins of the fourth-century church of St George outside than there were in reception, the coffee shop or even the bar.

From there I wandered around Alexander Batanburg Square, which is dominated by a string of enormous Stalinist buildings, including the old party headquarters which they tried to burn down and couldn't. It was deserted.

One morning I walked from the railway station, down the steps, along the arcade up into the bus station. In any other city, such a route would have been so packed I would have lost not only my wallet but my trouser buttons as well. It was empty.

One evening, for want of something to do (you know what it's like: a long trip, away from home, nothing to do), I sat on a hard wooden bench in a bar along Bulevard Vitosha, drinking the local beer. You would have expected the place to be crowded. It was the main shopping street in the city. If anything was going to happen in Sofia, it would happen in Bulevard Vitosha. I was almost the only customer.

The barman started telling me what it was like living there. He was lucky, he said. He had water every third day. Hardly anybody had any hot water. Most people rushed home to make the most of the daylight. At night they lived by candlelight and huddled together behind thick brocade curtains to try and keep warm. And that was during the summer. I didn't dare ask him what they did in the winter.

One evening, as is my wont, I went to the opera. It was cheaper than buying a beer. It was frozen. The opera, I mean, not the beer. They couldn't afford to turn the heating on. Which is obviously why they stuck to good old-fashioned, rip-roaring, fully-clothed *Travatore*, and not some less-dressed modern like *Salome* or *Les Huguenots*. Judging by my experience, by the time they got to the end of Act I Scene 2, more than their tiny hands would have been frozen, I can tell you.

Afterwards, in another bar – Sofia is that kind of place – I asked another barman what life was like in winter. But he had to go. He told me he had another job driving a taxi, which he shared with his sister. She drove it during the day, he drove it at night. I was left to do the only thing anyone can do in a bar in Sofia in the evening. I watched the traffic go by. As a result, I'm proud to say, I am responsible for the first-ever downtown Sofia traffic survey ever carried out in the history of the new Bulgarian state. The findings: Moskvitchs, 13; BMWs, 3; Skodas, 12; Audis, 9; Trabants, God bless them, 3; dirty great Russian lorries, 4; Volvos, 6; trams, 4; Rolls-Royce Silver Shadows, chauffeur-driven, with flag on bonnet, 1. Which apparently belongs to some Bulgarian American in the property business. Although over another beer I was told by another barman who during the day was a teacher that that was unusual. Most successful Bulgarian businessmen had more than one Rolls-Royce. He had been told that one member of the group of thirteen had not only a Rolls but three Mercedes 600s, one sports Mercedes 600, a Porsche Carrera, a Dodge Stealth, one Range Rover, a Mercedes Jeep, a Toyota Jeep, two Mitsubishi Pajeros and a Wrangler Cabriolet as well.

I thought he was kidding. But he said he was deadly serious. 'In Bulgaria,' he told me, 'we now have 1,000 millionaires and five billionaires. All socialists.' He laughed. 'There are more communists running Bulgaria today than when the Russians were here.'

The only other man in the bar, who was wearing a brown leather jacket – brown is OK; black means Mafia – and drinking white wine with a Bloody Mary chaser with so much Worcester sauce in it it was practically black, came up and joined us. Trouble was, he told me, that not only did the group of thirteen have too many cars and too much money, they didn't know how to spend it.

He gave me an example. When the Bulgarian football team came fourth in the World Cup, they immediately became national heroes. 'Do you know what some of the members of the group of thirteen did?' he asked me.

I did what one is expected to do in the circumstances. I shook my head and ordered another round.

He took a long gulp. 'They wanted them canonised by the Church as saints. What's more,' he said finishing the glass, 'they went to the Archbishop, dropped him US$5,000 and told him to use his influence with the Pope.'

Now I'm not saying Sofia's boring. It's just that the only excitement you get is when the occasional car explodes which is full of petrol, literally full of petrol, on its way to the border with Yugoslavia. So professional have the smugglers become and so much money are they making – don't whatever you do tell the United Nations – they no longer smuggle MiG29 jet engine fuel in Coca-Cola bottles or cartons of soap powder. Instead they are actually rebuilding cars with hidden petrol tanks specially fitted behind the back seat, as well as smaller ones hidden under the front seats. Unfortunately, however, some of them get so excited at the amount of money they are making they just can't stop themselves from lighting a cigarette to celebrate. Then whoosh! Another burst of excitement.

One evening on my way back from Lulin, way out on the

road to Belgrade, I turned a corner past the post office. There, right in front of me, were a whole gang of Bulgarians and, I guess, Serbs, trying to break the world record for stacking plastic petrol cans into a coach. Backwards and forwards they were going, quite openly. It was crazy. It was also highly dangerous.

Another bus behind was also loaded. Under every seat was a case of Heineken. All along the overhead racks were cans of Coke. Down the aisle in the middle were sacks of cement. On all the seats were cartons of cigarettes.

The man behind the whole operation turned out to be a mild-mannered, peace-loving biology teacher with a long thin face, glasses and what could have been a military raincoat.

'But if you are a peace lover,' I said to him, 'why are you doing this?'

'For money.' He shrugged. 'We all need money. How else is there to make money?'

I asked if he had been in the army.

'Not in the army,' he said, 'but I was in the cadets. But we didn't have any money. We couldn't afford bullets.'

'You mean, you never learnt to fire a gun!'

'Not once.' He grinned. 'But we did learn how to take apart a Kalashnikov and put it together again. We did that all the time.'

Did he ever see any action?

'Not once,' he said.

Did he get a certificate at the end of the course? Maybe one in red, black and turquoise?

'Oh no,' he laughed, 'no certificate.' I was about to sympathise, blame the system, point out the shortcomings—'But they made me a major instead,' he grinned.

'A major!' I couldn't help laughing. 'For being able to dismantle a Kalashnikov!'

'Of course,' he said, proud of himself. Which made me feel guilty, though just for a moment. 'Why not?'

Why not indeed? Just imagine what the world would be like if everybody followed the diktats of the Bulgarian army and handed out commissions not for killing people but for taking weapons to bits.

'What is more,' he added, stiffening his shoulders ever so slightly, 'I'm now a member of the Military Club. I can go into the Military Club in Sofia with all the other old soldiers.'

By now they had packed their plastic containers on the floor of the coach and on all the seats, and were starting to push them through the windows. It was time, as they say, to leave. I didn't want to be around if this attempt on the world record suddenly blew up in their faces.

Compared to Sofia, Plovdiv, Bulgaria's second largest city, is equally volatile and explosive. But only in the social sense.

The old Roman capital of Thrace – remember your Greek history? No? Oh well, never mind – its outskirts are pretty rough, especially around Stoliponovo, virtually a no-go area, where kids run around barefoot and beatings and murders are not uncommon. The centre, however, is as safe as houses: houses built by Bulgarians with money they made from the Serbs. It is relaxed, friendly, full of tree-lined streets. There are lots of restaurants, bars and cafés. Even though the place is full of BMWs and Audis and Volkswagens, there are still plenty of horsedrawn carts and carriages around, which gives it an almost eighteenth-century feel. I've only been there once, by very fast slow train from Sofia. But I could happily have spent a week there.

The main street, Knyaz Aleksandar, is nothing but fancy shops and bars and restaurants; more Italian than Bulgarian, and definitely unlike anything in Sofia. It's lined with trees, and packed with people day and night. What's more they actually seem to be having fun, laughing and enjoying themselves.

The main square, the Tsentralen Ploshtad, is the absolute opposite. It's Stalinist. The enormous, rock-solid Hotel Trimontsium was obviously built to last a million years. Most of the staff look and behave as if they're already halfway there. The square is full of slow, thick, stolid figures who look as though their idea of a Marxist heaven is to spend a day and night pouring over monthly production figures for machine tools between 1923 and 1929. Left-hand drive, of course.

After that everything is interesting. The Greek amphitheatre, the ruins of a Roman stadium where once they ran chariot races and organised huge wrestling competitions; the Ottoman mosques, especially the famous Friday mosque with its domes and fancy minaret. But for me the real find was the old bazaar quarter, which dates back to Byzantine times. It's a maze of cobbled streets, tiny alleyways and fascinating little courtyards, all still very much lived in and in full working order. Wandering up and down the streets is like turning the clock back and living in eighteenth- or nineteenth-century Bulgaria. The other thing I liked about it was, it didn't have any cars exploding with petrol or people trying to break world records.

But don't get me wrong. Whether you're in Sofia or Plovdiv or halfway up the Pirin mountains, you've only to go inside any office, factory or farm to see how badly they are suffering from post-Robert Maxwell trauma.

Offices are still pre-Greek. They're old, dusty, decrepit. I went to one company just outside Sofia which was trying to do business with a big British construction firm. In the car park outside I counted eight and three halves of cars of varying makes, shapes and sizes, including one of those stretched American limos that seats about 350 people, all rotting and rusting away; two vans, one and, I think, two one-thirds of lorries; a broken-down petrol tanker that looked as though it had been used for carrying milk, although bearing in mind the business to be made selling petrol to the Serbs it was probably the other way round; about a couple of hundred steel girders; goodness knows how many oildrums, a couple of dustbins, heaps and heaps of rubbish and one of those carpenter's benches, complete with wood on top and a saw, which had rusted into the wood.

Inside, the building looked like those temporary toilets you get at country shows. Everything was made of flimsy plywood.

Doors were hanging off hinges. There was even graffiti along the corridor. In English. Which I suppose proves something. One slogan was 'Skate or Die'. The other, don't ask me why, said 'House of Pain'. I tried to find out whose office it was referring to but my Bulgarian was somewhat lacking.

The factories are pretty much the same; either closed down or running at 20 per cent, even 10 per cent of capacity. Loading bays are stacked with boxes, packages and raw material either rusting, rotting or being eaten by rats.

In one factory I went to, the goods train outside had actually rusted to the tracks. Weeds, creepers, even bushes were growing over it. A warehouse on the outskirts of Sofia had been taken over by a pack of stray dogs, who seemed to be having the time of their canine lives.

Electricity is on-off-on. Water rationing is the order of the day. Streets are pitch black at night because not only the lamps but even the cables have been stolen.

The following day I went to another factory, in pretty much the same condition. Except this time two telephones were working. Although not at the same time. They made some kind of clever electronic bonding system for the armaments industry. I knew a Germany company was interested in representing them, being their agents, even putting money in and building up the business. Were we welcomed with open arms? No way. We got post-Maxwell trauma full in the face.

They were frightened of doing any kind of deal, not only with my German company but with any outside company, for fear of being closed down.

'But why would somebody do a deal with you, put money into you and then close you down?' I asked someone who looked like a manager.

'Because they are frightened of us. They want us out of the market. They want to take away our business.'

'But you are already losing your business yourself. You can't supply your customers now. You are only operating at 20 per cent capacity,' I said.

'Yes,' he said, drawing himself up to attention. 'But 20 per cent is better than zero per cent.' And that was it. End of conversation.

A French banker told me a similar story. For over four hundred years Bulgaria has been the world leader in rose-oil production, a vital ingredient in just about every big name perfume, as well as in a whole string of pharmaceuticals. Everybody wants to throw money at them. The European Union wants to help them improve their production facilities. A worldwide chain of perfume companies wants to help them improve their technology, research and marketing. But the Bulgarians only see them as a thorn in their flesh. They think they will lose their independence. They are frightened anybody will make more money than them. And while they've been slamming the doors and battening down the hatches, the Turks have overtaken them in production, made enormous leaps and bounds in quality and started getting the kind of prices, around US$5,000 a kilo, that only the Bulgarians used to get.

You see what I mean about still suffering from Robert Maxwell? Before he arrived, of all the East European countries, they were the fast-track developer. Now they've fallen way behind Poland, Hungary, the Czech Republic. If they don't buck their ideas up they will probably fall behind Albania as well.

On my last day I got an invitation – an invitation! – to visit a textile factory in a tiny village halfway up a mountainside about an hour's drive from Sofia. When I finally got there I was greeted by a group of men playing football on a rough dirt track. Geese were waddling around all over the place. Old women huddled like flocks of emaciated turkeys on the grass growing through what once, I assume, was pavement. A young boy herded a flock of equally emaciated sheep through the remains of the car park to a field at the back. The factory itself had very few windows, its doors were hanging off their hinges and only one telephone worked. The plant had not produced anything for five years. But it was listed for privatisation.

Was that what they wanted to talk about? No way. The manager wanted me to help him get a job with Tetrapak, the Swedish packaging colossus which, heaven help them, was trying to open a plant in the country. They were looking for an engineer, someone in his early thirties, who was fluent in English. The manager was an engineer. He was pushing forty, if not fifty. And definitely English fluent was not he.

But what the hell! I rewrote his CV for him. Instead of saying he was an engineer, I said he was a technologist. Instead of saying he was whatever age he was, I said thirty. Fluent in English most definitely he was, said I. And what's more, I added that if he got the job he would very quickly be fired with enthusiasm.

Initially, the socialist in him protested. But once I got going he relented. By the time I had completed the form, he was more capitalist than you or me. He seemed to like the fired with enthusiasm bit. He kept repeating it, as if he was rolling a slug of Cheval Blanc '47 around his mouth, savouring every last drop.

Should I have filled in the form for him? I don't know about you, but forms are forms. The guys interviewing him would probably be Swedish. So maybe English their not so hot any way was. As for his age, he didn't look exactly broken-down and dissipated, probably because he hadn't had the opportunities we've had, so maybe he could get away with being thirty-something. Even if he couldn't, why shouldn't he have a go? Plenty of other people get good jobs even though they're not qualified. Why should Bulgaria be the only country in the world to be different?

On the train back to Sofia I met a train driver who trains train drivers. Except he is no longer a train driver and he couldn't remember the last time he trained anyone. 'I know the economy's not doing very well,' he told me. 'When I was a train driver, I kept driving these long, long trains to Russia. Now there are no long trains.'

Today, he is a teacher at a railway training school. Except there were no facilities, only a handful of students who were not interested in anything, and no trains for them to drive if they ever finished their training. 'We have no facilities. We have no books. Some days we don't even have any electricity.'

So what do they do?

'We play table tennis. That's all we can do.'

'You mean all the time?'

'No, no. Only two days a week.'

'Because you are working the other days?'

'No,' he scoffed. 'We only go in two days a week. There is nothing to do. Nobody is interested. There is no reason to go in. In any case,' he leant towards me, 'I must make money the other days, or we don't eat.'

His wife, he told me, was a biologist; a lecturer at the university. It was a good job, but even she had to work in the evening and at weekends so that they could afford to live – or rather exist.

'So if you're working all the time, and your wife is working all the time, who looks after the children?' I asked in a sudden attack of concern which, I admit, doesn't happen very often.

'No problem,' he shrugged. 'They look after themselves.'

We talked politics. What did he think of Russia? Of America? Were the Turks OK? Would they ever make friends with Greece? How about another beer? Then it suddenly occurred to me, I don't know why. 'Your children,' I said. 'How old are they?'

'The boy is four,' he said. 'The girl is only two.'

'You leave them to look after themselves? Evenings and weekends?' I must be going soft.

'Of course,' he said. 'What else can we do?'

I visited farms, or what had been farms; agricultural co-operatives, or what had been agricultural co-operatives, even vineyards; everywhere it was the same story: everything that could not be melted down or sold was overgrown or covered in rubbish.

The main roads were like the M25: overgrown, cracking up

and full of traffic cones, diversions, roadworks, single lanes, barriers, broken-down lorries. No, I tell a lie. They're nothing like the M25. They might not be as big and as wide but on a good day you can actually hit 25mph. Trouble was, whenever I was behind a lorry doing 25mph you could see great strips of rubber flying off the rear tyres. Which suddenly made the M25 seem quite attractive.

The country lanes were littered with cars that had either long since given up the ghost, broken down or were being frantically repaired on the spot before they fell apart again. Some trucks even had their engines balancing precariously on a couple of bricks in front of them.

The farms were basic. But basic. Scythes, pitchforks, carts, donkeys. And not the big, smart donkeys either; I'm talking about the tiny, pathetic, weak little donkeys. Not that that means they're bad farmers and unable to produce enough food for themselves. Under the Russians, whatever they produced had to go to Moscow. What Moscow didn't want, they could keep. But Moscow always wanted everything, so poor old Bulgaria never had enough for its own requirements and never enough to sell to enable them to buy new equipment, new machinery. Not even a new donkey.

'You remember the Moscow Olympics?' one old farmer asked me.

'Vaguely,' I admitted.

'Well, there was no food in Bulgaria the whole time of the Olympics. We had to send it all to Moscow. How else do you think the Russians could find so much fresh fruit and vegetables?'

As a result farms in Bulgaria are barely surviving, apart from one huge operation which was launched in 1993 with just US$200,000 and is today turning over US$20 million sales to companies in Russia, the United States, Europe and Australia. And because the farms are barely surviving, the dairies and food production companies are also on their last legs. Many of them, I was told, don't start work till late in the afternoon because they've got so little to do.

'But surely dairies start work in the morning?' I asked a farm manager who used to work for one of the old state co-operatives.

'Not in Bulgaria,' he said. 'Here it takes all day to collect the milk.'

'But how long does it take for a lorry to . . .?'

'A lorry,' he laughed. 'Here we have a horse and cart. Most of the farms are tiny – less than twenty, maybe less than ten cows.'

'So what about the food companies? You don't collect from the farms by horse and cart?'

'No, no, we collect by lorry.'

'So why does it take so long?'

'Because there are so few farms, and they are all a long way away.'

'But I thought Bulgaria was a big country for food, for cattle, for pigs . . .'

'It was,' he sighed. 'Until they privatised and handed everything over to small private farmers.'

'But isn't that supposed to make things better?'

'Not in Bulgaria. In Bulgaria they put bureaucrats in charge of agriculture. First, the bureaucrats sold off all the feedstuff. Then they gave the cattle to the farmers. But the farmers didn't have any feedstuff, so the cattle all died.'

Unbelievable but true. The year after they privatised the huge state farms and co-operatives, over 250,000 cattle, nearly 500,000 pigs and around two million sheep had to be slaughtered. Food production crashed 15 per cent. That's according to the official statistics. You can guess what the real figures were.

But what about the Bulgarian wine industry? From 1940 until the day Gorbachev banned booze from the Communist Party or the Communist Party from booze they were the official wine producers for the entire Soviet Union. They also built up one hell of an export business. Many's the time I've packed away one of their fierce Bulgarian reds or two for lunch. Or was it dinner?

But guess what I discovered. We were only able to enjoy so much good, cheap Bulgarian wine because of the harsh, brutal, repressive measures taken by Soviet planners way back in the late 1940s, when they destroyed all the beautiful little vineyards up in the hills which had been owned by thousands of peasant families, many for generations, and established huge, faceless industrial complexes that have been producing millions of gallons of the stuff ever since. Drive from Plovdiv to Sofia and you can still see up in the hills the terraces and south-facing slopes where the best grapes used to be grown before the planners did their worst. On top of that, everything was subsidised to the hilt, even down to drafting school-children by the thousand for the harvest – free. They were moved around by horse and cart, given one meal a day, and slept in empty schools.

And guess what else I discovered. Another example of the Maxwell effect. Bulgarian wine made its big international breakthrough in the 1970s when the chattering or rather the drinking classes decided to boycott anything to do with the oppressive regime in South Africa and switched their support to the equally oppressive regime in Bulgaria. What they didn't know was that the reason Bulgaria was suddenly able to produce so much good quality wine at such absurdly low prices in order to meet the sudden international demand was that they were bulking up their own stuff with good quality wine they were buying at rock bottom prices from the only country that had it coming out of their ears: South Africa. You think I'm kidding? Go around the vineyards, talk to the Bulgarians. It might take a couple of bottles. They'll tell you exactly the same. They were selling South African wine in Bulgarian bottles.

And more examples of the Maxwell effect: your Bulgarian sports stars, among them European Footballer of the Year, Hristo Stoichkov, and the women's high jump world record holder, Stefka Kostachinova, are setting up their own bank. I'm not saying a word. The prestigious Bulgarian-American Enterprise Fund's Young Entrepreneurial Excellence Award has gone to a young man who believes he can put Bulgaria on the world trade map. How? He wants to raise low-fat, low-priced rabbit meat for export. A disc jockey, Zdravko Stoianov, has just set a new world record for disc jockeying non-stop for 100 hours.

They are still pumping out Kalashnikovs by the million, from three factories. The Bulgarian Kalashnikov is of far, far better quality than the Kalashnikovs made in Russia. At least, that's what I was told one evening in the downstairs bar at the Novotel in Sofia by this guy wearing dark glasses and a black leather coat.

The petrol smugglers have diversified. The last I heard was that they were smuggling in oil-drilling equipment in the guise of hydrological research equipment for the Serbs and making even more money.

And I've never come across a country which is so full of viruses – in this case, computer viruses. Apparently they pump out viruses at the same speed with which Robert Maxwell announced crazy ideas to the world and then abandoned them. Ping Pong. Cascade. A million different versions of SMEG. So many viruses come out of Sofia, it's practically the Kummpbota Maxwell Ka!? of the Verrldd.

Computer manufacturers they are not. But software Maxwell geniuses they are. At least according to a very professional-looking guy I was introduced to in a bank in the centre of Sofia. According to him, scores of US companies get their software written in Bulgaria, including all the big names working for all the big names in the industry. Just as Swissair gets all its computer work done in India and the Chicago Mercantile Exchange gets all its admin handled in Dublin. Bulgaria is quick, reliable and very, very, very cheap. Trouble is, he grinned, whenever a US computer company cancels a contract, all the superintelligent nerds in Bulgaria get together and send another super-impossible-to-detect black-and-white virus over to them as a goodbye present. Why black-and-white? Because, he said, the Bulgarians might be the most superintelligent whiz-kid nerds on their

IBM 360 mini-computers, but apparently they're no good when it comes to being customer-friendly. The jazz still has to be added in the US. But by then the damage has been done.

As we walked along the near-empty streets back to the Sheraton, he told me they were now working on a scheme to swamp the Net and bury users in a mass of useless information. 'It could bring the whole thing grinding to a halt,' he smiled.

'So when are you going to let it loose?'

'As soon as they cancel another contract.'

He went into the Sheraton. No doubt to the Fantasy Nightclub. I went back to the bar opposite the American Club. There I met another computer expert, obviously a graduate of the Maxwell Business School. He told me, hush, hush, he knew a whole string of people in Sofia who could reprogram credit cards. How? First they run a magnet backwards and forwards along the magnetic strip to erase the existing information, then they tap in whatever you want.

I pretended I was vaguely interested. What else could I do? Then he asked me if I could get hold of any mobile telephones.

'Why?' I asked in all innocence.

'Because I know plenty of people here who can recycle the chips.'

'How do they do that?'

'Put them in a freezer. That wipes them clean. They'll then put anything you like on them, no problem.'

I said I would give him a call.

'If you're going to call,' he said, 'don't call yourself. Call a company with one of those computer answering machines, wait until they've given you all the options, then dial 9. That way you get into their computer system. You can then call anybody anywhere in the world and they will pay the bill.'

About a week after I got back to the office I got a parcel from the man whose Tetrapak application form I had filled in.

There was nothing saying whether he got the job or not. All there was was another famous Bulgarian-made product which at one time you could spy all over the world: an umbrella.

Bucharest

Mad, Vlad, and dangerous to go: that's the flip description of Romania. Mad because it shouldn't be there in the first place. It should be in Western Europe. Its history, its culture, its language, its Latinity, as they say, is Western not Slav. Not even Magyar. It's only where it is, in the middle of Eastern Europe, surrounded by a thousand incomprehensible languages, because a bunch of Roman legionaries went AWOL while on manoeuvres, stayed on, settled down, established themselves as Romania Libera, started making *infantes* and ended up by becoming a prized province of the Empire. As a result it's one vast mish-mash, like those soups you wish you'd never eaten in China. It's Hungarian. It's German. It's Saxon. It's Armenian. It's Szeklers. It's Jewish. It's also Czech, Turkish, Tartar, Ruthenian and, if I'm not very much mistaken, a tiny little bit Irish. I'm thinking, for example, of the first Romanian diplomat I met at their embassy in London who asked me, 'Are you a singular man living in London?' Me. Singular. It was the nicest compliment I had been paid for a long time.

It's also, of course, Catholic, Orthodox, Orthodox Orthodox, Russian Orthodox, Catholic Orthodox, Muslim, Muslim Muslim, Muslim Orthodox and the great spiritual caravan park for gypsies or Romanies all over the world. Although I gather there's no love lost between the Romanians and the Romanies. I'm not saying they go round smashing fiddles or washing boards over each others' heads in every lay-by in the country. But I was told that in Romania people who have a front gate have a sign on it warning the dogs to beware of the gypsies.

As well as being absolutely mad that the country exists in the first place, it's amazing the place has continued to exist, despite everything.

For one thing, it survived the Great Leader, our Hero of Heroes, the Great Conductor Ceauşescu, an inspiration to megalomaniacs everywhere, providing they are prepared to bring their wives along to criticise them for not being megalomaniac enough. Not only was he stark, staring, raving mad, the poor Romanians were also – I know it's easy to say – stark, staring, raving mad to put up with his antics, his posturings, his secret police state and, even worse, his missus – 'I am the Mother of you all' – for so long. It's unbelievable to think, first how long he survived, and second, how easily and quickly he was toppled.

Just look at what he did to the place. Romania has everything. It is the largest country in Eastern Europe after Poland. It is a superb location for breaking into both east and west Europe. It has plenty of natural resources: oil, gas, good arable land, a huge market, and a cheap, professional, well-educated and well-trained workforce, especially the miners who will turn out at the click of a finger and beat up anyone they're told to. It has Europe's lowest salary rates, and enormous tourist potential. Parts of the country are, in fact, so Gothic you could hang your bat on it. Instead, however, of building on his country's strengths, exploiting its location, developing its natural resources, building up its industrial base, modernising the agricultural sector and throwing the place open to tourists, Ceauşescu was obsessed with three things: sex, office blocks and not getting his shoes dirty.

Sex because he wanted babies, babies and more babies to grow up and become government aparatchiks, secret police-men and torturers. When you think they even imprisoned and tortured people for practising yoga in the privacy of their own homes, you can see why he needed more and more aparatch-iks, secret policemen and torturers. Which is presumably why nobody was allowed to travel. Travel would take their minds off the job. Driving licences were more difficult to get than passports. And passports were impossible to get. Television was only on two hours a day, and there were hardly any bars or pubs or clubs. Our Hero of Heroes who knew everything obviously thought that if he kept people hard at it, cut out all distractions and limited their consumption of the national drink (I always thought it was brown fruit juice with fur on top, but I discovered it was beer), it wouldn't be long before he had all the aparatchiks, secret policemen and torturers he needed. Unfortunately, or rather fortunately, like most forms of socialist planning, it didn't work. He got the babies, but they were the wrong type of babies. Instead of becoming aparatchiks, secret policemen and torturers, they were cruelly abandoned and left to rot in horrifying conditions in orphanages and children's homes that looked like concentration camps.

He got the office blocks, however. Enormous, never-ending office blocks. Some of the greatest office blocks ever built. Except that they are all empty.

As for keeping his shoes clean, he most certainly did that. While the poor peasants were up to their eyes in mud, he insisted on concrete paths. Concrete paths around his palaces, around his hunting lodges, even through some of the country's most glorious woodland. You've only to visit some of his official homes and castles to see at what cost. In fact, I reckon if you were to add together all the driveways and garden paths he had built to protect his shoe leather they would probably stretch halfway round the world.

During one trip I managed to visit one of our Hero of Heroes' old summer palaces at Sinai, up in the mountains in Transylvania. Everywhere there were concrete paths and concrete slabs and concrete paving stones to save the great man of the people from getting a speck of mud on his highly polished boots.

In the bad old days, I was told, the palace was surrounded by troops and barbed wire. Nobody could get near it, whether Ceauşescu was there or not. Come the Revolution the first thing everybody did was rush through the gates. Not to run all over the concrete paths, but to picnic on the grass. 'We wanted to show it belonged to the people,' an old man, who looked as though he could have been one of the original Roman deserters, told me.

But going into the house itself was another matter. If the Hero of Heroes' shoes were not allowed to come in contact with the soil, our boots were not allowed to come in contact with his floorboards. We had to put special slippers over our shoes to stop us from marking our floorboards and wearing out our carpets. In the new post-Ceauşescu Romania it seems that we workers have nothing to lose but our shoes. If, of course, it is post-Ceauşescu Romania.

As I was searching for my shoes one of the old retainers said to me, 'Of course, you know he's not dead.'

'Who?'

'Ceauşescu. He's alive, in Cuba. They've seen him. With his wife. With Castro. I thought everyone knew that.'

I didn't say a word.

The poor Romanians are one contradiction piled on top of another. I mean, at one and the same time, they were fierce nationalists who had nothing to be nationalistic about; arch-communists who had more friends in the West than in the East; and anti-fascists who were nationalists and imperialists and anti-communists as well. They believed Bolshevism was the most barbaric, systematic and scientific brutalization of humanity ever invented. Yet they destroyed their country, their countryside, shot people in the back and created one of the cruellest and most barbaric regimes the world has seen.

Then what did they do when they finally broke free? They went mad. At the time they had the lowest rate of inflation in Eastern Europe. Now it's the highest. When I first went there it was a modest 5,300 per cent. Buy a newspaper and there were too many noughts to fit on the cash register. They had the lowest prices. Now they have the highest. Other East European countries liberalised practically at a stroke. In Romania they wanted to do it their way: step by step, slowly

slowly, don't upset anyone; Keep the old bankrupt state enterprises going just a little bit longer. Let all the grossly inefficient operations run up just a few more debts. Postpone privatisation just a little bit longer. Put off laws on bankruptcy for a few more months. What happened? For three years it has had 200 per cent inflation and over. For three years any manager of anything whatsoever to do with the state has had a free hand to do, to spend, to stash away whatever he wants. The government indexed wages to inflation, which means the one is always chasing the other, and has refused to consider laying anybody off whether they work for what's left of the public sector or what's left of the private sector, even though, amazingly, the unions have been demanding job losses and factory closures. And as for the Securitate, Ceauşescu's notorious secret police, they let them get away with murder. And worse. Much worse.

Somehow or other, whatever they do, the poor Romanians seem to fall for con trick after con trick, scam after scam and sting after sting. Who's that driving a Mercedes? A former government minister who is supposed to be big in the arms business. Who's in that Porsche? An old member of the Securitate who's also got that big house in town and a villa in the country. How did he make his money? Selling petrol to the Serbs in what was Yugoslavia. And who's in that flashy Italian job? The general manager of that big state-owned company that should have been privatised this year but is now scheduled for privatisation the year after next. If there's any money left in it, that is.

You think I'm kidding? Look, which country puts tanks all round the runway at their international airport, camouflages them and leaves the barrels sticking out? In which country would you find four million people, about one-fifth of the population, putting their money into a scheme set up by an engineer which guaranteed to pay them back seven times the amount they put in – that's right, seven times what they put in – in three months?

And which country drinks red wine mixed with Coca-Cola?

*

Bucharest must be the empty-office capital of the world. The crying shame is that to build them, our Hero of Heroes, who was to architecture what the Borgias were to child-care, destroyed the heart of the old city. He ripped out old churches, bulldozed and flattened street after street after street. And for what? To put up an enormous, imperialist, glittering white Lego tower block festooned with balconies. The House of the People, three times the size of the palace of Versailles, the biggest building in the world after the Pentagon in Washington. The cost, a staggering US$15 billion, or 10 per cent of the country's GNP. It is so vast, apparently, it can be spotted, no problem, from outer space.

'Gee, what's that big office block down there?'

'That's Romania.'

The only reason I can imagine for putting up such an enormous building is that our Hero of Heroes must have thought that if one day it was stormed by the workers out for revenge, it was so big and had so many rooms he could hide in it for years on end, like the Phantom of the Opera, without being discovered. But, of course, when his time actually came he was standing on a balcony of the neo-Stalinist State Council building the other side of town.

And in front of this monstrosity is an enormous boulevard about as wide as the Champs Elysées is long. It could probably handle two jumbo jets landing side by side. To the French, who invented this kind of thing, it's just 'une folie de grandeur', because it wasn't built by Haussmann, is bigger than anything they've got and isn't in Paris. To the poor Romanians, of course, it must have set them back a thousand years.

While Ceauşescu was trying to out-megalomaniac all the other megalomaniacs, his countrymen were living in the most appalling conditions, struggling to survive on pickled eel and breaded pig's brain, cooped up in tower blocks, two families to four tiny rooms no bigger than a cupboard. No electricity. No heating. Leaking toilets. Leaking water pipes. Condensation running down the walls. Hardly any furniture. The whole place smelling like an open sewer. I went into one flat in Bucharest where the only way to switch on the single light bulb dangling precariously from a gaping hole in the ceiling was to somehow twist two live wires together without electrocuting yourself in the process.

This was not just happening in Bucharest, but all over the country. 'Systemisation', our Hero of Heroes called it. Anything that was in his way was systematically destroyed: people's homes, old buildings, churches and, of course, people. Suddenly bulldozers would appear on the scene and – bam – within minutes whole areas would be levelled to the ground, barely giving the inhabitants a chance to get out, let alone take their belongings. A fairly senior official in the ministry of finance told me that one morning the bulldozers turned up outside his father's house, or rather tiny little wooden shack, in the country. The mayor arrived, waving a piece of paper – bam – That was it. The house was flattened and his father was moved to a single room in a block of flats on the other side of town. All in a matter of hours. The most famous, or infamous example was Snagov, a village twenty miles north of Bucharest, close to one of Ceauşescu's hunting lodges. Whenever he went to the lodge, apparently, he got held up by traffic in the village. What did he do? He systematised it. Just like that.

Today, of course, things are different. Nothing is being knocked down. Everything is just crumbling into the dust of its own accord. Inside the House of the People the water pipes have burst, the marble halls are flooded. Goodness knows what's happened to all the gifts he collected on his travels: paintings from the Vatican, ivory from Africa, crystal from Poland, the Order of Lenin from the Russians; Most Favoured Nation status from the Americans; Solidarity from the Chinese; pay-offs from Israel and the Arabs and an honorary knighthood from the Queen. They're probably sitting on some secret serviceman's mantelpiece in Monte Carlo by now.

And what became of all the statues? Here our Hero of Heroes is charmingly holding a model atomic bomb in his warlike grip. There the Treasure of Wisdom is showing his solidarity with the workers by pretending to push a little plastic snowplough without getting his shoes dirty. Over there is the Source of Light driving an even smaller plastic train. One of my favourites was the Giant of the Carpathians which – I even said it at the time – looked like the Arc de Triomphe with Ceauşescu's head stuck on top. They've obviously gone the way of all those television reports that used to occupy one hour fifty-five minutes of the two hours of daily transmission, showing shots of The Leader goes Hunting and Kills the Biggest Bear in Europe with a Single Shot without Getting his Shoes Dirty squeezed between shots of The Leader Receives an Honorary Degree, The Leader Shakes Hands with Some Poor Guy Dripping in Medals, The Leader who Grew the Biggest Water Melon in the World and The Leader who Invented Popcorn. Honest. Our Hero of Heroes actually believed he invented popcorn. So did every Romanian.

As for the little bit of Bucharest that was not systematised by our Hero of Heroes, it is a little bit of everything to everyone. It's European. It's Roman. It's Eastern. It's Turkish. Its squares are not squares but bazaars. Its bazaars are not bazaars but squares. Some of the old buildings that are still standing look more Vienna than the Hofburg. Others look more Moorish. The back streets are so old and rundown and filthy, you could almost be in Paris.

Whenever I have the chance I like wandering around the Uniri district near the old Hanul lui Manuc Hotel. It's a maze of tiny alleyways packed with little shops smelling of garlic and smoke, selling everything from old watches to exotic little birds. There are women squatting on the pavement selling bundles of fresh herbs. Old men are playing chess on an up-turned box. Tiny restaurants are serving spicy soup, all kinds of spicy meat dishes and a wide range of spicy wines. There are kids everywhere. Just like a Turkish bazaar. The main shopping area, Bratianu, is always packed with people – not shopping, just looking. University Square is for the educated. You need to be highly educated to count the bullet marks all over the place unlike Herastrau Park, alongside one of the city's more imposing lakes, which is almost civilised. But wherever you go the streets are full of soldiers guarding buildings that have fallen down or are about to fall down; buildings destroyed by earthquake; buildings destroyed by the revolution or buildings that just happen to be on the spot where the soldiers get tired of wandering up and down doing nothing and feel like a cigarette. And for every soldier on the streets you can bet your life there are half a dozen official or unofficial secret servicemen ready to jump out on you from the next doorway, the roof of that building across the street or from the sewers in the middle of the road, to sell you a pair of jeans, cigarettes or a stack of old paperbacks.

But for all that, I have a soft spot for Romania. No, it's not because, as some people will say, it's the only country in the world where you can get an unbelievable 4,100 leus (pronounced lays) to the pound; it's because I always get Romanian-made shirts from our local agricultural supplies shop in Heathfield. They're very cheap, hardwearing and perfect for special occasions. Like taking the horses up the South Downs for a twenty-mile run.

Now for Vlad, or, to give him his proper name, Prince Vlad Tepes of Wallachia, the other improper, insane, bloodthirsty sadist, who used to go around impaling alive on stakes sometimes as many as 20,000 people at a time. I mean 20,000 people. Can you imagine it? All those trees. All that organisation. Digging them in. Getting the angle right. And all the clearing up afterwards. Although to be fair to him, Vlad did his bit to help. He would dip his bread in the blood of his victims to help mop it up. Afterwards he would have a wash and a brush-up and bathe in the blood of the latest crop of virgins. That's what I was told one evening somewhere in the middle of Transylvania. And I always believe everything I'm told. In the middle of Transylvania. Late at night. With bats and vampires flying around and Dracula's castle up the road.

112

Our Hero of Heroes thought himself the sanest, most reasonable man on earth. Yet when he was looking for a great Romanian to hold up to the world as an example of dedication, integrity, unswerving loyalty to one's country and a perfect role model for the new Romania, he seriously proposed good old Vlad. He was a prince. He played two of the big superpowers off against each other. It was all going to be a gigantic opportunity for banging the nationalist drum. Who talked our Hero of Heroes out of it, I don't know. Probably the guy in the tower block playing with the live wires.

Whoever it was, Vlad lost his chance. Today, most people associate Romania, or rather the bit of it called Transylvania, which is enclosed on two sides by the Carpathians and on the west by a chain of hills that give way to the plains of Hungary, not with Vlad but with Bram Stoker's terribly upright, courteous, dinner-jacketed Dracula (*dracul* is Romanian for dragon or devil) – even though any mention of Bram Stoker or his Dracula was forbidden by our Hero of Heroes. That hasn't stopped the Romanians pushing their Vlad, however. Just as in England every house over two hundred years old claims Queen Elizabeth slept there, and in Dublin every third house on the left past the pub is where Terry Wogan's mother lives, to be sure. In Romania, the doors, the windows, the horns of cattle, entire towns and villages, and the people themselves are all smeared in the blood of Dracula's victims, if not in garlic. Csejthe Castle, on the edge of the Carpathian mountains; Konigstein Castle, way up on the top where the bats come out to play; the fantastic castle at Hunedoara with its turrets and watchtower and great wooden drawbridge; Brnah Castle with its secret escape tunnel; Corvin Castle in Hunedoara; the Golden Crown at Bistriţa; practically every house in the sleepy old Saxon town of Sighişoara: I tell you every castle, mansion, hotel, two-bit bed-and-breakfast outfit and bus shelter claims that Prince Vlad sucked there, even if he couldn't have been within biting distance. In fact, I reckon there are about as many castles claiming that Prince Vlad sucked there as there are vampire travel agents and would-be tour guides.

For the living dead – oops, I mean tourists – there are also bloodcurdling Dracula tours; Dracula conferences; Dracula cocktails made of vodka and – I hope – red fruit juice, Dracula picnics of blood and brains, Bull's Blood or Hungarian Egri Bikaver red wine and genuine Romanian calves' brains which you're frightened to eat too slowly in case it congeals. There is even a Dracula hotline specially for the Japanese, who seem to like their Dracula more gruesome and bloodthirsty than anybody else, and a Dracula striptease, which I understand charges monster prices. Dracula, it seems, has made everyone in Transylvania a bloodsucker of one kind or another.

Me, I feel sorry for the Countess of Cachtice. Can you imagine, she tortured, killed and even cannibalised over 400 virgins and bathed in their blood, and still she wasn't considered wicked enough to be considered a Hero of the People? Doesn't it make you feel positively drained.

Now the dangerous-to-go bit. The biggest secret in Europe; a sleeping beauty; Europe's last virgin economy. Romania doesn't lack supporters, especially among the French who have almost colonised it. Guidebooks tend to rave about the place. But then most of them are written by people who know about as much about it as Bram Stoker, and the nearest he ever got to Transylvania was a couple of old guidebooks to the Austro-Hungarian Empire which went on about the place being full of misty mountains, howling wolves, growling bears and a million superstitions. Sure, parts of Bucharest make you feel as though a wooden stake has just been driven through your heart. But parts of it are also quite charming, especially out in the suburbs where most streets are lined with trees and the houses are full of bullet holes. The ones in the Nicholas Iorga Institute for History, I was told, date back to 1940 when the fascists seized power.

The countryside, if not exactly idyllic, is better than a bite in the neck. Well, a bite in the neck from Prince Vlad. It looks as though it came straight off a drawing board in some central planning department between Bucharest and Moscow. In the south Romania is flat, as flat as Holland and about as interesting. There is mile after mile of nothing; a vast, flat expanse with hardly any trees or hedges. The fields are not nearly as square as in Holland. Maybe the set squares and rulers in Romanian schools were supplied by the Russians. Although I suppose our Hero of Heroes would never allow any rulers into the country. Villages and towns follow roughly the same grid. Linking them all are empty roads. The land is rich, fertile and capable of growing crops, vampires, grazing cattle, mining, forestry, producing wooden stakes by the millions. You can still see a huge, shapeless bundle of rags disguised as an old woman lead a single cow down a single track so that it can spend all day eating two blades of grass. Then at night she leads it home and sticks it in a stable next to the house. Which is the nearest you'll come to central heating in Romania. Farmers still make hay the way they made it a hundred years ago. There are no tractors, no hay-making machines, no balers; just an old broken-down horse dragging an old broken-down cart. Skinny, moth-eaten cattle wander around everywhere.

'It's the revolution,' I was told again and again. 'Before the revolution, the farmer could pay someone to look after the cattle all week. Now they all want a day off. The farmer can't afford to pay someone else one day a week to look after the cattle. He just lets them wander.'

Talk about deserted villages. Parts of Romania seem to be crowded with nothing but deserted villages. Not because times are hard, although they are undoubtedly very hard, but because they are old German villages and the Germans have gone home, even though none of them had ever been to Germany before. And neither had their parents, grand-parents, great-grandparents or probably great-great-great-great-grandparents either. They first came in the twelfth century to protect the eastern flank of the Magyar Empire. And stayed. They built towns and villages, huge churches – the Lutheran church in Braşov is the largest east of Vienna

– universities, schools, opera houses and, of course, vast factories for making sauerkraut. As soon as the borders were open – zap – that was it.

One town, Nou, I was told, was once virtually eighteenth-century Germany, full of typical prosperous German homes. The people called themselves burgers and spoke their ancient Sachsen dialect. Now only one man lives there.

A village I went to high in the Transylvanian mountains between Braşov and Sighişoara was as deserted as it could be. The old gabled homes were empty apart from the occasional radio and porcelain teacup. Many of them had already started to collapse. Inscriptions on the walls, all in German, were beginning to fade. Signs were falling down. Gardens were overgrown. In the little Lutheran church where they sang their hymns in their ancient Sachsen dialect, men on one side, women on the other, the ancient organ was still there. The pews, without any backs to them, were still there. A pile of hymn books was still there. But nothing else, apart from the occasional bat dropping out of the rafters.

'It won't be long before it's inhabited again,' I was told outside by an old man who looked as though he had just escaped from his coffin for the day and was still having problems adjusting to the light.

'What, by Germans?'

'No, by gypsies. As soon as they see people moving out they move in.'

The roads are also deserted, but driving in Romania is still like playing Transylvanian roulette with the living dead, because whenever there are two cars on an empty road, they are trying to carve each other up. Not, I hasten to add, Mercedes and Jags and Alfa Romeos, but Dacias and Olteits – which is even more dangerous because there is no way one can ever pull out in front of the other and overtake. They haven't the power. What's more, if they try it, all the drawing pins pop out of the cardboard and the car falls apart. Unless, of course, it's a taxi.

Taxi drivers are still adjusting to the post-Trabant age.

Before the revolution, you only ever saw Trabants on the roads. Everybody knew how fast a Trabant could go, especially downhill. Everybody knew how to assess the speed of an approaching Trabant, or when to try and strain the poor old thing to overtake. Preferably stationary vehicles: overtaking a moving vehicle, even another Trabant, was an adventure. Now the roads are not exactly choc-a-bloc with Porches and Ferraris – that is, unless you're near a factory that the government is planning to privatise in three years' time. But to all intents and purposes an ordinary everyday Volkswagen in the hands of a Trabant-trained taxi-driver is a Porsche compared to what he was used to. It can swing out and overtake at the speed of light. Unfortunately, local drivers are unable to adjust to the increased speeds. A spot on the horizon does not remain a spot for long if it's another Volkswagen taxi coming straight at you, whereas in the old days, a spot on the horizon would remain a spot all week, especially if it was a Trabant. The result: the streets are flowing with as much blood as the bedchambers and dungeons of Transylvania. Not so much in Bucharest, where most of the roads are wide enough for ten lanes of traffic either side. But out in the country, between towns. Especially on the way to the airport.

If the driving gets to you, stop at a bar or hotel or restaurant. But be warned: you have to tell the taxi driver at least twenty minutes beforehand. They don't know how to work the brakes either. And wherever you are, ask for the local speciality. I guarantee whichever part of the country you are in you'll get the same vegetable soup topped up with vinegar, the same lining of cow's stomach with vinegar and still more vinegar.

'If the spoon does not stand up in it, it's not good,' a fat old lady in a bar told me. I tried to stand the spoon up in the soup. It disintegrated on contact. 'Before the revolution it used to stand up,' she said. 'Now people cannot afford the ingredients.'

On the way back to the car, take care. You'll be surrounded by enough gypsies and hordes of children to populate one of the deserted German towns. Some of them might be descendants of the fortune-teller who told King Edward his grandson would never be crowned king, and the one who told me I was going to win the National Lottery one day even though I never buy a ticket. But they're more likely to be descendants of the guy who lifted your wallet coming out of the railway station in Bucharest, or the one who was selling hashish outside the hotel in Braşov. 'Watch them. They'll take the fillings out of your teeth,' one barman warned me.

Foreign investors, you could almost say, are the other way round. They want to put the fillings into the great big gaping holes in Romania's economy.

The small investor is already there in his hundreds, from Pakistan, Egypt, Turkey, Bulgaria; from the Lebanon – naturally; even from China. In fact, there are so many Chinese now in Bucharest they are talking about forming their own Chinatown and building their own shops and stores as well as homes and apartment blocks. Part of the reason is that the small man, the trader, the wheeler-dealer will go anywhere he can see an opportunity. Part of the reason is that as a result of the Gulf War all the traders and wheeler-dealers had to leave Kuwait in a hurry and Romania looked like a good bet. And part of the reason is that, under Ceauşescu, students from countries nobody else wanted to know were welcomed to Romania, given free university places and treated like honoured guests. Now they are showing their appreciation by coming back and doing business, or swindling and taking jobs away from their one-time hosts, depending on who you're talking to and if anybody else is listening.

It is the big guys who are not coming. Foreign investment in Romania is the lowest of any of the old East European countries and 2.5 per cent less than in Hungary. And the Romanians can't for the life of them understand why. It can't be for lack of opportunity, they say. It can't be because they have probably the most inefficient industrial structure in the whole of Eastern Europe – well, maybe apart from the old Yugoslavia and Albania. It can't be because they still have a completely chaotic system of production and distribution. It can't be because they still have a collectivised agricultural sector, or because they still have a decaying infrastructure, a vigorous no-holds-barred Stalinist economy, an atomisation of society unmatched anywhere outside North Korea and an unqualified determination to push ahead as quickly as possible with a fast-track policy of gradualism. It can't be because the notorious Securitate, the worst of the worst in the old Eastern Europe, has been dismantled and replaced by no less than six different secret services composed of anything between 16 and 60 per cent of the old Securitate, depending on which minister says what to whom and where.

I mean, gee whiz, is it any wonder they can't find anyone to help them fill even their T-shirt quota to the European Union? Brussels says Romania can make and export no less than 26 million T-shirts throughout Europe. How many do they make? About six. And five of them say, 'My mum went to Bucharest and all the European Union would allow her to bring back was this lousy T-shirt.'

'Could it possibly be because there is no water after nine o'clock at night?' I was at a meeting of the Romanian Development Agency.

'Perhaps you're right,' said an official. 'I'll look into it.' He shuffled his papers around his desk again. 'We must do something.'

But of course they don't. As soon as the government spots a potential investor on the horizon, they immediately insist on tying them up in red tape, subjecting them to the mercy of any politician who wants to score a cheap political point and make them wait years for a decision.

Which is obviously why churches in Romania are so busy: they're full of foreign investors, bankers, lawyers, accountants, not to mention the vast mass of unemployed, all praying that somebody, somewhere will make a decision. I'm not joking. Look, I've been to churches all over the world, believe me, I know what they're about.

Once in Helsinki I dashed into a Lutheran church to have

a look. Standing facing the altar were two priests; one had close-cropped hair, almost shaven like a monk's, the other had long, flowing blond locks tied up with a bow. When they turned round – you got it – the bald one was a woman and the one with long flowing locks a man. The one with long flowing locks then gave what I suppose you would call a sermon. He strummed his guitar and chatted, played his guitar and chatted. During one of his chats I swear I heard him say, 'We have a lot of sex in the church in Nigeria.' Or maybe he meant, 'We have a lot of sects in the church in Nigeria.' Either way I shall never again be able to hear the Salvation Army belting out 'Come and Join Us' without thinking of him.

But the place for churches, or what they call in-your-face religion, is the States. They've got it all, from the Church of Richard Nixon in Texas to the First Church of Christ the Abortionist in Carnegie Mellon University. And they do it every which way. In New Jersey I once came across a First Lutheran church which was making a big deal about Express Worship: a greeting, a prayer, a hymn (or rather a song), a bible reading, all in twenty-two minutes; the length – surprise, surprise – of a television sitcom. I wonder why.

I can remember some yukky squirm-making Mother's Day family service I got caught up in in Williamsburg, Virginia, for eighty years the capital of the first New World colony and now virtually a Civil War theme park town. For some reason, halfway through the service we had to wave our hands over every mother in sight. Which I thought was pretty stupid, until I noticed the reactions of the family in the bench in front of me when one of their sons started waving his hands over his girlfriend's head. Judging by the look on his mother's face it was the first she'd heard about it. What made it hilarious was that they all obviously wanted to scream at each other, but they couldn't say a word. To cap it all, the fat lady with the kid next to me – I always get them, wherever I go – just wouldn't let go of my hand. When I finally broke free she kept patting my knee. Then, would you believe, when she got up to go to communion, she gave me the kid to hold. Me. I can't stand kids. I don't know anything about kids. I don't want to know anything about kids. I can tell you, it put me off the whole thing for ever. Take my advice, steer clear of Mother's Day services, especially in the States.

Also avoid something called the Peace Keepers, some American, male-only Christian movement run by a guy called Randy something-or-other, aimed at creating 'an environment of godly masculinity where a man's man is a godly man'. On one trip to Washington DC I almost got dragged along to a twelve-hour session of what they called fraternal bonding at RFK Stadium. But I got out of it. Luckily. Unless, of course, you like that kind of thing.

If, on the other hand, you get the chance to go to an Orthodox service in Romania, go. It's fantastic. I've been to Orthodox services all over the Middle East. Once in Amman, Jordan, I did an Orthodox church crawl and took in Greek, Roman, Coptic American, Russian all in a morning. But as far as I'm concerned, nobody but nobody does it like the Romanians. Especially in the one just down the road from the enormous square where a lot of the fighting took place during the overthrow of our Hero of Heroes. It was unlike anything I've ever seen anywhere. Even in the chapel at Toronto airport where everyone throws themselves about in what I can only think is an acute form of spiritual turbulence. In Romania, this was religion for real. Here you got the feeling they really, but really, had something to pray for.

The church was about the size of a large parish church and looked like an economy version mosque. There were no benches; strips of carpet ran from the door the length of the building. On either side were a huddle of broken chairs that would not have been out of place in a doctor's waiting room. All along the far wall, up three steps, was a glittering, gilt mosaic wall composed of seven arches. The centre arch was bigger than the others, and through it was the altar and a heavy Byzantine-ish crucifix. This was real Ark of the Covenant stuff. The three arches on either side featured a mosaic of your usual heavily bearded saint, a gilt door, then another heavily bearded saint.

Outside the door on the left was already a small queue of maybe a dozen old women, each holding a lighted candle and what seemed to be an offering for the priest. The priest looked like your typical old-fashioned, slightly doddery parish priest. He would stand at the door, take the candle and the offering, and dash back inside the door. Sometimes the old women would kiss his hand. The door on the right seemed to be the business entrance. Old men, young men, men in smart business suits and ties, would dash in and out as if they were busy running the orient.

I drifted over and sat on one of the doctors' chairs on the right-hand side. It was not so much dark as gloomy. Candles were flickering everywhere. All along the arches were candles. Through the gate in the centre I could see more candles. The women were carrying candles. In front of the arches, at the bottom of the steps were more candles. In the centre of the church under the great dome, still more candles.

Slowly people began to appear. Of course there were the old ladies, of all types; the ones who've been widowed since the days Prince Vlad could finish his soup before it congealed and are draped in black; upright, sturdy old ladies dressed in black but for some reason wearing white ankle socks: lots of the Women's Institute type and one old lady who was still unable to let go of the days before the war when she was the toast of Paris, Biarritz or wherever. She had an extravagant white hat, a thick white crust of powder and a dress that could have been a Barbara Cartland reject. In fact, she looked like a downmarket Barbara Cartland lookalike. But as the church began to fill up, as people stood higgledy piggledy around the candles (some had chairs; one woman brought a shooting stick), you could see everybody else there: young, old, very old: rich, very rich: poor, very poor.

Now I know we're not like the others, but suddenly I began to notice. As soon as anyone came into the church, got accustomed to the gloom, they were off kissing everything in sight. The bearded saints got kissed on the hand, the foot, on both hands, on both feet. That was no sooner done that the kisser was off to the next one: hands, feet, the book in his hand, his bishop's crozier. Then to the next one, and the next and the next. All round the church were mosaics and pictures of saints. They all got their full share. Some got the quick peck, others the real works. Some people even bent down and touched the ground once, twice, three times before they kissed the pictures. Then there was the way they kept crossing themselves. Now we make the sign of the cross on ourselves, more or less formally, from left to right. They were making it right to left which, I reckon, means St Paul was left-handed. Then they didn't bless themselves once, but almost all the time. I tried to work out a pattern, but couldn't. At first I wondered whether one kiss meant three blessings; one touch of the ground, five, and so on. But no luck. They just seemed to do it wherever and as many times as they liked.

The church was now reasonably full. Most of the chairs had been taken. There were a fair number of people kneeling in the centre of the church, not in neat rows as in a mosque, but haphazardly. The queue of women with candles for the priest was now about thirty strong. A number of young girls had joined them. A few old men were at the end.

An elderly man with long, flowing, well-cultivated locks, a tanned crinkly face and wearing one of those blue windcheater jackets sauntered up to the big, four-sided lectern in front of the chairs on the right, flicked over the pages of the book open upon it and, in a voice like rusty corrugated iron, let out a long, agonising, echoing wail like a cat on a hot tin church roof. We were in business. The service had started.

Now I'm no way a member of the chanting classes, but it sounded to me as if he had been doing this four times a day since David gave up the catapult and switched to the tambourine. His slightly modulated howl soared up to the top of the dome and back down again. It rushed around the walls.

It enveloped all the old ladies, as well as the young men, women and even children who were now going around the walls kissing everything. One old lady looked so frail and blind I thought for a moment she was going to kiss the grandfather clock in the corner. But she didn't. Mostly he would chant away uninterrupted for five, ten minutes at a time. Sometimes a voice would chant back at him from the other side of the centre arch, but he seemed to have the church floor to himself.

Now I'm not saying he wasn't doing his job properly – he was superb – but he had obviously been doing this a long time. First he would stand in front of the lectern. Now he would twist on one leg, lean all over the lectern and wash his face with his hands. Now he would take his glasses off and pick the hair out of his ears. An old friend would come up to him. He would greet him, shake him by the hand, sit him down in a chair by the lectern, without stopping the flow for an instant. Once when the chant was taken up by the voice behind the screen he managed to chat away to his old friend, who was about six-foot-six, twenty stone and looked like the owner of a Munich Bierkeller, without once missing his responses. It was fantastic.

He was joined by one of the deepest of deep bass singers I've ever heard. He looked just like his mother. He had great heavy shoulders, a big black beard and hair that he combed in all directions in a desperate attempt to avoid looking bald. Again, in between responses with the voice behind the arch, they greeted each other. Then they were off. It was spectacular. This is what religion is all about. The seven choirs of angels couldn't keep up with them.

More people were coming in. More young people, couples, young families, who obviously had more trouble getting up in the morning than the old people. Some smart suits arrived, and some very smart suits. But young, old, smart suit or not, everybody as soon as they came in did the rounds and kissed everything that didn't move. The church was now becoming quite full. The few chairs had long since been taken. There weren't many gaps.

Suddenly the gate before the central arch was opened and three priests appeared. The leader would not have been out of place in a laboratory or operating theatre. He was tall, slightly cropped grey hair, clean-shaven, the kind of man who could curl a minister of health around his scalpel. Number two was your typical Orthodox priest: heavy set, great thick beard, that slow, deliberate walk. Number three was the kindly parish priest the old ladies had been talking to. From the back of the church, a choir now appeared. The star of the show had been chanting nearly non-stop for over an hour. He had earned a rest, and a chance to catch up with his good friend. Which is what he promptly did.

The three priests were draped in splendid, sparkling, almost dazzling vestments. The scientist seemed to be wearing a cape of the finest gold; the typical Orthodox priest was in deep crimson; the poor old parish priest was wearing a poor old parish priest's type of vestment. But gold, crimson, or parish-priest nondescript, they were for real. They were not social workers with dog collars, and as for organizing whist drives, going to jumble sales and popping along to the Young Wives on Thursday evening for a cup of tea, forget it. They were on earth to do God's work and that's what they were going to do.

Backwards and forwards they went through the central arch as the choir continued chanting with all the heart and gusto and larynx they could muster. On one occasion they came back bearing a book, the gospels, which the scientist placed on a lectern in the centre of the church. Immediately every-body insisted on kissing it, once, twice, sometimes three times. Some touched the floor before they did so, once, twice, sometimes three times. Still the choir continued.

Once the priests came out not from the arch but from the little door on the left where the parish priest had been talking to the old ladies. They walked in procession down towards the centre of the church then turned and made for the centre archway. Everybody surged forward in a scrum. Everybody wanted to touch the priests: touch their vestments, kiss their hands, touch and kiss the cross, the books they were carrying. Everybody, young and old, men and women, were grabbing at them. Some people kept pushing forward through the crowd. Children were lifted up and passed to the front so they could touch the priest, the cross and the book. Then all of a sudden women started throwing themselves at the priests' feet and lying all over the floor. To get back to that central arch the priests had to step – try to step – between them, with everybody still grabbing at them. Poor old Father Keep at our local chapel would have a heart attack at the thought of such a thing happening in Waldron. So would I.

The priests back inside safe and sound, with the choir still chanting away, the women picked themselves up from the floor, everybody drifted back to their places, or started yet another kissing tour. The gentle old ladies grabbed the chairs. The star of the show took up with his friend again. The old lady who had once been the toast of Paris began reminiscing again. 'Chérie, when Josephine first rang me up . . .'

Another old lady now started the kissing tour. She was dressed in the traditional black, with a black headscarf, and looked as though she had never seen the outside of a church since the Council of Trent. Walking along politely behind her was a tiny little girl, dressed in an elegant, expensive denim suit. They were obviously from two completely different worlds. But the little girl was soon kissing the saints and patting the pictures as if she had spent all her life picking up sticks and walking behind donkeys.

A Romanian businessman had told me his daughter, who had just started school, had gone out on her own and bought a bible. Every evening she was reading one chapter, maybe two. 'Religion is something we know nothing about,' he told me. 'We were not allowed to go to church. We were not told anything about other religions. It's an area where we're completely ignorant.' But since the revolution, he said, their children had been discovering religion on their own, or maybe with the help of their grandparents.

The choir now stopped their chanting. The eager businessman type, who had been darting in and out of the door on the right, now dashed up to the pulpit, switched on the lights, tapped the microphone, gave everyone a headache and darted back behind the door. The scientist-priest gave his sermon, reading flatly from notes. I couldn't tell whether it was directions to the promised land or extracts from the latest government directive on when and when not to turn the water off. Then suddenly la Belle, the Darling of Paris all those years ago, leapt up from her chair, rushed across the crowded church and started hugging and kissing some long-lost friends she obviously hadn't seen for two days, first on the left, then on the right, then on the forehead and finally on the top of the nose. Nobody took any notice. The priest carried on preaching. This kind of thing obviously goes on all the time in Romanian churches. Something else I mustn't tell Father Keep.

The sermon over, the choir launched into another chant. More people set off on kissing tours. The star and the big bass singer started gossiping again. The toast of Paris, Biarritz or wherever, noticed some more friends she hadn't seen since last night and went off to hug and kiss them to kingdom come. Many people were still kneeling. Some had brought carrier bags to kneel on, which didn't seem quite right for a prayer mat, but I suppose they served the purpose. Two old men were still bowed over kissing the floor, for all the world as if they were in a mosque. The rest of us shuffled from foot to foot.

More chanting. Out from the central arch popped the scientist. He came right down into the crowd at the bottom of the steps and started what looked like a meet-the-people campaign. He would ask questions, a few would reply. Another question, a louder response. And another question, an even louder . . .

Then I noticed people had begun moving out of the church. The star of the show was at the back, deep in conversation with the toast of Paris. There were only a few people on the kissing tour. It was obviously time to leave. The service had started at nine, and it was now gone 12.15, but it didn't seem like it.

It was the only time during the whole trip that I didn't think Romania was mad, Vlad and dangerous to go.

Limassol

Well, I'll be jiggered, old Pongo's over there with Jimbo and the Major. They're all having a snifter with Comrade What's-his-nameski from Moscow, and the sun's not even over the yardarm yet. No sense of tradition, what.

Cyprus is not just the island of Aphrodite, old women in black, stone cottages, the occasional whitewashed villa, bitter lemons, spicy lamb taras (in other words pastry filled with cheese then dipped in syrup), and a state pathologist who when he is not carrying out autopsies is the most popular man on the island because of the way he dissects local politicians in his television chat shows and newspaper columns. It is also your typical jolly old spiffing four-sheets-to-the-wind ex-pat country. Not your let's-retire-to-the-sunshine watering hole, like Tunbridge Wells or Eastbourne. Or Florida Quays. Or the Costa del Crime. But your real, genuine, professional, retired colonel, Alf Garnett, Denis Thatcher, Long Live the Queen, God Bless Her, Oh to be in England, the overseas edition of the *Daily Telegraph* is my bible, worn out 78s of Count John McCormack's 'The Minstrel Boy' on the recording machine, empty Christmas hampers from Harrods thrown in the garage, the old country's going to the dogs, dyed-in-the-wool, Mrs Thatcher, gin-and-it, old boy, true blue, ex-pat wallah rolled into one and shrivelled to the size of a black olive by over 330 days of sunshine a year country. What's more you can bet your life in the afternoon, after a morning of gin-and-tonic, every one of them still dreams of a country full of 'old maids bicycling to holy communion through the morning mist' until somebody tells them it was never ever like that. It was all propaganda dreamt up by some socialist Johnny called Orwell, who was also a bit of an ex-pat himself, by jove.

You want to see the hang 'em, shoot 'em and flog 'em brigade, they're here, in their old King's African Rifles slouch hats, their faded khaki pullovers (officers' pattern), their ancient khaki shorts, their thick stockings and boots and, when they're on parade, their straw boaters, blazers and regimental ties.

The 'Discipline, that's what they need. Bring back National Service, soon knock some sense into them' gang. They're marching up and down the old promenade taking their constitutional as if they were rehearsing for the Trooping of the Colour.

And the most vicious of them all: the 'Castrate the lot of 'em, that'll teach 'em. Do it myself, I would, every single one of them.' They're here, in the same flowery dresses and hats they wore at Ladies' Day at Ascot before the War. The First World War.

Ex-pats. I've seen them all over the world. In the States; go into a shop, a bar, a restaurant, an advertising agency, a magazine office, a music company, even a nightclub, anywhere in Manhattan and as sure as Tea and Sympathy, the typical English tearoom on Greenwich Avenue near 13th, serves the best spotted dick in New York, it'll be run by ex-pats. Southern California seems to be full of them as well; especially the King's Head in Santa Monica on a Friday night when everybody in the place appears to be interested solely in catching up with the English football results. In fact, sometimes I think more Brits went to the States than all the Italians, Germans and Irish put together. In Canada you see them everywhere, along with the old Yugoslav taxi drivers. Throughout the Far East, they seem to be all over Tokyo, Taipei, Seoul and Bangkok and I don't just mean at weekends. Again they're all over South America. There's even a British pub in La Paz, way up on the top of the Andes. And, of course, they're all over Africa and the Middle East; the amateur ex-pat as well as the professional.

The amateur who, to me, always looks like a failed mystic hippy, tends to go overseas for a purpose: to teach in mission schools or universities or the ubiquitous English School or College; to nurse sick children deep in the heart of Africa or rich old Arabs about to realise they believed the wrong things all their lives; or to cheat, swindle and con the natives into parting with their gold for reject glass trinkets from Stoke-on-Trent. The professional, on the other hand, gives me the impression he has delved deep into the yawning chasm of his commercial skills and expertise and decided he has no alternative but to become an ex-pat. It's the only way he can get a job, the only way he can earn a living. Trouble is it generally turns out to be one hell of a glorious living, way, way above anything he could hope to achieve back home.

'I've got a six-bedroom house in the best part of town. I've got a house on the beach with a jacuzzi and a sauna. I've got a car. I go fishing every weekend, up country at least every month. I've got everything I could ever dream of. Why do I want to go back to Ashton-under-Lyme?' one ex-pat manager who was living the life of two Rileys in East London, South Africa, told me.

Similarly the guys down the line, office managers, clerks and back-up staff, who can't stand being restricted to one stale shredded wheat for breakfast, one hour and a glass of Perrier for lunch and a house full of dead cats. They take off for the sun and the life of half a Riley spent glued to the BBC trying to keep up with the latest Test match scores even though all day long they do nothing but perspire up and down their colonic tract.

The military ex-pat is, of course, in a rank of his own. 'With Monty in the desert. Best years of my life. I was a corporal then. Just up from a private. One down from a sergeant. Great times. Great times,' they bark at you in short, sharp, clipped tones.

The second best years of their life they live as though they're still at the Sandhurst they never went to: always immaculately dressed, always punctual, always the true Brit. A throwback from the days of the Raj, with a house full of servants, the full Monte for breakfast, their own valet and driver. Happy and relaxed with the locals – providing, of course, they remain servants and valets and drivers.

But it's not just the British ex-pat who is in Cyprus. There are also plenty of French, German, American, Irish, Indian, Chinese, Lebanese and Dutch ex-pats. And in the last few years Russians, Ukrainians, Byelorussians, not to mention those two Uzbechi barmen. In fact there are now so many Russians and East Europeans in Cyprus there are more stories about them in the local newspapers than there are about Western Europeans. Even some of the advertisements are in Russian, and not just the ones for the basic necessities like food, drink and nightclubs, but adverts for all those expensive, unnecessary little luxuries like auditors, accountants and international firms of management consultants.

But, crikey, of them all, the British are the worst. Because they are the best at doing what we are recognised for throughout the world – complaining. About the country they're in: 'If this is Aphrodite's island, she couldn't have been a goddess. More of an old hag, what.' The people: 'I'm not saying they're stupid. Damn fine chaps some of them. Most of them, though, you can only communicate with by tom-tom, what.' About the weather. About the mosquitoes. About the water. About why can't they just go behind a bush like everybody else. About why don't they wash their hands. About the people next door. About the sound of their radio. About the BBC. 'Don't listen to the old World Service any more, old chap. Always give more time to the antis. That's not what I pay my licence for, what.' About every possible local custom and some pretty impossible ones as well and why, oh why can't they do things like they do back home in the old country they never want to see ever again for the rest of their lives.

You name it, they've had meetings about it, written to government ministers about it, sent delegations about it, organised bridge parties, Christmas fayres and charity walks to raise money to continue their campaigns against it and even invited the local mayor – 'Silly old fool, who does he think he is with that lavatory chain around his neck, what?' – to declare them officially open.

Cyprus, therefore, came as no surprise. I landed at Larnaca, the main port, which is famous for its ruins. Most of which are at least twenty years old and used as hotels, restaurants and shops. It was my first trip to the land of Aphrodite which, apart from being given by Antony to Cleopatra, was a stopping-off point for the Crusaders and home of the famous Cyprus potato, without which no Sunday lunch or TV dinner would be complete. Over 2,000 square miles of mountains, cool, fertile valleys, forests, unrelenting beaches and one historical or archaeological ruin after another. Or, to use the local ex-pat lingo; the Big Olive, what.

What was the first thing I heard? Two old ex-pats – he looked like a pair of old riding boots, she like a million dollars, all green and wrinkled – creating a God almighty rumpus about what Dusty Miller told the Chief Wop to make the old solids hit the old whatnot. Which, I must admit, was not what I was expecting, Land of Aphrodite or not. From then on it was non-stop ex-pat blah, blah, blah, the whole time. In other words moan, moan, moan.

'Morning, Major. Still no news, I'm afraid. Big pow wow today, six bells, with, y'know, the one whose brother is the judge. Soon let him know what's what, what.'

The Major wanders around the bar. He either knows everybody or spends his whole life talking to strangers. 'Seen the *Daily Thatcher*? Old Bomber in there with some brassy tart. Goes on like that any more, he'll be somewhat non grata in our neck of the woods, I can tell you,' I can hear him shouting at one group.

'Brassy tart? You mean the Lady of Shallot,' says a crisp pair of khaki shorts and what looks like Baden Powell's original hat.

'The Lady of Shallot? What are you talking about, old chap?' says the Major, swaying gently. He points his King's African

Rifles slouch hat at some blowsy old blonde who looks as though she's used up two life memberships at Annabel's.

'Shallot. That's what she says after half an hour: That's shallot,' guffaws the crisp khaki shorts.

'Shallot. Ho ho. That's very good. I must tell old Boozy, he'll enjoy that one. Hey, Boozy.' The Major now waves his King's African rifles hat at some figure across the bar and hobbles across to ruin the rest of his day.

'Hey, Chukka. Wait for me, you old cove. Ordered a bloody taxi three days ago, still not turned up. Just bloody typical. By the bye, how's the good lady?' A doddery old regimental sergeant major now shouts across the bar to a lieutenant-colonel type.

'Leg still playing her up. Seems to be getting worse,' he whinnies.

'Take her out in the bush and shoot her, put her out of her misery. That's what you're going to have to do. You know it.'

The lieutenant colonel nods slowly.

'Come on, don't worry. We all have to do it one day. Whatyagointahave?'

'Large one, what.'

'See old Tommo over there,' an NCO type says to me. He's bent practically double, two glasses of Scotch in front of him. 'Damn fine chap. Had a good war. Saved the regiment, y'know. Shot the cook. Whatyagointahave?'

Then there are some military types with an upper lip so stiff you can't understand what the hell they're saying

'Hu-hurr-hum-hurr.'

'Well, of course.'

'Whaaaaaa?'

'That's what I say.'

'Hu-humm, hrr-thrrrr.'

'Never would have been allowed in the old days.'

'Hrmygonnahah?'

'I'll have a large one.'

Larnaca is probably the most successful town ever created by the Turks. Because it hardly existed until all the Greeks in the north fled south; most of them, from what I can tell, to Larnaca.

'I'm a refugee in my own country,' a Greek businessman originally from Famagusta, which is now in the Turkish north, told me.

Since then Larnaca has doubled, trebled, quadrupled, quintupled, probably one-hundred-rupled. Today it is a glorious, sprawling, indifferent town, seaside resort and hotel zone, just this side of tacky. Or perhaps, with so many Russians in the place, I should say just this side of tackyski.

It's got all the pubs you could wish, or not wish, for: Neighbours' Bar, Terry's Pub, Fred's Pub, Steve's Pub, Shakespeare's Pub, the Old Country Pub and, of course, the Corner Pub. It's got a Tudor Inn complete with mock oak beams which is closed – typically British! – on Sundays.

It's got cafés: Andy's Café, Mike's Snacks, the Cod Father, Fish 'n Chips only £1.95, tomatoes stuffed with tuna fish, ice cream that's left out in the sun so long the only thing you can do with it is drink it, genuine Green moussakas made of chips and not much else, and forty-five minutes' wait for a tip-top salad which consists of two lettuce leaves. It's got a Royal British Legion: 'British Tourists with Children Welcome'. And the traditional British Legion menu: soup of the day, steak and kidney pie, cornish pasty, all served with chips, peas, gravy, good English cup of tea.

It's got shops selling English worsteds, Chiltern mineral water, great dollops of raspberry jam for breakfast which turn out to be cherry, Decca records, Big Ben souvenirs, T-shirts saying Button Your Fly and Christmas decorations in June. It's got bouncy castles, sunbeds for hire, singalongs on the beach, squeals of girlish delight over winning a couple of chewed-up matchsticks at yet another game of gin rummy, mini-golf courses, snooker schools, warm beer, air-conditioning that doesn't work because everyone leaves the windows open, Co-op Credit Societies, Belisha beacons, three-pin plugs, 220 volts, old-fashioned pillar boxes, driving on the left-hand side of the road, traffic lights in all the wrong places, roadworks all over the place, Group 4, and irritable wives complaining that the bill for £353.25 worth of tacky jewellery they will never ever wear is £3.25 more than it should be. So it's not too difficult to see why so many British ex-pats pack their kitbags and head straight for the place.

My first meeting is with an old contact I first met in Nigeria. He decided to move to Cyprus, he tells me, because in Lagos he was fed up with being rounded up by the military to watch executions on the beach. Does he complain about the Nigerians, about being rounded up by the military, about being forced to watch executions? No way. Instead he complains endlessly about the way the Cypriots keep cutting off his telephone for what the Cyprus Telecommunications Authority says is essential maintenance work.

'That's what they say,' he tells me, 'but I happen to know it's not true. It's because they want to put a tap on my line and they can't get it right. They have to keep coming back.'

I then go and see another old contact, again an ex-pat, who is working for a local bank. I first met him a million years ago in Freetown, Sierra Leone, where he made a handsome living looking after local politicians from the takings of the casino. He is complaining about the problems of getting a maid.

'A Cypriot maid? Are you joking? You can't get them. They don't want to do the work. It's beneath them,' he goes on and on and on. Since he is not planning to run for public office in the US, he is looking for a Filipino or even a Sri Lankan maid.

Another meeting, another contact; this one complaining, would you believe, about there being too many foreigners on the island. 'Drug them, then ship them out, that's what they should do; otherwise there'll be too many damned foreigners.'

'Like back home,' I mumbled.

'Like back home. That's why I'm here. If it wasn't for all those damned foreigners, I would have stayed at home, what.' A deep breath. 'I say, what will you have? I'll have another one, old boy. A large one.' I order two large ones. 'That and all those johnnies with two buttons on their suits.'

One morning early I go to have a look at the church of St Lazarus, where Lazarus himself is supposed to have been finally buried. It was, I felt, the least I could do for the poor man. He's one of the few people ever given a second go on the roundabout, and of all places he chooses to end his days in Cyprus surrounded by old ex-pats. It's enough to put you off resurrection for life. As I cross the courtyard to go in I spot two of them: both in khaki shorts, long, thick socks and little red cravats. Immediately I am nervous. No more complaints, please ... But, quite unBritish, they start off about how wonderful the weather is, how glorious the flowers are, how super their gardens are.

'Oh the flowers, they are just super. The Mediterranean y'know. Couldn't do this back home.'

'Season lasts from February to December. Non-stop sunshine, what.'

'Roses, wild flowers, cyclamen, primulas, hyacinths, irises, violets, bright yellow crown daisies, red poppies, gladioli, every kind of anemone – they have the lot. Bougainvillea – you'd never believe the trouble I have with my bougainvillea. They've got strong, thorny stems. Need a lot of handling, I can tell you. Practically torn my hands to shreds they have. But my goodness they're worth it.'

'Hibiscus, that's another shrub that does well over here. Grows like a weed. And buddleia – that attracts the butterflies. Masses of them. Sometimes you can't see the buddleia for butterflies.'

'Of course I have lots of poinsettias. Had lots back home, but not as good as here. Here they're much, much better.'

But once inside the church they change immediately from being pro-everything to being anti-everything.

'Take the traffic.' The one with the moustache is undoing the red silk cord that is obviously there to stop people wandering all over the sanctuary. 'No idea whatsoever. Traffic jams every Sunday evening, regular as clockwork, just as people are trying to get home after a weekend at the seaside, in the country or just out for a drive. I ask you. Why can't they do something about it? No idea. That's the problem.'

Now he is wandering all over the sanctuary. It's enough to make Lazarus turn in his grave. A second time.

'No respect, that's the trouble with these johnnies. Strikes. First the engineers go on strike, then the television cameramen. It's as bad as Britain before Mrs Thatcher sorted them out.' Now he is lifting up the curtain at the back of the sanctuary and peering behind it. 'We're getting riots now, night after night. That's not what I came here for.'

For riots read scuffles. In Nicosia, in Limassol, outside a couple of nightclubs. In the middle of summer, in the early hours of the morning. But it's enough to get them going.

I notice the tomb of Lazarus, and walk down the steps, towards it.

'No sense of responsibility. Playing bridge the other night with some of the locals. Shall I tell you what they did? They opened: three no-trump thanks to a six-club trick, two hearts and a spade. Four spades one of them put up. Four trumps. Ace and a spade combination . . . Nine tricks . . . Should have been ten . . .'

Whatever that means.

Then the other one joins in. Both of them are now climbing up the gallery at the back, booming down at me about the shops, the standard of service, the bars, why aren't they kept clean, the costs of running a car, the problems of getting it maintained, how they've no idea how to roast a leg of lamb, and as for the Yorkshire pudding, you can actually eat it. Which everybody knows is not what you're supposed to do with a real Yorkshire pudding.

After that I've got a choice: to visit the local cat sanctuary and a jeweller called Hitler and Son Limited, or head off for the Troodos mountains and see Patrick and Mary. If I can't go to St Lazarus without being set on by British ex-pats, what on earth will it be like at a cat sanctuary, let alone a shop called Hitler and Son? I decide to head inland for the Troodos mountains.

Patrick and Mary, whom I've known for a million years, decided a while back they'd had enough of living in the wilds of Sevenoaks, going backwards and forwards to London every day, running around all the time. They wanted peace and quiet. What did they do? They went to Vonni, a tiny village way up in the mountains, a million miles from nowhere and started – are you ready? – a donkey sanctuary. For old donkeys. For stray old donkeys. For broken-down, unwanted, stray old donkeys.

'Never been busier, old chap,' says Patrick, paddling backwards and forwards like a rural dean who knows deep down he'll never make it to bishop.

'Always so much to do,' says Mary, who looks like Laura Ashley on elderflower champagne. 'Don't know where the time goes.'

The time goes rescuing broken-down, unwanted, stray old Cypriot donkeys. Like Rowland, who is just 11.1 hands. For townies that's about four wine cases high. He is the smallest donkey they've got but he holds the Colditz gold medal for the higher number of escapes. Like George, who is blind in one eye and was abandoned by the side of a mountain road and left to get on with it. Like Georgie Girl, who gives rides to children in the village. Like a million others whose names I can't remember.

When he's not looking after donkeys, Patrick, who must be worth a small fortune, spends practically every waking hour on clearing paths; on fetching and carrying and cementing and building fences with pallet boards he trades for donkey manure with a local vineyard owner; on scrounging the length and breadth of the island for old china sinks for water troughs, half barrels for feed bins, old posts, planks and corrugated iron for building stables. He is also looking for a trailer with sides, or a horsebox, to fetch and carry his beloved donkeys. Besides all which, he has also taken it upon himself to teach the Cypriots, who've had a shade less than 6,000 years' experience of donkeys – the backbone of the country since 5800BC when the first Cypriots started doing business somewhere between Nicosia and Limassol – how to look after them properly.

'They've got absolutely no idea.'

'Yes, Patrick.'

'Once they've finished with them, they throw them out and leave them to wander around and fend for themselves.'

'Yes, Patrick.'

'That's no good.'

'No, Patrick, I mean, yes, Patrick.'

'They can't stand the rain and the sleet and the cold.'

'You mean it gets wet and cold out here?'

Laugh? I could have cried. They wanted to escape the rain and the cold, and to live a quiet, peaceful life with no hassle. Not only do they end up working their fingers to the bone looking after a bunch of old donkeys and being deafened at night by a flock of Greek owls called Scops which sound like a pack of overcharged mobile telephones, they are also frozen solid for the thirty-five days of the year the sun doesn't shine in Cyprus. It gets so wet and so cold, in fact, that the first winter they were there they had to send urgent messages back to Blighty for a couple of heavy-duty Barbours to be flown out tout de suite, old bean, to save them from catching their deaths.

Over a meal (I suggested it tasted like donkeyburger and was rewarded with an icy smile), I learnt lots more wonderful, exciting, marvellous, fascinating, thrilling things about donkeys. They take eleven months to gestate, not nine (a-ha). A young donkey should not be worked until he is four years old (yawn). A mule is the offspring of a male donkey and a female horse (zzzzz). A hinny is the offspring of a male horse and a female donkey (crash, apologies all round, I fell off the chair).

Then came the hints. Paths to be cleared. Dry stone walls to be repaired. Stables to be built. Labouring. Fetching. Carrying. Any time you'd like to spend a few days here, old chap, only too pleased. Catch up on old times.

Oh yes. There are one or two other things I would prefer doing in what little spare time I have.

Finally I have to ask the question: what do they miss most?

'Popping into Marks & Spencers,' says Mary. There's a Marks & Spencer in Limassol but it's not the same. Apparently it only stocks the things they think Cypriot women would want to buy, not the things ex-pats like Mary want to buy.

'Wandering around Oddbins, or even Threshers,' says Patrick. Cyprus may be full of wine produced with his donkeys' manure, but it's the wrong kind of wine: no Cabernets, no Zinfandels, no Merlots.

Would they ever come back?

'No way,' they say. 'We have our donkeys to look after.'

Yuck.

If Larnaca is the best city created by the Turks, Limassol is the best city created by the Russians. In fact, it's the Russian capital of the eastern Mediterranean. Not only are they the biggest ex-pat group in the place, they own the biggest, most expensive properties and have the fattest bank accounts. They have their own shops, bars, restaurants and clubs. They have their own newspapers, their own television channel, their own banks: six and still counting. There are over 1,000 Russian companies registered on the island. Some – nobody knows how many – are full to overflowing with SDPs – Specially Designated Persons – who are fronting for the Serbs and busily breaking every sanction in the United Nations Book of Rules and Regulations Impossible to Implement. The rest are just wheeling and dealing to their hearts' content. Like shipping stolen cars from all over Europe to the folks back home, stealing all the jewellery they can grab in Canada, running low-interest-rate credit scams for newly arrived Russian immigrants in Israel, not to mention smuggling nuclear materials through Poland to anyone who wants to buy and the more-than-occasional contract murder anywhere you want: Brighton Beach, New York, Seattle, your mother-in-law's flat. A few, and I stress I was told this in the strictest confidence, are even doing some business all legit and above board. But it is, I emphasise, just a rumour. I have no way of confirming such a completely unwarranted accusation against the Russian community.

'So how do you know the Russian mafia is on the island?' I asked a local businessman.

'They're the ones wearing ties.'

Which sounds absurd, because it's normally black leather jackets, but it's true. Suddenly you could see them all over the place: wandering in and out of offices, sitting in parked cars, lounging under umbrellas outside bars, leaning up against trees opposite banks: the men in ties. Not greasy old regimental ties, or threadbare club ties, or even old school ties held together by centuries of gravy, custard and cheap beer; real Hermès, Dior or Armani ties.

'I say, old chap,' another British Colonel Blimp buttonholed me one evening, 'heard the one about the two Russians?'

'Well, actually, I've got a taxi outside—' I began.

'Two Russians walking along the jolly old street, what, both wearing the same Johnny Hermès tie.'

'I've got—'

'One Russian chappie says to the other chappie, "Your tie, how much did they rush you for that?" "US$500," he says. "What," the other Russki chappie says, "US$500? They saw you coming. I got mine for US$1,000." What? What? Jolly good one, eh? Whatllyahave?'

A Russian Hermès tie, which looked as though it was worth US$750, told me later it was all untrue. They had nothing to do with the mafia.

'We Russians, we always get the blame. It's always Russians cause trouble,' he told me one evening in the bar of the Curium Palace Hotel on Lord Byron Street.

'So if it's not the Russians, who is causing all the trouble?'

'The Ukrainians, the Georgians, everybody else. But we get the blame.'

All I can say is, Cyprus is about the only country in the world where I not only loosened my tie, I actually took it off altogether. Why? Because with a tie I even had problems getting a cab. One day with a tie on I spent maybe twenty minutes frantically wandering up and down Limassol High Street trying to get a cab. They all looked the other way. I took my tie off. Three of them were begging for me to hire them. One of them even said he would throw in a free tour of the town. I didn't have time. I had to visit a printing company out on the industrial estate. But we compromised. On the way there we stopped off at the Archbishop's house to see the giant statue of Makarios which looks just like a huge modern version of a chess piece. The bishop, of course. It's like an enormous upturned cornet.

With a tie, I also had problems getting into offices, let alone having meetings. Without a tie, no problem – straight through the door, up to the chairman's office, straight in to see him. The only problem was getting out of the place.

An old Blimp I met with a tie – 'So what does the *Daily Thatcher* say today, Biddlecombe?' – told me he fled Britain because he thought we were going soft on communism. Today he spends his life lending cups of sugar to Ukrainians who are wheeling and dealing all over the world, and playing nanny to the children of Russian mafia hitmen resting between engagements.

'They make money, they lose money; they buy houses, they sell houses. They don't care. For them it's not money. It's not business. It's something to do. Then they go home.'

But sitting in a hotel watching the Russians or the Ukrainians or the Georgians or whateverski at play is not a pretty sight. They not only look like tanks in fancy dress, they move like them as well.

The door of the restaurant opens. In they come in formation destroying everything in their path. Tables and chairs are brushed aside, the floor quakes, chandeliers rattle. I'm no seismologist, but the first time I saw them get up to dance, I was convinced we hit 6.7 on the Richter scale. As for swimming, every time one of them threw themselves in the pool, I got soaked to the skin. And I was sitting on my balcony working – on the fourth floor.

As for the capital, Nicosia, I must say it looked the least

divided of all the divided cities I've been to. Unless of course you're talking about the division between the ex-pats and the Cypriots. You have to search to find the dividing line. The dividing line built by the Venetians in the sixteenth century, I mean. Then when you've found it, it's not as brutal and offensive and aggressive as you imagine. Neither, surprisingly, is the dividing line built by the United Nations to keep the Greeks and their would-be liberators apart. Sure, there's the occasional UN post. Sure, you see UN cars and Jeeps dawdling around. Sure, there's the occasional bit of barbed wire. But it's nowhere near as intimidating as, say, watching a small Dutch town preparing to host a football match at which England is the visiting team.

In the old Kennedy Hotel in the town centre, which has now been completely refurbished and transformed into a Holiday Inn, I can't even start talking business until these two old buffers tell me their problems.

'Posted a letter to a friend in Limassol in February,' the greasy regimental tie tells me before we even get into the bar. 'Do you know when it arrived? I'll tell you.' He thumped the table. 'It arrived the end of May. I ask you, is that service? Is that what we should have to put up with?'

The navy blue blazer even complained about the way they drink their ouzo, which I thought was pushing it a bit. 'Just add water, they do, and drink it down. That's not the way to do it.' He is tapping his finger on the bar. 'The correct way to drink ouzo is with cucumber. One sip of ouzo. One sip of cucumber. Slightly salty, if possible. There is no other way to do it.' As for the best ouzo, it should be slightly dry, not sugary. But we all knew that, didn't we?

I wanted to cross over to the Turkish side. All the Cypriots I met on the Greek side told me I should have a look for myself, see if I agreed with them. 'You'll never believe it. Twenty years, they've done nothing. Ruined the country. You should go look,' I kept being told.

An old foreign office type I first met in Cameroon offered to come with me to show me the ropes. 'Know how to handle these boyos, y'know. Years of experience. Got to treat them the right way, y'know.'

We march, left, right, left, right, up to the blue-and-white-striped hut by the old Ledra Palace Hotel. 'Now my good man,' he booms at this nice friendly guard with a droopy moustache. 'Want to show my chum the old Turkish side. Just pop across, have a quick look. Back in a couple of minutes.'

What happens? We get bounced. Which was hardly surprising.

And for all the US$8 billion the Russians are supposed to have stashed away in secret Cypriot bank accounts, the British ex-pats still beat them handski down. Why? Because, damn it, we know how to do things properly. They have even formed a British Ex-pats Let's-complain-about-everything Society. The jolly old Russkis would never have thought of that, what? Too damn democratic for them, what.

And what is the Society's greatest triumph? Rejoice! Rejoice! After twenty years of writing letters, lobbying officials and ministers, they have just achieved their one and only major historic triumph, that will live forever in the annals of Anglo-Cypriot relations. They have managed to persuade the Cyprus Ministry of Transport, no less, to change the tiny, insignificant sign along the road from Limassol to Paphos from the straightforward, no-nonsense English 'To the slaughterhouse' to the pansy French 'To the abattoir'.

Trouble is, the French ex-pats association are now writing letters and lobbying officials and ministers, insisting that if it is going to be in French, la gloire de la France demands that it should be a bigger sign.

What.

Istanbul

The only city built on two continents. A genuine bridge between east and west. The biggest border town in the world. The greatest crossroad city of all time. That's Constantinoupolis, Stambul, Gosdantnubolis, Kushta, Tsarigrad, Rumiyya al-kubra, New Rome, New Jerusalem, the City of Pilgrimage, the City of Saints, the House of the Caliphate, the Throne of the Sultanate, the House of the State, the Gate of Happiness, the Eye of the World, the World's Mistress, the Refuge of the Universe, the City of the World's Desire and His Stand Bull, as the girl in my local travel agency in Heathfield calls it.

No other place in the world can touch it. For over a thousand years it was probably the greatest city on earth, and it's still up there with the best of them. At least, as far as I'm concerned.

It's where history and geography and civilisation and religion and 1,001 vested interests meet. Or rather clash.

It's Greek. Or rather it was. It was founded by Byzas in the seventh century BC. Even today Turkey has more ruins of ancient Greece than Greece itself has. Take my advice (although, I warn you, not many people do): if you want to study Ancient Greece and you can't afford to get into the British Museum or the Pergamon in Berlin, don't go to Greece. The pollution will kill you. Go to Turkey instead.

It's Roman. Or rather it was. A thousand years after the Greeks arrived it was seized by Constantine in AD330. He made it not only the capital of the Roman empire but the capital of his Christian empire as well. Again, if you want to study Roman remains, don't go to Italy. One way or another the Italians will kill you. Go to Turkey instead. Not only has Turkey got more Roman remains than Italy, they look more like Roman remains as well.

It's Christian. Or rather it was. St Paul was there three times. Which must be some kind of recommendation. Santa Sophia, way up in Old Istanbul, was for a thousand years the greatest church in the world, with a dome so large it was impossible to build it at the time. Today, thanks to Ataturk who wanted Turkey to be more Western than Eastern, it is no longer a Christian church but a Muslim museum. But all over Istanbul, as well as all over Turkey, Christian influences remain. St Paul's visits were not in vain. I only hope he got the air miles he was entitled to. Few people do.

It's Muslim. Or rather it was. Or perhaps I should say, or rather it was much more than it is today, in spite of what the fundamentalists are up to. In 1453 Sultan Muhammad swept in with a vast army of fur kaftans and ostrich feathers, all waving their swords and scimitars, and made it the capital of the Ottoman empire, which at one time stretched from Morocco to Mesopotamia, from the Danube to the Persian Gulf, and from Poland to Yemen. It made the world tremble. Everybody rushed to lock up their wives and daughters. Well, maybe not their wives. To most people the Ottomans were devils incarnate. To Byron, who wasn't fussy about wives, daughters or even fellas, come to think of it, the city was heaven on earth. He said he had 'never beheld a work of nature or art which yielded an impression like the prospect on each side from the Seven Towers to the end of the Golden Horn'. Then he hobbled off to join the Greeks and died fighting for them against the Turks. Although, for reasons I suppose not entirely his fault, he did have a somewhat lopsided view of the world.

It's French. Well, any country that has lost as many wars as Turkey has must be a little French, n'est-ce pas? After all, look at what happened, or rather at what didn't happen in 1812, 1829 and 1878 between Turkey and Russia; in 1832, 1839 and 1840 between Turkey and Egypt; in 1827 between Turkey and

147

Greece, and since 1900 between Turkey and Bulgaria and Albania and Greece – again – and Italy and Serbia. And, if that's not enough, who chose the losing side in the First World War and lost Arabia, Syria and Mesopotamia in the process? What happened during the Second World War? The Turks say they deliberately remained neutral, which I very much doubt. With a track record like theirs I reckon neither side wanted to have anything to do with them.

Finally, God or rather Allah help them, it was British. Well, a little bit. The last Ottoman sultan was smuggled out by the British in 1922. Which just about says everything.

But that's not all. Turkey is also famous for inventing the outdoor restaurant, providing the best stockwood in the world for handmade guns and rifles since the French forests were destroyed during the First World War, and supplying more snails to the restaurants of France than anybody else in the world. The Turks, as you probably suspected, are also world famous for the size of their nuts. Talk to the dealers and merchants in Rotterdam who specialise in handling nuts, and they will tell you stories about the size of Turkish nuts that will bring tears to your eyes.

On the other hand, I suppose you could say Istanbul is the biggest it's-not city in the world.

It's not Byzantine, it's not Greek, it's not Roman, it's not Christian, it's not Muslim. It's not East, it's not West. It's not Europe, it's not Asia. It's not rich, it's not poor. It's not first world, it's not third world. It's not French. It's got no connection with turkeys. Turkeys, or turquois, come from Mexico. And it's most definitely not British. I mean, have you seen the state of their kitchens?

It's also not the kind of country where if people agree with you – a rare experience for me – they nod their heads up and down. If they agree with you they shake their heads from side to side. Like the wife does when you get back from a long hard trip where, solely in the interests of boosting Britain's balance of payments, you've dragged yourself from one bar to another and from one five-star restaurant to another, and on your hands and knees you ask her if you can go down the lodge for a night with the boys. And if they want to annoy you they don't, as your mother-in-law does, suddenly arrive and announce they are staying until whenever. They simply blow their nose at you. Which I find far preferable.

But however you look at it, the Turks, by sheer hard work, engineering skills, grinding attention to detail and total dedication to quality, have built up the richest and most powerful country in Europe. Trouble was, it wasn't their own country. It was Germany. Some Germans reckon that without the Turks they would have to increase taxes by a staggering eight per cent. I won't tell you what the others say.

To me, Istanbul is quite simply one of the greatest cities on earth. Just think; it has witnessed 3,000 years of history. It has seen empires come and go. It has seen religions come and go and come back again. It saw the Persians come, only to be sent packing by Alexander the Great. It saw the Crusaders come, admittedly not all at one time, and it saw them go again. For a thousand years it was a mega-city, with a population of over a million, while its nearest rival was less than one-tenth its size. What's more, it makes the most fabulous teeth-rotting multi-million-calorie desserts on earth. Two bites and the cholesterol is running out of your ears.

Today, of course, it's facing every which way. To Europe. To the Balkans. To the Caucasus. To Arabia. To Central Asia and all those Turkic-speaking-stans. Nearer home it's looking at all its next-door neighbours: to Azerbaijan, Armenia, Bosnia, Bulgaria, Cyprus, Greece, Iran, Iraq, Russia, Syria. It's no wonder Turkey wears out on average four foreign ministers a year. The poor dears are in such a fez. They know they don't want to be an Ottoman stuck in the corner and covered with dirty washing. But they can't make up their minds whether they want to be East or West or neither East nor West; Christian or Muslim or neither Christian nor Muslim; rich or poor or neither rich nor poor, or whatever.

The great Kemal Ataturk, the Father of Modern Turkey, (who incidentally was born in Greece, but don't say a word;

it's a bit like reminding Mrs Thatcher she signed the Single European Act) decreed when he became president in 1923 that Turkey had to turn to the West. He abolished Islamic law, curbed the power of the Muslims, barred all religious orders, closed all the madrasas or seminaries, stopped men from wearing skull caps and from having more than one wife and, because they then had to have something else to do in their spare time, he ditched the Arabic alphabet and introduced the Roman alphabet, so it would be easier for them to read the sports pages and do the football pools. Since not so many wives would be needed to ruin the lives of their husbands, he gave women the right to stop wearing the veil and, instead, to vote and stand for parliament, so they could ruin the life of the country instead.

A kind of Mrs Thatcher with a thick bushy moustache, as opposed to a light fluffy one, Ataturk also had enormous respect for Western parliamentary traditions. As a result, he relentlessly pushed all his ideas through regardless of anybody else. In fact, so determined was he to introduce Western ideas and culture into Turkey, he decreed that any concert which took place in Istanbul should be given by two orchestras, one Western and the other Turkish, which should play alternatively, first Western music, then Turkish music. I don't know about you but not only would this have turned me off the whole idea, it would most definitely have forced me to spend even more time in the crush bar than I do now. But from the ruins of the Ottoman empire, he was convinced this would somehow set Turkey on the road to becoming a modern nation and a Western-style democracy.

However, it was not to be. Now they want to change it all back again. Or at least a growing number of them do. Turning to the West, they say, was supposed to make Turkey rich, but it didn't. Turn, therefore, to the East and we'll all be rich: QED, or whatever the Arabic equivalent is. What's more a Muslim Turkey would also end Eastern slavery to the West, liberate Bosnia, Chechnya and Jerusalem, and free six billion people. To some, this is the view of crazed, lunatic, fundamentalist fanatics intent on turning the clock back to the days when Ottomen were Ottomen, women wore the veil and every man had four mothers-in-law. To others, it's a valid point of view which in a democracy deserves to be discussed, debated and decided. That after all was what Ataturk was on about when he was trying to turn Turkey from the East to the West.

The four-mothers-in-law party looks as though it is winning. In the old days you could party till dawn in the cafés, restaurants and clubs of Istanbul. Not any more. Bars are closing down. The Malta Palace in the nineteenth-century Ottoman mansion in Yildiz Park has gone. So too I reckon have at least eleven others, all, curiously enough, in property owned either by the city or the government. In the ones that are left, the music is turned off at midnight during the week and at the dangerous and shocking hour of one o'clock during the weekend. And when you get back to your hotel, what do you now find in your room? A pair of slippers, so that you can get up early and go to the mosque. Which is definitely not like the old days.

Foreign television channels have been severely curtailed. There are now only four hard-core porn channels compared to one where people do nothing but bang on about politics. Various statues have been discreetly removed. Too rude, they say. Kissing has been banned in some areas. At least between men. Not very sanitary, they say. Which particular areas are not very sanitary nobody would tell me. Neither would they tell me if there were any sanitary aspects involved in kissing between men and women. And, if so, in which area. Up by Santa Sophia? Along by the Petra Palas? Down by the Galata Bridge?

Even going to a café can be dangerous. Just before one trip, two people were killed and twenty-five injured when Islamic fundamentalists opened fire on four coffee houses in Gaziosmanpasha, a working-class area. Their crime? Watching football on television.

But probably the most dramatic fundamentalist gesture of all – apart from holding a Miss Europe beauty contest in the

Greek Church of the Divine Peace, one of the oldest Christian churches in the city – was the banning of mini-skirts from the Turkish parliament. So whether or not MPs continue to make speeches that are short enough to cover the essentials but just long enough to be interesting, they now have no excuse but to concentrate on solving the fundamental problems facing the nation. Although it's a bit rich, bearing in mind that the biggest individual tax payer in the country is a woman: Matild Manukyan, who for three years running has also won the prestigious gold plaque presented by the Istanbul Chamber of Commerce to the most successful businessman/woman in the city. Her job? She runs the biggest, most successful brothel in Istanbul.

Between the two extremes are others who say it can be either, or, I suppose in Turkey's case, neither. Neither Byzantine nor Greek. Neither Christian nor Muslim. Neither East nor all the rest of the stuff. Good old blond, blue-eyed Kemal Ataturk – something else we don't talk about – established Turkey as a secular state. It worked up until now. It can continue to work in the future. What's more, they should establish closer links with Europe. It will force them to pull their socks up, toe the line, get their house in order. It will give them an opportunity to become the European stepping-stone into Central Asia, that huge southern underbelly of Russia, the Balkans as well as the Middle East. It will also be a balance against way-out extremist militant Islamism.

But the odds, I reckon, are against them also. First, because when good old blond, blue-eyed Kemal Ataturk – oops, I shouldn't have said that – was introducing all his Western reforms he somehow forgot to stop paying the imams. Even though mosque and state were separated, the Turkish Department of Religious Affairs continued to pay their wages. As a result, being an imam is one of the best jobs going, and has been for a very long time. Second, even though he banned madrasas he didn't actually stop religious schools being established for the training and education of teachers and priests. Today there are over 400 such schools, turning out every year far more qualified Muslim teachers and imams than are needed. The surplus do what everybody does when they can't get a decent job: they join the civil service. Which, of course, means that every year the civil service, and inevitably the government, becomes more and more Muslim.

So too, as Allah made little coffee beans, does the population as a whole. The trouble, however, is not just that 99 per cent of the population are now Muslims but, as with everything, there are two kinds: the Sunnis, who make up about two thirds of them, and the Alewites. The Sunnis are a bit Church of Englandish. They know what they believe in, roughly speaking; they're prepared to stick to some pretty general rules; but they don't want to make a big deal of it. The Alewites are a bit like the charismatics. They actually believe in what they say. They believe in Hazreti Ali, a nephew and son-in-law of the Prophet Mohammed. They believe he should have taken over from Mohammed after his death in 632. And they want to get on and do things.

To me, however, Istanbul is all these things, and more. It's East, it's West. It's Christian, it's Muslim. It's rich, it's poor. It's everything else you want to say it is. Upside down, inside out, back to front, and none of them. But whatever it is or isn't, it is or it isn't in the Turkish sense of the word. So it's got to be one of my favourite cities, full of intrigue and mystery. Especially driving a million times over the Galata or even the Ataturk Bridge at sunset trying to find an office in a street off an alleyway off another dirt track.

'But,' you say to the driver, 'you said you knew—'

'No problem, dottore,' he says.

You drive for another hundred miles, past a mosque, underneath another bridge and somehow alongside a street market.

'I thought you said . . .'

'No problem, dottore.'

Past the Bosphorus Hotel, perched on a hillside in twenty-six hectares of parkland. Past what looks like the remains of some spiral column. And past the Ottoman-style Sumengen Hotel where I'm not saying what happened.

'I thought you said . . .'

After I get out three times to visit a baklavaria to regain my strength I eventually find the place myself.

'No problem, dottore. I told you,' says the driver leaping out of the cab, grabbing my briefcase, adjusting my tie and demanding enough Turkish liras to buy himself an *A-Z* for every major city in the world, including Istanbul.

If that's not enough mystery and intrigue for you, it's also got 2,000 odd mosques, or rather it's got approximately 2,000 mosques. Mustn't say anything that might upset the fundamentalist four-mothers-in-law party. Just in case. Then there are all the glorious slim, towering minarets. Richard Hannay called them factory chimneys. The low wide domes. The ships lining up to go through to the Black Sea. The ferries shuttling across the Bosphorus serving apple tea in dirty, narrow glasses. The Galata Bridge. The mass of tiny alleys. All the crumbling buildings. The sagging roofs, rotting beams, collapsing balconies. The millions of worn-out stones and steps. The call of the muezzin. The flea markets. The tea sellers. The water sellers. The hustlers. The kids. The beggars. The two moth-eaten, broken-down old bears which I used to see being dragged along the Sahil Yolu early mornings overlooking the Sea of Marmara. The noise. The continuous hassles with shopkeepers, street traders, corrupt politicians and dodgy civil servants. Not to mention policemen. The polluted air. The polluted water. The polluted everything else. The whole place is buried in rubbish up to its non-existent fez. And when it comes to rubbish, let me tell you, there's no rubbish like Turkish rubbish, because as far as I can tell they don't even recognise the concept of rubbish. They still think they are nomads; what they throw out or leave behind doesn't make any difference. It's not theirs. It's somebody else's problem.

At one office I visited in Sultanahmet, the oldest part of the city, they were just piling stacks of loose papers and files outside their front door. No plastic sacks, no string around them, nothing.

'What is rubbish if you are moving all the time?' one of the partners said to me.

'But you're not moving all the time,' I said. 'You've been here for over a hundred years.'

'Yes, but we probably will soon,' he said, emptying another bin of loose paper all over the street.

Similarly there is no traffic like Turkish traffic, no death-defying drivers like Turkish death-defying drivers and no non-stop traffic jams like Turkish non-stop traffic jams. Istanbul is the only city I know where they regularly pack six lanes of traffic jams onto a four-lane highway. And that's not including the pavement. And don't ask me how, in one of the most dangerous cities in the world when it comes to road accidents – more people are killed per head as well as per car per thousand population than anywhere else – there's no such thing as a driving test. At least there wasn't until a couple of years ago. Which means, when you think about it, that 95 per cent of vehicles now on the road are driven by people who just jumped behind the wheel and sped straight into their first traffic jam. And since they have introduced tests, the whole thing is even more of a nonsense. Most examiners, I was told, are too scared to sit in a car driven by a complete stranger, so they pass nearly everyone automatically. Even more absurdly, taxi drivers are exempt from taking any tests whatsoever.

But I don't care, I still love the place. To me, it's the most glorious disaster on earth. It is also the one place in the world where, don't ask me why, everybody calls me dottore, even the first time I see them.

One day, I keep promising myself, I will arrive at Istanbul by boat, at dusk, along the Bosphorus, though I know it will scare the hell out of me, not yet having experienced the delights of being taken hostage by Chechen guerrillas. But I always arrive by air.

'Dottore,' says the guy as I step off the plane.

'Dottore, nice to see you,' says the guy on immigration.

'Dottore,' says the customs officer.

I grab a cab outside.

'Dottore, you've come back to see us again. I knew you would.'

I arrive at the hotel.

'Dottore, welcome. Nice to see you again, dottore. The usual room, yes, dottore. No problem, dottore.'

They are also very helpful and friendly. 'You are nice man, dottore,' they keep saying to me. If my tie is momentarily dislodged they think nothing of straightening it for me and tightening the knot a little as well.

'You are dottore,' they say as we shake hands. 'You look like dottore, I can tell. Yes?'

If there is the slightest hint of dust on my jacket, they will insist on brushing it off. 'No problem, dottore. For you is a pleasure.'

Why dottore? Why me? God, I mean Allah, alone knows. I don't look anything like a dottore. I haven't got an expensive suit or expensive shoes. My ties are ordinary. And as for my bedside manner, I doubt whether I'm much of a dottore in that respect either, at least judging by the number of cases I've read that come up before the General Medical Council disciplinary committee. But to all the fat pashas and wheeling dealing businessmen and merchants and taxi drivers I'm a dottore. Especially to the taxi drivers.

The first time I visited Istanbul I was met by a solid phalanx of taxi drivers, all looking as though they had served as foot soldiers in Troy, and all calling me dottore. Behind them was another phalanx of battered taxis, or dolmushes as they call them, which as far as I can gather is Turkish for 'O Mighty Allah, please don't let the string break until I can get to the garage and steal another bit'. They weren't modern cars; they were pre-historic. They were Dodges and Chevrolets and Packards that were old when the Ottomans were still Otto-boys. I chose a car that was all big headlights and long swooping fins. It looked as though Al Capone used it for weekend breaks.

'American?' I said as I tried to squeeze myself in.

'No, dottore,' said the driver. (See what I mean; it was the first time I'd set eyes on him.) 'German.'

'But it looks—'

'German gearbox.'

'But the rest of it is American?'

'No. English engine, Russian tyres, Bulgarian exhaust, ashtrays come from Italy.' A pause. 'Dottore.'

I gave him the name of the hotel, but of course he'd never heard of it. I always think Turkish taxi drivers are New York taxi drivers on vacation. They never know where you want to go, where it is or how to get there. They rarely speak your language. If they do you can hardly understand a word they say. All they seem able to do is drive backwards and forwards across the Bosphorus Bridge smoking one packet of cigarettes after another until you have the courage to point out that, maybe, haven't we, I think, perhaps been this way before. Providing you haven't got cancer by then and are stretched out on the back seat gasping for breath. Although in fairness, one of the reasons I know and love Istanbul so much is due to the taxi drivers' unfailing ability not only to get totally lost on the simplest journey, but to charge you two arms and a leg for doing so. I must have visited most of the 2,000 mosques in the place – not because I have a particular thing about mosques, although many of them are quite spectacular, but because I discovered it was the only way of shaking off your typical Turkish taxi driver and avoid getting more polyps at the same time.

'How much to wherever?' I would ask.

'Sixty, maybe seventy,' they would say, stroking the walrus moustache. 'It's on the meter.'

You climb in and discover the meter is not working. Odd bits of wire are curling out waving at you from where the meter is supposed to be.

'But there's no meter,' you mumble.

'No problem,' they grin. 'Lets say about 200,000.'

Two hundred thousand! That would buy enough baklava to keep every dentist in Europe busy for a fortnight.

'Hey,' you shout. 'That's not what you—'

The taxi rockets forward. You're trapped. However many

times you ask politely, beg, bawl your heart out, they refuse to stop until, ha, ha, you've gone backwards and forwards across the Galata Bridge a dozen times, around the old town twice, out to the airport once and have developed a definite throbbing in your left lung. They finally come to a stop outside the wrong place, in the wrong street on completely the wrong side of town.

Do you shout, scream, stamp your foot and lose, or do you just give in and lose anyway without wasting all that energy? Me, I'm one of nature's losers, so what's another defeat to add to the long list?

Until I discovered the mosque dodge.

'Hey,' I screamed at a taxi driver as yet again the price accelerated almost as fast as the car with clouds of smoke whirling around the roof and the prayer beads hanging on his rearview mirror lashing wildly all over the place. 'What mosque is that?'

'Beyazit mosque,' he said. 'Very nice mosque.'

'I'd like to visit it,' I panted, taking in enough smoke to fill the Albert Hall. 'I like mosques.'

What could he do? He had to stop. There was no way a devout fundamentalist like him would risk the wrath of Allah. I leapt out, walked reverently up to the mosque door, bowed my head, took my shoes off, and, hiding them inside my jacket, tiptoed inside. Once inside I took in the details: built in 1506 by Sultan Beyazit II, the son of Mehmet the Conqueror. A quick look at the decorations. Oops, mind the old man with a stick! I then raced for the opposite door, out into the street, and straight into the first passing taxi. It worked a treat. I saved a fortune. I'd saved a row. I'd fought off the big C. And I was free.

Most times I managed to put my shoes on. Sometimes, however, I just leapt barefoot straight into the back seat. On one or two occasions, I admit, I tore my feet to shreds. But it was cheaper to buy three tins of elastoplast than pay 200,000 lira. In any case it was a small price to pay to become the world's leading expert on the mosques of Istanbul.

Only once did I get caught. We screeched to a halt outside this mosque in Sultanahmet. I leapt out and did my usual. Within thirty-seven seconds I was out the other side. A cab came round the corner. I waved and leapt in. It was just as I started pulling on my shoes that I realised it was the same driver. He couldn't park outside the mosque so he was driving round the block to avoid the police.

'Aha.' He grinned at me. 'I understand. You are political man.'

'Yes,' I said weakly, wondering what was going to happen now. 'I am political man.'

When we got to the hotel, he only wanted 40,000, not the original 200,000 he had demanded. But he insisted on giving me a receipt for 380,000. 'I understand,' he grinned. 'You are political man. All political man the same.'

Now of course, I'm an expert not only on taxis but also on mosques. But whatever I do I know I'm going to be taken for a ride. I know I'm going to be taken everywhere by the scenic route. I know it's going to cost me a fortune. I know one day I'm going to stop spitting up blood. What do I do? I stick with the same guy all the time. That way there's less aggro, less wear and tear on the old feet, not to mention the insides, and less cost. Usually.

On my last trip, I landed on a grey, dark, foggy morning. I'm not saying the first cab driver I saw at the airport was rough. It's just that he didn't look the kind of person you would want to leave alone in a room with your wife, your daughter, your son or even, come to think of it, your dog. His cab, another one of those battered, broken-down American limos, looked as though it had been used to chauffeur St Paul on his first visit. It stank, not of smoke but of air freshener. It was like sitting in the middle of a student riot with tear-gas grenades going off all round you. And, guess what, he called me dottore.

'I am your driver, dottore. I am your guide. I am at your service, dottore. For you, dottore, no fare. I am pest taxi driver in Istanbul. You bay me what you think it's worth. You bay me too little, no broblem. You bay me too much, no broblem. So long as you are happy, dottore, I am happy. I am pest. I am pehind you. Yes?'

Well no, actually. That's not what I had in mind. But I wasn't going to argue. Except when I saw his cab. Then I thought he should be paying me for having the courage to get in the damn thing. But did he know his way around? He did. Did he wait when I asked him to wait? He did. Did he come back at the time I asked him to? He did. Did he smoke? He didn't. Trouble was, he kept getting his b's and p's mixed which, OK, I could live with. The really big broblem, I mean problem, was that wherever we went, whoever I met, he wanted to drag me off to some stall or duty-free shop or bazaar where he knew somebody who would give me 'Good brice. Very good brice. Brice specially for you, dottore.'

My first meeting is in Beyogku, on the north side of the Golden Horn, the European end of town. It's not exactly the most difficult place on earth to get to. Except with this guy. Every five paces he wants to take me to some shop or stall or hole in the wall where he has an aunt, an uncle, a brother or sister who will give me 'Good brice. For you, dottore, good brice. I bromise you, dottore. I am your friend, yes? I am pest. Yes?'

'But I want to go to—'

'You will like, dottore. This is—'

'But I don't—'

'It is cheap, dottore, very cheap. Much cheaper than the hotel. Just look.'

'But . . .'

'I am your friend, dottore, yes? I am pest. Yes?'

'Yes,' I say weakly. 'You are my friend. You are pest.'

Well, what would you do? Get out and go through the whole rigmarole again with another taxi driver and probably end up with somebody a million times worse?

Three and a half hours later I arrive at my meeting, having visited every shop, stall and hole in the wall owned by six generations of his family, all no doubt prepared to give him 50 per cent commission on business he brings them. At least I think that's what he gets. Every time we went anywhere he would open the door for me, usher me in, close the door firmly behind me then leap up to whoever was handling the cash, crying, 'Half ber cent. I want half ber cent.'

It was only after the thirty-third stop I realised he was trying to say 50 per cent. At least I hope so. There was no way he could survive on $\frac{1}{2}$ per cent commission on what I was spending.

The first place we went into was exactly the same as every other place I've ever been in Istanbul. In the middle of the floor were a pile of kilims, or ruggies as Americans call them, a stack of cheap rugs and a heap of sheepskin jackets. Around the walls were enormous displays of plates and goblets and vases and candlesticks. There was jewellery and copper everywhere.

'Very good textile. Very good quality. You want to see?' his grannie says to me. I could tell it was his grannie. She had the same kind of moustache.

'No, thank you, I'm very—'

It didn't make any difference. She insisted on giving me the tour. 'Cheap prices. You like cheap prices? Yes?'

Twenty minutes later I'm dragged into another filthy hole in the wall, oops, I mean traditional Turkish shop, handed a glass of hot sweet tea and forced to study a pile of leather jackets.

'You like belt? Very good quality. Very—'

Now I'm being fussed over and mothered by some belly dancer who's run to fat in all the wrong places. Although it doesn't seem to make any difference to the taxi driver. He obviously enjoys living off the fat of the land.

'No thank you, I've got a plane to catch in five minutes.'

It doesn't make the slightest bit of difference. I have to look at a whole year's production of leather jackets before I can escape.

The next stop looks like an underground cave full of kilims. They're all over the walls, all over the floor. Some are even hanging from the ceiling. Now I don't know much about anything. That's what I'm always being told by guess who. But I do know one thing about kilims. Beware the pink ones. They're not for real. Something to do with making up the colours or something. I spot three of them. But of course I don't say a word. Instead I pretend to rummage around, and discover hidden in a corner a saddle bag, a pile of prayermats, a Dagstan cradle cover and what looks like heavily embroidered tent bands. Then I do the usual. I ask the price of the saddlebag, offer half, settle for two-thirds and promise to come back the following day with the money. As I race back to the cab, I can hear the driver going on about half a ber cent.

Which obviously did the trick. For the rest of the time I was there, it was – zap – straight to my meetings then – zap – straight to wherever I wanted to go. No arguments, no getting lost, no problems. I reckon I saw everything. Well, everything I could see between meetings and lunches and dinners and generally working my fingers to the bone as you do every waking second of the day you're away from home in some exotic location surrounded by all kinds of, well, things to do. I also reckon I crossed the Bosphorus so many times I should be given either the freedom of the city or a gas mask. Given the choice I'd take the gas mask.

The only trouble was that the 'pest' of all taxi drivers in Istanbul kept wanting to bractise his English. Which I didn't mind so much because there was no way I wanted to talk Turkey all the time. He was so determined to speak English, he told me, he used to get up at four o'clock in the morning to watch American football on Sky Television on a next-door neighbour's set. Which is certainly dedication over and above the line of duty. Trouble was, on top of the b's and p's broblem, his English was not exactly, well, English, if you see what I mean. He kept talking about caringness and wellness and embathise. Rain was not rain but brecipitation. A watch was a timebiece. A ben, I mean a pen, was a writing instrument. He didn't decode anything, he made a determination. As for taking chances, he didn't. He made them. Which, I can tell you, he did often, so often I reckon it ruined my wellness for ever. But it was still a small price to pay. I went everywhere and I saw everything.

I went through Besiktas and Macka where most of the hotels are located. I went to Bebeck, an upmarket district on the Bosphorus European side. I wandered through Fatih, a nice middle-class area. I went round Beyogku, the old European quarter, once full of elegant town houses built by Italian and Prussian architects for Greeks and Americans and anyone lobbying or serving the court of the Ottomans. Today it's full of potholes as well as Albanians, Bulgarians and Kurdish families who have fled the war. Sometimes, if you're lucky, you can hear their traditional drums and clarinets drifting through the evening.

I went to Memo's, the swish, violet-painted yuppie bar in Ortakoy, and the Malto Kiosk Café near Yildiz Park where you could be anywhere in the States. It was full of glamorous yuppies, fashionable clothes, moustaches, mobile phones and long fashionable beards. Newspapers were scattered all around. Outside there were Mercs and BMWs and loud music.

At the quayside, fishermen were still unloading sea bass and bonito. Old men were sitting counting their worry beads. Old women were wandering around complaining that the men do nothing all day but drink raki. On Sundays the area is one enormous street market. Bars are packed. Nobody can hear, let alone listen to the cries of the muezzin from the Mecidiyic Camil mosque nearby for the noise and the music.

Another evening after yet another hectic day, I wandered around the Sultanahmet district, the world capital of doner kebab, where the main shopping street, Istiklal Caddesi, originally known as the Grand Rue de Pera, was full of embassies until Ataturk in a further bid to turn the country to the West transferred the capital east to Ankara, and they either shut up shop or turned themselves into extravagant, expensive consulates. Now it's one long pedestrian precinct with two old trams trundling back and forth and a mish-mash of faded hotels and scruffy modern buildings.

I turned into the Greek Pasaji or Flower Alley or Passage or

Back Street which was crammed with cheap bars and noisy cafés and restaurants and street singers and magicians and dancers and acrobats and hustlers. Everybody was troughing away on such delightful delicacies as fried sheep's intestines, deep fried mussels smothered in tomatoes and chillis and some translucent splodge which looked like millions of raw jellyfish eggs. First thing in the morning, unless you're in a rush to get back to your hotel, it's the place to be. The fishmongers are doing a roaring trade in bass, octopus, red and grey mullet, a thousand different types and sizes and shapes of squid, and a mass of things I have never seen elsewhere.

At the end of Istiklal Caddesi, is Taksim Square, the Piccadilly Circus of Istanbul, which is surrounded by casinos à la Turca; in other words, sordid nightclubs and drinking clubs, every one of them complete with statutory belly dancer. If you want to try something more arty, and perhaps more risqué, you could take in Club 1001 or Valentinos, where I'm told you can have it both ways. But I warn you, you're on your own. I'll see you back at the hotel.

Me, a philistine to the end, I went to the Ataturk Cultural Centre in search of a ballet, a concert or some grand opera. But there was nothing doing. Instead I spent a riveting evening studying the joys of irregular metric in traditional Turkish poetry.

For ballet, for a concert and especially grand opera all rolled into one, I went round the corner to the Pera Palas Hotel. To get in involved a bit of a pas-de-deux as I wasn't King Zog of Albania, the Sultan of Zanzibar, the King of Montenegro, the Emir of Mecca, the Maharajah of Behupral Biki Begum, Mata Hari, Kim Philby or even Agatha Christie, although why any hotel should want to boast that all its best and most famous clients are now dead beats me. I mean, what's wrong with their kitchens?

Once inside, it took me at least two and a half Scheherezades and three Allelujah choruses before I could get a drink. No, I couldn't have one in the enormous baroque fantasy of a lobby which looks as though it was designed and decorated by a William Morris gorged on Turkish delight. Would I care to go to the Oriental Express Bar? Said bar was a mass of dark Oriental carpets, dark green pillars, pink marble, giant mirrors, gilded ceilings, high latticed windows, enormous crystal chandeliers and creaky doors. It was empty apart from one old crone, dressed in black from head to toe, who looked like Agatha Christie come back to prove us all wrong. Three or four barmen were standing around looking at each other. A piano was playing languidly in the corner. Just as we were into the second Allelujah chorus one of the waiters shuffled across to me. Did I want to see Room 101? he asked.

No, I said, I'd prefer a large Scotch. I'd been waiting . . .

Room 101, he said, was where Ataturk stayed. After all these years, his panama hat, his coat, even his pyjamas were still there just as he left them.

Well, if that's the standard of service in the hotel I was glad I wasn't staying there, I said.

He just looked at me.

The dining room, let me tell you, was grand opera, pure and simple. Not only did the waiters look as though they were there to welcome the very first Orient Express in 1892, the place was scattered with a string of dead bodies which obviously escaped M. Poirot's attention. It took three acts of high drama and spell-binding tension before I could even get a menu. I'm still waiting for the wine list.

Seven and a half weeks later, when I had finished my meal, I stepped out of the hotel and was immediately set upon by two taxi drivers. One looked like an ayatollah on sick leave. The other was slightly more restrained. He looked like an ayatollah who had taken a holiday job to earn some extra dinars.

'You nice man,' said the ayatollah.

'You dottore,' said the holiday relief. See what I mean?

They shook me by the hand. They straightened my tie. They brushed my suit down. They practically tore me in two. Call me a coward, but I fled back to the bar, waited another two and a half weeks to be served, and downed a couple or three vodka vishnas, a lethal mix of Turkish vodka and cherry juice.

Most people rave about the Pera Palace as one of the great hotels of the world. I can't see it. First, it's much smaller than you think. Now I agree, size is not everything. Although it is as far as Turks are concerned. Second, it's got atmoshere. But it's definitely the wrong kind of atmosphere. The Orient Express Bar is supposed to be legendary. Trouble is by the time you get a drink you're beginning to feel a bit of a legend yourself for having waited so long. As for the restaurant, Istanbul normally gets very hot in summer. Third, it's terribly English. So English, that immediately you step inside the door you feel at home. You have to wait for everything and you're frightened to say a word about it.

But whatever Agatha Christie did holed up in Room 411, there is more to Istanbul than the Pera Palace.

Santa Sophia, Hagia Sophia, the Cathedral of Holy Wisdom, or whatever you want to call it, is unbelievable. How could they build such a thing in 537? And in just five years, too. It's enormous. The dome, which is the size of a football pitch, is supported entirely by the whites of God or rather Allah knows how many eggs binding the walls and marble and everything else together. To walk from one end to the other is practically a marathon. At the time it was built, at the height of the Byzantine empire, it was not only the greatest church in Christendom, it was also the biggest building in the world. Since then it's been a model for St Mark's in Venice and for almost every other Orthodox cathedral ever built.

It's no longer the greatest church in the world; now it's the greatest Turkish museum in the world. Instead of icons there are huge plaques everywhere. Instead of Christian names the building is full of the names of Allah and Mohammed and various caliphs and imams. But wander around it in the shimmering candlelight, a muezzin wailing in the distance, a group of peasant women with shawls up to their eyeballs following each other around in a long conga-like crocodile, and a huddle of old men in suits that look as though they were donated by Oxfam before the Dardanelles standing at the back. Somehow the marble walls and mosaics and galleries and colonnades and huge empty spaces seem to exert this fantastic hypnotic calm. Unless, of course, you're trapped by a couple of typical English tourists.

'Can't trust them,' the voice of Virginia Water pierced the candlelight. 'Leave anything anywhere and it will be gone.'

I wandered over to the mosaics which remained hidden during Turkish rule. They followed.

'And then,' I heard the wife – she couldn't possibly have been anything else – announce to the world, 'we keep it in our pockets all day.'

I crossed over to the gallery. They followed.

'And then we use it again,' the husband confided.

Instead of climbing up to the gallery I dashed round to the so-called sweating pillar in the north nave.

'By then it's all crusty,' said the wife. It was too much. I collapsed on one of the ledges. 'It's horrible when you think about it,' the wife was going on.

To me Santa Sophia and the Sulayman mosque are a pair. They're both huge, both built to last to the end of time. And they're both serious. I mean, some churches and mosques and basilicas are, well, chocolate-boxish. Especially some Italian ones. Not these two. They're the big, solemn, heavy type. Not for them charismatic services, guitar playing and women priests. Their God is the real God of Abraham. No questions asked. No doubts even anticipated let alone tolerated.

Just as at one time Santa Sophia was the church to beat all churches so, I reckon, the mosque of Sulayman the Magnificent with its great dome and its four minarets is the mosque to beat all mosques.

The Blue Mosque, by comparison, so-called because of the millions of unbelievably blue hand-painted iznik tiles, not because of the colour of Constantine the Great's language when he realised it was going to be bigger than his beloved Santa Sophia, is somehow more friendly, more accessible. More parish church than cathedral. In spite of all its minarets and domes and semi-domes, it's somehow more elegant and slim. Maybe it's the lamps hanging low all over the place. Maybe it's all the mother-of-pearl inlays. Maybe it's the wall-to-wall carpeting and the eighteenth-century prayer rugs. Or maybe it's just the friendliness of the tour guides who come rushing up to see you en masse as soon as you set your stockinged feet inside the door, waving their official tour guide badges at you. One particularly eager old man waved his badge so close to my face that I couldn't help noticing it had expired thirty years ago. It wasn't quite enough to make me turn Muslim. But if it was, I would make it my local, no problem at all.

Between the Blue Mosque and the Topkapi Palace is Sogukcesme Sokagi, once a delightful, beautiful, traditional Turkish area: in other words, a rat-infested slum of broken-down, burnt-out wooden shacks. Today it's been well and truly gentrified. It's been rebuilt, refurbished and completely restored to its nineteenth-century glory, when it was home to foreign diplomats as well as the usual collection of court hangers-on who all wanted to be within walking distance of the sultan. But instead of restoring it to its original private homes, they've restored it to a collection of guesthouses and small, discreet hotels. One guesthouse, however, is a library containing every book written on Turkey by Western writers over the past 400 years. A fantastic source of material on Istanbul. I must use it if ever I have to write something sensible about the place.

As for the Topkapi Palace, let me tell you now: if you want to keep your fantasies, don't go there. Go to the Firebrigade Museum instead. It'll do you more good. It's also much warmer.

Talk about the Forbidden City in Beijing – the Topkapi is about half the size of Monaco. It was home to over 5,000 people: civil servants, eunuchs (which I suppose are pretty much the same), official turban winders and I suppose official turban unwinders, slipper-toe curlers, slipper-toe uncurlers and so on. Built on the site of the old Byzantine acropolis, it was the very heart of the Ottoman empire. It was also home to no less than twenty-five sultans. From here for over 400 years they ruled an empire stretching from the borders of Italy, Austria, Hungary and Russia all the way to Egypt.

Once inside the walls, it was claimed that any taste or preference or desire known to man could be satisfied. Food, I mean. The kitchens, which employed over 1,000 people, boasted they could feed 10,000 people a day: soups, pilafs, kebabs, meat, fish, vegetables. They had over a hundred recipes for pilaf, over 150 for aubergines, but only one recipe for flavoured yoghurt. Oh yes, which reminds me. They also had a harem, which is really only a girls' school with a particular emphasis on, I suppose, physical education. There the girls were trained in the arts and crafts, music, religion, making apple tea and what they called household management. Which I admit covers a multitude of sins. You think I'm kidding? The Turks have turned the old harem in the Ciragan Palace into a girls' school. So what's the difference?

Before I went, I thought I was going to see golden thrones, towers, columns, enormous walled courtyards, majestic reception rooms dripping with gold leaf, a sea of deep red cushions, gilded mirrors, mosaics, huge Japanese vases, copper braziers, Ming porcelain, imam chants before Mohammed's sword and coat, emerald-encrusted daggers, the 86-carat Spoonmakers Diamond, jewels the size of hardboiled eggs, the skull of John the Baptist, the green porcelain plates the sultans used to dine off which changed colour if there was poison in the food, and the regular midday beheading. I thought it was going to be the ultimate grown-ups' theme park. Instead it was a cross between a dirty, dusty, provincial museum and a redundant Turkish bath. The size of the palace – over 400 rooms – surprised me. I never imagined it covered such a large area. Neither did I realise it was, in fact, a complex of different buildings. I always thought it was a single building. The harem was almost a village within a village. I must admit, it was not my idea of a harem, but perhaps that was because some vital ingredients were missing.

Because time was short – I could only manage to snatch a

couple of hours between meetings – I joined the Deutsch tour rather than wait half an hour for the English one. All the key words I could understand, like Fräulein, jung, Nacht, ja, schnell, danke schön. Which surprised me. I never thought my German was that bad.

I saw all the old Imperial costumes – not all over the floor, in display cabinets – a million examples of Turkish embroidery and various collections of armour. The jewel room with the famous Topkapi dagger was closed. Which is usually the way it goes if I visit a museum. I also learnt lots of things about harem life I never knew; like why there were so many taps and fountains all over the place. Running water makes it difficult for people to overhear what you're saying. Fancy, all these years I thought it was a trick invented by James Bond to stop SMERSH from bugging him. I was also told the women in the harem could say nein. Although whether they ever said anything else after that the guide couldn't tell me.

One guy, Sultan Ibrahim, can you believe it, actually got bored with the whole lot of them and had every single one of his 299 concubines bundled into concrete sacks and thrown into the Bosphorus. Most people call him mad. Others said mad he might have been, but at least he made sure he could watch the racing on television without 299 women nagging him to go and cut the grass. You don't believe me? Any evening you're in Istanbul with nothing to do, and you're not yet bored out of your mind with your personal harem of 299 concubines, go and stand on the edge of the sea and I swear you can actually hear the lot of them still nagging away at old Sultan Ibrahim to their hearts' content.

It wasn't until the end of the tour that I discovered none of us actually spoke German. Dutch, Italian, French, a smattering of Serbo-Croat, we spoke all those. Not even the three fat old ladies covered in black from head to toe could speak German. Which surprised me because I could have sworn I'd seen them before in, was it Hamburg?

Which goes to prove Biddlecombe's Third Law of Tourism: it doesn't matter what the guide says, nobody is listening anyway. If you're interested, you'll get more, more accurate, information out of a book. And if you're really interested you won't go there in the first place. Impressions are always better than reality. Seeing the thing you love is the sure way of losing that love. Tout de suite.

As we came out, the English tour were waiting to go in.

'Attaboy,' shrieked an American. 'Gee, what a life these boys had. Yippee.' His wife looked as though she would never forgive Germaine Greer from being born twenty-five years too late. I almost regretted not waiting for them.

After that, everything else was exciting, or chilled-out, as the taxi driver kept saying. If Topkapi didn't look like a harem, the Grand Bazaar or, to give it its proper name, the Kapali Carsi, which is Turkish for Don't Even Think of Coming in Here Unless You're Prepared to be Parted From Every Penny You Own, certainly did. It looked as though it was designed by William Morris stoked up to his eyeballs on hash. It was way-out, riotous, a mass of colour.

In 1880 it had, according to a contemporary survey, 4,399 shops, 2,195 ateliers, 497 stalls, 12 storehouses, 18 fountains, 13 mosques, a school and a mausoleum. Nothing has changed. Today – I've counted – it has over 4,000 shops, 2,000 workshops, 500 stalls and 500,000 pedlars. It has its own restaurant, cafés and, yes, toilets. Modern. Just like, well almost like the ones back home. It has its own school, bank and, of course, its own mosque. It also has exactly 2.75 million people eager to part you from whatever money, cash, credit cards, IOUs you've got or are ever likely to have. Jewellery, carpets, leather, ceramics, genuine Louis Vuitton suitcases, Turkish-made sacks of red grenadine, rugs from the Caucasus, Turkmenistan and every other 'stan you can think of. It's a real Muslim shopaholic's paradise. And if that's not enough to get the old wallet going, try the Egyptian spice bazaar, or Yeni Carni, opposite the Galata Bridge. It's called that not because the spices come from Egypt, they don't, but because of the Egyptian method of doing business there, which has remained unchanged for generations.

You wander around examining mountains of red chilli powder, yellow saffron and peeled almonds. You rifle through great sacks of sage, camomile and henna. You check out huge hunks of honey from combs the size of elephants' ears. You drool over the Turkish delight, the pistachios, the sweetmeats, the cheeses and the dried fruits. You look at the tins of caviar at £10 a throw, all the different leather goods, and a million thises and thats to take home to the wife to stop her from complaining because you're off again on another trip next week. Or, at least, to try to stop her from complaining.

You make up your mind. A packet of dried fruit for the wife. A tin of caviar for the secretary. You go up to the guy. 'This. How much? Total. Altogether. Lira. Turkish lira.' You talk to him in his own language so there's no possible chance of a misunderstanding.

'Well, let me see now, that will be 25,000 lira, actually.' He obviously has problems understanding what you are saying.

'Twenty-Twenty-Twenty-five thousand? Joking. You must be. I'm not a Frog, you know. British. I'm—'

'Well if that is the case, my dear sir, for the sake of the old empire, God Bless Her, shall we say 15,000?'

'Fifteen thousand? Now look here, mate, I haven't come all this way – I'll give you five. Not a penny—'

'Shall we say ten? For the sake of friendship.'

'OK, mate. Ten thousand. Done. That's what I like, a fair deal.'

You give him a 50,000 lira note. He gives you 20,000 lira change. You put the money straight in your pocket without looking at it because you know you beat him down.

And how much is 25,000 lira? About £1.

Now it's time to celebrate.

Reading a Turkish menu, I always think, is a bit like reading the Song of Songs: kadim gobegi (lady's navel), a kind of lemon cake soaked in syrup; belle lips, a cake soaked in even more syrup; sultan's delight, a kebab with egg-plant purée, soaked in still more syrup; and my favourite, imam bayeldt, 'the priest has fainted'. Lamb rissoles, nightingales' nests, kebabs, dolmasis, they're all fantastic. I think the only dodgy meal I've ever had in Istanbul was in the Pandeli by the Golden Horn, which is supposed to be famous for its sea bass cooked in paper. Mine tasted as if it had been cooked in the *Sewage Workers' Weekly*. But that's another story. If I live long enough to tell the tale.

Whether you have kebabs or dodgy fish, nobody can finish any meal without a couple of huge chunks of Turkish delight, which many people, usually those with false teeth, claim is not just the absolute nectar but the absolute nectar in velvet trousers, the best sweet in the whole wide world, and the most sinful concoction known to man. In all four religions. The ingredients, from what I can gather, are pretty run of the mill: a little bit of this, a little bit of that and about two and a half tons of 100 per cent pure, unalloyed, concentrated sugar. The magic apparently is in the heating. Boil it for too long and you could use it to lay a concrete path. Boil it too little and it oozes all over the place. Boil it at 300 degrees Fahrenheit in a filthy black copper cauldron for the length of time it takes to mutter the odd word of magic, cut it into seven strips, roll it seven times in the direction of Mecca, leave it overnight bathed in the full moon and it's the second most enjoyable thing this side of paradise. Not my words. The words of one of the taxi driver's five gummy old grannies.

'A signet ring, dottore. She say wear a gold signet ring. That way you make always the pest Turkish delight. The pest,' he told me one evening on the way back to the hotel when we popped into yet another hole in the wall to meet yet another of his grannies.

But whether it's made with a signet ring or not there are a million variations and a million reasons for them. Coconut to cheer you up. Pistachio, Napoleon's favourite, is supposed to be good for the heart. Lemon, Queen Victoria's favourite, is good for the liver. Cigar-smoke, Churchill's favourite, makes you forget the Dardanelles ever took place. Then there's rose petal, dried fruit, sugar almonds, pineapple, vanilla, chocolate and what the hell have we got left over we want to get rid of?

And the best way to eat it? Granny, or at least her six double chins all said, lemon tea. Not coffee. Especially not the heavy aromatic Turkish coffee. It kills the taste. Me, I prefer it with cognac. Preferably a couple of large cognacs. Whatever granny says.

The following day, having seen the European and the Asian sides, I saw the other side of Istanbul, the enormous townships or squatters' camps which are growing like wildfire on the outskirts.

The population of Istanbul, they say, is around 10 million, although I reckon if you take the amount of rubbish that's less than 1,000 years old and add to it the number of excuses for not doing anything about it, it's more like 15 million. Either way it's growing at the rate of more than a thousand a day. Yes, a day. That's around half a million people a year, which must make it one of the fastest growing cities in the world. They come from eastern Anatolia, driven out by the war against the Kurds, from all along the Black Sea coast, and from the whole of the old Soviet Central Asia. In twenty years' time it is bound to have more than doubled. Most of them end up in these camps in tiny mud and concrete huts, with no water, no heating, no nothing. There are no roads, no jobs, no schools, nothing but enormous rubbish tips. Apparently the build-up of methane in them causes more explosions and deaths than the whole Turkish army has managed to achieve against the Kurds.

All the people who live here have is a desperate wish to survive – and the backing of the fundamentalists. I don't care what you say about them; if they are gaining support they deserve it. In all the squatters' camps and poor areas of Istanbul I saw, you could see them hard at it. OK, they're vote-catching; Turkey is a democracy, so there's nothing wrong in catching votes, anybody can do it. It's just that the other parties can't or won't. That's their problem. But more important, the fundamentalists are actually helping the people. They're giving them food, and the basic necessities. They're giving them hope. If St Paul was to come back for a fourth visit even he couldn't argue against that.

At one time Armutlu, an illegal camp a stone's throw from the Bosphorus Bridge and home to 60,000 people, was a no-go area for police. The only way people could cook and eat or keep warm was by burning rubber tyres all day long. Now the fundamentalists have moved in, they're getting roads and pavements of sorts. They've opened up hundreds of tiny coffee shops. They've also shown the locals how to get electricity by stealing it from the city's power lines. But don't tell anyone I told you.

The biggest division running right through the middle of the city, is, of course, the Bosphorus, which is a million times worse than any squatters' camp. I was told again and again that it is so bad people have given up trying to commit suicide by throwing themselves into it, because there is so much sewage, dead cats and second-hand torture equipment in it – government issued, one owner, used only once – they would be more likely to break a leg on impact than drown. In any case, they reckon they could float on it so long, by the time they were rescued their leg would be healed again. On top of that, it's already so busy you can't imagine it getting any busier. But it will. First, because there will be an enormous increase in traffic from the east as the Black Sea countries and Central Asia states open up even more. Second, because once all the canals in Europe are linked up to the Danube there will be a similar increase in traffic from the west.

Be that as it may, catching the Galata feribot across the Bosphorus from Eminonu near the Sirkeci railway station, and zig-zagging up to Rumeli Kavagi on the western bank where you can gorge yourself to your heart's delight on fish, fish and still more fish, is still a magical experience. It's magic that you get across without hitting or being hit by anything. One of the busiest, and one of the most dangerous seaways in the world, there's no radar controlling what goes on, let alone what goes up and down. It has twelve major turns. Its narrowest point is only 500 metres across. That doesn't make any difference. Everything just ploughs backwards and forwards at will: the ferries, the huge tankers, the big steel-hulled fishing boats, those enormous vessels containing liquid nitrogen gas, the occasional battleship, and of course the millions of tiny wooden pop-pops. It makes going through the English Channel blindfold in a giant oil tanker in a force 10 gale a piece of baklava.

Undaunted – stiff upper lip and all that – I decided to check the tiny fishing villages. Wherever I went the picture was much the same: barrels of mussels, all kinds of fish and crabs lying on slabs of ice, old men with snowy moustaches mending their nets and talking about the catch, little boys fishing off the harbour; restaurants serving turbot, bass, mackerel, tuna, sardines, red mullet, swordfish, calamari, shrimps, blue fish, red fish, white fish and tons of fresh anchovies, all washed down with gallons of raki. Everywhere women complaining.

Klumkapi, I think, was my favourite. There are restaurants all over the place. The streets and pavements are blocked with tables and chairs. On summer evenings they even close the streets to traffic. There are old timber houses everywhere. It also somehow still feels more like a fishing village than a tourist spot.

Now it's the last day of my trip. The taxi driver is taking me back to the hotel. Everything has been fantastic: I've made all my meetings; I've been around town; I've seen the sights. Suddenly he brakes sharply and pulls into the side of the road just by one of the five-a-side football pitches on the Sea of Marmara.

'Dottore.' He turns round to look at me. Oh hell, he's remembered that damn saddle bag I said I was going to buy in that tiny underground cave. Gee, and I thought I'd got—
'Dottore,' he says again. 'Are you a real dottore?'

What could I say? If I said no, I'd shatter all his illusions, probably be arrested by the police, be charged with fraud and deception ... 'Yes, of course,' I muttered, adjusting an invisible stethoscope around my neck.

'Dottore,' he said. Oh, no, I thought, what now? He knows

it's a lie. He's going to report me to the Turkish Medical Council. He's going to accuse me of— 'Dottore,' he repeated, 'my leg hurts. What can I do? You help me, dottore?'

His leg! Of course I can help him. 'Three glasses of raki,' I said briskly, 'three times a day. A bottle of raki to be taken as soon as you get home.'

Thrilled. He couldn't have been more pleased. His face broke out in a million smiles. He lunged towards me as if to give me one of those slobbery Yasser Arafat kisses, but I managed to pull back in time.

'Dottore,' he said, jamming the car into gear and shooting off at about 300 miles an hour, 'dottore, you are pest.'

Amman

How can I say this without upsetting anybody? I just can't help it – to me, Jordan is just too nice, too polite, too courteous, too pleasant, too friendly and too helpful. I'm sorry, but that's the way it is. And it takes some getting used to.

The first time I went there I was expecting all the usual joys and thrills of modern travel. What happened? Not one policeman, in order to protect my privacy, offered to take my wallet back to his office so he could check whether I had declared all my foreign currency. Not one customs officer wanted to check my passport in case I had left a US$10 note in there by mistake. There was no enormous scrum at the airport with millions of people offering me taxis, wanting to be my friend and trying to take my shoes off so they could clean them for me. There was no fight with the hotel to get the room I had booked and paid for a month earlier.

There were no rows with taxi drivers because they turned up three and a half days late, took me the long way round and failed to wait when they had said they were going to wait, and had been paid to do so. There was no bribing lift attendants half a week's wages to take me to the fifth floor when the damn thing was automatic anyway. Not one restaurant accidentally overcharged me so much they could buy the Trump Tower for cash. Nobody tried to sell me genuine Roman remains which their father had made that morning in his backyard.

There were no hordes of little boys chasing me down the street screaming baksheesh, baksheesh; no guys selling ten postcards for the price of five, and their sister round the corner if I'd like to meet her; no guides, official or unofficial, willing to show me for a special price what everybody else sees for free; no dealers willing to change my dollars into any currency under the sun at rates which would make Shylock blush. Not once did I get a gippy tummy. In fact, I reckon you could stay in Amman for the rest of your life and never get a gippy tummy. And on the way out the check-in clerk at the airport didn't charge me a departure tax when – you got it – there was no departure tax.

I know you don't believe me, but I tell you it's true. They don't hassle you. They don't pester you. They don't swindle you. Leave £100 in notes on a table in a room with a bunch of Jordanians, when you come back it will still be there. What's more they will have washed and ironed each note and arranged them in numerical order. Leave 100 pence on a table in a room with a bunch of Egyptians and when you come back not only will the 100 pence not be there, neither will the table, the chairs, the carpets or probably the room as well.

It's the same with Jordanian hotels. They're all very clean, very pleasant. All the rooms have the furniture and fittings you expect, including electricity, light bulbs, hot and cold running water, a door and a lock that works.

Taxi drivers turn up when they say they're going to and take you straight to wherever you want to go. No getting lost. No mucking about. Straight to the door. And they charge you the correct fare. No mumbling about 'whatever you want to give me, sir. You decide. You're the boss.'

Lifts work when you press the button. Receptionists and secretaries don't expect to be paid for telling the man you've come halfway round the world to meet that you've arrived.

All the tourist junk is good tourist junk. That includes all the rugs, brass coffee pots and necklaces you see everywhere, as well as all the prints of old Arabia by David Roberts, the nineteenth-century failed Scottish theatrical set designer who virtually cornered the market in chocolate-box Arab art.

In fact, Amman is so civilised that there are only three

decent bars in the whole place and just one nightclub. Which is so civilised and respectable nobody bothers to go there. A night out in Amman, as a result, is sipping sweet tea – a hubbly bubbly is too noisy – nibbling kinafas, which taste like baked shredded wheat marinated in thick syrup and doused in half-melted salty goat's cheese, and talking about the things that didn't happen to you during the day. A night in is watching television – one South African-made programme after another – nibbling gooey pastries and wishing you'd gone to the new kosher restaurant, the Istanbul, in Shmeisani, the classy, upmarket area around the Ministry of the Interior.

'It's the first kosher restaurant in the Middle East,' a British diplomat told me. Which didn't seem right somehow. But who am I to argue with the collective Arabists' knowledge of the Foreign Office?

Taking everything into account I don't reckon it's bad, for a country which was nothing but a heap of sand until it was created by Winston Churchill on a Sunday afternoon in 1923 between finishing his daily bottle of Bolly and hitting the cigar box. You wonder what the place would be like if he had taken all day. Alternatively, if the Founding Fathers had got on with the job and, instead of talking for months on end, sewn the whole deal up in a morning, maybe the United States would be a whole lot different than it is today. Either way, Jordan was a pleasant surprise. Somehow I thought that a more or less artificial country in one of the world's most dangerous, turbulent and unfriendly regions would have big problems, given the nonsense they had to put up with from the Assyrians, the Hittites, the Nabataeans, Alexander, Pompey, the Persian hordes, the Crusaders, the Muslims, Allenby, Glubb Pasha (who I'm sure I used to see towards the end of his days shuffling in and out of the library at the Centre for African and Oriental Studies in London), and, of course, Lawrence, who was obviously one of the few people who did not find the Arabs impenetrable. Or rather Orance, as he is known in the back streets and bazaars of the old city. But they don't seem to hold it against him. At least, not the ones I met, who all seemed to have immaculate headdresses complete with leather thong, beautifully pressed khaki jackets, polished open-leather sandals and a batch of press clippings showing that they, their fathers and their grandfathers all rode with Orance.

Jordan, in fact, is almost Boy Scout country – old-fashioned Baden-Powell Boy Scout country, not this new-fangled, chummy, long-trouser Boy Scout business. They want to be friends to all and a brother to everybody under the sun. The brotherly sun, that is.

The pattern is set by the Chief Boy Scout himself, friendly old King Hussein, the West's oldest Arab ally, who has ruled his friendly kingdom in the friendliest possible way for over forty years. So successful has he been that to almost the whole world the idea of King Hussein being nasty is about as intimidating as Yasser Arafat being friendly, and slobbering all over you.

To the British, Hussein is still the ultra-loyal Sandhurst cadet who took over from his grandfather, friendly old Abdullah, on 2 May 1953. If loyal is the right word. Not only is his UK pad virtually in the shadow of Windsor Castle, he refers always to the royal family, and therefore so does everybody else in Jordan, as the Windsors. Not the Queen. Not Her Majesty the Queen. Not that crazy gang of hangers-on. Always, the Windsors. During one trip, I was practically followed by the Duke of Kent who was opening factories or whatever. All the time people referred to him as one of the Windsors. On another occasion the *Jordan Times* reported Prince Charles visiting a cosmetics factory in England and afterwards asking if anybody wanted to lick mango butter off his royal Windsor personage.

To the Palestinians, of course, Jordanians are either cousins, uncles, brothers, aunts, nephews or nieces. When Israel was created, nearly half a million Palestinians just upped and made for Jordan. Palestinians are, therefore, all over the place: in government, in the military, in business, in banking.

To the Syrians, the Jordanians are just too co-operative and too, too eager to be friendly. The Syrians have always seen themselves as Israel's most powerful enemy and neighbour. Today, of course, there is not so much emphasis on the enemy. But they don't like the Jordanian approach. And they don't like the way they are always being outmanoeuvred by Jordan.

To the Israelis, they are either friendly, very friendly or very, very friendly. Until 1948 Jordan was very, very friendly to everybody. Come 1948 and the creation of Israel they started being just friendly. When good old friendly King Abdullah seized the part of Palestine the Israelis couldn't get their hands on they became very friendly. Today, I would say they were heading towards being very, very, very friendly.

To Iraq, they're Now-would-you-like-to-have-a-cup-of-coffee? You-must-tell-me-all-about-the-Windsors, are-they keeping-well? Throughout the 1980s, of course, they were very, very friendly. Jordan was the main supply route for Iraq. Everything was fine, everybody made a lot of money. Come 1990 and the Iraqi invasion of Kuwait, poor friendly old Jordan was betwixt and between. It was neither really for nor really against. It wriggled this way and that and sat on the fence for so long trying not to upset anybody that when it climbed down it ran away in all directions, upsetting everybody in sight – the Iraqis, the Kuwaitis, all the Gulf monarchies, the Americans, the United Nations. Poor old Hussein didn't know what to do with his woggle, and whatever he did was wrong.

Since then, things have got better. Well, marginally so. The Kuwaitis still refuse to have them back in the country. The Gulf States still refuse to give them any oil or financial assistance. The Americans are still not as buddy-buddy as they used to be. They are even insisting they repay some US$488 million debt, which is peanuts in international aid circles – about half the cost of a UN seminar on eliminating poverty, I would have thought. But relations are more friendly than they used to be. Certainly, as far as I could tell, Iraqi businessmen, or at least all three of them that are left, have started coming back to Amman in their raggy old suits and cardboard shoes.

They still talk about doing business together. But both sides know it's a long way off yet.

The result is, trying to talk politics to the Jordanians is like trying to fight your way out of a very nice, very friendly, very pleasant sack of candy floss. By Appointment to the Windsors, of course.

Ask them if they are a democracy.

'We are, of course, a democracy,' they will tell you. 'A Western democracy. The only country in the region with a Western-style democracy.'

'So, ministers sit in parliament?' you ask innocently.

'No, no government minister sits in parliament,' they say. 'But we're still a democracy.'

'But parliament takes the decisions and sends them up to the King for his signature?'

'No,' they say, 'The king actually takes all the important decisions . . .'

'On the advice of the government?'

'No. On his own.'

'But you are a de-mo-cr—'

'Yes, of course. Why not?'

'So parliament appoints all its own ministers?'

'Well, no, not . . .'

'The King appoints . . .'

'Well, it's like this. The King is responsible for appointing ministers. But if anyone causes trouble the King automatically appoints . . .'

'Because you're a . . .'

'. . . Because we're a democratic—'

'In that case you must be more democratic than Is—'

'Please excuse me. The palace. I have a meeting at the . . .'

It's the same trying to ask them about their Muslim Brothers, the friendly Jordanian name for the fundamentalists whom they tend to look upon more as teenage children going through a difficult period rather than mindless extremists allied to the devil as some countries do.

'So how extreme are they?'

'They're not really extreme.'

'But aren't they followers of Iran?'

'No, I don't think this.'

'I thought they wanted to overthrow the existing structure and establish a fundamentalist Muslim state?'

'But they can't do that. They have signed our national charter, which specifically forbids . . .'

It's the same with the students. Can you believe it? Jordanian students are constitutionally incapable of being angry. I mean really angry. Some of them go on about the Americans, how they should never have come to the aid of nasty old Kuwait and inflicted all that damage on friendly old Uncle Saddam; how wicked old Saudi should never have invited the terrible old United States to do its worst against a fellow-Arab neighbour. But you get the impression they don't mean it. It's almost as if the wily old King has paid them to criticise him so that he can prove to the States how Jordan is truly democratic so they can throw lots of dollars at him without him complaining.

Hey, I've just realised. Maybe that's why Amman is full of roundabouts, or circles, as they call them. They don't want to be seen taking sides with anyone.

Try going from the Inter-Continental to get some kinafa in, say, Shmeisani, the up-town area. You ring up to place the order.

'Please, you want them made with rosewater, pinenuts, pistachios . . .?'

'Just regular will be fine.'

'Please, we don't do regular. We do rosewater, pinenuts, pistachios—'

'OK, I'll have one of each.'

'Please, we do sixty different types. Our regular ones are rosewater, pinenuts and pistachios . . .'

'OK, give me one rosewater, one pinenut, one pistachio . . .'

'Please, sir. They'll be ready in five minutes.'

'OK. Give me your address, I'll be there in ten minutes.'

'Please, where you now?'

'In the Inter-Continental.'

'OK. You come out of hotel. Turn left. That's first circle. You go to second circle. At second—'

'Yes, but what's the address?'

'I tell you address. At second circle, you—'

'I don't understand. What is second circle?'

'I tell you. At second circle.'

Again, because they don't want you to think they're unfriendly because you don't know their address they refuse to use any addresses at all. Instead everything is based on the eight circles. Which is obviously fine if you know where the eight circles are and can tell one circle from another by looking at them. But it wasn't fine for me. I spent half my time going round one circle after another, and all the Jordanians I asked for help either did not understand them themselves or were too friendly and polite to point out what an El Charlie I was for not understanding their oh-so-simple and friendly system. The result is I am probably more of an expert on Amman than I am on my local village high street.

So it is without any fear of contradiction I can tell you, in the friendliest possible way of course, that as a city Amman is no great shakes. In fact, it looks like a goody-two-shoes city designed by Rotarians for Rotarians – probably, I will admit, because it's only really existed for fifty years. In 1945 it was home to barely 500 people, but it's made enormous concrete gains since then. Mostly in the form of cement-rendered breeze blocks used to construct some pretty faceless, anony-mous-looking straight-up-and-down hotels, office blocks and housing estates, many of them only recently built to house all the Jordanians who were thrown out of the Gulf. Oops, I mean, to accommodate the returnees. Which is a good thing in one way, as it should save them from one thing that would test their friendliness to endurance and beyond: tourists.

At present, let's be honest, there's not much for your average tourist to photograph and then forget what he photographed, when he photographed it and was it before or after Granny's eightieth birthday. There's a few sheep grazing on the occasional building site. There's a pretty little shop by the bus station. And somebody told me some friendly old Arab is supposed to be building a model of the Abdulaziz mosque in matchsticks, but I may have misheard.

The big problem as far as tourism in Jordan is concerned is not Saddam Hussein but some nonentity called Dean Burgon and a single line of so-called poetry he scribbled without thinking a hundred years ago. For all friendly old Hussein's friendliness, for all the Jordanians' pleasant nature, if anything will blow their Boy Scout country sky-high it will be Burgon and his rambling.

The first time I went to Jordan there wasn't a tourist to be seen. I was able to go everywhere undisturbed, see what I wanted to see without being jostled by people going on about why can't they get a decent cup of tea, did you see how much they charged us to get in and how long is it till the next bingo game. I was just about the only person in the Roman ruins, which include a spectacular 6,000-seat amphitheatre carved into the side of a rock, a full-size street and a forum, all about two minutes from the centre of town.

I was the only person in the King Abdullah mosque. How did I know it's the King Abdullah mosque? Because it's not grey or white. Admittedly, I was with a carpet salesman, who was trying to sell them a single carpet that would cover the whole inside, which is about the size of a football pitch. But he was too late. They had just fitted the most superb, thick, almost bouncy, outrageously expensive carpet in deep red with extravagant patterns. What did they do to indicate the lines where people were to gather for prayer? They put huge, thick black lines all over it with what looked like ordinary paint. It was heartbreaking. All the same I got a personal tour of the building, the balconies on top, even King Hussein's private mini-mosque outside where he stays until the time is right for him to join the public events inside.

I was also the only person in the National Archaeological Museum which, to be honest, was not surprising. I only went there to have a look at the view over Amman. The museum was open, so I thought, why not?

Now it's all changing fast. The hordes are coming with a vengeance. And I am told the Israelis are the worst. Not only are they vandalising all the holy shrines, including the Jewish ones such as Aaron's tomb, they are stealing everything which is not screwed, locked, bolted and welded to the ground. So bad has it got that the Israeli government has been forced to apologise publicly to the friendly Jordanians for their behaviour. Not that the friendly Jordanians are worried about the odd shrine and a couple of pictures. They're just terrified that if the Israelis continue this way, they won't have to invade Jordan next time. The whole country will already be in their backyard or on their garden patio in downtown Jerusalem.

As a result, I very nearly didn't go to you-know-where which is half as old as you-know-when. But early one morning, very early one morning, I gave in as I usually do and headed south out of Amman on the four-lane highway to Aqaba and the Red Sea where, unlike in other Arab countries, goats have the right of way. See what I mean about them being friendly.

With the sun rising over the desert all I could see were clapped-out twenty-seven-wheel tankers selling all the Iraqi oil they could to the nice Jordanians. Which is not what I expected. I expected to see super, clean, modern Jordanian trucks shipping everything they possibly could into Iraq. But presumably that will happen one day.

Slowly, however, the trucks disappeared and we were hurtling through a wide open biblical landscape. Mile after mile of dry, sunburnt grass, flocks of sheep, the occasional modern house, dead donkeys by the side of the road. We stopped at a petrol station. Even friendly Jordanian taxi drivers never think of filling up before a long trip. Behind the pumps was a large tent. Alongside it was a Toyota pick-up. All around, sheep were grazing on what little tufts of grass they could find. After that it was non-stop for four hours to what I thought would be one of the greatest travel experiences of my life.

One of the greatest travel experiences of my life! At the

entrance, deep in the Wadi Araba valley, there were horses everywhere. Some were tied up under cover, to protect them from the sun; others were being lined up ready for the next batch of French or Italian or German tourists all dripping with cameras; others were wandering off trying to dodge their place in the queue and two or three were being raced backwards and forwards by eager little boys who had obviously just learnt that there is more in life than racing donkeys backwards and forwards. None of them looked anywhere near as good as old Lad and Little Herbie back home. Lad is getting on now, but in his day he could have outrun every single one of them, even on three legs. Similarly, Herbie, who is about as big as the lot of them put together.

All around them, clustering like flies, were thousands of old women complaining about how thin the horses were, the condition they were in, why are they standing like that with their heads down, look at that's one feet, when was the last time they brushed his mane, the ambassador will get a letter from me the minute I get back to Budleigh Salterton.

'Oh no, I'm got getting on that one. He's too thin. I'll try that one.'

'No, no, how many times have I told you? It's got fleas.'

'Poor dear, just look at its tail. Hasn't been brushed for years.'

And in a welter of promises to send entire family fortunes to the Brooke Hospital for Distressed Horses in Cairo, off they all eventually shuffle, banging and kicking and thumping their poor, pathetic, undernourished horses to catch up with the others.

Reluctantly, I join in. I've come so far, I'm not going back. On and on we plod: me, my horse, my Bedouin guide, my guide's horse, my guide's horse's guide and my guide's horse's guide's horse. They all insist that even though I've been riding for 173 years, I still need them all to hold the fraying bit of rope dangling from my horse's scrawny neck.

At first, it's just an ordinary sandy trek. Then as we plunge deeper and deeper into the mountains the track becomes a gap in the rocks, in some cases only wide enough for two horses. The rocks either side become the height of maybe a twelve-storey building. It's like a cross between a grown-up Cheddar Gorge and the Grand Canyon. With culture. I ask the Bedouin guide the name of my horse. I thought he said baksheesh, but I may be wrong. He obviously wasn't a Jordanian.

Further on we plod, five, ten, fifteen minutes. The passageway has now opened out. The rocks are not as tall. Running along the wall is a primitive water supply system. Closer and closer I come to one of the greatest travel experiences of my life. The greatest is to get on the escalator at Victoria tube station on a Monday morning and find it's working. For years I've been dreaming of this moment. That first glimpse of the . . .

What happens? I tell you what happens. Everybody starts going bananas for their cameras. For their cameras! I mean it's not as if the thing is going to move. It's been there practically 2,500 years. It'll be there a bit longer, for people to flash off the odd hundredth-of-a-second blurred photo with their cheap Japanese cameras to forget to collect from the chemist when they get home. Then when they finally get them they won't remember whether it was the Prado in Salt Lake City, the leaning tower of Eiffel in Shanghai or a visit to the set of *Indiana Jones and the Lost Snark*. Nevertheless, it's instant tourist photo pandemonium.

'Vite, vite. Camera, ma chérie.'

'Hey, listen to me, willyah? What damn f-thing do I put this thing on?'

'Mama mia, it's a da comin. It's a da comin.'

The guide, the guide's guide and, of course, all their guides' guides' guides' guides' horses get caught up in the pandemonium and start rushing up and down, making matters a million times worse. Even Baksheesh starts getting wound up in the commotion. He flicks his left ear a couple of times. Which probably burns up all the energy he's been storing for the past 2,500 years.

'Sir. Sir. Monsieur. Camera. Quick.'

'Lady take picture, yes?'

'I hold horse, you photo.'

I haven't got a camera. To me, cameras are for people with bad memories. But the guide keeps insisting I should take photo.

'Why you no have camera?'

'I don't want a camera.'

'I get you camera. Everyone has camera. I get . . .'

The guide's guide and the guide's guide's guide now start shouting and screaming at me as well. In the end there is this great heaving and shoving and shouting and screaming riot that bursts round the corner like an entire rugby crowd hitting the turnstiles at the same time. The Frenchman is screaming, ma chérie. The American's shouting because an Italian with a big hat has blocked his view. The Italian is screaming for his mother. I'm on poor old Baksheesh jammed up against some stall with six people hollering at me and offering to write my name in a bottle of sand. All around me are half a dozen guides and guide's guide's guides trying to get me to take cameras they have somehow conjured up out of the thin desert air. There in front of me for the first time in my miserable soul-destroying life, carved out of the rock, is the Treasury.

And this was going to be one of the great travel experiences of my life. Like seeing Venice for the first time, or wandering through Cracow of an evening, or having a glass of champagne in the Crillon in Paris, or knocking back my first real, but real, dry martini in that bar I can't remember in New York.

But from what I can recall, even in the hubbub, the view is spectacular. The building itself is much higher than I imagined; maybe nine, ten storeys high. Six columns, a niche on either side, a pediment. Above that more columns, an urn. Most people say it was the Treasury, others the Temple El Khazna Faraoun, and still others the Treasure of Pharaoh. The area in front is about the size of half a polo field. It's all rough sand, no paving, just a dusty old camel who seems to be posing for another John Roberts print. Which adds to the impact.

You can imagine Herr Johann Burckhart in 1812 to the sound of cannons and for the price of two horses' shoes, the amount of money he paid a local guide to take him there because he wanted to sacrifice a goat on the top of Mount Aaron; you can see him coming along the very same track and suddenly turning the corner and seeing it there in front of him. It must have been like discovering Victoria Falls or bursting upon the Pyramids.

It's also definitely not whatever the colour was supposed to be. Burgon when he wrote that poem must have been colour blind, or else like most poets he didn't know what on earth he was talking about. For my money, it's pink and white and orange and maroon and dark red and yellow and gold and even black. But I suppose you can't make that rhyme with anything.

I clamber off old Baksheesh and climb the steps. They are not the original steps. Neither is the first pillar on the left. But you just can't help being impressed by the scale of the thing. I mean, you would have thought that life was tough enough in those days in the middle of nowhere without trying to carve great buildings out of the side of a mountain. After all if you haven't got drills and dump trucks and tractors, it's a pretty stupid thing to do. If, however, you're not interested in the practicalities and you are determined to cut huge great buildings out of the solid rock, then this is undoubtedly the way to do it. And again not just your ordinary buildings, but colossal buildings, giant columns, enormous steps, doors twenty-five feet high, which would not have been out of place in Rome or Athens.

All the other buildings are equally spectacular, but they are not as stunning and impressive as the Treasury because you've lost that shock of the different. You've got used to it.

Once you've got your breath back and fought off the tourists, you plod through another tiny passageway between towering cliffs. The area now opens out into a wide plateau.

On the left is an amphitheatre. It's not in such grand condition as the one in Amman; built the Greek as opposed to the Roman way, the seats at ground level form a perfect semi-circle. The seats above are set back slightly and extend further than a semi-circle. On the right facing the amphitheatre are the shops. On the left are all the Roman credit card machines and cash dispensers.

Two thousand five hundred years ago, this was big stuff: a city of 35,000 people, the New York of the whole region. What is it today? Nothing. The ancient capital of the Kingdom of the Nabataeans, once a major centre for the caravans running between China and India and Gaza and Alexandria, is just one glorious tourist venue. Which is probably a warning to all of us.

Another guide approaches. He is to be my local guide – at least that's what he and all my other guides and guides' guides' guides tell me. It's OK by me. I've dreamed of visiting this place for so long, I want to see as much as I can. Trouble is, while he speaks perfect English, he speaks it with, how shall I say, a less than perfect accent, as if he learnt it from a book or from watching too many Meryl Streep films. Women, for example, comes out as war-man. Which gave me a slight turn when he first told me that he had four war-men at home and each one was war-shipped by the others. Only once did I really flip. That was when we'd climbed 527 steps to the High Place of Sacrifice and he turned round and asked me, 'You are turd, yes?' I suggested that before we leave, it would be wrong not to make a sacrifice to the gods. But he wouldn't co-operate.

In order to try and concentrate on matters in hand and stop myself from fantasising any more than usual on the way down I kept asking him why they built such enormous buildings. A small building I could understand. But why such huge build-ings? The guide said it wasn't difficult, which presumably meant he was descended from a long line of pyramid builders.

'In froze gays, brock not lard, brock loft. Today lard because feather change. In froze gays beasy,' he said.

Beasy or not, it was one hell of an operation. First,

presumably, the local architect had to work out what he wanted: the size, the dimensions, the decorations. Then he had to reverse it all.

'You smoke?' he suddenly said.

'No thanks, smoking is—'

'Smoking is hood. You spell. You sell warman you smoking. She sell OK. No problem.'

After that he told me about his daughter. At least I think he did. 'They tied and flailed. It not right. But what can I do?' I'm afraid I had no suggestions to offer. I mean, so ended what should have been one of the greatest experiences in my life.

On the way back we drove to Mount Nebo from where Moses stood, saw the Promised Land stretched out in front of him and in those immortal words said, 'OK fellas, the final lap.' It really was beautiful. It was real Old Testament country, full of shepherds who still watch their flocks at night and old men trotting along the roads on donkeys. From the top I could see not only the Dead Sea but glinting away in the distance the golden spires of Jerusalem. But the best thing of all was the silence, the complete absence of tourists and guides shouting and hollering at you.

Madaba, one of the little towns nearby, was originally involved in the carve-up among the twelve tribes, but it only really hit the big time when it was run by the Romans. Since then it's just coasted along. We parked in the main street. The driver went off to have a beer. I wandered around. Apart from this little shop, downhill on the way to the mosque, which sold some fantastic kinafas – so sweet I was frightened to shake my head in case my teeth dropped out – the only other thing I discovered, in the Greek Orthodox Church of St George, was a huge mosaic map over 1,500 years old showing Palestine and lower Egypt as well as the Nile, the Dead Sea and Jerusalem. Why a mosaic map? Why in Madaba? Nobody could tell me.

It was the last afternoon of my trip. The Jordanians I had met were so kind and considerate that we finished our meeting way ahead of schedule. Because of all the delights and attractions of

Amman I decided there was only one thing to do: make for the Dead Sea. Or, rather, descend to the Dead Sea. It's nearly 400 metres below sea level and the lowest spot on earth.

Dead, I can tell you, is the word for it. The road there, a four-lane motorway that twisted across the mountain, was nothing but a death trap. Especially as, coming in the other direction, everybody seemed to be driving as fast as they could to get as far away from Jericho and Yasser Arafat as quickly as possible. Dead dogs and donkeys I've seen alongside roads, but not as many as I did alongside this one. Then there were all the military checkpoints.

'Please not to worry,' the driver kept telling me. 'These people, they are my friends. I know them.' And I could understand what he was saying. All the same I don't think I've seen so much hardware in such a short space of time, primed and ready to be used, since that board meeting when the non-executives finally plucked up courage and got rid of the chairman.

The Dead Sea looked uncanny. It was much bigger than I had thought, and a kind of pale turquoise. I had imagined it to be grey, don't ask me why. It was also as still as a mirror. I didn't go in myself. Partly because I'm allergic to water, partly because I didn't want to risk the salt ruining my tastebuds. After a lifetime devoted to developing an appreciation of the finer things I was certainly not going to risk blowing it all in five minutes. Instead I assumed the role I normally assume in such circumstances. I sat by the bar and heaped ridicule on everybody I saw. And after an hour of seeing all kinds and shapes and sizes I do have the utmost admiration – for the Dead Sea itself. How it could possibly support some of them is a miracle in itself.

After so much salt there was only one thing to do. On the way back to Amman between the third dead donkey and the fourth dead dog I stopped for icky-sticky-gooey-syrupy kina-fas. I was halfway through my second one (don't tell my dentist) when I met this very friendly Jordanian businessman on his way back from Aqaba.

The British, he told me, supported the United Nations blockade on Aqaba. What did the Jordanians do to get their own back? No nonsense, he told me. No second thoughts. They immediately slapped a unilateral, 100 per cent ban on importing into Jordan – English chocolate.

So now do you believe me when I say they're too nice and too pleasant and too friendly? And what's more, did you realise I'm the first person in history whose written about you-know-where without mentioning whatever it was you-know-who said about it?

Bogotá

Well, I did it. I got in and I got out again. Alive. No bullet holes. No scars. No signs of needles being plunged into me when I wasn't looking. Nobody planted drugs on me. Or even in me. Nobody slipped a burundanga, a borrachero or even the more deadly cacao sabanero into my beer, into that one single glass of whisky I had the whole trip or even into the chocolate left on my pillow every evening. But I will admit I'm still nervous about opening the post in case any of those little heat-sealed packets of white powder fall out. Not that you would know about that kind of thing.

You might think differently, but I reckon that's not too bad, considering Colombia, Britain's largest supplier of carnations, is the world centre of the multi-multi-billion-dollar cocaine business, the most violent and one of the most dangerous countries in the world.

Huge chunks of it are not even controlled by the government. The old Soviet-backed Revolutionary Armed Forces of Colombia and the once Castro-backed National Liberation Army between them control almost all of the north-east, north-west, the centre and south of the country. The drug barons control the rest. There are over 1,000 kidnappings, over 1,500 terrorist incidents and 94 murders every single day of the year. In the past ten years alone four presidential candidates, 23 judges, 63 journalists and over 3,000 soldiers and policemen have been shot, bombed or horribly murdered. Taking into account the size of the population, the murder rate is eight times higher than in the US and a staggering fifty times higher than in the UK.

But don't get the idea they have no respect for law and order. They have. So much so that when Pavarotti arrived in Bogotá for one of his big sing-ins he was told quite firmly that it would be illegal for him to sing in Italian, French or German. Under Colombian law, the Spanish language was supreme. He could only sing in Spanish. A lawyer even slapped down an injunction to ban the show altogether. But with minutes to go, it finally went ahead. The judges decided that cultural activities were outside the law and then rushed to grab the seats they had been given in the front row, while somebody no doubt made the necessary arrangements with the lawyer.

Not surprisingly, therefore, everybody says you shouldn't go there. The Foreign Office goes on about fifty years of civil war: the longest-running guerrilla war in the world; blackmail, kidnapping, bombings, private armies, warlords, men with great big bushy moustaches, drugs. But the government, our ambassador told me, was determined to crack the problem.

The US State Department call it 'volatile and dangerous', 'a hotbed of terrorism'. Visitors should stick to the coastal resorts and 'avoid Bogotá' at all costs.

Even that guide book which never recommends expensive places to eat says it can be 'very dangerous'. Armed robbers are 'more common every year'. It isn't the safest of countries. But if you've got to go, you've got to go.

I've been to plenty of dangerous places in my time, including Moss Side, Manchester, where for a long time everybody complained it was too dangerous for them to go out on the streets and sell crack to merchant banks in the city on a Friday afternoon when everybody is racing to get down to their weekend place in the country. But none of them carried so many government health warnings. In the circumstances, I thought, if I've got to go, I might as well go prepared.

First, I learnt the local lingo; useful everyday words like snow, mardies, smack and skunkweed. Then I thought I'd better learn some handy phrases like Chitral Silver, Special

Pearl, Silver Haze, Master Kush, Early Girl, Red Bird, Northern Lights and Durban Killer. Then I thought I should master the kind of words that come in handy at receptions and cocktail parties like whooooeeee, screamin' cheetah wheelies, cheeba cheeba, pothead pixies, arepas, buñuellos, sancocho Robert de Niro, aguardiente ... No, wait a minute, they're local delicacies. Arepas are maize pancakes filled with egg or cheese, about the size of a doorstep. Buñuellos are fried cheese balls rather like small hard grenades. Sancocho Robert de Niro is a thick chicken and vegetable broth, so-called because that's all he would risk eating while he was there filming *The Mission*. Aguardiente is a strong, sweet, killer anisette liqueur made from coconut. As for whooooeeee, screamin' cheetah wheelies, cheeba cheeba and pothead pixies, they're all ... they're all ... Do you know, for the life of me I can't remember what they are. All I know is ... Oh yes, I remember now. I also learnt the one word without which no trip to Colombia is possible. Perico.

'Perico? How much you want? Ten grams? Fifty grams? Half a kilo? A kilo? A container load? I fix it.'

'No, thank you. Not today.'

'What do you mean, no thank you? Nobody says no thank you to Enrico. You want to meet my partner, yes?'

Then I studied the local currency: one gram of cocaine equals 200 grams of marijuana; 200 grams of marijuana equals one gram of amphetamine; one gram of amphetamine equals one kilogram of marijuana; one kilogram of marijuana equals one gram of heroin; ten kilograms of marijuana equals one gram of something called ice; 20 kilograms of marijuana equals one gram of crack; and one suitcase of crack equals one hell of a Swiss bank account and no problems for the rest of your life.

Next, I thought I'd better pack the right clothes for the climate. Out went my lightweight, non-crushable, washable, bloodproof Airey and Wheeler tropical suit which I'm sure they call Airey because it's so big and loose. Out went all my shirts with the starched collars. Out went the pith helmet and all my medals. Well, you never know if you're going to get an invite to a local British embassy reception. Instead I packed all my old clothes. Well, the ones that are older than the ones I normally wear: the jeans I wear when I'm mucking out the horses; that filthy old shirt from Romania which I picked up cheap at the South of England Show five years ago and has never yet been washed and, of course, the old stand-bys – a bullet-proof sweater, a bullet-proof jacket, a bullet-proof briefcase complete with false bottom, a bullet-proof wallet and a bullet-proof folder containing details of my blood group – 95% proof; a photograph of my beloved – my horse, Herbie; and details of who should be notified in case of an emergency – Michael Broadbent, Christie's Wine Department, London SW1, so he could arrange to sell off my cellar full of fine wines in order to raise money to ensure Herbie could spend the rest of his days happily munching away on the very best Kentucky blue grass.

Finally, something I never do. I checked with the security experts. Don't take any risks, they said. Don't walk around the streets. Go everywhere in an unmarked car with the doors locked and barred and bolted and the windows jammed tight. Don't look as though you've got two pennies, or rather pesos, to rub together. Don't carry any valuables. Don't shake hands with anyone. It's the quickest way to lose your watch, your rings, the little finger on your left hand. Don't take your jacket off in bars, restaurants or even in any office no matter how hot it is. They deliberately turn the air-conditioning off so they can grab your wallet out of your jacket when you're mopping up the perspiration.

If you're stopped by anyone anywhere, in the street, in the lift, in the mini-bar in your room, don't argue. Give them whatever they want. Give them whatever they don't want. Give them everything you've got, down to the number of that bank account you opened years ago in Luxembourg when you were attending that conference on tax evasion and that even your wife doesn't know about. If a policeman comes up to you waving and shouting and gesticulating at you like mad;

don't take any notice. It's one of the oldest tricks in the book. He's probably a crook dressed up like a policeman. Ask for his identification card, his serial number and the last time his wife agreed with anything he said or did.

And so it went on. Don't stand still. Not because they'll mug you, but because they'll slip something into your pocket, drop something into your bag or squeeze half a ton of something into the heel of your shoe. Never accept a drink from anyone. A stranger, the guy you met on the plane, the Lord High Archbishop himself. Especially if it's odourless, colourless and slightly powdery. It could knock you out for days at a stretch. You could wake up on the beach, in a shack in the middle of nowhere or in a back street with a thick head and an empty bullet-proof wallet. If, of course, they've left the bullet-proof wallet behind. Some people have even come to and discovered that while under the influence they've visited their bank, withdrawn all their money and handed it to this nice man who promised to give it to Mother Theresa.

I wanted to go to Cali, out towards the coast, where everyone swoons over the churches and museums. Don't, I was told. I wanted to go to Medellin, where everybody goes around with big smiles on their faces. Don't, I was told again.

OK, I said, how about Villa de Leyva, a tiny colonial town complete with cobblestones and whitewashed houses? No. Then what about Cartagena de los Indes, the capital of the old Spanish colony of New Granado, the home of Gabriel Garcia Marquez, which is supposed to be one of the most beautiful cities in the Americas. Better even than Providence, Rhode Island. Never.

'Okay,' I said. 'In that case it's got to be Bogotá. Hullo. Hullo? Are you all right? Can you hear me? Have I said something I shouldn't have?'

So you can guess what happened when I got there. I'm the only person in the whole city of seven million people racing from my taxi to the hotel, across reception, into the lift, along the corridor, into my room and then locking, barring, bolting and piling everything in the room up against the back of the door. Everybody else is strolling casually along the streets, wandering into hotels and sipping pisco sours at the bar.

I'm the only person sweltering in a bullet-proof sweater with a bullet-proof jacket two sizes too big. Everybody else is immaculate in Hugo Boss suits or Ralph Lauren polo jackets or Versace outfits.

I'm the only person going around asking every tourist, traffic and military policeman, every soldier, commando and presidential guard, every security man, everybody with wrap-around shades and a heavy modern stick hanging loose beneath their jacket to identify themselves and give me name, rank and number. Everybody else is giving them a 'buenos dias' or a 'buenos tardes' and generally treating them the way everybody treats the police or the military in a South American country that has known nothing but civil wars, dictatorships and one coup after another for about a hundred years.

I'm the only person in El Sandwicheria around the back of the Plaza de Bolivar, the main square, who throws himself on the floor when some kid drops his can of Coke and it explodes. Everybody around me just carries on as if for all the world they were in the Coffee Shop in Belfast during the height of the troubles. I'm the only person in the country sitting in boiling, stifling offices with my jacket on. Everybody else is in shirtsleeves, flimsy dresses and the tiniest and tightest of tank tops. Which come to think of it is why I'm boiling over in the first place.

I'm the only ... Hey, wait a minute. Is that guy following me? Didn't I see him outside the Capitolio? And wasn't he also in the Sandwicheria when ...? No, maybe he wasn't. But it could be his brother.

And I'm the only person in the country limping around without a watch, cufflinks or even a pen in my pocket. Everybody else is dripping with Rolexes, rings, pearl neck-laces and gold chains the size of tow ropes. Why am I limping? Because all my money, travellers cheques, credit cards, the key to the hotel safe, my passport, my airline tickets and Michael Broadbent's business card are hidden in my left shoe. That's why I'm limping.

Did I look inconspicuous? Did I melt into the background? Did I look as though I wasn't worth the cost of a used razor blade, a blunt knife or even a bullet? What do you think? Which is why I'm convinced accepting advice is a million times more dangerous than ignoring it. Take my word for it, therefore, not the word of the ex-pats. Bogóta may be dirty and filthy. It may be riddled with corruption. The water system, the sewage system, the transport system – none of them may work. But it is no more dangerous than playing cards with your brother-in-law, making the slightest comment on your wife's cooking, or any car park around London, where as soon as you get out of your car you are surrounded by a group of smart, enthusiastic young men who, for a small consideration, are more than prepared to ensure nobody lays a finger on it until you get back. Except that Bogotá is crawling with pickpockets, thieves and muggers, and violence is endemic. There are on average fourteen murders a day. Grass is everywhere, not just on front lawns and tennis courts. Go into a lawyer's office and somehow you come out feeling lightheaded and willing to pay whatever they ask.

What's more, the place is riddled with poverty, destitution and the fear of practically anything that moves. You've only to walk out of your hotel, run like mad a couple of blocks and it's staring you in the face. Old men crunched into doorways so thin you can hardly believe they are still alive. Women wrapped up in sheets of polythene, stretched out on the pavement. Children – the locals call them los Gamiles, which they say is the polite name for human vermin – living on the streets; living in cardboard boxes; even, would you believe, living under the streets in the sewers. Many of them are already drug addicts. Most are consumed by every disease known to man. Every day, I was told, on average five of them are found dead – lying in doorways, slumped in the middle of the pavement, blocking a sewage pipe. Even worse, if anything could be worse, every night teams of vigilantes roam the streets clearing them up. Exactly what 'clearing them up' means, I couldn't find out, but I've got a pretty good idea, even though the police are now bragging that not only are a record 3 per cent of all crimes now going to court, but in addition they have dramatically improved their rate for solving murders from zero to a staggering all-time high of 1 per cent.

But Bogotá does not just have the highest number of problems in the world; the highest number of casualties for any civil war anywhere in South America; the highest death rate among presidential candidates, judges and the police force, and the highest acreage of cocaine production in the universe: it is also one of the highest capitals in the world. At 2,800 metres, it is squeezed between two mountain ranges, so as it grows it grows lengthways, with the result that it looks more like – I suppose – a syringe than anything else.

Years ago, when it had a population of just 150,000, it rejoiced in the title of the Athens of South America. Now it's grown to over six million, and has one of the most polluted environments – environmental, political, economic, cultural – in the world, it is called many other things. To me, however, it is also the world capital of metal railings. They're everywhere: around shops and offices, houses and apartment buildings, around car parks. They're even on top of houses and apartments and car parks, forming huge zoo-like cages. Except in this case, I suppose, the animals are on the outside trying to get in. If Lord Beaverbrook was ever to be reincarnated as minister of aircraft production for Colombia, he'd have the time of his life ripping them down and building all the Spitfires he could ever dream of.

As for taking drugs, as opposed to producing them, I'm no expert – the nearest I've got is the occasional glass of herbal tea – but I would have thought Bogotá had one of the lowest rates of consumption in the world. In the States drugs are everywhere. Wherever you go, it's bread and cannabis jam for breakfast, hashish brownies for lunch and an Ian Moore (champagne and a reefer – didn't you know that?) for dinner.

In New York, in Washington, even in the middle of nowhere like Champaign, Illinois and Erie, Pennsylvania.

At any lunch or dinner party, everyone is tucking into space mushroom pie, hitting the narcotics dish, spouting their pseudo-zen nonsense and telling jokes about wherever President Clinton goes he is greeted by military bands playing In-hale to the Chief. In-hale to the Chief! Most of the Americans I meet at dinner parties look as though they've never exhaled in their life. By the end of the meal they're driving 'n' crying: in other words so Rolling Stoned out of their minds they are praising the US government for the firm line it is taking against the twenty-six countries which it says are responsible for the worldwide drugs problem.

In Europe, of course, it's different. Nobody takes drugs. They always pay for them. In London if you are unfortunate enough to be invited out to dinner, Melissa and Sebastian are going on about rolling paper joints while they did the cooking and how already they've given their eldest daughter the teeniest of teeny puffs. It won't do her any harm, of course. After all, drugs are no more dangerous than alcohol.

'Quite right.' Everybody nods.

I, of course, always ask the one question I shouldn't ask. 'So how old is your daughter?'

'Seven,' says Melissa.

'Six,' says Sebastian.

Parents never get anything right when it comes to bringing up their children.

Afterwards Sebastian offers me a little something. 'Take it. You won't sleep for days. Not even during the AGM,' he says.

'It's only £5 a gram. Cheaper than buying dried milk,' adds Melissa.

In Holland the situation seems to be totally out of control if you're not Dutch, but totally under control if you are. Years ago you had to hang around railway stations for a smoke. Now it's as much part of the Dutch way of life as a slice of Edam, a lump of Ouderkirkenagel and never ever buying anyone a drink. There are even radio programmes giving you

the price of the stuff. As for the number of times I've seen
people sitting in coffee shops or bars sprinkling marijuana
over their tobacco, rolling it up and taking a drag, I've lost
count. In some coffee shops – some are even owned by the
local town council – there are special drugs menus to choose
from.

'Grass?' (in other words, marijuana leaves). 'No, I'm sorry,
sir, that's off today. Try our hash [cannabis resin] instead.'

'Is it a good year?'

'Yes, sir. The very best.'

'OK, I'll have a pint. But make it quick, I'm in a hurry. I've
got to give a speech on the evils of smoking.'

'Yes, sir.'

And I'm not talking about sleazy dives. These are
respectable hang-outs. Go into the Little Balloon, one of
Amsterdam's oldest and quaintest coffee shops. There for all
the world to see are drugs dealers sitting at the pine tables
selling their little thirty-gram packets of hash and marijuana
with names like Purple Skunk, Swazi, Sputnik or the locally
produced Nederweed which is supposed to be grown under
special high-powered lights in lofts and garden sheds all over
the country.

'So how much does it cost?'

'For you, £10,' one dealer told me. 'Enough for ten
cigarettes. It's the best quality heroin in Europe, and the
cheapest. Better than you get in Marseille, Hamburg, even
London.'

Who says the Dutch are not traders? And they don't just
smoke it themselves and bring their children up on it. Even
worse, they give it to their pigeons. During one trip to
Holland, I was told the Dutch Racing Pigeon Association had
decided to start testing their birds for dope. Somebody had
discovered that if you give drugs to young pigeons they lose
their feathers during moulting which means they can fly much
faster. Now everybody was doing it. At one local meeting of
Dutch racing pigeon fanciers, I was told, officials discovered
more drugs than on the train that runs seven times a day

between Venlo in Holland and Cologne. Which, believe me, is some quantity of drugs.

As for the rest of the world, it's the same story wherever you go. In Morocco, not surprisingly, you can now see more acres of kif, or marijuana, which is supposed to produce the best hashish, than of dates. I've seen the poor farmers shaking the pollen out of the dried tops of the plants, squeezing it into a tiny black ball, warming it up with a cigarette lighter and watching the tiny drops of oil bubble out.

'Un bon vendange?'

'Pas mal.'

Wheat, corn, marijuana, farmers are la même chose the world over. In Lomé, Togo, I once saw a kid standing by a wooden table opposite the Hotel Ecole de Benin openly selling bags of cannabis about the size of packets of tea. In Pakistan, I'm told by a friend who is an addict (of travel, not what you think), at Ormara as well as at Mckran you can hardly sleep at night for 250 camels shuffling on to the beach to offload their, ahem, merchandise onto motorboats eager to make for waiting ships. So don't bother with Ormara or Mckran if you are looking for peace and quiet. Unless, of course, you are looking for a special type of peace and quiet.

In the headquarters of the élite Central Police Unit in Tel Aviv, another addict (travel again) told me he actually saw a marijuana plant growing happily away in the public reception area. Whether it was under protective custody or whether they were innocent victims of the crime, he couldn't tell me.

You even find kids behind the bus shelter in the High Street in Heathfield, our nearest town, smoking the stuff, appropriately enough, in the bottom of cans of Coke, and doing a roaring trade in transfers. You haven't come across transfers? You can now buy them impregnated with drugs. Stick them on your skin and you're on a high for the rest of the day. No pinpricks, no needles, and you can roll your sleeves up without worrying about getting caught.

Once I realised, therefore, that Bogotá was not quite as

dangerous as the experts said it was, I was off. Slick-haired macho hombres in their lizard-skin cowboy boots; thieves with long knives hidden up their sleeves ready to chop your finger off at the first sign of an expensive ring; beautiful young mulattos gliding hand-in-hand along the street – I couldn't tell you which sex they were – looking for likely pockets to pick; even scruffy kids pushing chico de tinto from a thermos flask which they kept in a wooden box: none of them worried me a bit, although one morning I did get a little nervous when I was followed around town by an old soldier who kept showing me a photograph of himself when he was in the presidential guard, and giving me a long lecture on the history of Colombia. Every time I stopped before what looked like a mildly interesting building he would leap up and down in front of me going, 'Boom boom. Here big fight. Boom boom.'

To be on the safe side – you see what Bogotá does to you – I got up extra early another morning and wandered around watching the locals doing all the things everybody does all over the world at the start of another day: sponging down the guard dogs; greasing their rifles; turning off the alarm systems; unlocking the doors and windows; rolling a spliff, lighting up, taking a long, slow puff, keeling over and passing out; and beginning the long process of taking down the metal grilles. I wandered through the back streets of Candelaria, which is a bit like Andalusia without the tourists – old Spanish-style mansions, oak balconies, tiny, narrow streets, geraniums, magnolia trees, and, of course, bougainvilleas. I strolled among the shops and stalls selling gold, diamonds and emeralds. I went in and out of sandwicherias, and cafeterias. I even went into a snack bar called the Broasted Chicken. All on my own. By myself. Nobody else with me. One evening I couldn't resist it, I'm afraid; I just had to go to a restaurant called El Horno, where I risked all and had a home-made fruit juice. I even – but don't tell my mother – undid the top button of my bullet-proof jacket.

Another day I took a cab, not an armoured tank, and drove

with the windows down to the south of the city. We drove around Ciudad Bolivar, a vast collection of shacks that stretches way up into the steep muddy hills, which is home, if you can call it that, to farm dwellers and peasants driven out by the big landowners as well as by the guerrillas. After that I drove to the north of the city where the upper and middle classes live behind their brick walls and security guards. And, I'm sorry to disappoint you, I got back safe and sound.

By the end of the week, without a care in the world, I was visiting offices and companies and factories as far away as Cajica and Zipaquirá, two towns around fifty kilometres north of the city. I even went to an enormous flower plantation which is helping to ship over twenty tons of flowers a week to Britain: carnations, lilies, chrysanthemums and something called Queen Anne's lace, making us one of their biggest export markets.

On the green plains just outside the city, growing conditions were perfect: sunshine, constant temperatures, constant hours of daylight the year round, hardly any frost. The downside was that the place looked as though it was run entirely with child labour. Children were watering, weeding, pruning, spraying pesticides (many of which, I discovered later, are banned in the United States and Europe because they can cause respiratory problems, paralysis of the nervous system, epilepsy, cancer, miscarriages and all kinds of mutations). Safety procedures and controls were non-existent. There were no masks or any kind of protection for the children. Often they were mixing the pesticides with their bare hands. After that they were cutting and tying the flowers into bundles ready for packing and shipment.

Children are cheap to employ. They are paid next to nothing, and there are millions of them. Most are living on (or under) the streets. In the morning they are collected in buses from Madrid, Funza and Mosquera, the barrios or slums, and shipped into the plantations. There they work virtually non-stop for 10, 11 or even 12 hours, depending on the time of year and the number of flowers that have to be shipped.

'We have to otherwise we would never make any money. Even employing the children, eliminating pathways and growing as intensively as we can, we hardly make anything,' one of the managers told me.

I looked surprised.

'It's true,' he said. 'Eight big plantations have gone bust this year alone. That doesn't help anyone, especially the children. What's more their hands are tiny. They can get in and out the bunches of flowers without damaging them. Adults can't.'

In addition to paying the children next to nothing, many plantation owners, I was told, as a sign of appreciation allow them to take home cuttings which they have sprayed with their deadly insecticides so they can feed them to their animals and pets.

On the way back to the hotel I will admit I did have a scare. One of those big, heavy Harley Davidson motorbikes drew up alongside us. The guy on the back, all in leather with a red scarf tied tightly around his face, suddenly started waving us into the side of the road. Oh, oh, I began to think. Maybe everything they said was . . . But he only wanted to tell us the back door of the car wasn't properly shut.

I learnt a lot about drugs in Colombia. Out of academic interest, naturally.

Ten years ago Colombia was only in the refining business. Coca, the raw material for cocaine, was grown in Peru and Bolivia, and the paste was flown in for refining and onward shipment. Today that's all changed. Thanks to a bug which has destroyed most of Peru's coca fields – who says Fujimori can't organise things? – in just two years Colombia has become the biggest producer in the world with over 80,000 hectares under cultivation. The area round Cali alone is said to dominate the world market through a branch of the Sicilian Mafia based in Venezuela, and supply over 75 per cent of all cocaine sold in the States.

Shipping the stuff out used to be as easy as pushing a needle into your left arm: US$60 a month to a dog handler here; US$220 a month to a lieutenant colonel there; US$25,000 to an airport manager or air traffic controller per flight. At one time, I was told, they were using specially converted 747s, which gives you an idea of the size of the operation. Or if that wasn't possible, they used to land fully authorised, genuine passenger jets for special deliveries on dry lake beds near the Baja village of Todos Santos on the southern tip of the southern California Sur without anyone – passengers, crew, customs officials – saying a word.

Today it seems to be lots of little Piper airplanes taking off from lots of tiny airstrips in the middle of the jungle and flying in to lots of other tiny airstrips in Mexico or the US or both. To avoid being detected they fly out first to Cuba, then north across the Gulf of Mexico and turn right to Florida. To make certain they don't come up on US radar they fly just a few feet above sea level. Then the clever bit. To ensure they also land without being detected, a second Piper airplane reports to air traffic control and takes off from Florida in the normal way for a day's flying up and down the coast. It then rendezvous with the first Piper and both fly back and land in Florida together. Except that they fly so close together air traffic control thinks it is just one plane. They get away with it, I was told, because there is never anybody on the ground double-checking what is on the radar screen. But still they are looking for other ways of getting the stuff out. They tried traditional Colombian handicrafts, but they were rumbled. A DC6 loaded with 4.1 tonnes of cocaine disguised as handicrafts was discovered at Lima's Jorge Chavez International airport in Peru. Half the officials said it was the real stuff, the other half said it wasn't fake. Colombia wasn't even mentioned on the flight plan. One idea I was told they were working on was to bond cocaine with fibreglass and plastic, then ship it out as flat fibreglass sheets, or any shape product you like. So be warned. If one day you're sitting having dinner on your new imitation oak fibreglass table and you begin to feel a bit woooseeee, it's not the Cheval Blanc '47, it's the table. Although your wife will never believe you.

As for prices, people used to pay for cocaine through the nose, if that's the right expression. Today – the latest market information – wholesale prices in New York are running at around US$20,000–25,000 a kilo, way down from the boom days of the early '80s when it was around US$50,000 a kilo. In Miami, it's cheaper. In Los Angeles, it's cheaper still. Around US$15,000–20,000. So now you know the best place to do your shopping. But pity the poor farmer. He gets less than a 200th of the price it fetches on the streets of New York, or even behind the bus shelter in Heathfield.

In Bogotá, however, the nearest I came to seeing any sign of drugs was along by the Parque Santander. An old man shuffled up to me, a dirty, crumpled sheet of newspaper in his hand. 'Señor, señor,' he said.

This is it, I thought. THIS IS IT. Just look even mildly interested and every cop in South America will be on my back either because I've been set up, the innocent tourist abroad, and they want every last penny I've got on me, or it's for real and they're going to chuck me in gaol and throw away the key. But it wasn't. He was pushing cheap emeralds.

As for being hustled, the closest I got, much to the disappointment no doubt of the Foreign Office, the US State Department and what's the name of that book, was in the Museo del Oro, which is supposed to contain the most marvellous collection of pre-Spanish gold jewellery and decoration. It is also supposed to be the safest, most heavily guarded place in the country. I was wandering aimlessly, as you do, from one showcase to another, in what looked like an enormous bomb-proof, volcano-proof, earthquake-proof strongroom. I was in the furthest corner. It was pitch black apart from the light from the showcases. Suddenly, out of nowhere, one of the armed guards was standing beside me.

'Señor,' he said, swinging his gun towards me. 'Dollars, señor. You have dollars?'

That apart, I had a great time in Bogotá. When I left I only had two pounds in my pocket. But it was great stuff. No, I'm kidding. I don't do drugs. Instead, I'm afraid, I'm addicted to champagne. My only hope is that one day it will lead to caviar.

Quito

Ecuador is a funny old country. They claim they are at the centre of the world – Ecuador, Equator – get it? But nobody takes any notice of them or knows anything about them. You don't believe me? OK, so where do Panama hats come from? Wrong. Ecuador. A good one you can roll up and push through a wedding ring. Where is the condor's favourite patch? Peru? No, Ecuador. Which country produces the best, most haunting Andean music? Bolivia? Nope, Ecuador. Which is the most dangerous place in the world when it comes to driving? The US? Italy? Hong Kong? No way. Ecuador.

At one time they were hailed for their lush, extravagant, wedding-cake style of architecture and the skills of their artists and sculptors and craftsmen. The light of America they were called. The Florence of South America. Now they can barely put one brick on top of another without both falling over.

And in 1835, most famous of all, with the arrival of Charles Darwin on the Galapagos Islands, they invented evolution. Which is when, I reckon, the whole place stopped evolving and started de-evolving, if that's the correct word.

Today, instead of just jumping off a boat and wandering ashore accompanied by the occasional turtle, things have de-evolved to such a state that you have to queue for hours at an immigration desk only to be told you've filled in one form when you should have filled in two.

'But I was only given one form. The lady back there said—'
'You should have two.'
'She said only one.'

'Two.'

'She said they've changed the rules. It used to be two, now it's . . .'

So back you go to the lady. 'He said I need two forms.'

'One. He is wrong. It is only one. He does not know anything.'

'I know, but . . .'

So what's another form? You fill it in and queue up for another two hours. And what does the guy do when you give it to him? He doesn't even look at it. Which is just as well because as a minor protest at being shuffled between the two of them, where it asked for my profession I put 'housewife'.

Then there's the luggage. Instead of being dumped on the beach in a matter of minutes, things have now de-evolved to such a peak of organisation and efficiency that it takes at least thirty-five minutes, give or take an hour, to get to you.

You get to the hotel. Again de-evolution has been at work. Instead of throwing a few sticks together, setting light to them and boiling a mug of tea, you have to wait two hours for room service to bring you a beer from their own personal supply because the restaurant is closed because there is an election taking place.

As for taxis, they've perfected the art of de-evolution down to the equivalent of a flesh-eating stingray. The taxi drivers have spent so long in their taxis they don't know where anywhere is any more, and what's more they don't know how to ask anyone for directions. You spend hours driving up and down the Avenida 10 de Augusto looking for the Museo del Banco Central when it is actually slap bang opposite the Parque la Alameda. Why did I want to see the Museo del Banco Central? Because it's the only Central Bank that I know in the world that actually displays not only the instruments of torture they use to deal with teams of World Bank economists trying to negotiate a structural adjustment programme, but also the twisted, mis-shapen bodies of their victims. Of course, they tell you they are merely early examples of the advanced surgical instruments used in Ecuador hundreds of years ago, and the bodies are the bodies of patients. But have you ever heard of a Central Bank that was interested in anybody's health and well-being and was actually responsible for carrying out operations? They might think I've started de-evolving like them, but I haven't. The whole thing is enough to make Charles Darwin revolve in his grave, if that's the correct word.

And yet, compared to many countries, Ecuador was originally dealt a fantastic hand. The land itself is spectacular. It has beaches and rainforests. It has the mighty Amazon. It has jungles and mountains and glaciers. It is supposed to have more types of animals and plants than anywhere else in the world: over 100 different bats, over 1,500 different birds – twice the number we have in Europe. And, as if that's not enough to be getting on with, over 20,000 new species are being discovered every year. On top of all that, it has the Galapagos Islands, Darwin's 'broken field of black basaltic lava, thrown into the most rugged waves and crossed by great fissures, everywhere covered by stunted, sunburnt brushwood which shows little sign of life', which is home to I forget how many plants and animals you won't find anywhere else.

Ecuador has also been civilised, so to speak, for 10,000 years. Which is a darn sight more than you can say for some countries in that part of the world. A bunch of Indians called the Quitus (hence Quito, the name of the capital) drifted down or, I suppose, up from the north Pacific, liked what they saw, and decided to do all the things one did in those days if you liked the look of a place. You built your house, planted your seeds, spent Wednesdays, Thursdays and Saturdays out hunting and worshipped the sun. Presumably on the basis that, whatever happened, you wanted to continue going out with the Wednesday, Thursday and Saturday hunt no matter what else came up. According to some people – and there are inevitably a million who disagree – Ecuador was the first major settlement of importance in all South America.

By the time the Incas arrived there were towns and cities all along the coast as well as up in the mountains, and people were beginning to complain about hunting. Especially as it now included people as well as animals. But the Incas were undeterred. Quito they made their centre of operations. They then did all the things they did wherever they went. They built a temple to the sun, a palace for the emperor with hot and cold running virgins, known to everyone as the House of Pleasure, and a masonic lodge, although it was apparently difficult at the time to tell which was which.

When Atahualpa had his set-to with Huascar for the control of Tahuantinsuyo and won, he again made Quito his head-quarters. Such was the attraction of hot and cold running virgins. And up went more buildings and palaces and masonic lodges.

When the Spanish came in 1526 things could have gone any which way, but they decided to have nothing whatsoever to do with Opus Dei. They didn't like the idea of ladies' nights. But it was too late. As soon as the Incas knew they were beaten, the big chief Ruminahui hid all their gold and treasures (which have still not been found; this can only mean they are filed somewhere in the British embassy), and set fire to the whole city. The Spanish, however, liked the look or rather the charred remains of the place and decided to start all over again. As they were in a new country, in a new part of the world, in a totally different environment vis-à-vis climate and geography, they decided to lay it out exactly as they laid out any Spanish city: a central main square where all the major buildings are located – the governor's palace, the archbishop's palace, the cathedral, the town hall. Then, running from the main square, completely contrary to what nature and geog-raphy intended, they built a series of long, straight, narrow streets. Talk about San Francisco. Building these streets must have entailed filling in no end of ditches, gaps and ravines, and building I don't know how many walls and bridges. But if that's the Spanish way of doing things that's the Spanish way of doing things.

In 1534 it became a Spanish city. Officially. In 1541 it got its own coat of arms from the King of Spain: a silver castle stuck on top of two mountains with two black eagles holding up a golden cross. Which was not bad considering Quito was famous for gold, not silver. It was not on top of two mountains, it was between them: Pichincha on one side and the rolling hills and valleys of Los Chillos, Tumbaco and Guayabamba on the other. And the two eagles should have been condors. But who's arguing? The truth should never get in the way of a good story. In any case, they got the cross right.

The Spaniards than gave it all they had. They gave it religion. They built no end of churches, monasteries and convents. The cathedral was the first colonial church built in South America. They gave it education: schools, colleges and universities. They gave it the Spanish language, Spanish philosophy, Spanish culture and Spanish siestas. They gave it organisation, administration, management and corruption. In 1563 the Spanish made it a 'Real Audiencia'. A president and three judges were appointed to run the city, the surrounding countryside, and anything else they stumbled across. They gave it health care. In 1565 they built the Misericordia, which is now the San Juan de Dios Hospital, the first hospital built in South America. They told patients how much they had to slip the doctors in order to get treatment – and still the place has been grossly inefficient and over budget ever since. They gave it technology. In 1815 they built an astronomical observatory, the first in South America. They trained a team of local astronomers and showed them how they could make extra money by hiring it out to students who wanted to get a closer look at the nurses' home next to the hospital. They also gave Ecuador the banana. No, seriously. Until the Spanish came along there were no bananas in Ecuador. Now they're all over the place. Bananas, I mean.

But more than anything they gave it style. Not just Spanish style, but a wonderful, unique mix of Spanish, Arabic, Renaissance, baroque, rococo, Indian, and rich, golden, luscious candy floss. So much so that from the sixteenth century to the nineteenth century Quito was famous the world over. Its workshops were bursting at the seams with wood-carvers, sculptors, carpenters, goldsmiths and candy floss makers. Its streets were flowing with treacle. Its churches were the wonder of the world and the envy of every wedding cake designer in creation. For they didn't just decorate them, they turned them into the most gorgeous extravaganzas: fabulous, towering red and gold columns; wonderful, lavish altars decorated with every intricate fiddly bit known to man; ceilings richly covered in gold and criss-crossed with every design imaginable; bright, colourful, magnificent paintings; delicate, fragile statues; glorious stained-glass windows. And everywhere, not just the glint but the 2,000-watt glare of gold.

San Francisco, the first building to be started in the whole city – work began a few days after the Spanish turned up in 1534 – was a mass of baroque carving covered in gold leaf. The high altar, the side altars; there was no better example of baroque carving in the world. It stood facing the biggest plaza in the city, a wonder of design and decoration. To the left and right were the monastery buildings crammed with still more paintings and decorations.

La Campania, across the plaza, was even more ornate, more richly sculptured, more completely overlaid in gold. The high altar, the side altars, the balconies, the lamps, the screens, the carvings – everything was covered in intricate Arab lattice-work and overlaid in gold. Some people estimate over seven tons of the stuff was used to decorate it, making it one of the most beautiful churches in North or South America.

Down Avenida Sucre four blocks, turn right into Avenida Flores, and across the plaza facing you is Santo Domingo, which boasts no less than 50,000 square feet of more ornate, intricate, lavish, luscious decoration.

And so it goes on. San Agustin, where Ecuador signed their declaration of independence on 10 August 1809; San Diego, with its huge wooden pulpit carved by the famous Indian wood-carver, Juan Baptista Menacho; the Sanctuario of Guapulo, at the bottom of a steep valley on the edge of town; El Belen, where mass was celebrated for the first time in Quito: every-where the fanciest, the most elaborate decoration imaginable.

Quito took everything it was given, learnt how to do it

better, then in 1592 turned the tables on the Spanish and demanded they run the place themselves. It wasn't until 1809, however, that they finally got their way. Again, it was another first: the first revolution in the whole of South America. But it didn't last long. It needed General Simon Bolivar and his sidekick, Lieutenant Antonio de Sucre, to finally fix it. Which they did on 10 August 1830 at the battle of Pichincha on the outskirts of Quito. At the time you'd have thought it was set for life. With its long history, its dramatic growth, its worldwide reputation for art, design and decoration, anyone would have bet a couple of gold decorated churches it was going to evolve into one of the leading, one of the most civilised, most cultured countries in South America. But Ecuador blew it. Its evolution into a major world player stopped dead. Things almost immediately began to go wrong.

First, they couldn't agree the borders with Peru. One side said one thing. The other side said something different. This went on until 1942 when both sides sat down and decided to resolve the issue once and for all. Which they did. They then immediately afterwards fell out again over what they had just agreed. Even today, they are at loggerheads. Ecuadorian maps say one thing, Peruvian maps something else. Hundreds of books have been written on the subject. The Ecuadorians say 507, the Peruvians say 203. When fighting actually broke out again between the two sides early in 1995, Ecuador estimated it was costing them both US$10 million a day. Peru said US$7.5 million. But talk to people in Aguas Verde, the border town at the centre of the dispute. They don't know what all the fuss is about. They are still wading backwards and forwards, wheeling and dealing and doing business across the open sewer running through the middle of town which is supposed to be the border between the two countries.

Today it's all gone – all the glory, the splendour, all the hope. Quito is still there, of course, 8,500 feet up in the heart of the Andes, at the northern end of the Valley of the Volcanoes, the second highest capital in South America after La Paz in Bolivia. But only just. For the time being, at least, it's still clean and fresh. The sun still shines almost all the time. On March 21 and September 21 it shines directly overhead so there are no shadows. When it rains, it's winter. When it's dry it's summer. Although, I suppose, it won't be long before even the climate evolves and the whole place is blacked out by thick, heavy, sulphurous clouds.

As for the once glorious, beautiful, Spanish-style city crammed with churches, dripping in gold, it has now evolved into a scruffy, dirty backwater beset by chronic unemployment, desperate poverty and an almost complete inability to do anything about it. I was only there for a few days, but in that short time I saw a march by Indians evolve into a protest about unemployment, low wages and what the oil companies are doing to their villages. I saw a protest by telephone and electricity workers evolve into a scuffle about privatisation. And when I saw a bunch of oil workers turning the corner at the far end of the street, I thought it better to go back to the hotel than evolve a broken leg. But I was out of luck. The electricity was off. It's known as Quito roulette. Wake up early and there might not be electricity to make coffee. Get to the office on time and none of the typewriters or computers will be working. Arrive back at the hotel too late and the mini-bar will have flooded the room. Any number can play. And a game can last for twenty years.

The tiny narrow streets are still there, but they are choked with traffic. The huge, wide open plazas are still there, but they are crammed with cars and stalls and pigeons and beggars. Many of the original Spanish buildings are still there, with their thick stone walls, their windows barred and latticed, their courtyards and gardens and fountains and red-tile roofs. All the churches are still there. But because the Ecuadorians are eager to let as many people as possible share in their past glories and traditions, and because they want to increase tourism and boost their foreign exchange, they have evolved a special new policy of keeping the churches locked, barred and bolted. Or at least most of them, most of the time. I'm game for a church crawl any day, but by the end of my trip,

I was lifting up my eyes to the upstairs bar in the Hotel Colon rather than to anything else. Anybody else would have been so desperate they would have turned Church of England. (Which is pretty desperate I can tell you.)

The number of times I tried to get into La Campania I cannot tell you. Early morning, lunchtime, evenings, weekdays, weekends. Even Sunday. It was always closed. I asked at the hotel if they knew when it was open. They had no idea. I asked the tourist office. No idea. I asked the policemen walking up and down outside. No idea. It was the same with Santo Domingo. Always closed, closed, closed. And nobody knew when it would be open. The cathedral I did manage to visit. It was stark and bare, covered in dust and rubble, practically falling down. San Francisco I also managed to get into, but it's badly showing its age. It's also been knocked around by the occasional earthquake. The gilt is still there, but under several thousand layers of dust. The floorboards sway and creak as you walk along them. Its statues are sadly in need of a lick of paint. Its paintings are rotting away. Once I even popped into El Sagrario, but it was second-division stuff.

San Agustin, San Diego, Sanctuario of Guapulo, El Belen – I spent so much time going back and forth trying to get into La Campania and Santo Domingo, I didn't have time left to go and see them. Such are the results of evolution.

But the government, having successfully developed this policy of attracting people not to look at their churches, are not stopping there. They are now evolving a policy to turn the whole country into what they call a tourist spot. Which means, no doubt, before long all the hotels will be de-evolving their services and evolving the size of their bills; the restaurants and bars will be de-evolving the size of their meals and drinks and evolving their charges; and taxi drivers will evolve from being friendly but useless to being out-and-out hustlers playing the meter when you're not looking and useless.

I blame not the Ecuadorians, however, but the French. They started the rot. In 1884 the British invented Greenwich Mean Time. This made the French hopping mad, not because they hadn't thought of it first but because it meant the British would get the credit for coming up with the idea. Although it looks as though the old Meridian lines are not as sacrosanct today as they used to be, what with one Pacific Island after another playing games with them and shuffling them around at will just to ensure they are the first in the world to welcome in the year 2000. What did the French do? What they always do; they set out to make sure they got the glory and not the British, even though every other country supported the British, over 70 per cent of the world's maps were based on Greenwich, and the United States (at the time divided into five different time zones) also based itself on Greenwich. First, they refused to accept the world decision to back the British. Second, they launched Paris time, which they set at nine minutes behind Greenwich Mean Time. Third they sent groups, missions, delegations, all over the world claiming they had invented le Greenwich Mean Time and taking the credit for the idea, so that even today French schoolchildren are taught that Greenwich is a small town north of Paris.

You think I'm joking? Let me tell you. In San Antonio de Pichincha, twenty-three kilometres north of Quito, on the exact line of the equator, they painted a red line on the ground. Today it's evolved into a tribute to the intrepid French explorers, French technology and la Belle France itself.

The red line is still there. But across the centre of it is a huge, solid, five-storey Soviet mausoleum-type monstrosity. On top of it is a giant globe. On the side is the simple inscription: 'Latitude 0°0′0″ Longitude West of Greenwich 78°27′8″ Altitude 2,483 m'. Leading up to it – this is true, I'm not kidding – is a massive Soviet-style Avenue of the French Heroes with – you're not going to believe this – a more than lifesize bust of each of them on top of a series of rock-solid plinths: each proud of their triumph, proud of their technology, each proud to be a servant of La France. I swear, walking along the Avenue I could actually hear the distant strains of the 'Marseillaise'.

Of the poor British guys who invented the thing, surprise, surprise, there's not a word. Which I suppose is our fault for being the shy, quiet, modest, reserved, unassuming, charming, sophisticated people we are. It is also I reckon our fault for calling the damn thing Greenwich Mean Time. Why didn't we call it London Mean Time? Or, better still, London Generous Time? Then the whole world, every second of every day on every longitude and latitude, would have marvelled at our triumph. You can bet your life, if the French had invented the thing they would have called it Paris, le commencement du Monde, or something like that.

Once I had reached the end of the Avenue, got my breath back and recovered my equilibrium, I came across the only connection the area could possibly have with Britain: a queue. Right in front of me was an American showing off to this kid – his son, presumably. He was going on about which was the capital of what country. Norway was the capital of Sweden, that kind of thing. 'Kid should know where he's at.' He turned round and grinned at me. 'You agree?'

'Yes, of course,' I said politely, wondering which was worse; sticking behind the American or going back down the Avenue of the French Heroes. 'That's quite right. Very important.'

'Go on then, you ask him a question,' he suddenly said to me. 'A question about geography. So he know's where he's at.'

Now I was trapped. It was the last thing I wanted to do. Then it came to me. 'OK,' I said, 'which is the most westerly state in the US?'

'Hey, you're a buddy,' the American slapped me on the shoulder. Then he turned to the kid. 'Go on, kid, tell him. What is it?'

The kid stared at me. I stared back.

'Oh hell,' said the American, 'it's Hawaii. Tell him it's Hawaii.'

The kid continued staring at me.

'OK,' I said, 'which is the most northerly?'

'Hey.' The American slapped me on the shoulder again. 'It's Alaska. Tell him, kid. Tell him it's Alaska.'

The kid just continued to stare at me.

'OK,' I went on, 'which is the most easterly?'

The American looked at me. 'It's got to be New York State,' he said slowly. 'Can't be Rhode Island. Not far out enough.' He looked at me again. 'Yup, reckon it's got to be New York.'

'Wrong,' I said. 'It's Alaska, Alaska and Alaska.'

'Hey, how can it be? Hawaii is way out ...'

'Easy,' I said. 'The lines of longitude. Have a nice day.'

They turned and walked away. 'You did that deliberate. In front of that guy. Making me look a ...' I could hear him shouting at the kid.

Why I went up the thing I don't know. From the top all I could see was the Avenue of the French Heroes and stalls and shops and carts and trolleys selling enough Centre of the World ponchos, T-shirts and bowler hats to go all the way round the world and back again without reaching a sale. Whizzing all over the place, past the delicatessen Monte Verde, past the Planeta Disco bar and past all the shops selling Centre of the World ashtrays, Centre of the World mirrors and live Centre of the World snakes in filthy Centre of the World bottles, was a Centre of the World train ride for kids who were obviously bored out of their minds being at the Centre of the World.

Back on the ground, I spotted a Japanese tourist who must have been geographically dyslexic. While everybody else was being photographed standing feet either side of the north-south red line, he was photographing his wife and kids standing feet either side of an imaginary east-west line.

My only regret was that Michael Palin didn't discover this place when he was doing his Mickey Mouse north-south travel series. He could have wrapped the whole thing up in thirty seconds and saved us all a great deal of embarrassment.

After that I wandered across to a 'Geographical Exposition', simply because it was the only way to avoid walking back down the Avenue of the French Heroes. It was a collection of huts, showing how the Indians lived a calm, quiet, civilised life before things started to devolve, complete with rats, two motheaten goats and a couple of turtles that looked as though they were around when Charles Darwin first hit the Galapagos – one place I deliberately did not visit in Ecuador.

To me the Galapagos is unique. For over three million years it has been left on its own to evolve and develop. It should be left that way. Let tourists in and they'll destroy it. It's not as if they're actually interested in the place; all they want to do is gawp and gape and make silly remarks and fill in the time between lunch and dinner and have something to bore people about.

'Ah, but tourism is strictly controlled,' we are always being told back home. 'Only a certain number of tourists are allowed in. When the quota is reached, that's it.'

Oh yes! Tell that to the iguanas. Out here it's a case of Darwin or lose. And at the moment it looks more as if people are going to win and the animals are going to lose. Practically everyone and his condor is selling trips to the Galapagos – travel agents, tour operators, airlines, bus companies.

'But I thought it was difficult to get in?' I asked one operator.

'Difficult? No, sir. You want to leave Friday? No problem.'

'What about the quotas?' I began to ask one airline.

'Quotas? What are quotas? You want to go, you go. There's no quota.'

There are cheap, cut-price tours, luxury tours, and of course dozens of pseudo-study scientific tours. In the old days barely 10,000 people a year visited the islands. Today it's well over 50,000. The population as a result has also increased. In 1950 it was around 1,000; today it's over 12,000 and growing at nearly 10 per cent a year, the fastest growth of population in South America. And is that because they are interested in the fauna and flora? No way. They're interested in selling ice creams and candy floss and Coca-Cola.

With that kind of growth taking place, and bars, restaurants, discos, shops selling T-shirts and even banks opening up, how long will the blue-footed and masked boobies nest wherever they want to on the ground, the marine iguanas run along beside you or the Sally Lightfoot crabs curl up by your feet and go to sleep? And with the harbours filling up with luxury cruisers complete with built-in swimming pools, flash catamarans and motor cruisers, and more and more ships going backwards and forwards, how long will hammerhead sharks cruise offshore? Not long. Already the rare giant tortoises, including Lonesome George, the only Pinta Island species left in the world, have been fenced off to protect them. Marine life has started to decline. The rare large sea cucumbers are almost gone – and once they're gone there is nothing to help purify the water and provide larvae for the fish. On top of that, one of the island's biggest colonies of flamingoes has virtually been destroyed to make way for a new airport.

Then there's the problem of the cats and dogs and goats and chickens and donkeys the shopkeepers and bar owners and bank managers bring along with them. Not to mention the problem of the fleas and nits and things the cats and dogs and goats and chickens and donkeys bring along with *them*, and the increase in the number of flies and ants and rats and other things they generate. Already some rare species have been affected and others are threatened.

As I see it, it's just not worth the risk. It's not as if there is nowhere else in the world where tourists can gape and gawp and make silly remarks. The whole thing is a nonsense. As far as I'm concerned one more visitor is one too many. And there was no way I was going to be that one.

On my final evening in Quito, I decided to go to a Swiss restaurant nestling just below the massive statue of the Virgin of Quito on the top of Panecillo Hill overlooking the city. I was told it had a fantastic view, besides being the best restaurant in town.

It was closed. It had become so popular it had attracted petty crooks and thieves who roamed around attacking people on their way in and out. The police said there were too many for them to deal with. In any case they had too many problems to sort out elsewhere to concentrate on just one restaurant. So people stayed away, and the place closed down.

Such is the funny old way evolution evolved in Ecuador.

Guatemala City

Just imagine. If it hadn't been for an earthquake in 1773 Guatemala could today be the greatest country on earth, stretching from Alaska in the north to Patagonia in the south. On one side its authority could stretch to the easternmost state of the US: Alaska. And on the other side to the westernmost state: also Alaska. You haven't forgotten the lines of longitude, have you?

The world could be run by elegant Don Josés. We could all be living in palacios dripping with Velazquezes, Goyas and El Grecos. We could all be eating paellas and anguillas and, better still, cordero asados. We could be drinking gallons of Rioja, being serenaded by señoritas and making elegant little jokes about El Cordobes. I could have as many horses as I liked. I could wear fancy leather boots and a big hat. I could ride up and down all day. Thursdays and Sundays I could go to the bullfight.

Instead Guatemala is a filthy, poverty-stricken, two-bit military dictatorship and I'm dragging myself around the world in order to try and rub two pennies together.

The Conquistadors under Pedro de Alvarado moved in around 1523 and set up shop first in Ciudad Vieja. After that was flattened by a mudslide in 1543 they moved up the road to Le muy Noble y muy Leal Ciudad de Santiago de los Caballeros de Goathemala. Or Antigua, as it is known today. Which makes you wonder why the Conquistadors never invented the typewriter. Can you imagine having to write that name out in longhand every time you sent a postcard home telling the wife and kids what a miserable time you were having, how it kept raining cats and dogs and how, promise, you would definitely be home to see them in the school Nativity play.

Situated at the foot of three volcanoes – to the south-east Agua, to the west Acatenango, and to the south-west Fuego, which still puffs out smoke by day and spits fire by night – Le muy Noble y muy Leal Ciudad, oh what the hell, Antigua, really is one of the oldest and most beautiful cities in the Americas. It not only has all the old Spanish churches and monasteries and convents and universities and hospitals and parks and gardens and vast colonial mansions you would expect, it also has all the atmosphere. I mean, I can sit having a drink in the Parque Central, the main square, and I can actually see Don José on a fabulous white horse riding out of the Palacio de los Capitanes, the old government HQ, which for over 200 years more or less ran Central America. On the other side of the square I can see a line of fabulous carriages, and Don Luis and Don Fernando and Don Miguel rushing into the Palacio del Ayuntamiento, which today, shame of shames, is the town hall. I only hope that with all that baroque decoration dripping over it, it doesn't symbolise the speed and efficiency of its organisation. Although knowing town halls the world over it probably does. Next door I can see Don Fernando popping into the Museo del Libro Antiguo, the old books museum, to check a quick reference. And of course, sitting over there under a jacaranda tree pretending not to notice me, is Doña Isabella ...

Trouble was, though the Conquistadors could do many things and rule many countries, they couldn't rule the volcanoes, which erupted time and again causing an enormous amount of damage. But so much did they like Le muy Noble y muy Leal, hell, you know where I mean, that they decided to stay put. Until, of course, that fateful day in 1773 when Fuego did its worst. The Conquistadors had no alternative. They had to leave. But they didn't go far. They moved about forty kilometres down the hill to the present site of Guatemala City.

Over two hundred years later, you can still see why they

didn't want to leave. All the magnificent old Spanish colonial buildings are still there. The long cobbled streets are still there. So are most of the houses, painted in light pastel colours and decorated with enormous wrought-iron grilles. Some even have massive wooden doorways you could easily ride through on a horse. Most of the churches and monasteries and convents are still there, many of them still as churches and monasteries and convents, although some, inevitably, have collapsed or been converted into luxury homes or hotels. The Catedrale de Santiago on the east side of the Parque, however, is a shadow of its former self. Built in 1542, it has been earthquaked and rebuilt almost as many times as Guatemala has been ruled by a military dictator. The Iglesia y Convento de Nuestra Señora de la Merced (La Merced for short) is probably the best of the lot. It's as baroque and as Spanish as they come; especially, I'm told, on Palm Sunday when, with the first of Antigua's Easter Week processions, the whole town turns back the clock, dons deep purple robes and takes part in one big procession after another.

The Iglesia de San Francisco has been restored and restored so much that the only bit of the original that remains is a chapel dedicated to one of the Spanish monks, Brother Peter, who founded a hospital for the poor, and the poor today, judging by the crowd surrounding his casket, seem as grateful as they must have been then. The Convento de las Capuchinas, on the other hand, originally built in 1736, is now a museum with, I must admit, some pretty gruesome reminders of what it was like to be religious in medieval times, although I personally am not against the practice of women being bricked up inside their own little cell for the whole of their lives. In fact, without thinking, I could suggest a long list of possible candidates right now.

Trouble is, the place is packed with tourists and language students. The tourists amble around with their cameras and money pouches and that vacant how-can-we-stretch-this-out-to-dinnertime look on their faces. The students are trying to dodge out of shops and restaurants without paying.

And because the tourists are there, the Mayan Indians are there, the poor lost descendants of that once great civilisation that I suppose almost out-Egypted the Egyptians until they virtually disappeared off the face of the earth around 1500 years ago. Mathematics, astronomy, architecture, agriculture, they knew it all. Enormous monuments, like the great Temple of the Giant Jaguar, and Tikal, with its wide, almost vertical stairway to the stars, they built them all over the place. Books – they came up with best sellers like *Popol Vuh*. But by the time the Spaniards arrived, they had disappeared. Zap. Just like that.

Things have changed, however. A Mayan Indian in his fancy trousers, red shirt and straw boater has only to appear in the Museo del Libro, or outside one of the churches and convents and – zap – it's the tourists who disappear. Which probably explains the disappearance of the Mayans. While they kept this mysterious power to make people disappear directed towards other people, they were safe. But as soon as they used it against each other – zap – they were done for. Except, it seems, in Guatemala where today they make up over 70 per cent of the population.

Most of the ones you see in Antigua come from the shores of Lake Atitlan, about forty kilometres away, which they believe is the navel of the Mayan world. Where their traditional Mayan handicrafts come from I don't know. Certainly the hats, shawls, blankets, blouses, dresses, even jazzy waistcoats, seem to have that distinctive, genuine, original Mayan design. Especially the waistcoats. As for the ceramics, they say that glazed, painted or just plain white ceramics were introduced to Guatemala by the Spaniards. All I can say is some of this stuff looks distinctly non-Spanish, let alone non-Indian. The wrought iron? The gold, silver and jade jewellery? You tell me. The wicker baskets, the hammocks, they look Mayan. So do all the horrible wooden masks. And what I want to know is, how come they all look like my mother-in-law? I think I should be told.

I'll tell you what also struck me about the Indians. No matter how much they sell or do not sell, they never smile. Not even when they are drunk. Now that might, of course, be a direct result of meeting my mother-in-law and using her face as a model for all those masks. If so, I know exactly how they feel. They don't have to explain a thing.

I once saw a group of Indians staggering out of a cantina in down-town Antigua, presumably as a result of selling two tablecloths and a straw hat in a single week. They were bombed out of their minds. Were they laughing and joking and slapping each other on the back? Were they hell! It was like watching a bunch of Dutch funeral directors on a night out, worried about who was going to pay the bill. Occasionally, I'm told, they do venture the slightest of smiles. Like when on November 1, All Saints Day, they flock to their nearest cemetery with huge, brightly coloured kites measuring up to ten feet in diameter to try and make contact with the spirits of their ancestors hovering overhead.

The descendants of the Conquistadors are, however, very much with us and to be found in the seedy, dusty old Club Guatemala down in Guatemala City, where they sit and sleep and dream all day long of the times that might have been. Not that they've got much to worry about. For the whole country, I was told, is owned and run by just 500 families of, no doubt, Conquistador descent. With a little help from the military, of course. Which is one reason why the whole place is in such a stinking mess. Own the country or not, the top 500 have flatly refused to pay taxes. Guatemala, as a result, collects less tax than anywhere else in South America. Talk about public squalor amid private affluence. You ain't smelt nothing till you've been to Guatemala City which, with a population of two million people, doesn't have any sewers.

'Who needs sewers?' one of the 500 told me. 'We have deep ravines below the city.'

Guatemala City, therefore, is one place in South America where you don't try too hard to look below the surface because you never know what you're going to find.

Take the construction industry. Why is it, if there is no

money in the country, life is one big construction boom? Is it because the 500 would rather put their money into concrete than into the banks? Or what about beer. If Guatemala believes in free trade, how come there's hardly any foreign beer sold in the country? And how come you hardly ever see Indians doing anything other than the most menial tasks?

'They don't know how to work,' any of the 500 will tell you. 'That's why we use Salvadoreans. They know how to work.'

So is it true that even today some towns are 'white' and some, like those way out near the Atlantic coast, are not? 'Not true,' another of the 500 told me. But did I know that the Conquistadors would never let an Indian ride any of their horses, and neither would he?

Which makes you wander what the world and Latin America would be like if the Conquistadors were still running the show. Given their undoubted organisational ability, their military and diplomatic skills, Latin America would, I reckon, either be stuck in some pre-Reformation time-warp or, if not way ahead of the rest of the world, certainly way ahead of where it is today. The whole thing would be a single market. There would be none of this Shall we form our own Common Market, or mini-Common Markets, or Shall we join the US-inspired North American Free Trade Area. It would be a major trading bloc in its own right, exporting all over the world. It would be in the forefront of any diplomatic initiative going. Say what you like about them, the Conquistadors were diplomats. They knew how to set up a diplomatic initiative and they knew how to shoot one down.

As it is, Latin America three hundred years after they left is still wallowing around trying to make up its mind what to do with itself. Of all the countries, Chile seems to be way out in front with, at last, a stable political base, a thriving economy and a no-holds barred commitment to economic reform. Mexico, at one time America's second largest trading partner after Japan, is still suffering from its tequila hangover, and likely to be for a few years more. Brazil has made a start, but they've still got to get their public finances, and especially inflation, under control. They've also got to take some of the excitement out of the political system, and I don't just mean the president whooping it up with a naked go-go dancer during Mardi Gras.

Argentina, on the other hand, seems to be coming round. At last. Growth is steady, inflation is way, way down. There are worries about the exchange rate which is linked directly to the dollar, but given the problems they've faced in the past that's hardly very serious. Uruguay and Paraguay, the other two members with Brazil and Argentina of South America's own common market, Mercosur, are each doing their own thing. Uruguay is coming round – for the good. Paraguay is slowly coming round – for the worse; still a million years behind the rest of the continent. They have barely any roads, or services, or hope of anything.

Colombia? Well, we'll have a smoke and wait and see what happens.

Peru is a big, big success. President Fujimori's only problem seemed to be his wife. Now he's solved that one there's nothing stopping him. Peru must be the success of the 1990s.

Bolivia is all systems go and privatising everything in sight, yet they still have problems, especially with the students who still hero-worship Che Guevara.

Venezuela has just disappeared off the map, thanks not just to a banking crisis but the way it was handled.

As for Central America, they all seem to have their problems, but the totally grand disaster has to be Guatemala. Far from inheriting the mandate of the Conquistadors, it is known today for its marimbas, a funny zylophone-type instrument; chicle, chewing gum to you and me; and its infamous death squads who, some people say, during nearly forty years of civil war have been responsible for the deaths of over 100,000 people and the disappearance of another 40,000. Even though the squads are slowly being wound down, the killings seem to be going on, either by the military doing their own thing or by illegal paramilitary groups carrying out freelance assassinations or running one drugs or crime racket after another. For in no other country in Latin America are the military and their friends as strong as they are in Guatemala. Not only are they a dominant political factor, they own their own bank, their own television station and even five per cent of the national airline, Aviateca. At least that's their published investments; goodness only knows the extent of their private investments.

It's not surprising, therefore, that violence is everywhere. Bombs go off all the time – outside the president's house, outside government offices, outside the university. Flights in and out of Guatemala City are often delayed because of explosions at the huge arms depot on the military base alongside the airport. I was once in a cab on the way to a meeting. At an intersection a driver refused to give way to us. The taxi driver, all greasy hair and silver teeth, screeched to a halt, grabbed a machete from under his seat and leapt at the car slashing its tyres and smashing its windows. I did what any self-respecting Englishman would do in the circumstances. I didn't move. I just carried on reading my three-week-old copy of the *Financial Times* trying not to notice. After he had finished he came back to the taxi, put the machete back under his seat and – olé – carried on as if nothing had happened.

Almost everybody you meet has been robbed, beaten up, assaulted, brutally attacked, or knows somebody who has been. Which, come to think of it, is a bit like being at home.

In one stockbroker's office I visited everybody had been robbed, beaten up, assaulted or brutally attacked. The senior partner had been attacked and robbed in his home. Two other partners had been beaten up and mugged in the street. I forget how many secretaries had been assaulted in car parks. Even the old lady who cleaned the office told me that only the previous evening she had been set-on by a gang of women who tried to grab her handbag. She was covered in bruises. But she still had her handbag. None of them blamed their fellow Guatemalans, however; they blamed the Americans. The senior partner, who looked like a Rambo gone to seed, told me he was trained by the US at La Escuela del Golpe in Panama. The coup school, he called it.

'Low intensity operations, counter-insurgency, psycholog-ical warfare, commando operations, interrogation, persuasion techniques, everything: the Americans taught us everything.' What's more, he said, they taught them by some kind of macabre programmed-learning system.

'I remember one question,' he said. 'We had been fighting all day. We had sustained heavy losses and captured enemy soldiers. The squad leader tells us we should take care of them. What should we do we obey the order and shoot the lot of them? Do nothing? Pretend we don't understand and ask for clarification? Do as he says but later report him to the military authorities?'

'So what did you say?' I asked.

He grinned. He didn't say anything. Just grinned.

People who have two Beretta 92 FS-9s to rub together live in constant fear. There are locks and bars and gates and security systems and security guards everywhere. Especially security guards who, everybody says, are either guerillas having a spot of R and R or sussing out the place for their next hit.

Go into an ordinary-looking office. It will take you ten minutes to get through security. Go to the Chamber of Commerce at the top of the Avenida la Reforma. It's like landing at the airport in Johannesburg where every month they collect thousands of knives and guns from arriving passengers. There are signs all over the place telling you to hand in your weapons before you even go through the security system. Visit an embassy. By the time you get past the guards and the gates and the cameras, the guy has left because you weren't in his office on time and didn't think you were coming.

I was once invited to an embassy reception. I did the usual British thing and turned up the statutory five minutes late so as not to appear too pushy or too desperate for a drink. By the time I got through the security checks half the guests had already left for fear of walking back to their cars in the dark and most of the booze had gone.

Get an invite back to someone's house, forget it. In other countries, it's a courtesy, maybe even a sign of friendship. In Guatemala City it's an obstacle course. First you have to find the place. I was invited home by a big banker. I had the address, I had one of those maps you scribble on the back of an envelope, I had a driver who told me he had been born, bred and survived in the City for forty-five years. Could we find the place? Could we hell! The whole street was one non-stop, twenty-foot-high brick wall. There were no doorways, no gates, no entrances. Not even any signs or bells to ring. Round and round and round we drove. There was no way of getting in. Back to the hotel we went in desperation. I telephoned, but only got an answering machine. The following day I went there again to see if in daylight I could spot the way in. I couldn't. It was a continuous blank wall. To this day I don't know how to get in.

Guatemala City is a dump; quite literally, one enormous garbage dump. It's full of fumes, broken-down buildings, pre-historic American school buses belching out more fumes. And garbage. Mountains of the stuff. It is, I reckon, the world capital of garbage dumps. Around the city, which has barely two million inhabitants, there are no less than 115 different shanty towns built on seven separate garbage dumps – no, garbage mountains – which are home to another 700,000 people. So famous are they that, would you believe it, one or two enterprising (is that the right word?) people run conducted tours of them. They have also been featured in photographic essays and painting competitions. An American photographer once mounted a series of exhibitions of photographs taken by the children living in the dumps.

I've seen some slums in my life – in Bombay, in Chicago, in Moss Side, Manchester. But these, I can tell you, are horrifying. Maybe not as horrifying as slums and shanty towns in other parts of Latin America where people, an aid official told me, actually eat human remains to stay alive. 'In parts of Brazil, in Recife in the north-east, they eat the bodies of people who have been murdered and just dumped in the garbage. Some of them even eat the remains thrown out by hospitals. It's terrifying,' he said.

Here they don't eat people. They eat, live (if that's the right word), and sleep on ravines; not ditches, but ravines full of filthy, stinking, rotting garbage. Flies are everywhere. Turkey-vultures or buzzards flap around tugging at everything they can reach. There are beetles eager for the chance to tunnel into your skin, lay their eggs like mad and leave you within a few days looking as if you had a double dose of AIDS.

Underneath the garbage, seeping into the soil, is . . . no. It's too much to even think of. But in spite of this, in some shanty towns people have got together and started their own schools. In Colonia Landiva, one of the big slums two miles from the city centre, I couldn't believe it, they have their own artists' studios, their own potteries and even their own theatre. But I have to say this is the exception.

I'm not normally put off by the stories of violence you hear wherever you go, but this time I didn't get around and see as much of the place as I would normally. But what I did notice, from the relative safety of a series of battered taxis with badly fitting windows, bonnets held down with string and grease stains all over the plastic seats, was that the whole place was really a vast mish-mash of self-contained areas or zones.

Zone 1 was, I suppose, downtown. It was full of shops, cheap hotels, crooks, pickpockets and more guns and rifles than there are hidden away in Northern Ireland. Zone 2 was home of the Hippodrome of the North, a vast relief map of the country which took over twelve years to make, as well as crooks, pickpockets and more guns and rifles than there are hidden away in Northern Ireland. Zone 3 was just full of crooks, pickpockets and more guns and rifles than there are hidden away in Northern Ireland. Zone 4 was the civic centre with the town hall, the National Theatre, crooks, pickpockets and more guns than there are hidden away in Northern Ireland. And so on.

But I did manage a quick glance at the tiny stock exchange and a quick dash inside the Church of San Francisco. Well you've got to have your priorities right. Especially in a place like Guatemala City. From the top of an office block I saw the army parade ground, which is surprisingly small for a country which has been ruled by the military for God knows how long. Hence the Second Biddlecombe Law of Military Planning in Latin America: the smaller the parade ground the more the military will want to exercise their skills on the streets. So the answer is simple. Build bigger parade grounds. Preferably on the tops of volcanoes. The First Biddlecombe Law of Military Planning in Latin America? Don't make jokes about military planning.

I saw the presidential palace, which many people call the 'enchanted castle', because they claim whoever is elected president and moves in is forever after paralysed by the spirits of Guatemala of the past and does nothing about it. The most dramatic example, they say, is the current president, Ramino de Leon Carpio. Before he became president he was the government's human rights ombudsman, with an international reputation for fearless and independent speaking, especially against the military. But since he's been president what has he done? Nothing. Not a word has he said against the military, not a hint or a suggestion. Not a single human rights case has been pushed, not even the murder of his own first cousin and close friend which happened shortly after he took over. Not the slightest power let alone rubber stamp has been grabbed back from the military. It's almost as if either the real Ramino de Leon Carpio has been killed by the military and a dummy put in his place, or he has just caved in after having 111 cigarette butts stubbed out on his back and being lowered into a pit full of human bodies.

I also got to know the area close to the airport, Zona Viva, which is nothing less than a rich man's ghetto: truly luxurious hotels, fantastic modern office blocks and a host of sparkling new shopping centres choc-a-bloc with all the fashionable upmarket names. Zipping around on jazzy motorbikes, chatting away into their mobile telephones were all your Guatemalan yuppies.

239

Call me suspicious, but there can only be one reason why Zona Viva is so close to the airport, apart from it being a quick get-away point in case of emergency. One day they will have to build a new airport further out of town, which will mean two things. The Zona Viva will expand further out to the new airport. Somebody will make a killing selling the land for the new airport to the government. Now tell me, if you dare, who is already buying up the land on which the Zona Viva will expand, as well as the land for the new airport? Wrong. Not the military but some whiz-kid derivatives junkie I came across behind locked doors on the third floor of a pretty nondescript office block slap bang in the middle of the Zona Viva.

You don't know what a derivative is? OK, I'll tell you. It's $\Delta t + et - a \sqrt{rt}\,^2 + 3$. And what is the point of it? O. E $(\Delta t + et) - et\,!+1$.

Is it risky?

$$\frac{H+E+L+P}{BANK+\ RUPTCY} \times SUICIDE$$

You got it? No? Well, how about, derivatives are products you don't buy with money you don't have in order to make real-life losses. Or if you're unlucky, profits. Copper, cotton, hogs, treasury bonds, a heap of beams, blackboards. You can play the derivatives game with anything you choose. In Guangdong Commodities Exchange I've even come across a soy-meal derivatives market. The day I was there, there were 100,000 contracts out on over one million tons of the stuff. How much was actually on the market? Just over 5,000 tons.

So how do you play? Simple. First you get yourself a broker. In the derivatives game a broker is someone who leaves you broker than the day you were first told he was an investment genius who would make you a multi-billionaire. Second, you sign across to him every single thing you possess or 50 per cent possess in the world. Third, you learn the jargon, like bullish and bearish. Bullish is when a broker says to you, I feel very confident today, give me your money and I'll lose it all in one go. Bearish is when a broker says to you, I'm terribly sorry but it took me two days to lose all your money. And a crash is what you create when you throw yourself off the roof into a street full of traffic.

So what does the broker do with your money? He goes out, has fun, drinks champagne, flies to Vegas, Rio and Monte Carlo and develops his own 'top down' or 'bottom up' investment strategy. In other words, how much money is required to persuade young ladies of a particular persuasion to remove either their top clothes or their bottom clothes first. Oh yes, and in between, when he gets a chance, he plays the market. Say for example there's a contract going for selling sand to the Arabs: 25,000 pounds of the stuff at US$1.25 a pound. That's US$31,250. The margin is, say, US$1,250, US$1,500 or even US$1,750. What the broker does on your behalf is, as the Bank of England once put it graphically, to 'stuff the brokers'. In other words to put up the margin, have another drink and wait for the money to roll. At least, that's what he tells you. But as far as I'm concerned, all it takes to play the derivatives game is timing, self-confidence, an instinctive sense of the odds, a firm grasp of the fundamentals, a US$1 billion ego, a fast pair of running shoes and a timetable of flights out of the country to the nearest place without extradition treaties. Although I knew one derivatives addict who made over US$250,000 in two weeks buying US Treasury futures every time the price went up by even a fraction of a fraction of a dollar. Which is about the same as you would make in, say, a Lloyds syndicate specialising in nuclear power stations. But without the emotional fall-out.

'It's like playing Russian roulette,' he told me afterwards, 'with the chamber full of bullets. Every time the music stops you pull the trigger.'

So now you understand? No? Well, take these three buttons. Oh forget it. Just take my word for it. It's a game for big boys like Japanese oil companies, German engineering groups, British merchant bankers, who can afford to lose money: US$1.5 billion here; US$1 billion there; another US$1 billion over there in Singapore. It's also getting more and more complicated. Some contracts are so complicated nowadays they can't even be described in words. They can only be described by computer. Or rather computers. One derivatives contract put together by Merrill Lynch, the mega US brokers, took thirty-two computers a whole week to explain.

So to find a derivatives trader in the Zona Viva was, I admit, a shock. I always thought derivatives traders were quants, or quantitive analysts, astrophysicists, rocket scientists, mathematical geniuses, PhDs in plasma physics, chess grandmasters or just smart street traders and wheeler-dealers who are a dab hand at poker on a Friday night. I also imagined them in banks, on trading floors, glued to their computer screens, running one mathematical model after another, spinning one mathematical formula after another, producing a never-ending stream of regressions and charts, and turning anything that moves into a computer program and sending out for pizzas round the corner. Not in Guatemala City, just down the road from some of the biggest, most horrifying slums in the world. But there he was, complete with red braces and white socks, juggling ten-year swaps against floating ones, hedging them with a string of futures and going across the road to get his own burger.

He started, he told me, by buying three-month call options on takeover targets for about 10 per cent of the share price. He then sat back and waited for the bid to be announced and pocketed the difference. After that he graduated to US dollars, Swiss francs, Norwegian krona and even things like highly volatile mortgage-based derivatives which even some Wall Street high-flyers or rocket scientists don't understand. He played them all, he told me, and more. To him, buying and selling the world's most complicated financial instruments was as easy as crossing a cheque. Plenty of people, he admitted, got burnt, but he was doing very well thank you. Hence his airport plan. As I left, he told me he was planning to turn his attention to what he called over-the-counter equity derivatives.

'Why?' I asked. 'Isn't life complicated enough?'

'No way,' he said. 'I can mirror-trade.'

'What on earth's mirror-trading?'

'Simple.' He grinned. 'I can get my grips on a company's equity stock without buying any.'

'So how do you do that?'

'By buying an aggregate derivative and selling its components off one by one apart from the company I want to hit.'

'But, excuse me,' I said, trying not to appear too stupid. 'Why is that important?'

'Because that way using inside information I can build up a big stake in a company without anyone being able to detect me.' Another big grin. 'Beautiful. Yes. You agree?'

'But why can't they trace you?'

He twanged his red braces. 'How can they trace me? First, the market is unregulated. Second, it's huge: US$12,000 billion. Third, how can they possibly monitor every transaction? It's impossible. You want to join me?' He twanged his braces again. 'How much do you want to put in?'

But in spite of my experiences of Guatemala (which incidentally comes from *guhatezmalha*, an old Indian word for – you're not going to believe this – 'the mountain of vomiting waters' a reference, I guess, to the fact that the country straddles thirty-two volcanoes), I know plenty of people who rave about the place. And none of them are either Guatemalan military or Guatemalan derivative traders. Some even claim it is the most beautiful country in the world and rave about its lakes and volcanoes and tropical forests, which cover at least two-thirds of the place. The ruins at Tikal, the largest city ever built by the Mayans are, I'm told, spectacular, although why Maximon, a cross between one of the Mayan idols and a Christian saint, wears several coats and lots of hats all at the same time, nobody has ever been able to explain to me. Pray to him and he is supposed to bring you good luck, love and lots of money, although how he can do anything with all those clothes on beats me.

And me? Yes, I agree. Guatemala is the most beautiful

country in the world. Now, if you'll put that gun down and untie my hands, I want to call my broker. I've heard someone's opened a book on the next volcano to hit Antigua.

San José

If you're a raw food vegan with a pasty indoor complexion, rope sandals, a grass polo-neck sweater and an insatiable desire for rainforest crisps ... If you live in a house built of soyabean flour and recycled newspapers and believe all babies should be born with a tag saying 'Made from 100 per cent recycled skin and bones' ... If you are hooked on Sierra Crunch muesli, organic red leaf lettuce and yak's milk yoghurt, then Costa Rica is paradise on earth.

Everything is eco-this or enviro-that or conserve-the other, providing it doesn't blow a hole in the ozone layer. And did you know – cue for furrowed brow and jabbing finger – it takes two-thirds of a pint of aviation fuel to get a Florida orange onto the shelves of a European supermarket? In fact, it's the kind of place where if you don't go around talking to the trees and communing with nature they reckon you're an eco-nutter. The locals themselves are known as Ticos because ask them anything and they immediately say, 'Momentico', which loosely translated means 'So what's the hurry? Let me go and kiss a few more trees then we'll have cup of llama's milk and talk about it.'

If, however, like me, you believe that not every business-man is hell-bent on polluting this planet to kingdom come, that once-damaged forests are being restored, that not every animal is on the brink of extinction and that it's not necessary to share a bath with your next door neighbour's daughter more than once a week to save water then, as I live and try to breathe without taking in too many noxious fumes, Costa Rica is an environmentalist hell on earth. In fact when I go there I develop acute symptoms of anoraksia nervosa. Whenever I see an anorak I get so nervous I have to stop what I'm doing and go and hug the nearest bottle of champagne.

But the irony is that Costa Rica, which was discovered in a haze of cigarette smoke by Christopher Columbus in September 1502, when he was greeted in the nick-o-time by a pack of old fags puffing in his face, is now on probably the biggest macrobiotic, bio-degradable eco-trip in the world. Having downed a quick slug of carrot juice, swallowed a mouthful of corn pudding and stuffed itself to the gills with vegetable peas, it has decided to turn itself into the world's first pilot project for 'sustainable development'. Whatever that is.

A lawyer I met downing a quick Scotch in a filthy bar off Culture Square in downtown San José told me that he personally knew twenty-four academic definitions of sustainable development, and could easily come up with another 257 without too much trouble, but he couldn't face the responsibility of all those trees being cut down just to prove a point. Anyway, the Costa Rica government has decided: sustainable development it is.

Trees will be planted all over the country and, in a bold initiative to stop children and young people hanging around unsustainable street corners doing nothing, they will all be planted by children and young people. Rubbish will have to be sorted into biodegradable, recyclable and Jeffrey Archer by householders before it is collected by sustainable dustmen or, rather, environment protection agents.

Because they point-blank refuse to build coal-fired power stations, let alone mine any of the coal they have in the country because it will damage the environment, electricity will have to be used far more efficiently than ever before. Bulbs will have to be put in all the sockets to stop it from leaking out. Anyone who pollutes will have to pay the price. Whether he is a businessman, an industrialist or a farmer, he will not only have to pay for any environmental damage he has created, he will also have to have a bath with his neighbour's daughter at least twice a week.

They have even passed a law guaranteeing every citizen the right to a healthy and ecologically balanced environment. How many trees will have to be cut down to produce how much paper to make it stand up in the courts is another matter.

Wherever you go, there are Citizens' Commissions for Environmental Defence. Every hotel seems to be hosting courses on developing natural policies for the protection of the ozone layer or round tables on Advertising and the Environmental Challenge, Accountancy and the Environmental Challenge, or even Environmentalists and the Environmental Challenge.

Visit any company, and everybody is at some in-house training session. I went to a firm just outside San José where they were teaching their refrigerator repairmen how to prevent the escape of dangerous gases into the environment. Another company was running courses to help their staff tell the difference between endangered and non-endangered rainforest plants. It was an electronics company. I was about to ask the managing director what on earth printed circuit boards had to do with rainforest plants when I spotted the rope sandals. I didn't bother. I have the rest of my life to live.

Another firm I went to was deep into geo-lifestyles. All their furniture, they told me, was 'environmentally certified' by the Smart Wood Programme of the Rainforest Alliance and had come from 'a small-scale, community-run project in Papua New Guinea'. One of the directors told me that whenever he visited Europe or the States he made a point of going around sniffing park benches.

'Sniffing park benches,' I said guardedly.

'It's the only way to discover if they're made from African hardwood,' he said proudly.

'And if they're made from African hardwood . . .' I repeated slowly.

'Then I notify the Rainforest Action Group. They write to the town council and complain. It's the only way we can make people aware of the damage they are doing to the environment.'

And use up more trees, I thought, although of course I didn't mention it.

For lunch we tucked into a biotechnology salad consisting of genetically engineered tomatoes and strange, crooked-looking squashes, which had even less taste than the usual salad, and talked about the relative merits of different corn-based golf tees and whether one day steering wheels would be made of soyabean oil.

I took copious notes with a biodegradable pen they gave me, on recycled paper which came out too white so they had to add grey colouring to it. Before I left I had to promise in future to use a toothpaste made with sorbitol and paste the empty tubes on the bathroom wall in order to cut down the worldwide non-recyclable toothpaste-tube mountain which every year increases by over one billion tubes.

At another company I met a crack team of scientists working in conditions of the utmost secrecy to develop an environmentally friendly trap to capture an environmentally friendly creature which they told me had a huge mouth, an enormous stomach, disgusting eating habits, looked revolting and was sex-mad. A million possibilities immediately sprang to my mind. But it turned out to be the Mediterranean fruit fly, which was starting to destroy their environmentally friendly crops. Trouble was the whole project had been delayed. They were waiting for equipment to be delivered by truck all the way from Florida. I was about to make the obvious comment when I suddenly realised I was surrounded by rope sandals and muesli sandwiches again, so I didn't bother.

At the Ministry of Finance I was told they were working on an ingenious plan to sell off huge chunks of rainforest to companies who are happily polluting other parts of the world, on the basis that one hectare of rainforest will offset the effects of 200,000 tons of carbon dioxide.

'It is quid pro quo,' an official in the Ministry of Natural

Resources told me. 'A carbon exchange. They produce carbon dioxide. They buy trees which absorb carbon dioxide. It is right, yes?'

The last time I was there doing my rounds, they already had one multinational practically signed up. Unfortunately the company was already heavily in debt and they were wondering whether the banks and shareholders would go along with them spending even more money on trees in Costa Rica instead of leaning on them to cut costs and get the company back into shape, however much it might contribute to saving the world. My opinion in a nutshell: no way, San José.

The crazy thing is that all this emphasis on the environment, the ecology, the quality of life, is relatively new. At one time Costa Rica (which is Spanish for the Rich Coast; Puerto Rica is Spanish for the Rich Port) pretty well led the world in technology. San José was the third city in the world after London and Paris to have electricity. But you would never believe it. It's as if as soon as they flicked on the switch they realised it was not for them and decided there and then to turn their backs on the modern world and all its works and pomp, and concentrate on everything pure and green and environmentally friendly. As a result even though in many respects it *looks* like plenty of other towns in Latin America, with its US-style shopping malls and department stores, it isn't.

It's peaceful; so peaceful it looks as though it's had a conservation order slapped on it. It doesn't have an army. The army was disbanded in 1948 and the barracks turned into a fine arts museum. It is politically neutral, so neutral that one of their presidents was awarded the Nobel Peace Prize in 1986. But, far more important, from their point of view it's the home of 179 types of orchid, some of which, like the sobralia, can grow to over four feet high.

'An urban island in a verdant agrarian sea,' one Costa Rican writer drooled over it. Others call it the Singapore of Latin America, with perhaps more emphasis on the carrot than the stick, if you see what I mean. Stories about the opening of yet another permanent organic-produce market rate more attention and more publicity in the local biodegradable press than a story about how a disabled pilot used his crutch to prevent his plane from crashing. He leant out of the window and thumped the landing gear with it. This somehow released it, and the plane landed safely. But nobody was interested.

Houses are not sold because they are lux des res with dbl bed, lgne, flf kit and large din area. Own pkg. But because they are 'stress and pollution free'. They have their own spring water, or failing that their own community water. So conscious are they of the environment that nobody says their house has been rebuilt or repaired; they boast it has been remodelled.

Golf clubs don't promote the quality of the greens or the size of the bunkers, or even drop discreet references to the nineteenth hole. They emphasise that they have 'clean air' and 'good water' and are more environmentally friendly than the one down the road.

As far as visitors are concerned, tours are not just tours, they're 'ecological tours', 'ecological expeditions', 'ecological experiences', or in some cases 'the greatest ecological adventure known to man' – providing, of course, he's wearing rope sandals, a grass polo-neck sweater, and lives in a house built of soyabean flour and recycled newspapers.

Photographers are not bad-tempered guys obsessed with their apertures who go around all day snapping at people. They're 'specialists in ecological photography', 'dedicated environmental observers and recorders' and even 'professionals' when it comes to birds.

You can't even go for a stroll in the woods any more. All the walks are nature trails, or tidal pool walks, or jungle walks. And all along the nature trails and tidal pool walks and jungle walks are animal shelters and bird boxes and huge long lists of the birds and animals found in the woods or the pools of that particular patch of jungle.

One morning, before throwing myself into the usual string of meetings, I was so sick to death of the muzak they were playing in the hotel – 'A Month in the Brazilian Rainforest: A collection of forest sounds' – I thought I'd try a quick walk in the woods near the hotel. Now my idea of a good time is not exactly traipsing through some hot, sticky rainforest trying to catch a glimpse of a bird who is no longer there, or the bottom of a howler monkey which is, so that shows you how desperate I was. However, it was not to be. By the time I'd finished reading the rambling nonsense at the start of the woods telling me about the animals I was going to see – an orphaned sloth, a brown pelican, a rather cheeky little boa constrictor, a couple of poison dart frogs, a rhinoceros beetle, a greenbacked heron and an egg-eating racoon – there was no time for a walk. I had to go straight back to the hotel.

Worst of all, if you happen to meet someone, whether it's in the woods, racing back to the hotel, or even drinking a low alcohol beer (what else?) in a bar, all they want to talk about is the environment. In one week, I promise you, all I spoke about was the dangers of fishing-net floats, rubber slippers, hospital waste, shampoos, cups, why tourists should not be allowed to carry outboard-motor oil in plastic bottles, and, of course, why fizzy drinks cans should be barred because hermit crabs crawl inside them and can't get out. And it's all so deadly serious. One weak attempt at a joke about crabs, hermit or otherwise, and they're off down the local Environmental and Natural Resources Law Centre for free legal advice on how they can either hand you over to the eco-police or sue you for committing some eco-crime.

You think I'm kidding? I tell you, in Costa Rica they're terrified of burying traffic policemen when they die because they are scared that the lead in their lungs will leak into the soil. It's like being inside some great sterilised, tree-covered Wonderland run by the Body Shop, completely insulated from the Age of Sludge, Sewage and Toxic Waste, waiting for Snow White's grandmother to turn up.

As for San José, it's like an environmental Disney World run by David Attenborough. I had thought it would be your typical Latin American town: hot, dusty, nothing but wooden shacks, maybe a rambling old hotel. A couple of guys with sombreros and blankets thrown over their shoulders. Long, scruffy, filthy bars. A couple of hot-shot preachers. Gunfire in the distance. Tanks rumbling up and down the street at night. Soldiers hanging around street corners. Long queues of dull, silent people waiting for trucks and buses and God knows what else. No way. It's clean, neat, beautifully kept. In a remodelled sort of way.

As for places to visit, there is the entomological museum downstairs in the basement of the musical arts department of the University of Costa Rica, which has over a million different insects on display including thousands of butterflies. There is also the La Salle Natural Sciences Museum on the south-west side of Sabano Park with a couple of million more specimens from all over the world. Failing that, there is the Teatro Nacional, which is gilt, marble and – shame on them – genuine Costa Rican hardwood, probably the last wood they ever cut down. Built in 1897, it looks like a mini Paris Opera House. On the ceiling, bless their green little hearts, is an enormous painting to honour the two mainstays of both their environment and their economy: coffee and bananas. Except that the coffee is shown growing at sea level, which as far as I'm aware is pretty impossible, and the bananas are growing upside down, which I would have thought equally impossible. The artist, I can only assume, was green in more than one sense of the word.

The Gran Hotel Costa Rica, next door, is great fun providing you don't mind drowning in a sea of anoraks. Whenever I go there the place is packed with plastic rucksacks and plastic hats and a million plastic eco-feminists demanding veggie burgers and glasses of water and then complaining because they can't pay for them with their credit cards. Which, of course, are made not out of plastic but out of birch and biodegradable glue. It also serves, I'm told, the best environmentally friendly biodegradable black bean soup in the world. If you're into environmentally friendly biodegradable black bean soup, which I'm afraid I'm not. First, because it's black bean soup. Second, I just can't get over the boiled egg they stick in the middle of it. It looks like a bald head floating in a thick, black, fetid, Amazonian swamp.

On one visit I remember I was stuck next to some raving, vegetarian, fruitarian, animal rights feminists who, all the time I was chasing this bald head around my plate, kept going on about cruelty to animals, even though you can bet your life they were dosed up to the eyeballs on hormone replacement tablets made with urine from mares kept in impossible conditions. Such is the milk of human blindness. As I came out, a rather camp tourist guide who looked as though he had lost his flock was marching up and down, screaming at the top of his voice, 'Nature calls.'

For real excitement, therefore, I normally stay in my hotel studying the environmentally friendly notices stuck up all over the place: Don't sit here: Don't smoke there: This is a non-smoking rest room: Please turn the lights off when you leave.

Don't throw food in the waste bins. It makes it difficult for the mice to get at it. Don't use hot water in the shower. It makes the cockroaches hot and sweaty. Don't switch on the air-conditioning. A couple of rare fruit bats have been hibernating in there since Christmas.

And towels. How many signs did I see telling me not to use their damned towels? In the rest room, non-smoking, just off the reception area: 'Help us to be more environmentally friendly. Use please only one of the towels provided.' In the rest room, smoking, in the bar, where nobody touches alcohol: 'Use, please, the air drier provided. This avoids us providing towels and using chemicals to wash them.' And, of course, upstairs in my room: 'Help Us Save the Planet.' Who, me? 'Would you like to be part of our scheme to decrease waste into our environment? We cordially invite you to participate in a few preservation measurements directly from your room. These measurements even in a small proportion contribute to an extraordinary cause and a noble task.'

Oh yes, please. I'm jumping up and down with joy. 'You probably know that tons of polluted water is being dispersed of into our lakes and rivers daily.' Yeah. So is your English grammar. 'To help us decrease waste from the hotel ...' You mean you're going to start serving some decent food? '... we are asking you if it would be possible for you to use your towels two days?' Sure, and the bed linen the whole week. 'If you would like to, please leave the towels hanging. But if you leave them on the floor, we will change them during the day.' For what? Something else? A decent meal? An alcoholic drink?

In one hotel outside San José we were even given instructions about the bed linen. In four languages.

Bed sheets: A pillow placed on the end of the bed, please change.

Bed sheets: A pillow placed neatly on top of the bed, please do not change.

Towels: To re-use, please leave your towels hanging on the rack or on the hooks.

Towels: For fresh towels, place your used towels on the floor and we will bring fresh ones.

That's not all. They even refused to provide soap or shampoo sachets. Which, silly old non-green me, I always thought was pretty essential for any hotel. Especially if they expect everyone to sit on top of each other for breakfast, lunch and dinner, the way they cram people into their coffee shops and restaurants nowadays. Instead they jammed four huge plastic dispensers the size of dustbins over the bath containing what they described as 'hair and skin care products made of only the finest natural ingredients'. Trouble was the dispensers were so big and sticking so far out over the bath it was impossible to get in the damn thing. So where the hygienic bit comes from God only knows.

On another trip, in another hotel, the room was full of goody-goody signs and notices which must have cost half a rainforest to produce.

We have eliminated two million plastic containers from the waste stream.

We cut out polystyrene foam, plastic tableware, phosphates and aerosols.

We re-use all our laundry water.

If that's the case I'm definitely hanging on to my towels until the moment I leave.

In yet another hotel I was greeted by a sign in the bathroom the size of a billboard: 'Help conserve water. Please turn off faucets tightly. Thank you for pitching in.' By the time I'd toured San José in a cab to get a dictionary to find out what the hell a faucet was, I'm sure I'd used up far more of the earth's natural resources and done far more damage to the environment than if I had ignored the damn thing and had a drink instead.

In desperation, I tried still another hotel. This time the room was festooned with signs about how many trees they had saved by using only 100 per cent dioxin-free recycled paper; how many gallons of water they had saved by not having to wash so many towels; how many tanker-loads of fuel oil they had saved, how many plastic plates they had saved, how many tons of garbage they had saved, how many . . .

I mean, excuse me. I'm sorry for breathing and pumping all that carbon dioxide into your oh-so-pure environment. But aren't you supposed to be some kind of hotel? And aren't hotels supposed to cater to the every need and comfort of the world-weary traveller? If I wanted to be hectored and lambasted I'd have stayed at home, wouldn't I?

In any case, just look at all the damage these dirty great hotels do to the environment, not to mention our pocket, just by being there. It's bad enough not being able to turn the air-conditioning on because of those damned fruit bats. Now they're begging me to last all week on one grubby hand towel and turn their faucets off tightly. They're crazy. Give me the Savoy in London. There they positively encourage you to chop down trees. In every room there are dozens of brochures – more trees hit the dust – trying to sell you one of their traditional handmade wooden beds, crafted, they say, 'to the individual requirements of its owner' and 'fitted by hand'. Which does make the mind boggle just a little bit.

But Costa Rica being Costa Rica, they get to you. By the end of the day I'm feeling so guilty about all the pollution I've caused, all the damage I've done to their environment, the untold harm my mere presence has done to the integrity of their cultural heritage, that I'm not just hanging up my towels to save the planet I'm going round turning off every light in the hotel; gathering up all the 'How to use the telephone' leaflets so that I can take them home and recycle them. I'm even collecting up my bath water, drop by drop, in those little polythene bags they put around the chipped glasses in your room with their dirty fingers to tell you they've been disinfected, and carrying them along the corridor, into the lift – they're still playing A Month in the Brazilian Rainforest – across reception and out of the back door to this lovely little tree which looks as though it desperately needs a friend to give it a drink. By the end of my stay, what with all the water it's been getting and the heat, it's the size of one of those American redwoods. The roots have undermined the foundations of the hotel, split the reception area in half and somewhat livened up the air-conditioned indoor garden. One of the branches has broken through a window and people who had flocked to the restaurant on the top floor which was famous for its vegetarian cuisine are now complaining about the vegetation everywhere. The last I heard the hotel had to close down. Three hundred people lost their jobs. But the tree was safe, so my conscience is clear.

The whole country is crawling with not just ordinary greens, but your real egocentric greens with their own towels made of still growing grass, their own supply of mineral water to wash in, not to mention their own bed, bathroom, chemical toilet and wooden staircase full of sachets of nettle shampoo.

I'm telling you, you can hardly throw a can of Coke out of the window of the car without hitting some Green in blameless trousers, sinless sandals and unreconstructed woolly hat deep into the Berkeley tourist guides. Why Berkeley tourist guides? Because they are printed on recycled paper with soya-based inks and for every tree it takes to produce them, they plant a new one. You didn't know that? I mean, aren't you interested in saving our planet?

Walking around the Plaza de la Cultura I once got a lecture on, of all things, pigeons, from some eco-weirdo who kept telling me we were all 'earthlings'. 'That one over there, that's the common rock dove or *columba livia* or, as it is known here, *paloma domestica*.' She pointed out some crippled, one-legged pigeon. 'It was found originally in North Africa. The Egyptians, do you know, used to keep them 4,000 years ago? They ate them before they started eating chicken. Isn't that interesting? And over there . . .'

Another time I left the offices of some swish, US-style advertising agency, turned the corner and started looking for a cab when I was set on – why me? – by this girl who looked as though she would have been happier giving birth to Sumatran orang-utans than babies. What did she go on about? Muesli. Not just your ordinary muesli, but genuine Costa Rica muesli.

'Too much sugar, don't you think?'

'Excuse me, I wonder if—'

'Not enough shredded coconut.'

'I'm looking for a cab, I'm afraid.'

'Really. Or enough currants. I like . . .'

It started to rain stair rods. Within seconds I was soaked. But she wouldn't give up. 'You should make your own.'

'Really. I didn't know you . . . I mean. Why the hell aren't there any . . .?' I got to the end of the street. I was soaked. Still she kept on at me.

'Well it's easy. You get six cups of rolled oats, a cup of bran flakes, some sunflower seeds, a cup of honey . . .'

Suddenly I had a profound environmental insight. In that moment, I realised why animals eat their young. Then, just as suddenly, it stopped raining, a cab came around the corner, I jumped in. Peace and quiet at last. But not for long.

Back at the hotel, all I could get was a non-calorie, non-cholesterol, non-fat, non-nutritional dollop of nothing called a nature snack, which looked like two lumps of shredded wheat buried in bird droppings, and a coffee which tasted more like eucalyptus fruit cup with a dash of camphor to liven it up.

I sat down in the furthermost corner of the coffee shop, and had no sooner unpacked my papers than in came this guy who looked more like a vegetable than a vegetarian, with forward crawling hair. He headed straight towards me.

'Our cities are like cancer cells,' he said sitting down opposite me, 'growing out of control, destroying everything that comes in their way. They must be stopped. They must become like garden communities. Deserts must be reclaimed. The sun, the wind, the tides must be harnessed to man's will. Factories must no longer be allowed to pollute the air, the seas, the rivers.' He kept picking dietary fibres out of his teeth and telling me he was an ecological conservationist. I smiled weakly.

'Pollution is everywhere,' he went on. 'In the air, on the land, in the water. All forms of life – animals, plants, even human beings – are in danger. Every hour of every day over 3,000 acres of land are laid bare, ruined by modern technology, industry, greed, ignorance. Man must once again follow his natural physiological tendencies. He must become a vegan-vegetarian again. He must stop killing . . .'

In desperation to get away from him I did the only thing I thought I could do in the circumstances. I booked myself a late-night tour of all the vegetarian and health food restaurants in San José. Dedicated vegetarians and health food nuts, I reasoned, would know all the restaurants already. The only people on the tour would be drop-outs desperate to get away. I was wrong. The worst was a woman who looked like a hangover from the '60s; the 1860s. She had these strange clothes on which looked as though they had been washed in a mountain stream and hung out on the bushes to dry. Over her shoulders she wore a cape like a witch's. All she needed was a cat to complete the picture. She kept going on about something called the Via Holistica. Was I living in the moment? Was I aware of myself, of my thoughts, of my feelings? Was I looking for a change in perception? An increase in awareness? Did I want what was normal and routine to become special and unique? Then she went on about 'the harmonious interaction of all parts of you: your mind, your spirit and,' she paused, 'your body.'

For the first time in my life I gulped down my muesli fricassée, threw money all over the table and fled.

Now don't get me wrong. No way will you find me rooting for vegetarians, but on the other hand I'm not against doing my bit to save the world. In fact, I always write, well, scribble, on the back of sheets of scrap paper. If everybody did the same, only half the number of trees would have to be chopped down every year. Right? What I can't stand is not only the environmentalists' heavy-handed, battering-ram, eco-police, I'm-the-only-person-in-the-world-who-cares approach, but the way they make you feel as though it's your fault you weren't born a tree, and personally to blame for all the environmental and ecological damage that has been caused since the world began. If, for the sake of peace and quiet, you happen to say you agree, they still won't let up. Token agreement is not good enough, they say. They want 100 per cent, red-raw vegetarian agreement.

I reckon Costa Rica is the only country in the world where I couldn't see the trees for the would. I would have gone to Puerto Limon to see the banana trees and ride the 'banana train' all the way to Valle de la Estrella, through the heart of their banana country, but it would have meant pumping all those fumes into the environment.

I would have gone on a humid, tropical, sticky jungle trip to see the toucans, parrots, macaws, kingfishers, yellow-billed cotingas, not to mention a clutch of humming birds, a bunch of two-toed sloths, a gang of white-faced capuchin monkeys and flock after flock of those enormous electric blue morphos butterflies with their 15-centimetre wingspan, but it would have meant invading their natural environment. In any case, I was worried about jungle trips in Costa Rica. Far from being fun, like going on safari, they are heavy stuff. I was told you don't run a book on which animals you spot, or mark each other ten out of ten for spotting the rare ones, because that devalues their individual integrity and reduces them to a mere mathematical formula. Excuse me for breathing – or rather emitting used oxygen into the environment.

I would have gone to one of their millions of volcanoes but there were too many rules and regulations. Wear a mask to protect you from the smoke and acidic gases; wear a long-sleeved shirt to protect you from the sun; if you get a headache or feel sick, tell the attendants; bring plenty of water; don't drink water from the volcano. It didn't seem worth the effort.

I would have gone to a natural park, a biological station, a sugar plantation, a natural freshwater, or even the big turtle conservation centre out on the southern Caribbean coast near the Gandsca-Manzanilla Natural Wildlife Refuge and seen the green turtles, hawksbill turtles, loggerhead turtles and the most popular of all, the leatherback. But it would have meant using up about as many eco units as it takes to fly Concorde round the world twenty-seven times.

And the other thing; wherever you go, whoever you meet, all they want to talk is environment talk. In some countries I've been to, they have verbal diarrhoea. In Costa Rica, they have herbal diarrhoeas. You go into a cafetalera, where they make coffee. Some guy with a head-shave and a nipple-pierce deep into his organic frisée lettuce sandwich starts on about ivory nut carvings and the sympathy trees have for the world. You see some guy painting an ox cart. He goes on about natural pigments, blending nature with nature, the integrity of the planet. Damn it, it's only an ox cart. I've got carts like that at home. I don't go on about them, do I?

You see some plants. Everyone tells you about something called the garbage-can tree which, to the delight of all envir-onmentalists, somehow dissolves not only its old leaves but anything else that comes in touch with it. Which is the kind of tree I could do with back home. Maybe a full jungle of them.

You go into a restaurant and order the most expensive dish on the menu, which turns out to be casalo: beef fritters, plantain and rice. In a country more concerned with bathwater than wine lists, I somehow feel it's safer to have a bottle of mineral water than anything else. An American couple at the next table lean across and introduce themselves. They look like the kind of people who don't just invite you to a cottage-cheese dip and watermelon party but who also send you a little pink card saying, 'There are lots of unfortunate people in this world. Please bring with you some unwanted clothing so we can send it to the Kurds in Iraq.' They tell me they're from New York. They've taken part in the big Earth Day celebrations every year for the last twenty-five years, when New Yorkers dress up as garbage cans, smokestacks, endangered tropical birds and polystyrene tombstones listing the species close to extinction.

'Yes, sir, New York has the best tapwater in the whole of the US of A,' the old man tells me.

I'm amazed. 'I knew nothing good ever came out of New York,' I say. 'I always assumed nothing good went in there either.'

'Straight from the Catskill mountains,' the wife ploughs on. 'Straight from the reservoirs. Couldn't be purer. Not even filtered. Doesn't have to be . . .'

'Surely it has to be filtered? One has only to think of . . .'

'No, sir, not filtered. Better than champagne,' they say together.

I left them discussing which part of their beloved Catskill mountains they wanted to be buried in and whether it should be in cloth bags or biodegradable cardboard coffins.

That evening I don't know why but I got bounced out of the Teatro Nacional, even though I had my recycled ticket. So I gatecrashed a reception at the Corobici Hotel. Who should I spot across the crowded room? A guy I used to work with a million years ago in Stoke-on-Trent. What was he doing there? He had been made redundant, been recycled and turned into a green consultant. He was there advising the government on

261

some big plastics recycling scheme. I spent my last evening drinking low-alcohol beer and reminiscing about, of all places, Stoke-on-Trent. Which was the most exciting part of my trip. Apart from the morning when I came down for breakfast and the hotel had run out of muesli.

Montevideo

I tell you it was Lord Lucan. I saw him. In Montevideo. He was wandering around the casino in the Hotel Carrasco, a broken-down marble palace overlooking the dirty brown waters of the River Plate. The kind of place where they used to sign peace treaties. He was still upright, still had that military bearing, that languid, upper-class, hangdog look. The moustache was still there. The hairline had receded just a little. He was bronzed. Like a freelance arms dealer who'd been handling too many dodgy plutonium rods which had fallen off the backs of lorries coming out of the Sverdlovsk 44 Research Centre in the Urals.

Other people say they've seen him working as a waiter in San Francisco, drying out at an alcoholics' centre in Brisbane, lounging in a bar in Madagascar, at the races in Hong Kong, in the Cresta Riley's Hotel in Gaborone, in the changing rooms of a gym in the University of British Columbia in Vancouver, in a warehouse in Ontario, or even sipping a pink gin in Sunnyside Park, the quaint old English country house hotel in Johannesburg where – insider dealers, derivatives traders and pension fund managers take note – there is still no extradition treaty with the UK.

There are even more way-out stories about him. That he was captured by the IRA. That he is a fund raiser for the IRA. That he shot himself and asked a friend to cut him up and feed him to the lions at the zoo run by one of his old gambling chums, John Aspinall.

Don't listen to them. He's alive and well and losing money

in downtown Montevideo. I've seen him. In fact, I was just about to go up to him when I spotted what looked like a real-life clash of the titans across this roulette wheel. On one side, behind a mountain of chips like the Manhattan skyline, puffing the biggest Davidoff in the world, some guy who looked like Kerry Packer's elder brother. On the other, a grande dame who looked as though she had overdosed on amphetamines and tequila for twenty years. Between them, spinning the wheel, a reformed Clint Eastwood, without the blanket on his shoulder.

I don't gamble. Well, not any more. A million years ago I did, when I was young. But then I suppose I did lots of things when I was young that I don't do now. Sometimes I would win, more often I would lose. Often all my week's wages in one session. And sometimes the next week's as well. Then, like most of us, I took the biggest gamble of all. And that was it. I didn't have any money left to gamble. But I like going into casinos: to watch, not to play around. Because I just know, when the diceman cometh I wouldn't be lucky enough to lose. I'd probably win a fortune and bang would go my dream of dicing with failure.

When I turned round he was gone.

But I know it was him. I mean, it's obvious isn't it? The night of the murder we all know he visited Uckfield, just down the road from where I live. Later his Ford Corsair, not the car you would have thought for an upper-class roller like Lucky Lucan, was found abandoned at Newhaven, just down the other road from where I live. After that, nothing. So how did he get to Montevideo? From Newhaven he was whisked to a passing Greek tanker. Why Greek? Because the Greeks will do anything. Also Lucan counted many Greeks among his gambling chums. They would have done anything for one of their kind, and especially a lord, a drinker and a gambler. Look at how they helped him pay off his debts way before he disappeared. From the Greek tanker he was transferred in mid-Atlantic to another Greek tanker heading for South America. Simple.

Why South America? Because he had chums there, people who would help him disappear. Don't forget, Lucky Lucan was a wild right-winger. He had this superiority thing. He believed he was on a higher plane than the rest of us. He even collected tapes of Hitler's speeches. Hardly the hallmark of a Liberal.

Why Montevideo? Because it's dirty, seedy, cheap and full of drop-outs. Besides, it's the Switzerland of South America. Today it has almost as many foreign banks as yesterday it had cattle. As the cattle business collapsed, it was replaced by banking. Now they say it is home to cash from all over the continent. Not being able to speak Spanish there would not attract so much attention as in, say, Argentina or Paraguay. Plus, of course, the fact that Pastas Baccino makes the best pasta in South America. On a rainy Friday or Saturday night, the place is packed. In any case, plenty of other people have done it: Jacques Medecin, the one-time mayor and overlord of Nice, gastronome, ladies' man and rabid anti-communist who was accused of fraud and corruption: What's-his-name, the international swindler and master of disguise; and, of course, Robert Maxwell. You mean you believe the story about him falling off the back of his yacht? Come on.

So why shouldn't Lucan be in Montevideo? It makes as much sense as all the other theories put forward by all the Inspector Plods of the Yard and all the investigations they have carried out over the years which by sheer coincidence, I notice, always happen to take place in warm countries during the winter. He had no money, no passport, no papers. Only the bloodsoaked clothes he was wearing. What could be more natural, therefore, when you're in a spot of bother than to 'lie doggo', as he said in his last letter, with one's chums. Especially if they are the kind of chums who've had a lot of experience helping other collectors of Hitler's speeches disappear. Verstehen Sie?

As for changing your identity, a few telephone calls and you can get a new passport, a new driving licence and new credit cards. Thailand, Philippines, even Zaire, there are fixers everywhere. Alternatively, I'm told, there are one or two pubs around Bayswater where you can meet the right people. Which might be more convenient, especially if it's a new British passport you're after. Other passports are easier and cheaper to get, and to fix. But be warned. Forging the passport is relatively easy. It's fixing the photograph in place that's the tricky bit. Tricky, but not impossible – depending on how much money you have to spend.

Years ago I received three blank Togolese diplomatic passports in the post. Why I got them, who sent them, I don't know. All I know is it was too much of a temptation. With the office photocopying machine and a little bit of ingenuity, I was able to insert my photograph in the super-secure section you're not supposed to be able to insert it in and add all the necessary reference numbers and stamps and signature. No problem at all. Did I use the passports? Don't tell anybody, but yes, of course. Especially in far away countries where there are always enormous queues at immigration and there is no Togolese embassy. Oh yes, and once at Charles de Gaulle in Paris. I arrived with a Togolese minister. We were both stopped. The policeman asked us to wait while he made a telephone call. Had I been rumbled? Was I about to spend the next twenty five years in La Santé, the maximum security prison outside Paris? Not at all. Even with my bad French I could hear the policeman checking if there was such a country as Togo. Did the minister go bananas! He had been personally invited by President Mitterrand. The President was a personal friend of his. He knew Jean-Christophe, the President's son. Never before had he been so insulted. Heads would *tomber* for this affront to the national dignity of the great, independ-ent, sovereign nation of Togo. But I got away with it. The French guy stamped my passport without looking at it. I was in.

So the problem is not the passport, it's keeping your new identity intact. You have to say goodbye to all your loved ones: your horse, your dogs, the farrier, the vet. You have to force yourself to ditch the wife, all your family and friends. You have to say goodbye to everyone who'd helped you over the years: your secretary, the girl in the typing pool, the messenger in the broker's office who gave you all that inside information over the years. The last thing you can afford is a letter from the Serious Fraud Office or, worse still, a postcard from home. The break has to be absolute, total, complete. Which can be very, very difficult. Just think of it: no more family parties; no more holidays with the in-laws; no more get-togethers with the neighbours at weekends; no more desperate, embarrassing hanging around at Christmas waiting for your brother-in-law to break open a second bottle of bitter lemon.

As for spending the rest of your life in Montevideo, imagine a tropical paradise: a long sandy beach, an unending string of luxury hotels, exotic bars, friendly natives willing to jump at the first sign of a cheap glass necklace. Well, it's nothing like that. It's a sunny, hot, sweaty place for cold, chilly, shady types. It's down-at-heel, dusty, old-fashioned, fuddy-duddy. An old Spanish-colonial city that doesn't behave like one. The kind of place where Hispanics, not to mention the occasional German has-been, go to relive past failures, and elephants and broken-down playboys go to die. Which is odd, because even though it hasn't got the usual run of gold, diamonds and drugs that you find almost everywhere else in South America, it's not far from places that have. Squeezed between Argentina and Brazil, it's practically within commuting distance of Buenos Aires. In fact, come summer, it's overrun by Argentinians in search of excitement. Which, I think, says more about the Argentine than it does about Uruguay.

I'm no expert on the fun spots of the world. Sure, I've been forced to go to your Miamis and Cancuns and Marbellas, but I prefer the slightly seedy, slightly mysterious, slightly racy places like Ho Chi Minh City, Havana, whole stretches of Africa, India and the Far East. Montevideo I also like, because it's a bit like pre-war Berlin. In the sunshine. Or, I suppose, Naples, as over 40 per cent of the three million population are of Italian descent. Which is why Montevideo is the perfect hideaway.

Wandering into the bar at the Victoria Plaza Hotel is like wandering into an old, grainy, flickering movie. Its cheap, faded wood panelling has all the temporary excitement of an abandoned film set. So have all its cheap, faded guests. Whenever I go there I feel as if I'm walking into some murky, seedy, shady arms market.

The guy sitting in the corner looks like an ex-member of the SS Youth. I'm sure he chews ball bearings for lunch. The one at the bar has liquid Semtex-H running through his veins. If he hasn't he's been short-changed. And heaven help the guy who did it when he finds out. The rest all look as though they've got Walther MPK 9mm machine guns inside their jackets, 9mm Smith & Wesson automatics in their violin cases and briefcases full of nerve gas developed in secret laboratories in the basements of ordinary townhouses in Santiago, capable of causing death indistinguishable from a heart attack.

Psst. Want to buy some cluster bombs? Good reputation? Good references? Call this guy on this number. How about fuel air explosion technology? It's the poor man's nuclear bomb. Got the knowhow if you want it. For the right price, of course. Looking for SAM-7 missiles, AK-47 rifles or Barrett light machine guns which can cause big problems for helicopters? You can bet your life somebody in the room not only knows who to talk to, but how to fix the papers, which bank to use and how to hide the readies afterwards.

I wander across to a chair in the far corner. Two school-teacher types are debating the relative merits of Chinese and Israeli grenade launchers.

'Depends if it's hot or not.'

'You mean the fighting?'

'No, the weather. The Israeli launcher operates OK if it's hot: 10, 20, 30, even 40 degrees centigrade. Any colder and it jams up. It can't stand the cold.'

'And the Chinese?'

'No problem, hot or cold it'll operate. Look at what they have to put up with on the border with Russia.'

Almost facing them are three Central European types in

immaculate suits and one flak jacket talking about MM40 sea-to-sea Exocet missiles.

'So how do we get them?' asks one of the suits.

'Don't worry, we'll take care of it,' whispers the flak jacket.

'Yes, but how?' asks another.

'You don't have to know.'

'But you gotta give us a clue. I mean . . .'

'Well, we normally use Cyprus. We fly everything in there, then get this Russian to fix the paperwork – end-user certificates, everything. The place is much better, more efficient now the Russians are there.'

I settle into my chair. From behind me I couldn't help hearing what seemed to be Arab voices. Then I heard a German voice talking about a delivery to a small airport just north of Hamburg which he said was owned by the Iranians. 'Keep it under seven and half tonnes,' he was saying. 'That way we don't have any problems with customs. Over seven and a half and we get big problems.'

Then I hear other voices talking about supplying somebody in the Middle East with counterfeit Jordanian dinars. Jordanian? Israeli? Palestinian?

I swear, if somebody had rushed in and shouted 'Quick, quick, the police,' the whole town would have emptied in ten seconds. But none of that made me nervous. What made me nervous was that whenever I ordered a drink the barman kept saying 'Yes, my dove. Thank you, my dove. Will that be all, my dove?'

Outside, the Plaza Independencia seemed jammed with Oldsmobiles, Cadillacs and, of all things, Morris Oxfords and Austin A40s. The square looks to me as though it was built for protest demonstrations and revolutions. Without any trouble at all, I can see tanks rumbling up and down it, snipers darting from pillar to pillar and a suicide bomber hiding behind the big bronze statue of José Cervasio Artigus, their national hero, in the centre. It's not your Tiananmen Square-type square. It's a million times smaller. More a 'Small revolution in Uruguay. Nobody hurt' type of square. But size isn't everything.

I amble along the Plaza Cagancho looking at the bookstalls. (No, they haven't got secondhand copies of any of my books. Yet.) Cheap paperbacks, hardbacks, some leather bindings; rare first editions like *Dr No*, which would cost me £45 at this little bookshop I know in Seaford. Here it is on sale for a couple of bananas and a coconut. It's the kind of secondhand book market where for half the price of nothing, as the Irish would say, you can pick up books so old and forgotten, all you have to do if you're a minor member of the royal family is rewrite them in order to make a fortune. A book on helicopters for children? It'll never catch on. A novel about a vicar's wife running off to live with a supermarket manager? Never in a million years.

I stumble into the Banco de la Republica Oriental del Uruguay to change travellers' cheques. There is this Spanish or Italian-looking guy wearing a broken pair of glasses. One side has come away from the main frame, and he appears to have tied them together with an old shoelace. His friend could have been Moroccan, or Tunisian, or maybe even Egyptian. He had a beard and a bow tie. As they passed me I swear the broken glasses said something like, 'Directeur-Général . . . arranger . . . accident . . .' But I could have been mistaken.

As I stagger along the cracked and broken paving stones to my meeting I just know I am being followed by a face which is still recovering from a shotgun blast at point-blank range and a limp that looks as though he's got a Pershing missile down his trouser leg. In his left hand he is carrying a briefcase that looks suspiciously like an Iraqi nerve-gas bomb.

When not earning – or trying to earn – my daily bread, I while away my time outside the thousands of open-air cafés or confiterias – there's one called Manchester in the Avenida 18 de Julio – which all smell of absinthe, coffee and sweat, watching who's watching who. The Uruguayans are watching the Colombians. The Colombians are watching the US undercover agents. The US undercover agents are watching whoever will let them watch them. Wait a minute. Isn't that Lord Lucan over there climbing into a battered old taxi? But nobody is watching him.

Sitting at a rickety table outside the Santo Cataline, trying to kick the tequila habit, you get the impression that every other person in Montevideo in dark glasses is laundering money for the Colombians for a 5 per cent fee. And all the others are doing it for $7\frac{1}{2}$ per cent. And whether they are 5 per cent or $7\frac{1}{2}$ per cent merchants, they've opened a string of companies to handle the business. The first to export legitimate product to the States. The second to handle part of the payment. The third to handle the balance. The fourth to transfer the funds to Italy. The fifth to double-cross the Colombians and shuffle part of the action sideways into Panama or the Cayman Islands or even the City of London.

I can't help it. In the cool marble interior of the Ministry of Foreign Affairs, I have this idea that every Uruguayan has a khaki cap, a beard, looks like Che Guevara, and jabs his cigar at you as if it is a dagger. Then I realise they are, they have and they do.

The bar in the Hotel los Angeles is full of Dutch contractors paying off Saudi middlemen for huge Middle East contracts; guys from St Gobain giving a petit cadeau to guys with monocles and bald heads for big contracts in Nantes and other foreign countries – I could tell they were from St Gobain, I could see right through them – and a group of Americans planning to raise a German sub which sank in the Arabian Sea towards the end of World War II which is supposed to be choc-a-bloc with silver bullion.

Montevideo, as you can gather, is not the most exciting town in the world. There is the Palacio Salvo, once billed as South America's tallest building; but then I suppose two bits of stick and a sheepskin rug was also once South America's tallest building; the cathedral, the oldest public building in the city; the Teatro Solis, which is the leading teatro in the city. And that's about it.

Somehow, I didn't fancy the restaurants either. Call me sensitive, but I just couldn't get it out of my head that if it came to it, these guys would be prepared to chew me up and swallow me: fingers, muscles, what little fat I have, even my

... No. It brings tears to my eyes even to think about it. For don't forget who was in the plane that came down in the Andes when to keep alive the survivors actually got their teeth into their friends: Uruguayans. People just like that guy over there. Licking his lips. And staring at me.

I tried popping across to Punta del Este, Uruguay's answer to the French Riviera or Palm Beach. It has the same long sandy beaches, the same row after row of luxury apartments and multi-million-dollar houses, the same manicured lawns and gardens. Gotlero Avenue, the main street, has all the swish shops and trendy cafés – a single cup of coffee cost me US$5 – and bars anyone could want. But it was no good. Nothing seemed to happen until about noon or one o'clock in the afternoon. Which I suppose is not surprising, bearing in mind the shops don't close till around 2 am when the clubs and discos open.

In the end I decided to see if I could find old Lucky Lucan again. I mean, just imagine Biddlecombe succeeding where Inspector Plod of the Yard has failed. Where to start? The casinos. Of course.

In London, Lucan used to spend all his time either at the Clermont Club with Aspers or Takkers, or doing the rounds trying to borrow still more money to pay his debts. So night after night while I was in good old Monte I'd put on a natty waistcoat, one of those bootlace ties, roll a couple of double sixes just for the fun of it and hit the casinos. Now, as I said, I no longer gamble, but I've been to just about every type of casino in most parts of the world, from the stately, formal ones full of cobwebs, imitation Louis XVI furniture and walls dripping with hunting prints and pseudo family portraits, to the ones covered with faded red damask wallpaper that look like a tart's bedroom. At least that's what I am told. My favourites are the small, traditional, slightly dusty, slightly faded, old-fashioned ones where everybody still turns up in frills and ruffles and the women come wearing suits and collars and ties. Like Monte Carlo or Geneva or any one of a dozen small casinos in Italy. But the others are good fun too.

Prague, for example, seems to be casino mad. I once went into a casino which consisted of nothing but Double Diamond De-Luxe video slot machines where everyone seemed to be playing two, maybe three at a time. Another one I went into in the middle of the day was worse. There were maybe half a dozen people there each hitting six or seven video slot machines at the same time. Two or three others were playing American poker. But wherever you go in Prague, in hotel receptions, in restaurants, in pubs, in snack bars, in bus stations, in railway stations and even in your ordinary corner store, there are slot machines. Everybody is gambling. Not just slot machines. Not just roulette. Not just blackjack. One bar I ended up in very early one morning, everyone was busy backing some greyhound race at some exotic, exciting place called Hackney.

In Sofia, Bulgaria, I once came across a roulette session where there were so many chips constantly piling up on the table two girls spent the whole evening trying to count them. For a long time I was a regular in the casino on the first floor of the Hotel Sarakawa in Lomé, Togo, which was always packed with North Koreans, winning like crazy. I can also remember going to one of the less regulated casinos in Lagos where, instead of playing the numbers, I saw a gang of guys betting on whose meal would attract the most flies. And another casino, which I can never forget, in Minneapolis, St Paul, didn't serve alcohol.

There are also casinos which are no longer a gamble but an industry. I once went to Genting, the biggest casino complex in South East Asia, high in the hills outside Kuala Lumpur. It was enormous – the size of half a dozen football pitches. And it had everything: craps, roulette, every card game you can imagine, something called the Magic Wheel. Not to mention restaurants, bars, theatres, enormous lobbies, playrooms for the kids, a thousand computer games for the more grown-up kids. And guards everywhere. It was packed all day and nearly all night. Not with high rollers; they were all at football matches with mobile telephones with direct lines to Zimbabwe, but with your ordinary everyday gamblers. Most of them middle-aged, and most, I would guess, whatever is the Malaysian equivalent of middle-class, middle-income families. Many were from Singapore where Mr 'Nanny' Lee Kwan Yew has stopped them from having all the fun they would like. But all of them were serious, and I mean serious. More serious than they looked visiting the temple specially built halfway up the hill on the way there. Probably because the gods don't hand down their favours in casinos as much as they do in temples.

On the way back to KL, at the foot of the hill we drove past the prime minister's official country residence, a gift from the casino company, which didn't make me think you-know-what. Instead it made me wonder whether there are any gambling links with another prime minister's official country residence called, strangely enough, Chequers.

'So what did you notice?' the driver said to me.

'The atmosphere,' I replied.

'You recognised it then?'

'What? You mean the seriousness, the concentration?'

'No, the drugs, he said. 'Half those guys were smoking.'

But there is nothing to compare with Las Vegas anywhere in the world. Anywhere in the whole of creation, the whole gambling cosmos. Caesar's Palace; Circus Circus; The Mirage, which is more of a rainforest than a rainforest; Treasure Island, complete with galleon in its own lagoon; and Luxor, the enormous pyramid of black glass complete with its own River Nile. They're all so absurd, so enormous, so tacky and so unbelievably well done you can't possibly dislike them. Even if you remember the 1970s and the lavish Casino du Liban in Beirut with its three enormous gaming rooms and its spectacular million-dollar floor shows which, apart from the usual, used to feature wild horses and even elephants. It always strikes me as odd, though, that to the Americans it's got nothing to do with gambling. To them, it's gaming. The punters who pack the place day and night are not gamblers, they're players. And the building they're in, especially if it's next to a rollercoaster or a water ride, is not a casino but a family entertainment centre.

But big, small, indifferent, or Las Vegas, to me the atmosphere in any casino is invariably the same. Flashing lights, bells, the constant whirr, whirr of the wall-to-wall slots, the sudden gush of coins as yet another machine pays out, the whoops and shrieks. The games are the same: roulette, blackjack, poker, sometimes something called pai gow and pai gow poker, baccarat, bix six, Caribbean stud, super pan 9, and, or course, video poker. Then there are the punters, oops, the players. Now and then, purely and simply in the interests of research, you understand, I've been to casinos where you expect James Bond to turn up any minute. The men are wearing their Jean Paul Gaultier outfits. The women look as if they've just lost at strip poker. On purpose, of course. Like always. The lights are low. Music is playing discreetly in the background. Everybody is sipping champagne. There's money, big money, in the atmosphere.

But more often than not it's bubblegum, baseball caps, Coca-Cola bottles and blue rinse. The high rollers are wearing white shirts and gold medallions and spend all evening chomping on hamburgers, feeding the slots and playing jackpot jungle or the fourth of July. The women are all as big as beer barrels with gold rings on every other finger the size of the Luxor Pyramid. The fake one in Las Vegas. It's bigger than the real one. The bartenders are all in pink, the waitresses in black. The place is crawling with guard dogs or blue coats or whatever the latest bland politically correct word is for beefy, in-house security men who would cheerfully break your neck as you accidentally trip over their foot on the way through a plate glass window.

Huddled around the roulette wheel are always two tiny wizened little Chinamen or Malays or Indians looking as if they haven't two pennies to rub together. But when they think nobody is looking they plunge their hands into their dirty black plastic bags and pull out another thick wad of notes. Lounging by the blackjack table are always tall, thin professor types who don't appear to have been in the outside world since Afghanistan was invaded by white Huns in the year 200. Then wandering from table to table there are always two Arabs. What are they talking about? Mark Thatcher? Saddam Hussein? Who is going to win the Derby next year? And that group of Indians watching the roulette. How much have they been able to launder so far this evening? What did the minister tell them about the contract? How much it is going to cost to slip . . .? Wait a minute! Was that an Italian accent? No, maybe not. It's just that whenever I go into a . . . Yes, it was. There it goes . . . No. It could have been . . . No way. Yes it was. It was Italian. Does that mean the whole place is run by . . . or under the influence of . . . or maybe it's just an innocent outlet being used by . . .

Hey, wait a minute. Is that guy with the dark glasses and shoulder pads following me? I amble across to the roulette wheel. He comes and looks at it as well. I shuffle across to the blackjack tables. He wanders across after me. I stroll down the long, long corridor of slot machines. He strolls down after me. I wander across to the bar. He starts to . . . Then all of a sudden he's deep in conversation with this tall, thin, pasty-looking guy with a pigtail and a limp. The next second, he's gone.

When I was in the gambling business at least I had fun, even when I lost all my week's money in one go. But not these guys, they're all oh-so-serious. They sit there with a poker face as if they're suffering from third-degree gambler's burn-out and their whole life depends on the next card or roll of dice. Which in some cases it probably does. There's no flicker of interest let alone excitement. No tension. Certainly no drama. It's as if they've all been hypnotised by the coloured lights. Although in Dublin I once saw a guy dressed completely in black sitting by the roulette wheel, like a raddled old journalist waiting for his sixth gin and tonic. In front of him was a pile of chips like the Dublin skyline and he was whispering, 'Oh Jesus Christ, God's only Son, may the price be 10–1.'

Or are they just bored out of their tiny minds? Bored by being there, bored by the whole monotonous process. Putting their money down, watching the wheel spin or the card fall. Then losing, losing and losing again. Or maybe even winning. Except maybe they don't go there to win. Maybe they go there just to recycle cash for somebody who's somewhere else really having fun. Or maybe it's just to get away from the wife's mother who is coming round again for dinner to poke her nose into things that have nothing to do with her.

Even if people drop down dead at the table the game goes on. An Arab once told me he was in Atlantic City one night when the guy sitting next to him rolled off his chair, dead.

'So what happened?'

'Nothing.'

'Didn't they call a doctor or something?'

'Sure, they called the paramedics,' he said. 'But we carried on, even when they were rolling the body up and carrying it out. After all, it was right in the middle of the game.'

So in big, lush James Bond casinos, or in small boring, provincial ones, how do you tell the successful gamblers? Easy. They're the ones who always leave with the blonde. The losers are not only stuck with the brunette, they have to hand out tips to all and sundry as well. Even that's not without its risks. I was told that one famous American gambler once had a fantastic night at the tables in Vegas and went around tipping everybody in sight – including an FBI undercover agent, who promptly threw him in gaol for six months for trying to bribe him.

My chances of finding Lucky Lucan, therefore, you might think were about the same as hitting a stand-off with two fives, a handful of dice and a baseball bat. Not true. I wasn't just looking for him on a win and a prayer. I had all the necessary qualifications.

Poker I can play. That's easy. I could remember the rules from the old days. Just about. Nobody says a word to anyone all evening apart from to bet, raise or deal. If anyone does say anything it has to be in English. Foreign languages, especially when spoken by foreigners, are not to be trusted. For each new hand, the cards are shuffled by the person on the dealer's left and cut by the person on his right. The dealer then deals, keeping the cards on the table the whole time.

Then when you play whatever you play all you have to say is, 'Uh-oh.' The dealer looks at you. 'Uh-oh.' He throws you two tens. You split them.

'Uh-oh.' Two more. Both twos.

'Uh-oh.' Two more. Both threes.

'Uh-oh.' Two more. Both fours.

'Uh-oh.' Two more. Both tens.

You then put the gun into your mouth. 'Uh-oh.'

Even though I've spent my life up to my neck in it, craps I find a little bit more difficult. Especially if you play it according to the American rules. The shouting, the screaming, the hugging, the kissing – that I can just about manage, depending largely on how much I've had to drink. I can even recognise a shooter, a stick-man, a dealer and a boxman. Or at least I think I can. My problem – one of my problems – is the rules. I always thought, whatever the game, if you kept betting on the sixteen one day you'd come up trumps. No way. Similarly, I can never remember whether the come-out roll is seven, eleven or 307 or all four. And what's all this about Come and Don't Come? It always gives me problems. Especially the Don't Come. And what on earth do they mean by Betting the Horn? Then there is all this business of the shooter's point and if you roll a three, a seven or a 2001 whether you've won, lost or passed everything on to the next player. And what about all this business of not-passing? If I roll a seven, an eleven or a 1066 on my first shoot does that mean I've won or lost? And what the hell is a stand-off? And I promise I won't ask you again, but what do I do if I get a seven before the shooter's point?

You'd have thought losing a fortune was simple, but they try to make it as complicated as possible. Roulette, for example: I always thought you lived or died on the spin of a wheel. Not so. Apparently you've got 18/38 chances of the ball landing on your number. In blackjack, it's more complicated. I always used to think the chances of being dealt two aces one after the other was $4/52 \times 4/52$ – the number of glasses of champagne you've had. Again not so. It's $4/52 \times 3/51$ plus the number of bottles of whisky you've been able to put on somebody else's hotel room. At least that's what this guy with an aggressive tie and a short-trousered grin told me. And as the bulge under his shoulder was a million times bigger than the one under mine I tended to agree with him.

On the other hand, I'm also the world's other leading expert on explaining what the house percentage is. Are you ready? Say the house percentage is 5.26 per cent per bet if you play in combination, that means, if you take the combination first, if you put one chip on each of the eighteen odd numbers on the inside in single-number bets paying 35–1 and if you put eighteen chips on the outside on odd in an even-number wager and if you then split two chips across the 0 and the 00 at 17.1 you are, in effect, betting 38 chips on each spin. This means in an ideal world each number will come up and you will have bet 1,444 chips. Say each of the single-number bets wins once, this will give you a profit of 648 chips, the bets on odds will win eighteen times, giving up a further 648. The split bet on 0 and 00 will win twice giving you 72 more chips. That gives you a total of 1,368 less the 76 you lost and the three bottles of champagne you can't remember buying which is – surprise, surprise – 5.26 per cent. OK, so instead of going in combination, say you play the same 38 chips per spin all on the outside bet on odd. Each win will give you 76 chips – 38 in winnings, 38 in wagers retained. If, again in a perfect world, you win, 18 times your winnings come to 1,368 chips including the sports car you promised that girl wearing, well, a big smile, which is – guess what? – 5.26 per cent.

Clear? Good. Next week I shall be lecturing on how to interpret video poker strategy charts and avoid being lynched when you query your drinks bill.

Whatever the game, I find deciding on the stake the easier part. The minimum bet is always too much, the maximum is . . . Quick, tell me. How did old Lucky Lucan get away with it? In between it could be anything from a couple of dollars if you're playing with grown-ups and, if you're in the Lucky Lucan stakes and you're doing the private rooms of the oh-so-discreet London clubs, we're talking about £10,000 for an ordinary game to as much as £25,000 for the grown-up version. Per hand. And how many hands did you say you wanted, sir?

Every evening in Montevideo, therefore, I stuck to the same routine. The waistcoat. The tie. A couple of tequilas in the bar at the Victoria Plaza with the arms dealers and drugs barons and sinister men in raincoats. Then the casinos. But I was about as lucky at spotting him as he was at winning at baccarat with Aspers and Takkers in the old days.

My last evening, I decided to give the Casino Carrasco another whirl. It was packed, which was unusual. Most evenings it was about as busy as a whist drive in the village hall run by the local Darby and Joan. Some faces I recognised. Similarly other bits and pieces hovering around the tables. The two Titans I'd seen my first evening had gone; one of them to buy the half of Manhattan they didn't already own, the other to blow their brains out.

From one hall to another I wandered. I got to one table as this big Texas cattle baron was filling his pockets full of chips.

'Hey, aren't you goin' tip the dealer?' this blonde – see what I mean about winners and blondes – was asking him.

'Hell, he doesn't tip me when I lose,' he said, sweeping her up and heading off.

In another hall at a poker table I saw two guys locked in mortal combat. One looked as though he had been put together with a stack of Semtex-H, C-4, a couple of pounds of gunpowder and a sack of match heads. The other obviously dealt in the kind of goods that are shipped in plain wooden boxes in C-130s which land on mile-long blocked-off sections of two-lane highways fifteen miles from the Iraqi border. I didn't understand what they were playing, but whatever it was, it was for real. Neither of them spoke. Each watched the other intently. All they seemed to do was nod slightly. There was no money on the table, no chips, nothing. It was eerie.

As for good old Lucky Lucan, I couldn't see him anywhere. I had a couple of drinks, then a couple more, then a couple more. One of the guys at the bar, who was also staying at the Victoria Plaza, told me he was in security printing, and was negotiating to print even more useless banknotes for Zaire. He offered me a lift back. As we walked across the car park, he kept putting his hands in first one pocket then another, then another. We stopped by this flash American car. A Chevy, I think.

'Hell,' he said, 'I've lost my keys.'

'No problem,' I began. 'We'll get a—'

In a second, he had snapped the aerial off the car, pulled out the thinnest section, twisted the top, pushed it through the door, caught the lock and pulled it up.

'Where did you learn to do that?' I asked.

'Naples,' he said.

Then as I climbed in, I saw him. The moustache. That hang dog look. The military bearing.

'Hey,' I shouted. 'I just want to see that guy over—'

We screeched away. As I turned round I could see two men waving at us, perhaps a trifle more vigorously than you would expect. But we didn't stop until we reached the hotel.

I might go back to Montevideo again, when I've been wearied by all my 'careless days and my luxurious nights', search old Lucky out, have a go at the tables, and lose a fortune. It would be a darned sight better than living in a tiny one-and-a-half room flat in New York's Lower East Side or going to ground in Fez in Morocco like Sebastian Flyte. With or without a German bodyguard.

On the other hand, it would be a hell of a gamble.

San Salvador

Well, shoot my kneecaps, El Salvador is missing out. Belfast is doing it: Beirut is doing it: Vietnam is starting to do it, and the Americans have been doing it for years. Running civil war tours, I mean. Believe me, El Salvador could make a bomb.

In Belfast, you clamber on board a gleaming double-decker and you're off: 'This is where Gerry Adams lived. This is where he worked in a bar and learnt his politics listening to journalists waffling on over pint after pint of Guinness. This is where he attended that funeral. This where he stood at the barricades. This is where, when the ceasefire was declared, he had the barbed wire and the reinforcements put up around his party headquarters so he could deliberately give press conferences standing outside on the pavement showing the world how he was prepared to ignore the instructions of his security advisers and risk his life to talk peace,' goes the commentary.

Falls Road, Shankhill Road, Suicide Corner; along the Peace Line where so many people were killed trying to attack the Henry Taggart security forces base. Gaeltacht, the sprawling estate where Irish is still the first language. Into East Belfast, the Protestant stronghold, past bars with nicknames like the Wounded Knee, the Cracked Cup, to the almost continuously bombed Robinsons Bar and opposite it the almost continuously bombed Europa Hotel.

'But why did the IRA keep bombing them?'

'Because that's where the journalists were. They used to drink all day in the bar, then stagger across the road and sleep all night at the Europa. They knew the best way to get publicity was to take the news to the journalists. They also knew that the journalists wouldn't complain because they not only got their news stories, they were also able to convince their news editors it was dangerous being in Belfast, so they still warranted those unlimited expenses and all that extra danger money.'

Of course. How silly of me to ask!

In Beirut they don't only run civil war tours, they also run hostage tours; for a small sum – there is no set charge. You know what the Lebanese are like – some very keen young men will show you not only where Jackie Mann, Terry Waite, John McCarthy and all the others were kidnapped but also where they were holed up for years on end. One man who looked like Yasser Arafat's younger brother even promised to show me where Terry Waite spent all that time chained to a radiator. But I politely declined. Partly because it was in the middle of Bir al-Abed, the Iranian-backed Hizbollah stronghold at the top of the Corniche, almost opposite where the old St George's Hotel used to be. Partly because I thought the emotional experience would be too great for me. I mean, all that time. The poor radiator.

In Vietnam they've gone a stage further still. Not content with showing tourists the damage caused during their war, they are now rebuilding some of the buildings that were totally destroyed in order to partly destroy them again so that they've got more things to show the tourists. The same applies to the Ho Chi Minh Trail, which ran through the Truong Son mountains in central Vietnam, eastern Laos and Cambodia, as well as the enormous complex of over 200 kilometres of tunnels at Cu Chi just outside Ho Chi Minh City, which was at one time home to over 5,000 troops. They are rebuilding whole sections which were destroyed by the Americans in order to give tourists more value for money. You scoff. But they want to do the same thing in Berlin. I read in a French newspaper that a group of German businessmen want to rebuild part of the Wall, including watchtowers and guard dogs, as some kind of amusement park. Which, if it's true, must deserve the Martin Bormann Award for Bad Taste.

As for all the civil war memorials in the States, most of them are bad taste. Not because they don't commemorate major historic events and important battle sites. Not because they don't do it well. In most cases they do it very, very well. But because they reduce the whole thing to a Walt Disney experience, slosh it over with little bits of fact and a lot of fiction, drown it in treacle and pretend nothing nasty ever happened.

Now I'm not suggesting that El Salvador, the smallest, most densely populated and most industrially developed country in Central America, should go as far as that. But what I am saying is they could go at least halfway. After all, they've got all the ingredients.

First, the name. For anyone who has trouble remembering the names of capital cities, it's a dream. El Salvador is the country, San Salvador is the capital. Or is it the other way round? Whatever the capital is called is also the name of the volcano towering above the city. If that's not straightforward enough for you, the old capital is called Nueva San Salvador. Or is it Nueva El Salvador? See what I mean? On the other hand, you could say even though it's called after the Saviour, it doesn't exactly follow the Saviour's precepts – turn the other cheek, do good to those who hate it and love its enemies. In fact, you could say it's pretty anti everything the Saviour stands for. It makes you wonder if things would have been different if it had been called El Diablo.

Then the movie. How many countries are the subject of a complete all-singing-all-dancing Hollywood movie? Trouble is it was made by Oliver Stone, the man who brought us such gentle, elegant little cinematic triumphs as exploding skulls, dismemberments, crucifixions and that glorious scene where a head which has been cut off with a chainsaw is dropped neatly onto the middle of a plate in a busy restaurant. I'm no expert on films – the last time I went to the cinema the piano broke down – so, I admit, at first I thought any Oliver Stone movie had to be bad news. The only ones I've seen I've seen on planes, and usually within minutes they've had me crying out for less: *Platoon*, which seemed to be about a bunch of guys blasting anything that moved to kingdom come; *Born on the Fourth of July*, which seemed to be about a bunch of guys being blasted to kingdom come; *JFK*, which seemed to be about a bunch of guys blasting each other to kingdom come, and the one that showed Arnold Schwarzenegger ripping a vulture's lungs out for, I think, lunch. But I may be wrong, there was a lot of turbulence on that particular flight.

Salvador, it seemed to me, was about a bunch of guys blasting some deadbeat, photo journalist to kingdom come because all he wanted to do was get away from the wife and have some virgin sit on his face for seven bucks. The only good thing I can say about it is that the flight on which I saw it had a particularly friendly hostess who dished me lots of wine and port and cognac so, thank goodness, I slept through most of it. But from El Salvador's, or should it be San Salvador's, point of view, it couldn't have been better. Because everybody who saw it obviously realised that, like all Stone's movies, it must be totally back to front. Far from being a hell-hole inhabited solely by sleazeballs and death squads and virgins who sit on your face for seven bucks, El or San must be a very pleasant, civilised sophisticated patch of dust in a continent that is otherwise a hellhole inhabited solely by sleazeballs, death squads and virgins who sit on your face for seven bucks.

The only problem is, El/San doesn't look as though it's been through a civil war. When I first went there, I didn't exactly expect to find the place full of gunsmoke, fighting in the streets, men with long beards and everybody wearing khaki. But I did expect some evidence of some kind of civil war. After all, it lasted twelve years and claimed over 75,000 lives out of a total population of less than five million. I mean, in Belfast, even when the peace process had started, there was still the occasional security sweep. Although I must admit nobody seemed to worry.

'Look, it's simple,' I was told one evening upstairs in

Robinsons Bar. 'If conventional troops are combing the area, they send in the helicopters, right?'

'Right.'

'So if it's serious and they send in the SAS, what do they do? They call off the helicopters so nobody knows the SAS is going in. Right? So how do we know the SAS is coming in?'

'Because there are no helicopters. Right?'

'Right. And it is a large one I'll be having, God bless ye.'

I order two more large ones. 'But the English can't be that stupid,' I begin nervously.

'Don't you believe it.' He downs the second or is it the third large one. 'Look, I'll tell ye. When the English send one of their men out on a secret mission what do they do? They give him a special secret radio so he can call for help if he gets into trouble. There's no point giving them ordinary radios, is there? They'll never get through, or if they do everybody will hear what they're saying. So they give them these special radios with built-in scramblers.'

'Yes,' I begin. 'That makes . . .'

'Except that the radios they give them are so powerful they blank out any other radio or telephone within thirty yards. So what do we do? As soon as we see a new guy on the block, drinking in the bars, driving around, we follow him with our ordinary radios. If the radios go dead, we've got him. Sure, 'tis another large one I'll be having, thank you very much.'

In Belfast, though the peace process still seems to be holding, there are signs of the Troubles everywhere. The old maid's chapel in Malone Road might have been replaced by the brand new St Brigid's Church, a sign of the growing wealth and influence of the Catholic community, but the Peace Line, the mini-Berlin Wall dividing the two sides is still there. The checkpoints are still there, though admittedly unmanned, and so are the enormous murals. Some with fresh paint. Very fresh paint.

In Beirut, the place is humming. There is building work everywhere, the streets are packed, bars, clubs, restaurants are doing a roaring trade. Syrian soldiers are everywhere. But you get the impression nobody goes around at night knocking on people's doors asking if they want to come out for a drink.

In Ho Chi Minh City the only sign that the war is over is the state of the bars, clubs and restaurants. Either they're empty or they've closed down and disappeared or they've been converted to coffee bars.

In El/San: nothing, nix, rien, nada. Not one soldier with a beard. Not one AK-47. Not even a simple US-built M16 rifle. No old FMLN commandants wandering around munching their pupusas – corn tortillas filled with beans or cheese or sausage meat. No big shots surrounded by gaggles of bodyguards. No peace lines. No checkpoints. Not even a single mural. Everything is clean and tidy. The shops are full, the shopping centres packed. There is hardly any space to walk along the pavement for all the stalls selling washing powder, slippers and funny-looking plastic dogs. The Salvadoreans were just too quick and too professional at fixing, repainting and rebuilding everything that had been damaged or destroyed by the fighting. In some cases it was done by the following morning. Not that I'm criticising; they had the best of intentions. But it's no way to cash in and create a civil war venue.

'It was propaganda,' a government official told me. A government official, I hasten to add, who was clean-shaven, immaculately groomed and wearing a suit that could have been pressed underneath a couple of tons of high explosives. 'The guerrillas said they were capturing the city. We said they weren't. As soon as they hit a building, we rushed round and rebuilt it as quickly as possible, repainted it and left it looking like new. In fact in some cases, the best-looking houses in the streets were the ones that had been hit by bombs and repaired. That way nobody could tell how much damage they were doing – not the local people, not the press. We had hundreds of journalists here; hundreds of reporters and photographers. They were always looking for an excuse to say the guerrillas were winning. But when they couldn't find the damage, what could they say?'

'They still said the guerrillas were winning,' I hesitated.

'The bad ones, yes. Not the good ones.'

Never one to accept anything I'm told, very early the following morning I decided to check him out and see if what he was saying was true. All I can say is, probably. Obviously I didn't go everywhere. I still had work to do – lunches, receptions, dinners. Oh yes and, of course, the usual meetings. But I did go around Soyapango to the east of the city and Meyicanos to the north, scenes of some of the fiercest fighting, especially during the final push when it was touch and go whether the guerrillas would win. Everything certainly looked neat and tidy. Just like any other Salvadorean area I've visited. Such as Arlington, Langley Park, Washington, where for some reason I can't remember I got caught up in some quinceanera party for someone's daughter, and parts of Irvine, California, on the fringes of Silicon Valley, where Americans seem to do the thinking and Salvadoreans everything else.

Soyapango, out towards the old airport, in the industrial part of town, is a maze of tiny brick, concrete and wooden shacks and bungalows. The part backing on to the big factories, the laboratories, the ferreterias, the agencias, the bancos, the institutos, the big, ugly distribuadoros as well as a Coca-Cola plant, looks like a grown-up shanty town. Nowhere near as bad as the shanty towns in, say, Guatemala City, or on the outskirts of most big South African towns, but the same type of thing. Tiny shacks; piles of pallet boards; broken-down trucks; rubbish; thick, choking fumes. Graffiti everywhere: FMLN, the guerrilla organisation; Vota FMLN; Libertod de Expression; P [for privatisation] means Unemployment. Further up, behind the football pitch, the wooden shacks give way to concrete blocks and the concrete blocks give way to bricks and mortar and garden walls and garden gates with brand new Yamaha motorbikes propped up against them. Here, instead of graffiti and political slogans, there are probably as many advertisements for, would you believe, Alka-Seltzer and luxury holidays in the Four Seasons Hotel, Antigua, Guatemala.

'See no bombsites,' my driver kept saying. 'No like in

London. I go to London. I see bombsites from war. War forty, fifty years ago. Not like here. Here no bombsites. Yes.'

Under the floormat in front of the driver's seat, however, I couldn't help noticing a revolver about the size of a machine gun which looked as though it could blast a considerable hole through somebody.

Late one evening after another gruelling round of bars and clubs and restaurants, I took another cab, this time around Meyicanos, the upmarket part of town. It was much the same – neatly painted houses, everything clean and tidy. The only damage seemed to be caused by lorries taking short cuts turning corners and smashing up the pavement.

But we could change that. Initially, I thought a few sticks of dynamite judiciously placed would soon re-create the type of genuine authentic bombsites that civil war locations require, and make the place look as though it's been through a rough time, not to mention over US$1 million of aid a day from the US. But then somebody told me that even though the country was now at peace they still had big problems finding jobs for the old guerrillas. Then it struck me. Give them jobs as bus drivers. Lots of Salvadoreans are bus drivers in New York. So it would only take a handful of ex-guerrilla Salvadorean bus drivers a couple of days of driving two abreast the wrong way down a one-way street, horns blaring like tug boats, ignoring traffic lights and swinging left in front of oncoming traffic, to have the city looking like New York. Which, let's face it, looks as though it's just coming out of a twelve-year civil war.

Alternatively, we could arrange another football match between El/San and next door Honduras. Don't forget the famous Football War in 1969 when El/San and Honduras were competing against each other for a place in the 1970 World Cup. Salvador, in a bid to push a broken bottle in the face of timid, law-abiding English football supporters and seize from them the world record for football hooliganism, actually launched a full-scale military invasion of Honduras. They tried to pretend it was something to do with opening up a route to the Caribbean. But nobody was fooled. Everyone knew it was the old tactic: retaliate first. The Organisation of American States blew the whistle on them and four days later called time, after over 2,000 people had been killed. Mostly Hondurans. Failing that, we could suggest a friendly match between El/San and England and let our wonderful, timid, law-abiding English football supporters do the job for us.

OK, so now we've got the place looking like it's been through a civil war, what about the tour itself? Where shall we begin?

It's got to be at the cathedral, where the archbishop, Monsignor Oscar Arnulfo Romero, was assassinated while saying mass on 24 March 1980, just a month after being appointed. Which, I suppose, started the whole thing off. Look at what Thomas à Becket did for Canterbury. There are not many churches in the world where archbishops have been murdered at the altar. If you've got one, you've got to use it.

Next I reckon, it's got to be the municipal cemetery to see the grave of Blowtorch Bob, Roberto d'Aubuisson, the notorious army major, coke addict, drug runner, torturer of political prisoners, murderer some say of leading archbishops, who ran the infamous death squads. There you could explain how it all began; how for almost twelve years left-wing guerrillas of the Farabundo Marti National Liberation Front fought the power and near invincible might of the US-backed government; how the death squads led by Blowtorch Bob with his skintight jeans and funny haircut went around kicking people's doors down in the middle of the night, smashing people's faces to smithereens with rifle butts, kicking them to kingdom come and then hacking them to pieces with axes and machetes; how people were stood up against walls and shot, heads cut off and stuck on posts; how women were raped and children beaten and skewered. You could also, if you wanted to risk perhaps not getting a government tourist grant next year, point out that in the office of the present president of El/San, Armando Calderon Sol – Ignoramus, to all his supporters – hangs a portrait of, you got it, Major Bob. On the other hand, you could forget to mention it.

Having set the gruesome scene, I think next it's got to be Soyapango first, to see some of the civil war damage that will have been created specially for tourists and to explain how for two years the guerrillas, under cover of dark, smuggled arms and ammunition into the area for their final, desperate attempt to grab the city. Their plan was from there to shell Meyicanos and hope the rich in their luxury pads would beg the government to give in before everything was flattened. Which they did. But the government didn't take any notice. They moved their own men and arms in among the luxury villas and started fighting back. Which upset all the guerrillas' calculations. It also upset lots of residents of Meyicanos.

For the other side of the story, it's got to be Meyicanos. We could tour the area, point out some of the more spectacular homes but, more interesting I think, over a quick lunch of corn tortillas and beans, would be to have a talk on kidnapping, because during the war it was about as popular as scattering somebody's brains over the back of a car. One after another, anyone who was anyone and had the readies to come up with the ransom was kidnapped. And they did it bit by bit. At different times of the day, different bits of the body would be returned until the ransom had been paid. Life for your typical Salvadorean businessman, therefore, was far from easy. You would say goodbye to your family in the morning and come home at different times of the day: a finger at elevenses, a hand at lunchtime, an ear at teatime and a cardboard box in time for dinner. Or you might not come home at all. Many families who got a ransom demand, and gave the money to the police to hand over to the kidnappers, never got their money or the victim back. At one stage so many businessmen were being kidnapped and held for ransom that it became a status symbol. If you hadn't been kidnapped you weren't important, and could never be considered a pillar of the local community let alone the mainstay of the golf club. In fact some kidnappers were so good and so professional everybody reckoned they were either members of the police or the military or were being paid by the businessmen themselves to divert suspicion, increase their standing in the community and ensure their re-election as treasurer of the golf club.

Now, I think, fortified by tortillas, it's got to be the presidential palace, then the zoo.

Armando Calderon Sol looks a bit like a nightclub bouncer who went to law school. To steal the books. A former mayor of El Sal – no, I mean San Salvador, the town – his big hero, don't forget, was the guy with the tight jeans and a nice line in death squads whose photograph hangs prominently in his office, which must be one hell of a dampener on any meetings where people are invited to give their views. If people are ever asked for their views by the new president.

Alfredo Cristiani, who held office towards the end of the civil war, was a totally different type of president. To me, he was the shy, quiet, modest, Abraham Lincoln-type hero of the whole thing – even though he comes from one of the fourteen families which are supposed to pretty well own and run the country – because during the worst of the fighting he managed to snatch victory for both sides out of the jaws of defeat. He's tall, thin, slightly stooping. He is very friendly and approachable and full of good stories, the kind of person who'd make you want to sign a peace agreement with him even though you'd never breathed a word against him.

How do I know? I once had a long session with him. I wasn't going to mention it. I was going to save it up for my Graham Greene-type book, *Getting to Know the President*, but I'll never find the time to write it. There's no way I can skip off to Cap d'Antibes for months on end. I have a living to earn. The meeting was arranged by the British embassy because – I'll tell you, if you promise not to laugh – they wanted to introduce him to a serious British businessman. Which tells you either how perceptive they are or how badly British books are distributed throughout South America. So while the dedicated group of British exporters I was with went off to make their calls: to room service, to the swimming pool, to that centre for visiting businessmen in the Zona Rosa, I headed across town all on my own – I had no Chuchu to hold my hand like Graham Greene – to see the man who, I knew from the papers, pushed moderation to the extreme in his efforts to end the civil war.

At that time, Cristiani had just stepped down after five years as president. When he first got in in 1989 the whole country was tearing itself to bits. When he stepped down in 1994 it was desperately trying to live in harmony.

He was full of stories about the international news media and how they cover or do not cover civil wars in the age of instant communications. 'I'm not naive,' he told me. 'I knew that the press were against us. We were the establishment, the guerrillas were anti-establishment. Whatever happened the guerrillas were right and had to be supported. What I did not realise was the lengths the press would go to to distort the truth; they even told outright lies just to support their case.'

He was great fun when it came to describing international negotiations and what happens behind the scenes. 'When I realised that we had to negotiate with the guerrillas, I knew that there was no point in me just saying I wanted to negotiate with them. I had to have the support of the international community. So I went first to see George Bush, in the White House. He listened to what I had to say, then said that I was obviously the expert on the spot, he would support me whatever I wanted to do.'

Visiting Mrs Thatcher was, by comparison, a bit like trying to sort out with the wife who's doing what at Christmas. 'I went to see Mrs Thatcher at No. 10. At first she didn't want to see me. She could see no reason for a meeting. Eventually she agreed. The meeting I will always remember. Before I could say a word she started saying, Never negotiate with guerrillas. Never. Never. Never. Never negotiate ... I kept trying to get a word in, but she kept saying, Never negotiate with guerrillas. Never. Never. Never. Eventually I managed to interrupt her. I said that not all guerrillas were guerrillas. Some were completely wrong, and we should never negotiate with them. Others maybe had a case. In El Salvador, I believed they had some points in their favour. First, we were not a true democracy and they wanted democracy. We had to listen to what they had to say. Second, it was better to let them argue their case within the democratic process than leave them outside with their guns and their weapons.'

'And did she listen to what you were saying?'

'I don't know.' He leant back and laughed. 'She still kept saying, Never negotiate with guerrillas. Never. Never. Never.'

I asked him, as an outsider, which European country he admired most; which one he thought had got its act together. His answer, perhaps not surprisingly, was Germany. He admired their federal structure. He praised their social market economy. He envied their democratic institutions. He also liked the way they do business, both political business and business business. 'They are organised. They have a plan. They know what they believe in. They know what they want to do. And they,' he paused, 'do it.'

After the presidential palace, things get a bit different. But hang on, I've got some ideas. Just to bring in the tourists, you understand.

How about knocking down the presidential palace and in its place building a replica of the White House together with a replica of Ronald Reagan saying one thing about El/San and doing the other?

No? OK, so how about, under the statue of El Salvador himself in the Plaza de las Americas, holding military training sessions for children; like they do at Williamsburg, where all day long loyal, God-fearing Americans dressed up as early eighteenth-century settlers drill innocent children up and down on the public square with mock weapons and teach them how to kill English soldiers, and then wonder why the National Rifle Association has such a strong hold.

'Aren't you teaching them how to kill people?' I asked one eighteenth-century settler.

'Shucks, nah. It's just kinda fun,' he said. 'We're just showing them what it's like in them old days.'

'But in them old days you all went around killing British soldiers who were just doing their job.'

'No way,' he said. 'You don't want believe what you read. It was nothin like that at all.'

OK, you'll like this one. What about turning the Cuartel, the sprawling military barracks behind the international exhibition centre, into a giant Oliver Stone Weapons' Park, a grown-ups' amusement arcade for real men who don't eat quiche, hate eating vulture the wrong way and love to go around skewering each others' eyeballs into the dust? There for the price of a corn tortilla with French fries tourists could fight the civil war all over again or, if they fancied something a little more gruesome, for a few dollars more they could do something even worse; they could do what they do in Stone's movies. In other words we could have Salvador: The Ultimate Oliver Stone Theme Park.

In Vietnam, just outside Ho Chi Minh City you can spend many a happy hour at an army shooting range blasting away with Kalashnikovs or AK-47s or whatever for a dollar a shot. In Russia, China and most of Eastern Europe, the military will hire you a tank for the day, or even a MiG for an afternoon, so you can have a go at starting World War Three all by yourself.

Target practice with a Kalashnikov, 30 cartridges: US$15; large-calibre machine gun, 100 cartridges: US$45; anti-tank guided missile, one shot in the right direction: US$750; anti-tank guided missile, one shot in the wrong direction resulting in the death of one's own colleagues: promotion to the rank of colonel in the US Army.

The Ultimate Oliver Stone Theme Park would allow you to kill, maim, or, if you haven't got the guts for it, just break one or two fingers of one or two innocent people. Now, as I said, I'm no expert on Stone's movies; I only see them on planes and then I'm usually too stoned to take much notice, but it would seem to me that to be successful the park must reflect his movies. To get in, therefore, you would have to have an enormous needle pushed into your buttocks (*Salvador*). After that there would be a series of displays proving that inviting someone to spend Christmas with you and your family is not necessarily the most hideous and terrifying thing that one man can inflict on another. We could illustrate, for example, death by chainsaw (*Scarface*): death by piano-wire (*Year of the Dragon*); death by crucifixion (*Platoon*); death by exploding skull (*JFK*); and death by being ripped apart by vultures (*Conan*). All in the best possible taste, of course.

One pavilion would be made to look like a Turkish prison (*Midnight Express*). To cut costs we could ask to borrow an old British pavilion designed by the exhibition division of the Central Office of Information for some international fair. Nobody could tell the difference. Except, being an Oliver Stone Theme Park, there would have to be a glass partition through the middle of it (*Midnight Express*). Exactly what the partition is for I don't know. I can remember this girl coming into the prison to see her boyfriend; I can remember them either side of the glass. After that I fell asleep. All I know is when I woke up the guy sitting next to me looked as though he'd spilt his coffee all over the front of his trousers.

The whole place would have to be staffed by witch doctoresses (*Salvador*); coke-sniffing whores who make a career out of sleeping with cripples (*Born on the Fourth of July*); sluts (*Scarface*); bimbos (*Conan the Future Republican*); groupies (*The Doors*); and nagging bitches (*Salvador, Year of the Dragon, The Doors, Wall Street, Conan, Talk Radio, Midnight Express, JFK, Scarface, Eight Million Ways to Die, Platoon, Born on the Fourth of July*, etc., etc.).

In the restaurant you'd sell raw vulture-heart burgers (*Conan*), decapitated head tartare (*Year of the Dragon*) and a special Oliver Stone cocktail full of bits of human skulls and heads (*Salvador, The Doors, Wall Street, Talk Radio, Midnight Express, JFK, Scarface, Eight Million Ways to Die, Platoon, Born on the Fourth of July*, etc., etc.) All designed to give you big problems with your urinary tract. Because as far as I can gather, watching Stone movies, all men end up having problems with their urinary tract (*The Doors, Born on the Fourth of July, Midnight Express* [50 per cent], *Salvador* [at least I think so. I can remember the machete hovering in the area. Then I fell asleep again]).

The price for admission: just seven bucks, with a virgin thrown in as part of the deal.

No? OK, listen. This is an even better idea. There's this multi-storey office block in the centre of town called Torre Democracia, the Tower of Democracy. Over ten years after it was built, it is still empty. Some say it's a symbol of democracy in El/San. Others say it's an enormous cenotaph to the thousands of innocent people who got caught up in the civil war and were imprisoned, tortured and killed. Still others say it's because there are so many agents and middle men and wheeler-dealers trying to sell it for cash to mysterious buyers with dark glasses that nobody knows who is representing whom, who is getting what, which bank is fronting the deal and who has to sign which bit of paper in which order. One evening at some bar or restaurant or club the local Lloyds Bank man introduced me to some guy who looked as though he had spent all his life in the slimelight. He was, he told me, a lawyer. Which proved my point. We gossiped about the usual things men talk about: the wife, the family, how it's a drag being away from home for so long. After three and a half seconds, I mentioned the building. He told me he was the sole agent for it. Under no circumstances should I talk to anybody else. The following morning, I got an enormous bill for his advice and services, and stating in to uncertain terms what commission he wanted, not if, but when the deal went through.

Now regardless of what he says – the following day I met two other people who told me the same thing – why don't we take it over and turn it into an American Military Aggression Exhibition. The idea worked wonders in Ho Chi Minh City, it could work wonders in El/San. Come to think of it, it would probably also work wonders in Libya, Panama, Somalia, or Haiti, where I'm told a travel agent made a fortune with the slogan 'Visit the USA before the USA visits you.' We could have big displays of all the arms and equipment the US didn't ship in; pictures of the US military advisers who were never there, and photographs of the damage that wasn't inflicted. We could have lectures on bomb making. We could show the progression from rubber bands, gunpowder and the tops of matches to deadly chemicals like ammonium nitrate, potassium chlorate and aluminium powder. The Americans would be bound to finance it. Look at all the money and children's homes and reconciliation and reconstruction projects they're throwing at Vietnam. And Vietnam is the other side of the world. Once the thing is built and the tourists are pouring in the Salvadoreans could go round the world selling their services to help other countries put up similar exhibitions. The whole thing could be a big money spinner.

Then how about alongside it, building one of those big simulator movie theatres, where tourists could have the ultimate virtual reality experience and fight the civil war themselves? Not like in Williamsburg, where only the kids get to fight without the intention of ever killing anyone.

And to round the whole thing off – you're going to love this – we've just got to have an El/San folklore evening. Every other town in every other part of the world has one. Why should we let El/San off the hook? We could start with a mariachi band – those are the ones with the blokes in black with buttons all down their trousers – marching along the Boulevard de los Merocs near the Camino Real Hotel. That could be followed by – another mariachi band marching along the Boulevard de los Heroes. Then by another, and another, and . . . Hell. I think I'd prefer to watch an Oliver Stone movie.

To wrap the whole thing up we must have a late-nite tour. First to the Zona Rosa for a meal. Any restaurant will do, so long as they serve *bombe surprise*. And we'll end up at that swish bar on top of the hill which to me, more than anything, proves that the civil war is over: it's run by Russians. When everything came to an end and the left-wing guerrillas won, well I mean, reached a positive compromise with the government, instead of going back home the Russians decided to stay on and sample the delights of freedom they did so much to destroy. And they are doing a hell of a lot of sampling, I can tell you. Oops, I mean, I am told.

When the bar opened, one rumour that did the rounds was that it was a KGB cover-up operation; partly because they seemed to be providing many of the services and facilities the KGB used to provide to top officials and foreign visitors. But the rumour is dead. Partly because everyone can see there is very little if any cover-up there. Partly because of the prices. They are so reasonable they couldn't possibly have been dreamt up by a KGB official. And partly because everyone who goes there says it's one hell of a place, so why knock it?

Right, that's the itinerary settled. Now the most important thing: what are the Salvadoreans like when it comes to handling tourists? For my money, they're friendly, helpful, courteous, the kind of people who help old ladies across the road, don't park where they shouldn't and have the patience to put up with the non-stop stream of stupid questions you get from tourists. Some people call them either the Lebanese or the Jews of Central America. They are hard workers, good farmers, good businessmen. Every morning at five o'clock, who's unloading their fruit and vegetables at the central market in Guatemala City? The Salvadoreans. Who are the third largest producers of coffee in the world? The Salvadoreans. They also have money – from the fruit of their labours as well as from the fortunes many of them made when they headed off to Miami for the duration of the civil war.

The difference between them and other Latin Americans who headed off to Miami during their troubles is that Salvadoreans are bringing the money home, to invest it in new business, new companies, new factories, anything that will make more money. In some villages and towns outside El/San you can see which ones came home and which have families still in the US. The homes are painted. Their floors are tiled. Churches have been rebuilt and redecorated. In one town I went to, there was even a town improvements committee channelling money from relatives in the US into all kinds of projects: repairing roads and refurbishing and rebuilding schools and hospitals, which everyone will tell you is amazing, because 90 per cent of them are mestizos of mixed

Spanish and Indian blood which some people claim is a recipe for disaster in Latin America. Look at Guatemala they say, look at Honduras. Look just about anywhere in the region. But here it's undoubtedly a recipe for success. Which tells you a lot either about the mestizos in El/San, or about the power and efficiency of the fourteen non-mestizo families.

When it comes to looking after foreign visitors, Salvadoreans are perfect. After all, one half looked after how many Americans and the other half looked after how many Russians for how long? Both sides enjoyed themselves so much they wanted to stay. Both sides wanted to give them more money.

Some Salvadoreans, however, are still a bit jittery – probably members of the fourteen families – and are only now getting used to going around without a bodyguard. You can tell because, apart from changing cars in the middle of traffic jams, wearing raincoats in brilliant sunshine and dark glasses when it's raining, they are always waiting for someone to open the door for them. Like one day during the height of the IRA troubles, when I was in one of the House of Commons bars and Gerry Fitt, MP for Belfast West, who for years was probably the IRA's number-one target, dropped in for a drink. Crash – the door burst open. Everybody looked up, but nobody came in. All the MPs went back to doing what they're best at: drinking and stabbing people in the back. Then – crash – in came two men wearing aggressive ties, great big lumps under their armpits and uncompromising raincoats. In the depths of the House of Commons. In the middle of summer. They threw themselves, one against the bar, the other against the far wall and started talking to the lapels of their suits. Three or four minutes later – flip, flop – in came a weakly smiling Gerry Fitt. El/San is a bit like that, but without the bodyguards. However, the ultimate test of a country's nerves, I always think, is to drop a glass in the middle of a crowded restaurant. Although I was sure it wouldn't send everyone diving under the table, I didn't dare risk it. But then I wouldn't risk it in Providence, Rhode Island either.

The other test is the 'Excuse me, I just want to make a quick call' test. You're sitting in a bar or restaurant, facing the door. You're deep in conversation about the need to cut import tariffs from 20 to 15 per cent and the benefits of reducing minimum tariffs on raw materials from 5 to 1 per cent and other such exciting subjects, when the guy you're with suddenly announces he wants to make a quick call.

'No problem,' you mutter through gritted teeth as you realise you're going to be stuck there. All alone. Facing the door. In a flash you wonder whether you should go with him. In another flash you realise you'd better not go with him. After all, you don't want him to think, ahem. So how about the old I-feel-like-some-fresh-air routine? No, that sounds as if you're waiting for him to ... Of course; the I'll-get-another-round-while-you're-gone routine. No thanks, he says. He's had enough. He'll be right back. You're trapped. You sit there nonchalantly, your eyes glued on the door. Not that you think for one moment anything so absurd ... After all, how many other people far less important than you have ended up in a ...

El/San – even the volcano of the same name – I have to report, passed the 'Excuse me, I just want to make a quick call' test. Otherwise I wouldn't be here to report.

On the other hand, in El/San I never run. Whatever the reason. If your pet dog is being attacked, or even your wife, don't run. Everyone will think you're running away from someone or something and, zap, that's another statistic for the records. Similarly if you're stopped by a soldier, a policeman, or your plain old-fashioned kidnapper, don't say anything until you see the whites of their eyes. Whatever you say, they'll misinterpret it. The closer you are to them the better for you. In fact, pray that if you are stopped you're stopped by plain old-fashioned kidnappers. You can at least negotiate with them. With the soldiers and the police, well you know what I mean. And never never never carry an umbrella. I don't care if it's the worst tropical storm in the history of the world, it's not worth the risk. Better a week in hospital with double pneumonia than a double shot between the hospital and the hotel. Umbrellas are funny things. Ask E.M. Forster. Carrying one along the street and suddenly turning round can make people do all kinds of things. None of them to your advantage.

As for hotel security, forget it. All hotels are bristling with security systems, cameras, guards on every other floor, landmines in the bars and barbed wire around the dinner plates; invariably a complete waste of time. You want to talk to someone staying at the hotel. The switchboard refuses to give you the room number. Easy. You call laundry, tell them you're Mr So-and-so, ask whether your shirt is ready. Can they deliver it to whatever number comes into your head? They won't understand a word you're saying. You ask them to check their records, maybe they've got you down for the wrong room. What number do they have? Bingo. Eight times out of ten they give you the number.

You want to get to the room? In most hotels there's no problem. In some hotels, however, they have special security floors. To get to the floors you need a special security card which stops the lift at the floor you want. Easy. Get in the lift. Wait till somebody puts their security card in the slot, then very quickly pretend you're looking for your security card, you can't find it so you press the floor you want at the same time as they do. Zap, you're in.

So what about El/San Salvador, then? Do you agree? Shall we turn it into a tourist venue? Or shouldn't I make jokes about— Aaach! My kneecaps! My kneecaps!

Samarkand

Guidebooks. I know you're not going to believe this, but there was a time when I not only read guidebooks, I actually believed what they said. Then, of course, in order to make ends meet I was forced to start travelling for a living and – surprise, surprise – I discovered that the most fascinating thing in Seoul is not the Walker Sheraton dance spectacular; that US dollars are accepted in Burma or Myanmar – there is an American Express desk in the Foreign Exchange Bank; and that 'Best Sleaze Pick-up Bar' is most definitely not Roppongs in Tokyo.

I also very quickly realised that the Calico Textile Museum in Ahmedabad is not one of the best museums of its kind in the world, even though they use different-coloured drawing pins to fix the sign saying the toilet is out of action, and that there is no mention of Yukio Mishima, one of Japan's greatest writers, in the Japanese Museum of Modern Literature, the Tokyo Metropolitan Museum of Modern Japanese Literature, or even the Kanagawa Museum of Modern Literature.

As for hotels, there's no way you should stay at the Selecta Hotel on Basildon Island. It is no idyllic coral-fringed island; the waters are not crystal clear; there are no blood-red sunsets. Instead, take my word for it, it's the headquarters of the Islamic fundamentalist group Abn Sayaff. The only blood-red sunset I've ever seen was in Tiananmen Square.

And as for local customs, contrary to what one guidebook advised me, the Confucian culture of South Cholla Province is not the big deal it used to be with North Koreans. They would rather talk about McDonald's. Neither is it rude to point in the Philippines. One so-called expert guidebook told me in the Philippines not to point but to 'indicate discreetly by pointing pursed lips in the direction you want'. I tried it one night in a bar when asking for the toilet and ended up with every guy in the place following me back to my hotel.

I also discovered that nothing in Cancun, Mexico is 'white, dusty and untouched' – at least not thirty seconds after it arrived it isn't – and that Cambodia is not 'hell in a hand basket', full of thieves, pickpockets and worse. In fact, the biggest thieves I've ever come across are the writers and publishers of guidebooks. I mean, if travel broadens the mind how come these guys know so little and demand so much?

As a general principle I reckon Michelin is the best when it comes to telling you where to stay, Baedeker at telling you where to stay if that's not possible, and Lonely Planet at where not to stay under any possible circumstances. Fielding tells you what to buy. Frommer tells you where to get it at the best price. *Time Out* tells you where you can buy what you can't buy at duty free shops. Insight Guides list everything you can't possibly see if you were to stay a month of Sundays, the Rough Guides everything to see on a Friday or Saturday night, Berlitz how to blame the taxi driver if you get caught and Fodor what to tell the wife you did the whole boring weekend you were forced to be away.

My favourite guidebook? *The Chivas Regal Traveller's Guide*. Not because I read it, but because I no sooner pick it up than I feel thirsty. After that I couldn't care less where I stay, what I see or where I end up.

Take Samarkand, for example: one of the holy capitals of Islam; the Mirror of the World; the Garden of the Blessed; the Fourth Paradise; the most glorious place on earth; the capital of the Conqueror of the World; the symbol of Tamberlane's – Timur-the-Lame's as he is known locally – power, prestige and splendour. The holder of the world record for royal weddings, where for a whole month 20,000 guests would feast on sheep's heads, horse croupes and tripe balls the size of a man's fist, and boozers were honoured members of society. Can you imagine it? Instead of reproving looks from the wife, they were hailed as 'bahadur', given a string of titles and a seat of honour – providing they didn't fall off it in a heap. As if that is not enough, Samarkand is also the dream city of Goethe, Handel, Marlowe, Keats and Neil Copson, a Liverpool businessman I know. 'Samarkand,' he sighs when he is not complaining about his back, his ears, his eyes or his latest client. 'One day I will go to Samarkand.'

According to the books, Samarkand, an oasis on the Zarasfshan river, has been inhabited for 40,000 years. It is choc-a-bloc with big noble houses, mansions and palaces. Everywhere there are exotic fruit trees. The place is dripping with gold, silver and jewels. Warehouses are packed with rugs, spices and giant bales of silk. One of the major pit stops on the legendary Silk Road, if not the most important, it is famous for its glass, its fine paper, its rich craftsmanship. Its schools are known all over the world. From the age of five boys study reading, writing and business management. By seven they all have MBAs. People drink from gold beakers, eat from gold plates and are treated in golden surgeries for gold poisoning. Oh yes and, of course, all the domes and minarets, all the mosques and madrasas, all the rich, intricate, colourful mosaics, all that turquoise and gold and royal blue. The delicate spring greens, the deep sapphires, the amethysts. The silhouettes. The golden haze. The twilight. The dying sun.

For years, in between dreaming of riding along the South Downs Way, getting a drink out of my brother-in-law and going to Petra, my diseased imagination would fix not just on the golden roads to the place but the place itself.

From Persia, from Syria, from Turkey, from Iran, from Russia, and from India, where he left behind five million dead, Timur-the-Lame brought back scholars, theologians, musicians, craftsmen, mathematicians, astronomers. Even businessmen. Before him, Genghis Khan came, saw and smashed the place to pieces. Not Timur-the-Lame. He came, saw and built as many buildings as he could. For somebody else to smash to pieces. Wherever, whatever he pillaged, back everything went to Samarkand. Also back to Samarkand went the men to do the job: bricklayers, tile makers, mosaic workers, ninety elephants from India and, the lowest of the low, the architects. Up went mosques and madrasas and mausoleums. And, of course, whenever he got back from a business trip, Timur-the-Lame did what any self-respecting businessman does if who is having building work carried out. He checked how his money was being wasted and how far behind they were with the work. If he liked what he saw, he would throw them a few chunks of fresh meat and tell them to get on with it. If he didn't, he would flog a couple of slaves, bribe some craftsmen, throw them some more chunks of meat as an incentive to get on with it and, the dream of anybody having building work done anywhere today, hang the architect. Slowly. In front of the building he had loused up. Then he was off again on another trip.

Some say he did it because he was as ugly as the sins he committed. He had one eye. His right leg and arm were crippled. He was supposed to be the ugliest man in the Muslim equivalent of Christendom. It is said that he once saw himself in the mirror and went bananas. God, or rather Allah, knows what he would have done if he had seen his picture in the *Sun*, the *People* and the *News of the World*. Others say he did it because he was a good Muslim who wanted to honour and glorify God. The fact that most of the buildings he put up are covered in humble, respectful prayers along the lines of 'You think I was the no-good, blood thirsty, son of a Mongol bitch and a Turkish dog so how come I could build this then?' makes me doubt it.

My theory is that, like all good dictators, having first signed up his PR man (Christopher Marlowe) to keep his name in the quality papers, he did it to keep everybody out of mischief. If you've got a 135-foot-high triumphal archway to finish by lunchtime, you ain't got no time to plot the overthrow of the tealady, let alone the Most High, the Most Glorious Builder the World has ever seen and the Scourge of God Himself.

As I read more up-to-date books, the picture changed. Samarkand, I was now convinced, was a dust-filled wasteland, a heap of sand in the middle of nowhere, fringed by a pale host of mosques and madrasas. A few ramshackle buildings, the occasional camel lumbering through, tufts of grass blowing in the wind. Lurking behind every palm tree a crazed fanatic with a long curled knife ready to leap out on any passing infidel and stab him to death. The book that particularly put me off the place was Colin Thubron's *Lost Heart of Asia*. According to him everything was faience this, faience that or faience the other. There were faience phoenixes, faience curtains, faience ribs, faience tears. There was pure faience, faience life and probably faience cheese and onion sandwiches in the faience boozer. By the time I got halfway through it – I only read half because I'm semi-literate – I wished he'd jump in the faience river and put us all out of our faience misery.

So what was it like when I finally got there? Nothing like they faience say in their faience books.

Samarkand is a semi-modern, semi-thriving, half-empty Russian-style ex-Soviet Legoland mess, full of broken-down cars, broken pipes and broken Soviet promises, with three or four spectacular blobs of history thrown in. As for being dust-filled, the only dust-filled things are the faces of travel writers who do their research in libraries instead of in the real world. Samarkand was a kind of smudgy grey: the people, the houses, the streets, even the eggs they serve for breakfast in the hotel. And to get there, all I did was get a bus. Apart from some guy riding shotgun with a plastic shopping bag full of rusty spanners, and a couple of holdups because the fanbelt snapped, it was no more exciting or dangerous than getting the bus from Buxted to Crowborough in the morning because British Rail have still not re-opened the line into London.

If there is a golden road to Samarkand, it is paved with fibs. I don't just mean the modern guidebook fibs. Take the great Marco Polo himself. Or, as my Irish geography teacher used to call him, Mark O'Polo. He writes about Samarkand. But I don't reckon he ever went there. As far as I'm concerned it's the one big hole in his book. First, because Samarkand seems to be way off the route he says he took from Palestine to Peking. Even for somebody who says he travelled further north than the north star. Second, apart from saying it's a 'large and splendid city' he doesn't go into any further detail, which is not what you would expect from a man whose eye for detail was such that he travelled through China for years without once noting how much they enjoyed their cup of tea. Third because he doesn't once use the word faience. But him I can forgive. He was a businessman. He was probably rushing around trying to do too much, like the rest of us, desperate to get home before the wife started complaining again about him being away all the time. Then there was Flecker with all this Golden Road stuff. But him I can also forgive. It's a great old-fashioned poem, great for reading out loud, slumped in the desert sand in the middle of the night after having drunk too much Chivas. Again.

The people I can't forgive are the so-called professional travel writers. If there was any justice in the world, these guys who scissor and paste their books together owe me a fortune for the money I've wasted on them over the years. To me, they are all thesaurus and no experience. Like wine writers and music critics. In fact, instead of travel writers grandly awarding stars to whatever they fancy, I reckon there should be some way we can award raspberries to travel writers.

Take the Registran, or forum, or town square, depending on which guidebook you foolishly bought. Years ago Lord Curzon called it 'the noblest public square in the world'. Here was a man who carried an inflatable rubber bath with him wherever he went, so I can only assume he was an experienced traveller and knew what he was talking about. Now it may no longer be the noblest square in the world but it is still quite impressive. Breathtaking, almost. Nowhere have I seen such a mass of sparkling, intricate, almost delicate blue, green and gold mosaics spread across such an enormous expanse of buildings. To me it's the Muslim equivalent of St Peter's, Rome,

St Mark's, Venice, and St Peter and Paul's in Vilnius, rolled together in one. Facing the Registran on three sides are madrasas – theological colleges or training schools for Islamic fundamentalists, depending on which newspaper you read.

What do the guidebooks say? 'Round its old market square, the Registran, are three madrasas ranked in near-perfect symmetry. It was almost deserted,' wrote Thubron. 'Once the centre of the world, it was now the centre of nothing.'

Market square! It's not a market square. It's the town centre, the equivalent of the Roman forum. Centre of nothing! The place was packed with people: locals strolling about; tourists gawping up at the mosaics and asking why the Nazi symbol was plastered all over the place; shopkeepers trying to push carpets; policemen trying to sell off chunks of the buildings as souvenirs. Facing the whole thing is one vast bank of nine rows of plastic seats capable of accommodating over 1,000 people for Soviet-style Son et Lumières. As for near-perfect symmetry, no way. Apart from the minor grammatical point that you either have perfect symmetry or you don't – there is no such thing as near-perfect symmetry – one building has a dome on one side but not on the other; one has two towers but not the others; and one is bigger and higher than the others. If that is symmetrical our scissors-and-paste experts should get a new bit of sticky tape to wrap around their glasses. Unless I missed something through the traffic fumes created by the non-existent traffic.

Sit on one of the almost empty 1,000-odd plastic seats. In front of you, the size of your average cathedral, is the Tilla Kari madrasa, famous throughout the world precisely because it is not symmetrical. It has only one dome, on the left. Go through the main door and you're inside a courtyard. Around the courtyard, there should be four blocks. Instead there's only one. Again, how that can be perfect or near-perfect symmetry beats me. Tucked away on the left is the Tilla Kari Mosque, the Golden Mosque, which was a last-minute decision of the ruler. It's some afterthought. Inside, you immediately look up. There is this fantastic dome, dripping with gold. It looks like a dome.

It's shaped like a dome. It's decorated like a dome. But it isn't. It's all a glorious Islamic practical joke, for it's a flat ceiling decorated and shaded with gilded leaves and flowers to look like a dome. Nice one, Mohammed. The rest of the building, which is about the size of a small cathedral, is a mass of blues and golds.

When Geoffrey Moorhouse dropped by he clasped his hands and gasped. 'Here was a richness of colour greater than I had ever seen anywhere before, a splendour of red beyond the opulence of rubies . . .'

No way, Geoff. You're either doing a Marco Polo or you need to get a colour blindness test. There is no red in the place whatsoever. At the time the mosque was built the only place producing red pigment was Greece and there was no way, Silk Road or no Silk Road, red pigment could have found its way to Samarkand. Orange, a dark, browny orange, yes. But not red.

The awful crying shame is that the Golden Mosque is falling apart quicker than the rest of the buildings. Not only is age taking its toll, but so are the results of the old Soviet dash to turn the area around Samarkand into the world's largest cotton plantation. In order to boost production they put in enormous irrigation channels which have affected the water table throughout the region. The result is unbelievable subsidence. Half the mosque is beginning to fall away from the other half. The whole length of the far side there is an enormous crack down one wall, all along the floor and back up the facing wall. And nobody can do anything about it. In the old days of the Soviet Union, the Russians pumped in archaeologists and cash to keep it and all the famous buildings in Samarkand in good repair. Today, with the Soviet Union gone, the Russians are no longer at their Uzbech and call. They have to stand on their own feet, and even though Uzbechistan is the third largest country in the old Soviet bloc after Russia and the Ukraine, they haven't got the money. What about UNESCO? Apparently to get money out of UNESCO you have to be a member and pay the dues. Uzbechistan is not a member because they are scared that if they scrape together enough to pay the subs they won't get their money back – and more – to pay for the restoration needed to keep things going. They think it will disappear into some vast UN-type machine and end up helping to pay for first-class air tickets for a bunch of over-paid bureaucrats.

I fight my way through the crowds back out to the near-deserted centre of nothing. On the left-hand side is the Ulug Bek madrasa, built around 1417–20. It stands gleaming in dark blues, light blues, yellows and greens. To the guidebooks, however, it is simply 'an ancient seminary decorated with a mosaic of stars over its enormous pishtak or portico'. This is the one built by Timur-the-Lame's grandson, Ulug Bek, an astronomer who was using the stars to calculate the length of a year to within a couple of seconds, two hundred years before Copernicus was thought of.

'The original decoration is still in place,' say the books. Still in place! Great chunks of it have dropped off. There's bricks, tiles, plaster, everywhere. Balconies are crumbling. In fact it was so bad none of the hundreds of people in Thubron's near-deserted centre of nothing were allowed in.

On the right-hand side facing it is the Shir Dor madrasa. It is supposed to be exactly the same as Ulug Bek, but it isn't. It's bigger and taller. It also sports mosaic lions which, say the guidebooks, are completely at odds with the Koran and all Muslim traditions. Wrong again. It must be obvious to anyone who has stumbled across *The Satanic Verses* in the local bookshop and very quickly passed over it as if it wasn't there, that the Muslims are no more a united church than the Church of England. The Shiites believe in decorations. The Sunni Muslims don't. The Shir Dor madrasa has decorations. The Ulug Bek doesn't.

The guidebooks also say that in colonial times it was a Russian hotel. They are talking out of the backs of their heads. It was a refugee camp for Russians evacuated during the last war, and I very much doubt it was anything like a hotel. Even an Intourist hotel.

After the Registran, the next almost deserted place to see is the crowded Gur Emir, the Ruler's Tomb, the burial place of the great Timur-the-Lame himself. Originally intended to be a mausoleum for his favourite grandson, the Crown Prince Mohammed Sultan, who was killed in the Battle of Persia in 1403, it ended up by being his own. He was on his way to bringing his own particular brand of the Pax Mongolica to China when, according to the graphic description of one of his doctors, he started coughing up his guts 'like a strangled camel dragged backwards with the rein'. That was it. Timur-the-Lame was now Timur-the-Dead.

Some books refer to it as his mausoleum. Others say it is his family's mausoleum, where 'cenotaphs of his family lie side by side'. Timur-the-Lame's was made of the largest block of jade in the world which split when Persian soldiers hacked at it two and a half centuries later.

Wrong, wrong, and wrong again. The Gur Emir is Timur-the-Lame's burial place. Well, they had to get something right. In any case it says so over the door: 'The Illustrious and Merciful Monarch, the Great Sultan, the Most Mighty Warrior, Conqueror of the World'. Which I think is a bit rich, bearing in mind he was responsible for the deaths of 17 million men, women and children, many with the utmost cruelty and indescribable brutality. Not to mention all the architects. But as far as I'm concerned they deserved everything they got. But it is also the burial place of various officials and retainers, his personal adviser and, stuck out in a far corner all by himself, some poor unknown soldier with what looks like a twenty-foot wooden stake through his head with a horse's tail hanging from the top.

The cenotaphs don't lie side by side, they are in three rows. They are not of his family. His adviser is actually in pride of place all by himself at the top. Timur-the-Lame is, in fact, at his feet. The block of jade was not split when in 1740 Persian soldiers under Nadir Shah hacked at it. It split when they tried to do unto Timur-the-Dead what Timur-the-Lame had done unto half the world, and take it home with them. They didn't realise it was in three pieces, so when they began to lift it the top slab broke; so they dropped everything and ran for cover. Since then, say some books, it has remained undisturbed, which of course is not true. The slabs have been patched up. What has broken off has been filled in with cement. In any case, drop the policeman on the door a couple of dollars and you can have a small chunk of your own to take home.

One book goes on about how, right across the interior of the dome, 'fanned a net of gilded stucco, which twined upon itself in mathematical delicacy dropping its golden creepers over the enormous spandrels, bays and pendentives and shed a soft blaze of light on to everything below'. What they don't say, either because they don't know or they couldn't find enough treacly words to say it, is that the dome is the first example in the world of prefabricated construction. Instead of doing the Michelangelo stuff and lying on your back for months on end, the decorations were prepared at ground level, taken up section by section and fitted together inside the dome.

Then there is the howling business. Thubron merely says, 'For a year after his interment, it was said, people heard him howling from the earth.' That's it. No explanation. Not even a guess at the reason behind it. It'll tell you why he was howling. He was crying out in protest at the poor quality of the building, because they didn't use the egg yolks and camel's milk he sent them to harden the bricks, and because he couldn't get his hands on the architect. After a year the howling stopped. Legend says it was when all the architects and craftsmen were released and allowed to go back to their homes to do their worst on their fellow men. I reckon it was when poor old Timur-the-Half-Dead realised that after a year of complaining to the Disciplinary Committee of the Royal Institute of British Architects even he wasn't getting anywhere, and like the rest of us who've had problems with builders he just gave up in eternal despair.

Finally, the legend of the tomb. Inside, etched around the top, are words to the effect: 'Lay one finger on me and I'll make you live to regret it.' Local people, as a result, feared that if Timur-the-Lame was ever moved the world would tremble. And what happened when, on 20 June 1941, in the pitch-black early morning for fear of upsetting local people, a group of Soviet archaeologists led by Michail Gerasimov dug down in the far right-hand corner of the mausoleum, entered the crypt beneath and took away the body for examination? Twenty-four hours later the Nazis invaded Russia.

Some books, to be fair, mention bits of the story, but they can never seem to agree on the date; on whether Gerasimov is an archaeologist or an anthropologist; on whether they simply broke into the empty tomb or entered the crypt; in which corner they dug down; on whether they took the body away and whether pigs have wings. And not one of them mentions the no doubt boring fact that Gerasimov was one of the archaeologists who helped piece together the only portrait we have of Rasputin.

All I know is, nobody is going to touch that thing again for fear of setting off World War Three. Well, you never know, do you?

Now we come to what's known as the Shah-i-Zinda Ensemble, which when I first read about it I thought was an Uzbechi string Quartet. As it happens it's where Timur-the-Lame buried all his women, and one or two others as well. Up thirty-six steps and you're in the Street of the Dead. You have to count every step, say the books, and get it right, otherwise you won't go to heaven. I made it thirty-nine, which tells you what type of books I read when I was young.

First on the left is the mausoleum of Emir Hussein, an ancestor of Timur-the-Lame – at least, that's what the guide-books say. Opposite is the Emir Zade mausoleum. Further along are the mausoleums for some of the women in Timur-the-Lame's life. On the left, the Shadi Malk Aka mausoleum to commemorate one of his nine wives and one of his daughters. The books simply say it is a 'tour de force'. Nowhere else in the world of ceramic art is there anything like it. In fact it seems pretty much the kind of mausoleum anyone would be more than prepared to build for one of their wives. Opposite is the Shirin Bika Aka mausoleum. Shirin, say the books, was one of Timur-the-Lame's nieces. The cupola rests on what looks like a sixteen-sided drum. The decoration is supposed to be Chinese or Chinese-influenced, depending on which book you were overcharged for at which airport. Further along on the left come three more mausoleums (or mausolea, depending on which school you went to and how much attention you paid during Latin lessons). Just before the arch is the tomb of Emir Burunduk, one of Timur-the-Lame's generals.

Through the arch, near the end, on the left is the mausoleum of Tuman Aka, another of the great man's wives. Outside, for the first time, suddenly you see violet decorations. Inside it's completely white. Or it was; today it's dusty and crumbling away. There's a tiny landscape painted inside the cupola. Opposite is the Door of Paradise, originally encrusted with gold, silver and ivory, now plain wood and hanging off its hinges, which must mean something.

Through the Door of Paradise, and instead of bumping into St Peter, I met one of Timur-the-Lame's original old retainers with bump, bump, bump, a crutch under one arm and walking stick in the other, a light blue greasy turban and a long flowing white beard. Did he send me to join the sheep or the goats? Neither. All he wanted was his photograph taken. Then through the passageway, which was obviously once covered in tiles, into the Russian ibn-Abbus mausoleum and finally into the tomb itself.

In the mihrab or niche or alcove on the western wall there is the slightest sign of soot on the wall. Ha ha, claim the guidebooks. This proves that in spite of everything the Arabs did when they conquered Samarkand way back in the eighth, ninth or tenth century, the locals, hidden away from the rest of the world, stuck to their Zoroastrian beliefs and continued to worship fire. No way. It means that people everywhere who want to commemorate or honour their ancestors light either a fire or, more conveniently, a candle. But you wouldn't expect guidebooks to understand something as simple as that, would you?

But if the guidebooks are wrong about Samarkand, no book has ever been right about Bukhara, which was at one time probably the most important staging post on the jumble of trading routes that criss-crossed Central Asia which some whoopy-do explorer in a designer jacket subsequently labelled the Silk Road although, as far as I'm concerned and I don't know anything about anything, calling a thousand different tracks and highways by the single name of the Silk Road is like calling every road between Land's End and John o'Groats the M1.

'A chalk-pale city, a mud-floored labyrinth ... ravines of brick and stucco ... occasionally a mangy Cerberus nested in an open doorway,' says Colin Thubron of Bukhara. He's out of his mind. Bukhara, which comes from either the Farsi word *buhara*, meaning source of knowledge, or the Sanskrit word *vihara*, meaning monastery – you pays your kopek and you takes your choice – is a Pillar of Islam and one of the holiest cities on earth. Not because of the natural piety of its inhabitants, the inspired preaching of its mullahs or the Wednesday morning market organised by the Muslim Women's Institute. But as a result of one of the most effective means of religious persuasion of all time: money. In 712 it was conquered by one Kutayba ibn Muslim. In order to get them to give up their fire-worshipping and switch to being Allah-fearing Muslims he decided that instead of them putting something in the plate they could put their hand in the plate instead. For attending Friday services at the mosque, he gave them two dirhams each. He also stuck a religious policeman in every home. The result, instant conversion and a habit of devout mosque-going that has lasted well over 1,000 years.

During the days of the Silk Road, Bukhara was choc-a-bloc with businessmen, merchants, camel drivers, camels and even, don't tell anyone, architects. Its warehouses were full of silk, brocade, cotton, carpets, gold and silver work. Its money market was the envy of the world with not a single derivatives fraud reported to the regulatory authorities. But it also had more than its unfair share of poets, artists and scholars. Its library was one of the most famous in the world.

Today it is still out of this world. If Samarkand has one or two historic blobs, Bukhara has them all over the place. If Samarkand has spectacular buildings crumbling into dust, Bukhara has them, in fantastic shape.

Trouble is the guidebooks still can't get it right. Most of them tell you to start at the Ark, or Fortress, or original Walled City, depending on which one you've wasted your money on, which is nonsense. The Ark is not why you go to Bukhara. It's interesting, but it's not the real thing. It's like going to Rome and starting with the English College. I always start my mosque/madrasa crawl at the Lyab-i-Khauz pool, go on to the Kalyan minaret and end up at the Ark or Fortress or original Walled City, depending on which book you wish you hadn't bought. It's the Muslim equivalent of wandering around Venice from St Mark's to Santa Maria della Salute. Or, if you like, checking out first the Confucian temple in Beijing and then the lama temple. The pool is great fun. It's surrounded by plane trees, under which, drinking shashlyk, plov, or just plain cups of chai, sits the open-air Bukhara equivalent of a London club. Here all the veterans of the town, ancient warriors with faces 1,000 years old, come to escape the wife, the constant nagging about having a shave, cutting the grass, repairing the hoover, and why can't they stay at home and watch television like all the other men in the town. Some of them look as though they rode with Timur-the-Lame himself: long pointed beards, leathery faces, crinkled old leathery riding boots. Some guidebooks call them 'turbaned neo-dervishes'. All I can say is, if they are 'turbaned neo-dervishes' I'm a one-eyed Rastafarian with a crush on Hildegaard von Bingen. Tucked away in the trees is a huge statue of Hodja Nasreddin, who some books say was a Robin Hood character. Any kid could have told them that, if anything, he is a Sancho Panza character. But that would be too easy, wouldn't it?

On the east side of the pool is the Nadir Divanbegi madrasa, built around 1620. One guidebook said it was all a mistake. It was really meant to be a caravanserai, a motel for camel riders. But when the khan declared it officially open he called it a madrasa so, as the khan never made a mistake, everybody had to rush around and turn it into a madrasa instead. But I couldn't find anybody to confirm the story. Certainly none of the old men around the pool had heard it, though most of them must have been around at the time. The guidebooks omit to point out the fantastic mosaics above the main entrance: there is the sun with a Mongol face; there are two strange birds; there is a goat. Like the mosaics in the Registran in Samarkand, these are not completely contrary to all Muslim teaching, only to Sunni teaching.

Opposite, on the west side, is a khanaga, a hostel for wandering dervishes. Today, however, it's an exhibition hall. On the north side is the Kukeldash madrasa, the biggest in Bukhara, with over 150 cells or rooms and an enormous courtyard inside. One book I saw had it down as a hotel. If it is, when I got there it had been closed for years.

From the pool and Hodja Nasreddin and the old men and their tales of raping and pillaging the length and breadth of Asia, I like nothing better than wandering through the mean Muslim backstreets. It really is like stepping back 1,000 years and living the life of a privileged Muslim. On the left, down a sidestreet, is the only synagogue in town. Straight ahead you come to the Taq-i-Sarrafan, the moneychangers' bazaar. Then there is the Magok-i-Attari mosque. Magok means pit, so you have to clamber down steps to what some books say is Central Asia's oldest mosque. Others say it was first a Buddhist temple, then a Zoroastrian temple. Today, however, it's a temple to carpets, which I suppose is no more surprising than wandering into St Paul's and finding it's virtually turned itself into an art gallery.

Along the street is the Tag-i-Telpag Furushon, the cap-makers' bazaar, where you can buy the best astrakhan hats and gold-embroidered skullcaps in Central Asia. That's not me speaking, that's the you-know-what. Me, I couldn't tell a good astrakhan hat from a bad one.

Past the semi-underground public baths, past the Abdullah Khan market, to the jewellers' bazaar; a quick right turn and you come to what is almost the equivalent of the Registran in Samarkand. On my left, the Ulug Bek madrasa, the oldest in Central Asia and the model for the much bigger, much more extravagant one built three years later in Samarkand. On my right, the Abdulaziz Khan madrasa, the newest in town.

The Ulug Bek madrasa in blue and white looks stern and mathematical. 'To strive for knowledge is the duty of every Muslim man and Muslim women,' it says, perhaps surprisingly; whether it includes reading a certain book by a certain Anglo-Indian author I have no idea.

The Abdulaziz Khan madrasa seems more relaxed. It is full of blues and greens and yellows. Over the pishtak or portico are – shock horror – a collection of phoenixes and birds with snakes' heads which is contrary to the principles of some branches of traditional Islamic art. Some guidebooks say it cost the artist his life, others that he was given an Arts Council grant. Which is worse, I hesitate to say.

Back through the jewellers' bazaar and along Ulitsa Kommunarov street to the Poi-Kayon plaza is another spectacle of spectacles: the Kalyan minaret, the famous Tower of Death. Nearly 50 metres high and 14 metres wide at the bottom, it was the tallest building in the world when it was completed way back in 1127. Anyone who has ever tried to cement one brick on top of another will also see it as a tribute to the bricklayer's art. For it features no less than fourteen different styles of fancy brickwork all the way up to the top. In its time it has been a minaret, a lighthouse, a place of, as one guidebook says, 'jaculation' – in other words of throwing common animals and unfaithful wives to their death – and, if another book is to be believed, the best place in town for peeping Abdullahs to catch the local townswomen without their veils, or probably anything else. Which may account for the fact that nobody is allowed up it any more, not even the mullahs.

From the tower is a bridge to the huge Kalyan mosque, which is almost the equal of the Bibi Khanym mosque in Samarkand, and can house up to 10,000 people. Originally built in the twelfth century, it was practically destroyed by the Mongols, then rebuilt in 1514–15. The courtyard is huge, about 125 metres by 80 metres. Around it is a colonnade of 288 cupolas resting on almost as many columns. At the far end is a hugh blue dome with a stork's nest on top.

Opposite, across the plaza, is the Mir-i-Arab madrasa, one of only two actual working madrasas allowed in the whole of the old Soviet Union. Built in 1535, today it houses 300 students; up from just sixteen in the days of the Soviets. According to which guidebook you read, it was built by a holy man, an architect, or a businessman who paid for it with the sale of anything between 1,000 and 5,000 Persians or Shiites enslaved for belonging to the wrong Muslim sect, or just being in the wrong place at the wrong time.

A quick left-right into Samani Park. On the right is Chasma Ayub, the Spring of Jacob, which is supposed to possess miraculous powers of healing. Some books, however, call it the Spring of Job. Through a pretty little park, turn right, and there is the only thing in this world ever left standing by Genghis Khan: the tiny tenth-century mausoleum of the Somanid Dynasty, which could have been built by the Michelangelo of bricklaying. I'm no Winston Churchill but I have built the occasional brick wall in my time, so I can recognise a good piece of bricklaying when I see it. This, I must tell you, is bricklaying that's out of this world. Put one brick on top of another? These guys came up with no less than eighteen ways of putting one brick on top of the other. The result is to bricklaying what Manley Hopkins is to Jeffrey Archer. When Genghis Khan and his Mongol hordes swept in in 1220, however, on the way to some massacre, he only had two things in mind, and neither of them was shopping, though they did manage to grab a couple of souvenirs before, like a gang of English football fans, pulling the place apart – with the exception of the mausoleum. Apparently as soon as the great man saw it, he clambered off his horse and wandered inside for a last look. As he turned to leave the wind blew inside, caught his hat and blew it to the floor.

'OK, Genghis, shall we let it have it?' yelled the demolition men.

Genghis bent down to pick up his hat. 'No, no,' he is supposed to have said. 'This little building is the only thing in the world that has made the great Genghis bow down in front of it. It deserves to live.'

And so it did, or so I was told.

The guidebooks say that if you walk around it three times in an anti-clockwise direction and make a wish, it will come true. All I can say is, when I got back they were still there. The guidebooks, I mean. And the scissors-and-paste merchants are as busy as ever.

A stone, or I suppose a brick's throw away, is the Bolo Khauz mosque, built in the eighteenth century. Even though it only has twenty pillars, it is known as the Mosque of Forty Pillars. Why? Because they are reflected in the pool in front of it, that's why.

Finally there is the Ark or Fortress or original Walled City, which contains royal apartments, reception rooms, stables, mosques, a treasury, police department, prison and hovels for 3,000 people. Or did. It was destroyed again and again in the tenth, eleventh, thirteenth and twentieth centuries when, some guidebooks say, the last Emir, Alim Khan, set fire to the place himself as he finished packing and prepared to flee the Bolsheviks.

The gatehouse is more of a tunnel containing, on the left, tiny prison cells which boasted not running water but running muck and manure which used to seep down from the stables above. On top is the nagorakhara. Some guidebooks say it's where the emir's private orchestra entertained the local people. Others say it's where the emir and his family gathered to watch public executions. What none of them say is that the whole area was covered by a single carpet weighing over a ton. Also on top is a large seventeenth-century djuma or Friday mosque. The pillars are made of karagachi, which some guidebooks say is a rare sycamore-like wood. Others say there is nothing rare about it, it is just wood. One book doesn't bother to mention it at all.

South from the mosque is the open-air korunishkhana or audience chamber where the emir sat on a marble throne, and his retainers and hangers-on approached on all fours.

But do the guidebooks tell you all this? Of course not. Most of them can't tell their Lyab-i-Kauz from their Nari Divanbegi, let alone distinguish the Khanaga, the Kukeldash madrasa and the Magok-i-Attari mosque. To most of them the Tag-i-Telpag Furushon is where you can buy skullcaps, the Ulug Bek and Abdulaziz Khan madrasas are where you can buy cheap postcards and the Kalyan minaret is where you can get paintings for next to nothing. The Spring of Jacob they call the Spring of Job even though they go on to refer to him as an Old Testament prophet. The tiny Samari mausoleum they say is a good place to rest your feet and all they tell you about the Ark is that in over 2,000 years the most famous prisoners were both British.

As for the decline of Samarkand and Bukhara from being two of the world's most famous religious and trading cities to being simply overnight stops for package tourists on their way to and from China, all they say is, 'The empire of the dead conqueror was disintegrating. Its economy was too shallow to support it.'

Which, of course, is wrong, wrong and wrong again. The reason the empire was disintegrating had nothing to do with the economy being too shallow. It had all to do with Europe being able to build ships, which made the Silk Route suddenly redundant. Instead of hauling everything by camel for months on end over a mish-mash of tracks in the desert, a single ship could do the work of 1,000 ships of the desert. Zap, it was finished.

How do I know all the books are wrong? Because Noila and Inez and Ziran, the guides who took the scissors-and-paste merchants round Samarkand and Bukhara, told me so. What's more Inez said she was hopping mad. They printed her private telephone number without her permission. If she had lived in England, she told me, she would have sued them, because they ruined her life.

Beijing

I know this sounds crazy. But Beijing, the capital of way over a billion Chinese, the spiritual home of more than half a billion overseas Chinese, and the world headquarters of the Beijing Square Dancing Club, is no more Chinese than an 18-carat gold, self-winding, water-resistant Omega Seamaster Professional with fully functional push-buttons made in Taiwan.

The buildings, the offices, the factories, the hotels, the motorways, the streets, the traffic jams – all look, well, nondescript. Faceless. Neither here nor there. Like in Eastern Europe or small-town America or a thousand other nondescript, faceless, neither here nor there places on earth I can't quite recall at the moment. The people, of course, are Chinese. Or, at least, they look Chinese. Although I suppose they could be Ani, Dai, Jinou or any other of the fifty-two ethnic groups that make up the People's Republic of China. The signs and the advertising are in Chinese, although a fair slice of them are in English, including most of the big road signs. But apart from that and the occasional pagoda-style turned-up roof, the whole feeling, ambience, atmosphere, mood of the place is definitely not, not to put too fine a glaze on it, China at all. In fact, Beijing I reckon has been subject to the biggest take-away in Chinese history. The Chinese have taken away all their old buildings and replaced them with great ungainly slabs of concrete. As for Turandot, I have news for him. The reason none shall sleep in old Beijing tonight, let alone any night, is because today everything stops for *chai*, the Chinese word for demolition. Every Ping, Pang, Pong in what was once the world's most horizontal city (nothing could be higher than the emperor's throne) is rushing around scrawling *chai* on anything with four walls and an up-turned roof, and two weeks later pulling it down and slapping up yet another monstrosity instead.

Gone, for example, are hundreds, maybe thousands of hutongs, those wonderful old traditional Chinese lanes and backstreets which used to forever echo to the pitter-patter of tiny feet (rats) – together with goodness knows how many traditional courtyard siheyuan houses, temples, bridges, ceremonial archways not to mention all those massive gateways and behind them the secret forests of willow, poplar, cypress and the exotic jujube and persimmon.

Gone is a huge swathe near Tiananmen Square which has been massacred, if that is the right word, to make way for an enormous office and shopping complex financed by Li Ka-shing, one of Hong Kong's mega-mega-rich obviously hoping to gain Brownie points from someone after 1997.

Gone is the Jixiang Theatre off Beijing's biggest shopping street, Wangfujing (for many the most famous opera house in the country, but not for me; to me Chinese opera is simply the Great Wail of China). In its place is coming a seventeen-storey shopping and office complex.

Gone, in downtown Xuanwa District, is the old Beijing Huizhong Hotel. Two months, that's all it took for the authorities to give the go-ahead for it to come down, and for it to be replaced by a top-class hotel, an eight-storey shopping mall and another seventeen-storey office block.

Gone is the Central Academy of Fine Arts, to be replaced by another – you got it – shopping mall.

Gone, or soon to be gone, even though it is less than halfway through an unbreakable twenty-year lease, is probably the most famous building in the city, the McDonald's also on Wangfujing. The biggest McDonald's in the world. A shrine to China's open-door policy. An icon for every Western-oriented Chinese kid who, in spite of all the problems and distractions of modern youth, has managed to bring his aged Maoist parents up properly so that he has all the money he needs to go there as often as he wants. It is within firing range of Tiananmen Square, seats 700 people and is constantly full. But if the developers say it's disposable, it's disposable, whatever the lease says.

Gee whiz, they even want to build on the site of Britain's only victory in Beijing, where in spite of the assistance of the French we burnt the old Summer Palace to the ground.

In fact, there are so many cranes and cement mixers ploughing up and down the Avenue of Eternal Peace all day long, I reckon it won't be long before it becomes the Avenue of Eternal Construction.

Today in Beijing there are no coolie hats, no rickshaws, and hardly any bicycles. Not like in Ho Chi Minh City, say, or Dhaka, where there are still millions in every high street, side street and back alley.

Gone are the little old ladies, bent double with yokes, staggering around carrying half the world on their shoulders. Gone are the old men who used to take their pet goldfish or budgie or whatever for a walk in its cage every morning. Usually in the middle of the street I was desperately trying to drive down in order to get to my first meeting on time.

Gone are all the people you used to see sitting outside their houses on tiny bamboo stools or squatting on the ground chatting, playing mahjongg, smoking a smokie, sharpening knives, selling prune juice, banging brass cups and drums and generally being Chinese.

Gone are all the loudspeakers in the streets and the sirens telling everybody to kill the nearest dog or cat or sparrow. Gone is the 168-hour Chinese working week, which used to run from one minute after midnight on Sunday non-stop till one minute before midnight the following Sunday. Instead the government is introducing the Chinese weekend. Not because they want everybody to have a day off, but because having got the big, heavy industrial sector firing on all twenty-seven cylinders they now want to get the consumer industry going as well. What better way of doing it, therefore, than giving people the weekend off? Just think what that will do for the wallpaper manufacturers, the paint industry and all those Chinese DIY companies.

Gone are all the seedy hotels, bars and nightclubs where old men used to hustle opium and young men anything you fancied. The hotels are now modern, friendly and very pleasant, even though everyone seems to be wearing a badge saying Tray Nee. The marble floors are highly polished. The chandeliers work. Wake-up calls come when you book them. Taxis arrive when you want them. And roof restaurants are roof restaurants, not places where people have something to eat while keeping an eye on things or waiting for a signal to move into Tiananmen Square. The bars are now full of one-time Red Guards slugging back the Tsingtao beer with their snake and chips before heading off to the nearest karaoke which, as far as I could tell, was always round the corner no matter which bar you were in or which corner you were around. And nightclubs! Today there are more nightclubs in Beijing than there ever were political education centres, where, in a complete break with their past, thousands and thousands of ordinary Chinese men and women are packed like sardines into tiny, dark, airless rooms and subjected non-stop to the same unending series of meaningless phrases.

Finally, gone are all the dogs. Well, almost. When it comes to dogs, the Chinese are barking mad. In Britain if a dog bites a human, especially if it's a rottweiler, it makes the evening news and everybody hollers for it to be put down. In Beijing so many dogs are going around biting humans, presumably getting their own back for so many humans going around eating dogs, the authorities decided there was only one way to solve the problem: eat all the dogs. They slapped a complete ban on dogs within the city limits. Trouble was they couldn't make it stick. Some Chinese actually liked their dogs as pets rather than as lunch. They then banned dogs from going out in daylight: they had to be exercised at night and owners had to take pooper scoopers with them. Now even that's not working so, last time I was there, they were planning to introduce dog licences.

As for that classless, sexless, shapeless symbol of the revolution, the Chairman Mao suit, that's practically gone as well. Occasionally you glimpse an old revolutionary wearing one. But that I reckon is more a tribute to the long-lasting quality of Chinese textiles than to the long-lasting fabric of Chinese society. After all those years of uniformity, in an effort to exert their individuality everybody now wears jeans, T-shirts, leather jackets, suits, collars and ties, and for the women, T-shirts, leather jackets, US$1,000 Italian suits, collars and ties, and drives around in BMWs or Mercedes waving their mobile telephones.

The only way you can tell you're in China nowadays is by the woks you see fitted on nearly every outside wall and roof, which the clever Chinese have managed to convert into satellite dishes for receiving overseas television programmes.

Which isn't fair. First because I always assumed China was China. Tokyo is still Tokyo, Paris is still Paris, New York is still New York, Budleigh Salterton is still Budleigh Salterton. Of all places, I was convinced China would be the last to surrender its natural identity. Second because, obviously wrongly (see, the wife was right, I do make mistakes), I assumed that Chairman Mao, one of the most powerful men who have ever lived, dominated the place so much that it would take 1,000 years to remove all traces of his existence. Yet in Beijing he is yesterday's revolutionary newspaper. There are almost no Maomorials to the great man apart from maybe the occasional centenary plate gathering dust in the back of a shop along that road at the back of the big Friendship Store. There are no Chairman Mao Squares, no Chairman Mao Boulevards, no Chairman Mao back lanes. Occasionally, I admit, you still see the odd statue – but only, as far as I could tell, in university courtyards. And all of them looked as though they had tears running down their cheeks. Which to me is odd. Very odd. I know he made enormous mistakes and ended up by being totally disgraced, as any man is who takes advice from his wife, but you'd have thought he would not have been almost obliterated so quickly. Gee whiz, there are more Chairman

Mao badges in the Brighton Museum Art Gallery than in the whole of China.

In fact, taking everything into account, I reckon our local take-away in Heathfield is more Chinese than Beijing. You don't believe me? I'll tell you how un-Chinese China is today. I couldn't find a laundry anywhere.

The state controlled straitjacket has been cast aside along with the Chairman Mao suits. They're now as capitalist as hell. Everyone is hustling something, obviously in a desperate effort to ensure that somehow the struggling Chinese economy maintains its staggering 12 per cent annual growth rate.

'Lookee, lookee, good plice. I give you good plice, yes?' In the old daysee, daysee – I mean, in the old days the Chinese were the oldest, doziest, most uninterested salesmen in the world. Go into a shop to buy deep fried caterpillars or underdone scorpions for lunch, nobody wanted to serve you. Today everybody is selling something: the young, the middle-aged and the old. Especially the old. There are over 117 million people in China aged sixty years and over and I reckon every one of them has tried to sell me a cheap silk shirt at some time or other. In hotels, in reception areas, in shopping arcades, in the corridors to the lifts – practically in the lifts as well, wherever you go someone is trying to sell you something. Even – a dramatic departure from the old days – in the shops.

On almost every street corner, and on all the straight bits, are hundreds, thousands – no, millions of Foo Ling Yews selling every type of goods and services you can think of and some it's best not to think of at all: silk, cashmere, jade, seals with your name in English and Chinese, assorted selections of antelope tendons, pigs' stomachs, tortoise intestines. To name but the most acceptable. They are even selling off, if not the family silver, the family itself. In one store they were actually selling original portraits of not only the Dowager Empress Gxi but of ten Qing Dynasty emperors as well. And no, it wasn't a Reject China shop, although I suppose it could have been.

It's the same in the food markets, which are like French

food markets except that nobody pushes in front of you. They are choc-a-bloc with the most amazing shapes and sizes. The food, I mean. Not the old women slopping the stuff out. There's frogs, tortoises, eels, spiced donkey meat, suckling pigeon, soft juicy rashers of dog, snakes' intestines, beetles' eyelashes, rats' tails and the most foul-looking concoction I've ever seen in my life which turned out to be a vegetable omelette. As if that's not bad enough they're doing the most amazing things to the food: pulling the legs off frogs, skinning eels, cramming millions of tiny worms into what look like old coffee jars, popping rabbits' eyes into dustbins, eating cockles and mussels without vinegar. And they're doing all this while the poor things are still alive, presumably to ensure that the food is sold in the freshest possible condition.

As for the proper shops, they are full of everything I can live without: smiling Buddhas hiding under tiny tortoise shells; Rokodile T-shirts; musical apples; fluffy pink dogs in a plastic heart; Great Wall of China cups and saucers; genuine Ding-Dong Dynasty bicycle bells; silk hats with built-in pigtails; 3-D pictures of the Great Wall of China made of velvet, cardboard boxes and 2.5 million matchsticks; tea towels – whatever they are; the Great Wall of China in a snowstorm in a plastic bubble the size of a football and silk shirts, silk shirts and still more genuine, Chinese, handmade, good quality, I-give-you-good-price silk shirts. But no matter how much they hustle me I refuse to buy silk shirts because I don't believe in supporting any industry that forces its workers to work all hours of the day and night in impossible conditions with total disregard for health or safety regulations. I mean the silkworms.

The supermarkets – there are now supermarkets in Beijing! – are well stocked. The fresh food is fresh and the frozen food is frozen, which wasn't always the case. Not so long ago, I was told, the frozen food was so fresh it practically got up and walked out of the door. The Chinese, being Chinese, ate the bits doing the walking and threw the rest away.

The big department stores might still look nineteenth-century but the selling is definitely twentieth-century. And I fear that in the book department in the Friendship Store on Jianguomenwia Dajie the collected works of Deng Xiaoping are outsold not only by Joan Collins but also by – shame of 1,000 eternal shames – Jeffrey Archer. Gee whiz, there's even a Rolls-Royce showroom in Beijing where ex-failed Red Guards are happy selling the arch-symbol of capitalism to their fellow ex-failed Red Guards.

And it's the same wherever you go. Like any businessman on a trip, I naturally try my best to avoid anything Forbidden. But for the Forbidden City I had to make an exception. For 500 years the centre of imperial power, until Peter O'Toole arrived on a bicycle with a dreadful Scottish accent and ruined everything, it's the biggest Forbidden thing I've ever seen. It covers a couple of dozen football pitches and contains exactly 999 rooms – nine is a lucky number for the Chinese. But to get anywhere near the place, you have to fight your way through stallholders, barrow boys, postcard merchants and great crowds queuing up for the sheer pleasure of having their hair cut by squads of outdoor freelance barbers; retired state barbers as well as freelances making extra money on the short back and sides.

Once inside, however, it was worth it. Especially to hear the story of the emperor who couldn't stand criticism. What did he do when he saw the peasants were revolting? He threw himself off the top floor of the nearest pagoda. Just imagine what the world would be like today if every political leader had the same principles.

It's the same at the Great Wall, which makes you weep when you think of the problems involved in getting a gold frame, let alone a conservatory built back home. Two thousand years old. A million miles long. Up hill down dale. It's unbelievable. But do you have time to absorb the atmosphere, appreciate the sheer stupidity of the thing? Do you hell. There are hustlers everywhere. At the foot of the wall, and all the way up the steps to the top; along just about every inch of the Wall itself. There's even a guy marching up and down with a loudspeaker selling certificates, in Chinese, which he will date and sign proving that you not only climbed the Great Wall but that you were a Big Big Charlie for buying the crummy certificate off him, especially at the price he was asking.

Although, to be fair, it's not all jungle. The Chinese are actually talking about un-Chinese things like value for money, honesty in advertising, protecting the consumer, honouring agreements, copyrights, patents and other silly things. The traditional wooden lever scales used by market traders all over China for over 2,000 years, for example, are being banned by the Municipal Finance and Trade Offices, by all Municipal Technical Supervision Bureaux and by the Administration for Industry and Commerce organisations.

Vegetables are no longer just a means of survival grown by full-time soldiers in the People's Liberation Army in complete contradiction of a mass of rules and regulations forbidding them from doing business. They are now sold with the producer's own trademark on them. Shoes are no longer made of cardboard. Beer bottles have stopped exploding like hand grenades. Liquor is no longer made with deadly methyl alcohol. And shop assistants are now forbidden by law to use such age-old traditional phrases as, 'I don't know,' 'If it's not on display we haven't got it' and 'Sorry, I'm busy. Can you ask someone else?'

Even restaurants, which in the old days used to be just good, bad and offal, are today being classified as good, bad and my God, what on earth is that? If you want to pig out on swine head braised in brown sauce and you want more ears, eyes and nose, no problem, sir, say when. Alternatively you might prefer offal stewed in chicken soup, offal braised in brown sauce, offal with tomato sauce or offal stewed with pork. If you want more entrails or intestines you can have it, and the Chinese will actually now guarantee you'll never get better.

Although what they'll do when they discover after all these years the Forbidden City only has 998 rooms and everybody wants their money back, I don't know.

As for patents, the Patent Administrative Bureau is busy suing everyone for any infringements they come across. When I was there they were celebrating their latest success. They had just forced two local plants and one joint venture to stop production of a whole range of air purifiers, destroy all their stock and apologise to Phillips publicly for infringing their patents.

To show you how bad, or rather how unChinese, they've become, they're training 1,000 new inspectors. They are talking about setting up a national network of film companies and cinemas to protect film copyright. The Supreme Court of the People has ruled that confiscating documents, snatching passports and kidnapping people and holding them for ransom even if they haven't paid their bills is wrong.

The legendary Chinese bureaucrats are also not only doing their thing, but doing it successfully. Tigers are being saved in the far north-east province of Liaoning. Smuggling has been banned. People dealing in tiger skins and bones are actually being arrested, charged and sent to prison. Food production is booming. Ansham, the big steel capital of north-east China, is now engraved on the stomach of anyone married to a vegetarian, for it has become the meat-eating capital of the world. Their farmers are doing such a grand job every red-blooded man, woman and child in the place is currently stacking away 47.5 kilograms of meat a year, nearly 10 per cent higher than the world average. With 1995 being the Year of the Pig, pig production is booming, although I suppose the pigs themselves are hoping their year will not be over that quickly.

The huge Taklimakan desert, the old Sea of Death, up in the north-west, the second largest desert in the world after the Sahara, is showing signs of life: some flora here, a bit of fauna there and no less than 277 different kinds of animals.

And their greatest success of all: cremation. When the communists took over in 1949 and Chiang Kai-Shek fled to Taiwan, nobody wanted to be cremated. Today they are dying for it and, according to the Chinese government statistical office, saving nearly 20,000 acres of land, three million cubic metres of timber and over US$1 billion every year. Who could possibly have imagined that would have been one of the great successes of communist rule?

What's even more frightening is that after all these years Chinese mandarins, who have never liked the idea of being named after an orange, have started telling jokes as well.

'Canton man come home for dinner. His wife give him table,' an official in the Ministry of Finance told me.

'Table,' I repeated nervously.

'Table,' he said triumphantly. 'Because Canton man eat anything with four legs. Yes?'

'Velly funny,' I said.

It's the same story in Shanghai, or Shankers, as we old China hands used to call it, which was the Sodom and Gomorrah of the Orient, the Paris of the East, the legendary city of a thousand brothels, a million dens dealing in what the Chinese called black mud and we call opium, gangsters driving around in bulletproof cars and furs so cheap even ordinary crooks would use them to keep their car engines warm in case they had to make a quick get-away. Some people say it was more decadent than Berlin, jazzier than New York and more crowded than Calcutta. But for Westerners only. The Chinese were not allowed to participate. One old China hand I know who hangs out in the Oriental Club in London swears there were signs in the parks saying 'No dogs or Chinese'.

Today after withering away for practically forty years – at one time Shanghai produced more films than Hollywood – the tortoise has become a hare. But a Western hare, not a Chinese one. The last coastal area to be opened up to the outside world (areas like Guangdong and Fujian had a ten-year start) it is now streaking ahead. Already China's principal port and the richest city in the country – it is the Dragon Head of the Yangtse river basin, which is home to over 300 million people – it covers just 1 per cent of China yet accounts for over 15 per cent of its revenue, and is growing at the rate of 15 per cent a year. Which to me is amazing. Judging by the sheer size and pace of the place, I'd have thought it would have been at least double that.

Some call it the third largest and greatest art deco city in the world, which is probably true. But to me the quality of the Mersey is not strained. Merely transferred. The bit in the centre, the Bund, the proud, granite waterfront boulevard, is right out of Liverpool. Even down to the beetles.

The Peace Hotel, slap bang in the middle of the Bund, is, I admit, an unbelievable art deco extravaganza, full of the Roaring Twenties. Originally Sassoon House, some say it was built on the backs of children working up to sixteen hours a day. In the days of the Cultural Revolution it was taken over by the Red Guards. One old retainer who looked as though he knew Sassoon when he was a boy, told me they didn't know how to behave. They never once used the restaurant, and totally ignored room service. They never once took coffee in the lounge. They ate, slept, drank and did all kinds of unmentionable things in the corridors. Today, however, it's back to normal. The corridors have been swept. Room service is back in business, although I never had a week to spare to try it out. And the whole place is a brilliant glare of 40-watt bulbs. But at least they've got bulbs, which is more than can be said for some Liverpool hotels. The view from the restaurant on the eighth floor across the waterfront to the huge red, white and blue Oriental Pearl Tower, the third highest in the world, is still spectacular, although by the time my meal arrived I knew it had been cooked by the Sassoons themselves.

Next door is the Bank of China, a seventeen-storey, stone-clad mix of art deco and traditional China drowned in soya sauce. Completed only in 1937 the long, main banking hall which is the safest place in town to change travellers cheques, has an enormous barrel-vaulted ceiling. The roof, however, is shaped like a pagoda with up-turned corners.

Further along is the old British consulate, which was obviously built when British consulates meant something more than cold tea, indifference, old school ties and Must-have-a-round-of-golf-sometime-old-chap.

Behind the Bund it is like a teenage Hong Kong: shops,

shops and still more shops. Not Hong Kong-type shops, Shanghai-type shops: the Cosmetology Haircut Company No. 57, the Mei Lee Women Articles Store, the Shanghai No. 7 Dispensary, The Shanghai No. 2 Optical Corporation, the Shanghai No. 3 Food Supply Corporation. There is even a shop called, in English, 'Pompous and Elegant. Your Ideal Home'. My dears, would you believe it! Virginia Water has come to Shanghai. And every single one of them is hustling like mad. One shop along Nanjing Road even has 'live' window displays, starting in the morning with hats and coats; dresses at lunchtime; swimsuits in the afternoon and I couldn't get near the place for the crowds to find out what was on display in the evening.

Live displays or not, the whole area is solid people – in the shops, outside on the pavements, blocking traffic; it's unbelievable. In 1937 a bomb went off in the Sincere department store in Nanjing Road. Over 500 people died. I hate to think what would happen if, God forbid, a similar thing happened today. Especially during the evening show.

On the pavements people are not just trying to push their way from one shop to another, they are repairing bicycles, cars, even office desks. Damn it, they are even queuing up to use the telephone. I went down one street and there, lined up outside an ordinary-looking home, were tables and chairs. On each table was a telephone. Because telephones are in such short supply, those who have them, especially those with more than their fair share, hire them out on a call-by-call basis.

In one bar I went into, they were serving what the menu said was Chicken Ting. I asked the waiter what it was.

'Chicken,' he said. 'We put it in microwave. Ting, it is ready.'

I got a cab to Pudong, which is virtually the second city within the city of Shanghai. Where, incidentally, the food was much better, because there wasn't so much of it. Years ago the journey would have taken two, maybe three hours on foot. Today, thanks to the new, 8,000-metre long Yangpu Bridge, it takes four, maybe five hours, such is the volume of traffic. But it was worth it. Pudong is not only one of the biggest construction sites in the world, it is also the world capital of brass plates. On every square inch of wall space where the cement has almost dried is a brass plate or three: Export Corporation; Construction, Decoration and Engineering Company; Supply Co; Trade Centre; Real Estate Company. I even saw a guy selling newspapers from a barrow, on the side of which was a brass plate: Newsstand Refrigeration Co.

Everywhere there are building sites, wickerwork safety helmets, bamboo poles and a million Chinese mixing sand and cement. Bridges, overhead inner ring roads, overhead outer ring roads; a new port, a new airport; power plants; a new underground system; another huge industrial zone. Offices, shopping centres, eighteen-storey car parks, hotels: there are over 5,000 building projects taking place in the city at any given time. In one year alone investment totalled over US$7 billion. Shanghai must be the only place in the world which has more surveyors and builders disappearing up their own atria than taxi drivers, let alone rickshaws.

And no matter where you go (if you can get there for the traffic), whether it's the Blue Heaven bar on the forty-third floor of Jinjiang Tower or the Get Rich Seafood Restaurant, famous for its savoury sea slugs, everybody is talking money, money, money, over breakfast, lunch and dinner. I once stopped a young man outside 76 Xingye Road, where in July 1921 around a table on the first floor a group of twelve angry young men sat down, drank tea and formed the Chinese Communist Party. I asked him the way to the Stock Exchange. He said he would tell me – if I paid him. Which shows you how far they've come in a short space of time.

You think the City of London is bad. When it comes to short-termism, the Shanghai Stock Market, I discovered when I finally got there, holds the world record. A return in two to three years? These guys don't just want to keep up with the Dow-Joneses, they want their money back before lunch. With profits. Or else.

Like the stock market in Shenzhen, it is based in an old Chinese theatre. Which must mean something or other. Unlike the one in Shenzhen, however, it holds the world record for high prices, the number of millionaires it has created, especially in 1992 and 1993, and the number of people it can pack onto the dealing floor. Which looks like a cross between the prize ticket exchange windows at the Beijing Horse Race Club on a Sunday afternoon packed with 'fun seekers' (they are not called gamblers, just as jockeys are not called jockeys; they're called, would you believe, intelligence testers. They test their intelligence against each other to see if they can guess which motheaten Mongolian pit pony is going to win the race) and Coates Wine Bar in London Wall on a Friday night in the old days when everybody was making money. Not for them all the agonies of the Stock Exchange Yellow Book and meeting after meeting while gaggles of lawyers argue about what the damn thing is supposed to say.

'Paragraph two, section four, sub-section 27 . . .'

'Little (a) or little (b)?'

'Little (b).'

'I hope you didn't mind me . . .'

'Not at all. It was a pleasure.'

'That's all right then. It's just that . . .'

'My dear chap, I assure you . . .'

'You're too kind.'

'Now where was I? Oh yes, paragraph 27, section two, sub-section . . .'

'. . . two . . .'

'. . . states quite clearly . . .'

Not for them the land of the fairies: trying to guess how many sub-sections would fit on top of a paragraph, and whether ringing your auntie in the Channel Isles from a public callbox in Wapping at 3.30 in the morning to gossip about why you couldn't ring earlier because of this takeover bid you're working on is insider trading or not. Not for them the gruelling late-night marathons trying to reach an agreement.

'I say, why don't we discuss this over a snifter at the club? Sun's over the yardarm, what.'

'I say, that's a good idea. Soon sort things out there.'

'Shoot?'

'Well, I do actually. Not awfully good though.'

'Tell you what, Bunty's coming down for the weekend. Come down as well and we'll have a couple of rounds.'

Not for them the little drinkie-poos in the downstairs bar at the Ritz where the finance director of Gin and Tonic up to My Eyeballs just happens to be talking to himself about this fantastic merger and how they managed to persuade the silly old duffer of a chairman of this company twice their size to sign on for next-to-nothing when – shock horror – who should be standing alongside him but this complete stranger of a City editor of a newspaper whom he has never seen before in his life since they had a drink together the previous evening in the Waldorf, when using information he had been given confidentially he put the knife in their intended victim and caused their shares to halve within minutes of the market opening that morning.

Not for them days out with the Duke of Beaufort's where the Rt Hon This of Moral Rectitude plc just happens to mention to Lord High Principles of Stockbrokers Unscrupulous that it would help jolly the old shares along a bit if some jolly old broker just happened to produce a rather whiz-bang report on them, and by the way, did he know anyone who could handle their pension fund. Not, of course, that the two are linked in any way.

In Shanghai things couldn't be simpler. The minimum purchase they accept, no matter what the regulations say about no minimum level, is US\$10,000. Maybe US\$5,000 if you're a good friend, but definitely nothing less, even if you tell them you're their long lost grandma. Dealing is as simple as ABC. Well, as simple as C-R-O-O-K-E-D to be precise. C shares are only available to Chinese citizens; R shares are local shares which foreigners can buy; OO shares are Chinese shares issued on the Hong Kong Stock Exchange; K shares listed on the London Stock Exchange and ED shares are shares of the odd one or two Chinese companies on the New York Stock Exchange.

As for the quality of their investment advice, on one visit I was strongly recommended, well practically shanghaied, arm-twisted and headbutted by a broker I'm sure was called Chee Ting Yew, into buying stock in a property development company selling land-use rights in the financial area of the city when prices were at their highest-ever levels. Another, far more civilised broker – 'Oh yes, old boy, do come in. Have a cup of tea, what?' – tried to cajole, threaten and then blackmail me into buying half the B shares in a washing-machine manufacturer, which he assured me was about to pick up a huge contract from the Ministry of Posts and Telecoms which would double, treble, quadruple its profits before its wheels even started spinning.

I was sorely tempted, but at the last minute I discovered a) they wouldn't accept a cheque, and b) there was the small matter of US\$25 to open a trading account; US\$20 every time I traded; another US\$10 a month if I wanted to deal by phone; stamp duty; some mysterious stock exchange charge which I didn't understand; and three more fees, which as far as I could gather were designed to keep the brokers in spring rolls, sweet and sour and soy sauce for a month. And even if I paid all that, they wouldn't send me a monthly statement showing how well my stock was doing.

'Not necessity,' the broker who was wearing a light green tracksuit with different coloured socks – one pale pink, the other light blue – told me. 'Stock always do well. No need check.'

And I had only popped into his office to avoid being hounded to death by a real live Chinese insurance sales-woman.

I was in the ABN Amro branch on the Bund with one of the managers, who obviously wanted to prove he was as Western as the next man. He had a red baseball cap on. Except it was too clean, on too straight and – shock horror – the peak was pointing forwards. As if that didn't make it difficult to concentrate, we kept being interrupted by agents pushing every kind of life assurance policy. Not that I'm an expert on life assurance. Being so young, that is. Finally, in through the door came a little old lady in a Western suit, smiling sweetly, with more chins that the Greater Shanghai telephone directory. She wanted to congratulate the manager on his birthday. Up he got to thank her, on two very good Chinese counts: first, she was a woman; second, she was offering him her good wishes. His baseball cap, however, remained firmly in place. Then – wham, bam – he was a goner. In two very capitalist seconds flat she slammed her thick black folder on his desk, ran her finger along a string of tables, convinced him he needed life assurance and signed him up. All in one go.

On my way out I spotted the sweet little old lady again. She was directing a team of sub-agents, with all the precision of what-was-his-name who led the Great March, to fan out throughout the building and sign up anything that moved.

'The boss, he buy insurance.' She darted towards me. 'Now everybody buy insurance.' Which is when I turned and, for the first time in my life, broke through a Chinese wall into the broker's office. To me, buying life insurance is not only crazy, it's the second sign of middle age.

That afternoon I was with a group of English businessmen. We had a meeting in Pudong, the modern half of Shanghai. In the taxi on the way there we were discussing the problems of doing business in the city and the short-term attitude of the Chinese.

'Short term,' the chairman of a big British public company, snorted. 'I'm retiring in three years' time. All I'm interested in is going while they're still standing up and applauding. After that it's somebody else's problem.' Then he fell asleep.

If the centre of Shanghai is old-fashioned, traditional, unbelievable China then Pudong is modern, up-to-date buildings all over the place, unbelievable China. The whole place is choked with traffic, yet that doesn't mean there are no accidents. Once, stuck without moving for a week on the way

341

to the big new exhibition centre, we were involved in three accidents. Two cyclists ran into the back of us even though we were stationary. The third accident happened when they started unloading the lorry in front of us. Because there was no room everybody kept walking across the bonnets of the cars. One unloader slipped and dropped a great pile of tin pans and plates over the front of the taxi, but nobody took any notice. The driver didn't even try to get out of the car. Which was probably just as well because we were jammed so tightly on all four sides he couldn't have opened the door. An emergency, as a result, is not a crash or an accident. It is when a trolley bus breaks down. Everybody then somehow gets out of the way, not for the police or the fire brigade but for the breakdown lorry.

Outside Shanghai, in the countryside, it's the exact opposite. If they drop a pile of pans and plates over your car they go chicken chow mein. Not because of the damage to the car, but because they can't sell the pans and plates. Well, not at their original price.

About the only place I came across that was still genuine old China was Xian, the walled city the Red Guards wanted to pull down before they decided to change sides and become stockbrokers in Shanghai instead. There everything was fast, fast, fast moving – and for sale. But the Chinese way, not the western way. Outside a shop selling tri-coloured glazed pottery of the Tang Dynasty which had a sign in the window saying 'They can be passed off as genuine', an old man was frantically chopping chickens' heads off, pouring the blood into a big chipped bowl and throwing the rest into a huge steaming pot. All along the main streets, down all the long, dark alleys, hundreds of cars and millions of bicycles were racing around. Old men were hobbling across the road. Rickshaws with complete homes stacked on the back were rushing about.

Out in the fields, where they grow more noodles than anywhere else in China, alongside a broken-down tractor which they cannot afford to run because of the price of petrol, a dozen wizened old women were stacking cabbages or guodong cai, food to survive the winter, at the speed of lightning. On the other side of the road peasants were rushing around tending their vegetables for all the world as if they were in the middle of rural China in the depths of the Ming Dynasty with no electricity or running water.

About thirty kilometres out of town was further evidence of the real thing: the hollow men of China – in other words, the Terracotta Warriors. I'm no expert on Chinese history – to me, it's just one Ming after another – but I must admit they are quite spectacular, although at first they did look like a bunch of non-executive directors lined up outside the chairman's office waiting to be told how to vote at the next board meeting. No guts, no brains. Nothing inside. I don't know about you but it also struck me as significant that a tomb built for so many people was reserved for men only. It's as if – and now I am being completely objective – they had decided they had been pestered enough by women in this world, they were determined not to be pestered by them in the next.

Whether you're in Beijing, Shanghai, Pudong or Xian, some things never change. One evening in Beijing, coming back to the hotel after seeing a rather catchy little Chinese opera called *Overturning the Armoured Vehicles*, I stumbled across the unknown army of what are politely known as soil collectors. Suffice to say they are to do with the fact that in spite of the enormous modern advances made by the Chinese, most houses are still not connected up to a sewage system.

As an old Chinaman said to me as we stood looking at the façade of the old Cercle Sportif Français in Shanghai (the rest of it is buried under the thirty-five-storey Garden Hotel): 'Prus ça chlange, prus c'est la même chlose.'

Windhoek

Mein Gott – das ist Afrika? I mean, this is Africa?

Everyone is polite, friendly, quiet, well-behaved. The streets are clean and tidy, the cars new or nearly new. They are driving calmly and sensibly along proper roads with proper pavements. Nobody is trying to cut anybody up, let alone overtake on the inside, on the outside or any side. Everybody stops at the lights. Pedestrians cross the road when the light tells them to. If you want a taxi you just get a taxi. There is no negotiating with half a dozen agents, sub-agents and sub-sub-agents. And the taxi doesn't have all its seats missing and half a dozen people already inside waiting to be driven all over town on your money.

At night – are you ready for this? – not only can you leave your hotel room, you can actually leave the hotel and wander around town without taking your life in your hands. Or putting it into somebody else's. Shop doorways are doorways, not homes to half a dozen families in cardboard boxes. The streets are not littered with people eating, drinking, living and, God help them, dying in the gutters. There are even signs in English saying, 'No loitering, begging, obstruction or harassment of public allowed. Offenders will be prosecuted.'

Meine Damen und Herren, willkommen to Windhoek, the capital of Namibia, although to all intents and purposes it could still be the capital of Deutsch-Sudwestafrika. For this, my brothers and sisters, I must tell you, is not the Afrika – oops, I mean Africa – we all know and love. This is Afrika

German-style. Which is as unlike any other part of Africa as it is possible to imagine.

First, the lay-out of the place. Running through the centre of town is Independence Avenue, which everybody still calls by its old name, Kaiserstrasse. On one side the official and administration buildings: on the other, shops, offices, restaurants, bars. High up on the official side, looking down on the city, is the gothic-style Christuskirche, an evangelical Lutheran church built in 1910 using local sandstone which looks as new today as it did the day it opened. Kaiser Wilhelm II himself donated the stained glass window above the altar. His wife gave the bible.

The parliament building designed and built three years later by the same man who built the church, Gottlieb Redecker, is still known locally as the Tintenpalast, the palace of ink, because of all the reports the Germans used to write there and send back to their masters in Berlin. *Plus ça change, plus c'est la même chose*. Or whatever it is in German.

Further along is the Alte Feste, the old German fort, the oldest building in town, which was thrown up very quickly in 1890 as headquarters of the local Schutztruppe, the German defence force. Thrown up! It's lasted twice – nay, ten times – as long and in far better condition than the buildings constructed all over Africa in the last ten years using the latest technology. Today it is supposed to be part of the state museum; as far as I'm concerned, it is the state museum.

Almost opposite is the original mess for the German military, Ludwig von Estorft Haus, named after the commander who ran the place from 1902 to 1910. Today the only food it dispenses is for the mind. It's the local reference library. A stone's throw away is another typische German building, built in 1905–06 as a residence for senior German officers and officials, which again looks as new as when it was first built. Probably because it is now home to the state ombudsman. And if he can't get things organised nobody can.

Wherever you look, everything looks German, breathes

Germany, is Germany. The Regierungschule, the old government school, with its funny pyramid-shaped tower, was built in 1911. Still its fancy weathervane is on top. Still it is working. Then there is Gatheman House with its funny pitched roof; the Schutztruppe Memorial unveiled in 1897 in Zoo Park; the Mädchenheim, built in 1914; the Hotel Kronprinz which dates back to 1902; the Pension Kleines Heim, ten minutes from the centre of town, an oasis of German tranquillity, built in 1911; the Hotel Fürstenhof, which won the African Chef of the Year Competition in 1993; the Thuringerhof and Hanse hotels which did not. They are all still there, still in perfect condition, still functioning. Still very much German.

Wander around the suburbs – if a town of 120,000 people can have suburbs. All the houses are smartly painted, their lawns immaculate, their hedges razor-sharp.

Most of the streetnames are German: Krupp Strasse, Daimler Strasse, Bulow Strasse, Srubel Strasse, Leutwein Strasse, Brahms Strasse, Schubert Strasse, Hofbahnhof Strasse, Florence Nightingale Street. Florence Nightingale Street? She wasn't German was she? Or maybe she was. Now that would be a good story.

The traffic is all German. In Windhoek you're not woken up at the crack of dawn by the cry of the coyote or the grunt of lions and tigers wandering the streets first thing in the morning but by the purr-purr of Volkswagens going off to work.

The shops are all German. Well, maybe apart from Rhino's Fast Foods. Most certainly have German names; Wecke und Voigts, the big department store; Kock und Schmidt; H. Becker & Co; Carl List Haus; Kessler Car Sales; Metje & Ziegler; und das Schneider Café, which incidentally seems to be the in place for a late Frühstück. Some of them have been in business for over a hundred years.

Every sign and every notice seems to be in German: Stadt; Geschäftszeit; Frisch; Brot; Kucken; Backwaren; Einfach gigantisch; Die Blumenecke; Autohaus; Bucksenmacher. The only ones not in German were in English and they were all telling people not to do something or other:

No skateboards
No bicycles
No dogs
No littering
No ballgames
No picking flowers
No fishing
No swimming
No alcohol
Stay out of flowerbeds
Persons damaging municipal property will be prosecuted

Presumably on the basis that only English speakers would think of doing such things. Not German speakers.

Then there are all the statues. They're on the green outside the Christuskirche, on the main Strasse, by the fort, near the shops. They are all sculpted by Germans, cast in Germany and shipped out, commemorating one German victory after another. The clock tower at the junction of Independence Avenue and the Post Office Street Mall, which is a copy of the one that used to be on the old Deutsch-Afrika Bank, is as German as a Schwarzwalderkirschtorte.

There are German charities, a whole string of German schools, a special club for German Shepherd dogs which meets Sunday mornings on the Farm Malabar at the back of the Daan Viljoen game reserve – bark twice before entering, Windhoek Karneval complete with thigh-slapping, Lederhosen, colourful floats and oompah bands, German radio programmes, and even a German newspaper which carries full-page in memoriam notices to German martyrs such as Rudolf Hess, Hitler's erstwhile Nummer zwei, who died in a Berlin prison in 1987.

In offices, people speak German. In shops, people speak German. In the bars which serve enormous glasses of German beer, in the restaurants which serve enormous portions, everybody is eating, drinking and speaking German. Gee whiz, in the large shopping centre where they place large chesspieces on a large board and everybody is eating large Bierwurst, Blutwurst, Currywurst, Meltwurst, Schlackwurst, Weisswurst, Zervelatwurst, Zungenwurst, Zungenblutwurst and every other kind of wurst, you hear nothing but German.

Talk to a cab driver, a hotel porter, a government official, a businessman, a banker, they all seem to have typical Namibian names like Leibenberg, Damaskus, Bradenburg, Blatt, Liszt, Eggert, Muller, Fischer, Fredericks, Ibenstein, Hoft, Luderitz, Schroder, Voigts von Finkenstein.

And, of course, there is the Bahnhof. Built in 1912, it couldn't look more German. It couldn't *be* more German. In fact, to tell you the truth, in the booking hall where some of the furniture is still stamped KDEV – Kaiserliche Deutsche Eisenbahn Verwaltung – I kept expecting to bump into Kaiser Bill himself with another stained glass window under his arm for another German church and his wife with another bible.

And what happens if a train is ever late? No kidding, it's a major national incident. There are stories in the newspaper, reports on television, explanations and apologies all round. I was there when in one carriage on a train from Windhoek to Keetmanshoop, the capital of the southern part of the country, the coffee machine broke down. You'd have thought it was the end of the world. The railway company, Trans Namib, immediately put out a public statement grovelling to passengers 'for the inconvenience they experienced on that particular journey and to give them the assurance that every effort will be made to iron out such problems as quickly as possible'. What nobody seemed to realise, my brothers, was that in the rest of Africa it would have been a major national incident if a train had run on time, and the coffee machine was still there and still working at the end of the journey.

Nor does the German influence stop there. Go inside any house or shop or office and you could be in Baden-Baden, or even Baden-Baden-Baden. All is light and cool and airy. Everything has a place, everything is in its place. Government offices in the rest of Africa are a mess. They're filthy. They haven't seen a lick of paint for a century. Doors are falling off their hinges, carpets have long since been eaten away by God knows what. If they haven't they stick to the soles of your shoes like icky glue. Everywhere there are piles of unread reports and papers, on desks, chairs, on the floor, keeping the walls upright and the ceiling in place – or most of it. In Windhoek everything is filed in alphabetical order in neat, clean, modern filing cabinets. Reception areas are reception areas and not family meeting places. I once called into a ministry in Niamey, the capital of Niger, where the reception was not only crawling with brothers, sisters, aunts, uncles and a million cousins all waiting to see the minister, but they actually had their bunsen burners out on the floor and were cooking meals. Windhoek offices are organised. Everybody has a desk. On every desk there is a PC. Every PC has a screen, a keyboard and, surprise, surprise, they work. Here even the paperclips were standing to attention.

These guys even think and act and behave like Germans. They believe in planning. They are already planning for the year 2005. How much foreign investment will they need? What will they require for high interest rate structures? Should they try to kick-start the economy artificially now to hit their targets in ten years' time, or should they continue the way they're going?

Discipline. Everything is ordered, managed, everything is done as it should be done. You don't believe me? This is the only country in Africa that passed a law telling schoolchildren how they should and should not have their hair cut. Out went the traditional 'panga' cuts for boys and the braids and other fancy styles for girls. Why? Because they were spending too much time on doing their hair and not enough time on their homework. And when the kids rebelled, what happened? The teachers went on strike until they obeyed the law.

They write reports on everything: on the economy, on private sector development, on the role of the public sector, on the free flow of funds for non-residents, on economic freedom, on labour mobility. You name it, they've written a report, probably three reports, about it. You think I'm kidding? I met a civil servant who was desperately trying to write a report on everything Namibia had in common with Iceland, to justify some exchange of diplomatic niceties. What's more, in the reports I've seen they keep talking about 'bulldozing' people to do things. Now is that a typical everyday African expression? Not that I'm bulldozing you for a reply, you understand.

And they actually believe in work! On a Saturday morning, one civil servant, in his beautiful office, surrounded by masses of books and files and paperwork, actually told me they were all doomed – his word, not mine – unless in Namibia they believed in 'the holiest of holies, work'. My brothers! My brothers! Does this guy know what he's saying? Is he trying to ruin it for the rest of the continent?

And is it any wonder that from the moment I arrived I couldn't believe my eyes? The plane arrived on time. I got through immigration in about two seconds. There waiting for me was my bag. Straight through customs – no x-ray machines, no unpacking and repacking my stuff twenty-seven times, no soldiers rifling through my briefcase, no nods, hints or suggestions, no waiting for hours because they want to check whether it's against the law to bring a 100-franc note into the country.

Out into the airport itself. No mass of people trying to help you carry your suitcase, put their hands into your pockets or take the shoes off your feet. The place is clean and orderly. I walk ten paces (did I say walk? There are some countries in Africa where you never walk) and I'm in a taxi heading to Windhoek. A taxi, I might add, which has all its windows, a roof, four doors which actually close, an engine that works and – this is going to come as a shock to you – four wheels. Four glorious wheels. With four tyres. Four tyres with treads on them.

The road is long and straight and in superb condition. No pot holes the size of swimming pools. In fact, no pot holes. What's more – another shock coming up – there are no dead sheep, cattle, camels or dogs rotting away at the side of the road. There are no broken-down cars, burnt-out oil tankers, clapped-out mammy wagons. A Mercedes appears slowly behind us, pulls out, overtakes and – whoosh – is gone. Mercedes are not unusual in Africa; just as in Germany every butcher must have a Mercedes, so in Africa anybody who has two dollars to rub together in a foreign bank account or knows anybody who has two dollars to rub together in a foreign bank account has to have a brand new Mercedes. How they get them or who pays for them is a mere detail. This Mercedes is an old Mercedes, but still bright, still shiny, still obviously cherished. We passed a real live genuine German castle, just like the ones along the Rhine, and I am in Windhoek. No hassle, no problems. This is unbelievable.

Namibia was Germany's first African colony, and their last. They bought it in 1883 from a local chief for £100 and 200 rifles. It was proclaimed a protectorate by Bismarck in 1884 and run initially by an imperial commissioner, Dr Goering himself.

Togo and Cameroon were also German colonies, but no way as German as this; in fact, I'd say they're no way German at all. Probably because the Germans moved into Togo and Cameroon to milk them for everything they could. Even before the First World War, daily production figures were being sent back by radio to Berlin. Not so Namibia. Here they went to settle. They could hardly do anything else since there was nothing there until, of course, April 1908, when a certain railway inspector discovered diamonds near Luderitz Bay. Then the place went stark, staring mad. Overnight Luderitz Bay became a boom town. Prospectors poured in from all over the world. Hotels sprang up, champagne was on tap. A stock exchange was opened for business. Houses, roads, schools were built. Street lighting was installed. Today it's back to normal, although most of the old German buildings remain: the post office, the Turnhalle, the Lutheran church – again, windows by courtesy of Kaiser Wilhelm II, vielen Dank – and, of course, the Bahnhof.

Swakopmund, on the edge of the vast Namib desert and

next-door to the open-cast uranium mine, is also much the same as it was when Captain Kurt von François and 150 Schutztruppen landed there in 1893. Most of the buildings are art nouveau German: the Bahnhof, the Haus Altonia, the Lutheran church, the old German school, the old post office, the Kaiserliches Besitzgericht, once the courthouse, now the president's summer house, the Swakopmund Museum, the Woermann Haus, the Alte Kaserne and, probably most famous of all, the old steam engine which used to run to Windhoek and back and which is known locally as the Martin Luther because of his famous comment, 'Here I stand. May God help me. I cannot do anything else.'

The Germans didn't just settle, they settled as Germans in their own little Germany with German standards, attitudes, and beliefs – and banks.

Whenever I manage to snatch a couple of days in Windhoek, I like nothing better than to nip down to the local country club, a five-star luxury hotel and casino complex just outside town built to host the Miss Universe competition and catch up on the local obituaries. My condolences, therefore, to the family of Herr Klaus Dieter Gutzeit, who died on board his yacht the *Cocona Star* while sailing in the Bahamas. Born in Gross Lindenam in Germany, when, as the newspaper reports delicately, 'Europe moved to the brink of war', he qualified as an engineer, arrived in Namibia and promptly bought 3,500 hectares of farmland for the then not insubstantial sum of US$500,000, a second farm for another US$500,000 and a house for a mere US$250,000. Who did he leave all his money to? To someone living in Tsumeb by the name of Paul Sutton.

My condolences to the family of Herr Daniel Booysen, a widower, formerly of Swakopmund, who seemed to be a laugh. His silver cutlery, video recorders, television sets and his car he left to his daughter, as well as a pencil sketch by a famous Namibian artist. To his son, he left some furniture and three paintings, one of a black-nosed impala.

My condolences to the family of Frau Anna Maria Retief, a widow and mother of six children, who died worth

US$3,500,000. And to the family of Frau Elizabeth Helene Bartholomae; you know, the one who used to be married to old Herr Karl Albrecht. She's just died leaving nearly US$9,000,000.

If nothing else, I suppose it proves the Germans have nothing to hide in Africa. In fact, I wasn't going to mention this but what the hell; I know for certain the Germans have nothing to hide in Africa because one Saturday afternoon while studying my obits in the bar of the country club I met a certain Herr Plutsick. Would I like to see some members of the local German community? he asked me. Some members? I reckon I saw every member of the German community in Windhoek, although some, I will admit, were much more leading than others. Now I'm not used to this kind of thing so I'm no expert; all I can say is, I've never seen sunblock used in so many places before: on legs, on arms, on faces, on backs, on the two bay windows in the front as well as on the garden porch and the back passage.

Herr Plutsick's idea of meeting members of the local German community was not my idea of meeting members of the local German community. Everybody was drunk. Everybody was roaring at the tops of their voices. Everybody was stark, staring naked. Out in the bush, up in the dry burnished land of the Kalahari, Laurens van der Post's romantic, wishy-washy dreamland of eternal spirits and makebelieve myths, they wear scruffy jeans, threadbare blue shirts and greasy old baseball caps, unless they are paid to strip off by tourists searching for what they call authenticity and I would call something else. Here they did it for free.

Being British I was naturally reluctant to shed my inhibitions. But I did so on the basis that I've never had anything to hide from anybody let alone a German, and in any case I knew that in a competitive society I had nothing to worry about. However, it was certainly a novel experience. Normally if I'm invited out to Saturday lunch I'm only used to seeing the salad served undressed. Not everybody in sight. All I can say is, I did my best to keep my enthusiasm under control, although as you can probably imagine, it was difficult at times. Especially when Herr Plutsick's Tochter asked if I fancied any of the local Spezialitären. All I can say is, she made a happy man feel very old. At the same time I feel honoured and privileged; after all there can't be many people in this world who know where the Germans don't put their towels.

What I also discovered, ironically, were all the things the Germans actually try to hide in Namibia. Like the deserts. Namibia has not only the oldest coastal desert, but also the highest sand dune in the world, all 300 metres of it in the Namib-Naukluft Park. It has savannahs. Africa's first and biggest national park, Etosha, out on the Atlantic coast, covers 8,500 square miles; about the same area as Wales. I discovered that although their constitution stresses the need for conservation and preservation of the environment, it is Africa's number one hunting ground. It is against the law, however, to hunt either on horseback, or by bicycle.

Namibia's famous wet, wild, lovely and dangerous Skeleton Coast, I was told, is renowned for its old wrecks. That is if they haven't beaten the habit and gone back to Berlin to become nuclear physicists or activists for Greenpeace. What bones are left, you can bet your life, are picked perfectly clean and shiny white and lined up in straight lines ready for inspection.

Fish River Canyon, somebody else told me (you must excuse me; I can't remember the faces), is the second largest canyon in the world after the Grand Canyon which, I have to admit, does not agree with me. The only time I went there I was – oh the shame of it – airsick for the first time in my life. Namibia is also home to 4,000-year-old baobab trees, the only white beetles and the richest diamond mine in the world. It was also the landing spot for the world's largest meteor, all seventy tons of it, which fell to earth in the early hours of 23 February 1986 to the strains, no doubt, of 'Edelweiss' wafting across the still, quiet desert.

But in the normal course of events, your average German living in Namibia will not reveal anything. Especially if he's sober and wearing his Lederhosen, let alone a collar and tie.

Not even the fact that to the south of Windhoek are the famous Eros mountains. They told me they kept quiet because they wanted to protect the environment and – oops! mind where you put that glass of beer – conserve the natural species. But I reckon they don't talk about it – hey, I said mind where you put that beer! – because they know they've got themselves this beautiful place to spread their towels in the African sun and the last thing they want is a bunch of foreigners coming in and ruining it.

Why, for example, did they call the place Windhoek, the Windy City? To put people off going there. It's no windier then walking across London Bridge on a bright May morning on the way to work. Then there are all the stories they put around about something called the Red Eye Gang, who are supposed to beat people up and steal their valuables. No way. It's part of their propaganda. Namibia is as safe as houses.

Did I enjoy my trip? No, I didn't. It's not the Africa I know and love. If I go to Africa, I want to go to Africa. I want the chaos and the bedlam, the lying and cheating, the risks and the dangers, all the agonies and heartaches and – my god, that kid's just got my left shoe. Hey come back here you little . . .

Cape Town

Call me naive. But I have never been anywhere in the world where people actually love – yes, I mean love – their president. Not just admire him, which would be unusual enough for any politician; not just respect him but honestly and genuinely love him. Neither have I been anywhere where everybody, well almost everybody, is genuinely, openly and honestly going out of their way to be helpful and understanding towards each other. It's unbelievable – but that's South Africa today.

'I just love that man,' a real old Boer, who looked about as civilised as a chainsaw, told me in his heavy accent one evening in some downtown bar in Benoni on the outskirts of Johannesburg. 'I know I shouldn't. I know he stands for everything I fought against. But when at the end of the world cup he came out wearing that green Springbok sweater, I just cried. We all cried. I couldn't help it. That's how much I love him.'

And all South Africans seem to feel the same way. Not just the calm, sensible, rational liberals like you and me, but even – but especially – the hardline Afrikaners who a few months ago thought that to be ruled by a black man was a fate worse than death.

'He's the most amazing man. All that suffering, all those years in gaol, and no bitterness. Not even to us, and we were the ones who did it to him,' a company director who used to be something particularly nasty in the Internal Stability Unit of the South African police told me.

In East London I got a lift to the airport from a guy in purchasing who looked like the kind of secret policeman who is surprised if he picks up a tapped phone and water doesn't come out of the earpiece. 'When he stood outside parliament that day, his hand on his heart, singing "Die Stem", I just broke up. I just couldn't help it,' he gulped.

In Durban I met a liberal Boer, who looked as if he ate cockroaches for breakfast. 'It's him, it's his fault,' he practically sobbed. 'I've even put a flagpole in my garden just to fly our flag, I'm that proud. The neighbours think I'm crazy, but I don't care.' He told me he was going to classes to learn Zulu, which would have been unheard of even three years ago.

Everyone I spoke to in South Africa seemed to agree. Amazing . . . sweet . . . magical . . . a miracle man . . . a friend . . . fantastic. People only have to see him to start crying. It's as if *Cry the Beloved Country* has become Cry the Beloved Voter. What's more it seems all this sobbing and rubbing their eyes has made them colour blind. Whites who previously would have preferred to die than to sit on the same park bench as a black man are now working side by side with them; going for drinks with them after work; going to the funerals of their new-found black friends and even standing up at rugby matches and singing the national anthem 'Nkosi sikelel i'Afrika' (God Bless Africa) at the tops of their voices.

The blacks are moving as well. They've recognised that the bitterness has gone, that everyone is now equal and has their part to play. So closely in fact are the two sides working together, I reckon they should ditch the Springbok as their national emblem and go for the zebra instead.

The only other man I can think of like him this century was Gandhi. Both were loved, actually loved, by millions of people. Both suffered enormous setbacks and trials. And both were deeply involved in South Africa. Which must say something about South Africa.

He is, of course, Mr Nissan Main Dealer. Or at least, that's what it sounds like to me in that awful South African accent.

For years I never went to South Africa. I travelled all over the rest of Africa, but for me South Africa, together with Outspan oranges, Stellenbosch wines and safaris in Kruger National Park were off-limits. And I mean off-limits. Not like for some Holland Park liberals I know who went on and on about never buying Outspan oranges or Stellenbosch wines in the shops ever again – and had them delivered instead.

On my first trip, therefore, I was more than prepared to discover that everything had changed and the old statutory system of apartheid with its horrors and violence had been replaced by a brand-new voluntary system of apartheid with all its horrors and violence. No way. All my prejudices crumbled into the dust, just as the sales of heavy-duty wire mesh, water cannon and riot insurance in inner-city areas have crumbled into the dust over the last few years.

I expected the whites to be going around saying they were sorry – sorry they weren't tough enough when they had the chance, sorry they hadn't fled the country and sorry the blacks had taken over. But the change was unbelievable as it was genuine and dramatic. In a matter of days almost the entire white population had swung round 180 degrees and were marching in exactly the opposite direction, to a different tune, under a different leader. With a colourful range of shirts. I can't think of a more dramatic, peaceful and immediate turn-around in history, apart from St Paul, perhaps, or that time my wife swung her mini-van round 180 degrees in the face of an oncoming tractor.

For the first time in their lives, the whites were leaving off their flak jackets and learning to drive at less than 55mph, buy food for their rottweilers and make a magazine last a whole week instead of a matter of seconds. The only black smoke you see drifting across the horizon nowadays is created by everyone having their braais, or barbecues, on a Sunday afternoon and using too many damp wood chips to cook their sausages wrapped in sheep's intestines. What's more, I was told, all the 'Whites Only' signs, previously treasured by the whites, were now treasured by the blacks. As a memento of the old days. And the only people who want to bring back the pass laws are, in fact, the blacks – to control the millions of black people who every year are illegally flooding into the country from the rest of Africa, and even from Asia and Europe. One black businessman, a salesman I saw in Durban, went so far as to tell me that today the language of the oppressors was Xhosa. But he was a Zulu, and I suppose you can't expect too much peace and harmony.

At the same time I was amazed at the size of the place. I knew it was big. But not as big as Europe.

The New South Africa, another Cape Town businessman told me, is made up of four distinct counties; the cities, the countryside, the bush – and Orange Free State. Which is apparently some typical South African joke. Ha ha.

Nor had I realised South Africa was so beautiful, as in luxury-motor-car-television-commercial beautiful. Admittedly in the past I had only seen photographs of squadrons of Eland 90 armoured vehicles glinting in the early morning sunlight, or Sharpeville bathed in a striking blood-red sunset, or silhouettes of car tyres. Actually being there and seeing it through bloodshot eyes was something else.

Table Mountain is spectacular. The view from the top, flanked on the one side by Devil's Peak and on the other by Lion's Head, even surrounded by a bunch of howling schoolkids, is fantastic. You can see the whole city, the whole peninsula way below. You can see the Cape of Good Hope which, when you think about it, is a wonderful name. You can even see Robben Island, where Mr Main Dealer himself was holed up for all those years when nobody loved him. Some days, I was told, you can even hear people talking 3,500 feet below. But that seemed a bit far-fetched. Especially as I could hardly hear what the person next to me was saying for all the flipping kids screaming at each other. And the ride down by cable car took my breath away. Partly because of the view and partly because at one stage a French couple at the back looked as though they were going to go for another kind of mile-high record.

All along the Cape coast, described by that well known travel writer, Sir Francis Drake, as 'the most stately thing and the fairest cape in all the circumference of the world', is some of the most beautiful scenery I've seen. Mountains, rolling hills, deep, rich, green valleys, little towns. Clifton, just under the Lion's Head, the upmarket, trendy, rich-rich end of town. Llandudno, which is squeezed between two hills and looks out on a rusty old wreck. Hout Bay, the centre of the Cape's crayfishing fleet, which at one time (typical Dutch) used to charge visitors for driving through the town. Chapman's Peak and across country to Fish Hoek, which is still dry today, over 200 years after Lord Charles Somerset decreed no pub should be built on his land. Glencairn. Simon's Town, the big South African naval base with its statue of Able Seaman Just Nuisance. Seaforth. All the gardens, most of them immaculate. The sea and all the little bays and harbours. The fishing boats. The beaches. The different colours. It reminded me of parts of Scotland or Italy. Then I saw some baboons and immediately thought of California.

'Do you know, there are more flowers and fauna here per square mile than anywhere else in the world,' some flower and fauna addict who looked like Gertrude Jekyll on Prozac told me.

'Really.'

'At least 1,500 per square mile compared to around 500 in the Amazon, and more are being discovered every day.'

'Fascinating.'

'Problem is we're now developing so rapidly that every day we're destroying more and more plants we don't know about.'

'Is that a – wait a minute. If you don't know about them, how do you know that every day you're destroying them?'

'But it stands to reason, doesn't it?'

'Why?'

I never did find out why. I didn't have ten days to spare. But I reckon it is because of the English gardeners. Cecil Rhodes spent a fortune hiring English gardeners to come to South Africa to help them plant only crops or flowers which could be harvested or cut at least twice a year. The fact that the place is overrun with the stuff must be a tribute to their hard work.

Of course I had to go to Stellenbosch, the only vineyards – oops, I mean winelands – in the world pestered by baboons from the outback as opposed to baboons from the customs and excise. When I got there I discovered it's not the best wine-producing area in the country; that's Paarl, further up the road. It's just that Stellenbosch gets all the publicity. It cost me a fortune hiring a car and a driver in order to find out. But in the past visiting Stellenbosch could have cost me my life, so I didn't argue.

The town itself, with its oak-lined streets, is full of Cape Dutch buildings. In many ways it looks like an old Dutch town which was uprooted in the middle of the eighteenth century and shipped out as a single job lot. At no expense to the Dutch, of course. Dorp Street has the longest row of historic buildings in the whole country. The Schreuderhuis, probably the oldest house in the country, is the same today as it was when it was built in 1709, thanks to the enormous amount the Dutch were prepared to spend on renovating and decorating their homes. The Blettermanhuis is a typical eighteenth-century Cape house with its H-shape and six gables: H-shaped because if there was a fire only one section would be affected. A Dutch trick to cut down on the insurance premiums.

Maybe the vineyards surrounding the town are not as immaculate as, say the vineyards in France or Germany. But certainly they are as colourful and as picturesque as in Italy or California or Australia. And after a couple of glasses of anything produced by this fantastic vineyard which goes by the glorious name of Meerlust – how can you not get addicted to wine with a name like that – everything looks fantastic.

In one vineyard whose name I can't remember – you see how I have been destroyed by Meerlust – I met a dotty old English professor who told me his wife had just died, he wanted a rest, so he was touring all the vineyards in the area. By bicycle.

'Why bicycle?' I asked. 'That'll take ages. You should go by car.'

'No,' he said, 'By bicycle. That way I know when I've had too much. I fall off.'

In Franschhoek, a tiny village settled originally by French Huguenots who fled religious persecution in France in the 1680s, in probably the most beautiful valley in the whole Cape, I met an Argentinian engineer also doing the rounds. He was planning to live in Cape Town when he retired. He said he thought it was the most beautiful place on earth. Which we drank to, of course. Again. And again. And again. And not once did he mention the name of what-are-those-islands-called?

But the thing that struck me more than anything about South Africa, even more than the three-foot electronic truncheon I saw some ex-policeman using to demonstrate crowd control techniques to his cronies in a bar in the back streets of Durban – I know this is going to sound corny – was the people. Maybe I was just lucky. It had to happen to me one day. Maybe it was because I was expecting everything to be so much worse, and it was all such a pleasant surprise. Maybe it was because I caught it at the right time. Mr Nissan Main Dealer was well into his presidency and wearing all the fancy shirts he could get hold of. South Africa had just won the rugby World Cup. Everybody was on a high. There was so much goodwill everywhere you could practically slice it up and chew it like biltong. Everyone was being genuinely friendly and helpful and understanding to each other. Maybe because they knew they had to be, there was no alternative, or maybe because everyone genuinely wanted to draw the line and start again. Either way, that's how it was, and for all I could tell they were enjoying being pleasant to each other. Gee whiz, they'd even started telling jokes again. In the old days, of course, they used to tell nothing but Van der Merwe jokes, which were a bit like the Kerryman jokes they tell in

Ireland, the Polish jokes in Chicago or the Newfie jokes they tell in Canada. South Africans also, of course, told political jokes:

A Zambian boasts of having a minister of naval affairs. 'But how can you have a minister of naval affairs?' asks the South African. 'You have no access to the sea. You're land-locked. You haven't even got a navy.'

'Well,' says the Zambian. 'You have a minister of justice.'

But now they were telling new, up-to-date jokes, about each other. Which I always think is a good sign.

'Mrs Main Dealer meets Mrs Thatcher. Mrs Thatcher says to her, "In England, you know, they used to call me the Iron Lady."'

'Mrs Main Dealer, she says to Mrs Thatcher, "Funny that. In South Africa, they used to call *me* the Iron Lady."'

'Mrs Thatcher takes one step back, looks at Mrs Main Dealer and says, "Tell me, who do you iron for?"'

Even when I tried to tell them that Lomu deliberately let them win the World Cup, they just laughed. 'Look, it's obvious,' I kept telling them. 'He'd have let you win even if you had one foot tied behind your back. Lomu destroyed the English team. How come he didn't do anything to the Springboks? He was hardly in the game at all. So it has to be because he wanted to let you win.'

Anyway, I'm hooked on the place. It's a long time since I enjoyed a trip as much as I did the one to South Africa. Even though it rained in Cape Town, was overcast in East London, cloudy in Durban and actually snowed in Johannesburg. Not much, but it snowed.

I arrived first in Cape Town, which the books compare to Sydney, Australia. No way, it's a million times better. Sydney is brash, modern, a bit flashy, a bit San Francisco. Cape Town is much more civilised. It is a mixture of Cape Dutch, Edwardian, Victorian and modern nondescript plate glass. It has cobblestones and tiny little squares and huge open air plazas. The Water Front, an enormous modern complex of shops, bars, restaurants, markets, theatres and a fantastic hotel, is built on one huge section of the old docks. The books say it is much better than Darling Harbour in Sydney. No way.

To me, Cape Town is one of those cities which has a style and a character all of its own. It's not just South African, let alone African, it's every nation under the sun. You come across old Dutch families; old German families; refugees from Angola, Namibia, Zimbabwe, Zambia, Zaire; emigrants from Portugal, India, France, Germany, Holland, even Britain. But no Australians. It is also in the most fabulous position, squeezed on the edge of a sixty-kilometre-long sliver of mountain on the very edge of the Atlantic. On one side mountain, on the other ocean. If it's not the most beautiful city in the world, maybe it's the most beautiful coastal city, or at least the most beautiful southerly coastal city in all Africa.

Many's the time while I was there I could see myself living maybe in Constantia, the horsey part of Cape Town, in somewhere like Dressage Drive. Table Mountain in the background. Going hunting twice a week in winter. Spending the summer going to the races down the road, the rest of the time dragging myself around the vineyards, oops, I mean winelands.

I stayed at the Holiday Inn on Market Square. Just around the corner was Archbishop Tutu's homebase, the great brooding St George's Cathedral, where police used to happily beat up student demonstrators taking refuge at the altar. Next door was a bookshop which boasted a sign saying, 'No Reading'. Which struck me as, well, interesting. But I did my usual and ate at most of the decent places in town. Top of the list, of course, was the Mount Nelson, or Nellie, as we regulars say, a grand old spinster aunt of a colonial hotel with a long, palm-lined driveway, a colonnaded gateway and guards in white helmets. I'd no sooner tucked into my first slice of ostrich carpaccio, which I found a bit bland and puddingy, than one of the waiters was adding to my joke collection.

'What do you get if you cross a rottweiler with a Rhodesian ridgeback?' I shook my head.

'A whites-only area.'

I was there for a week, but it took me nearly three days to get to the point: Cape Point, the furthermost tip of the Cape of Good Hope Nature Reserve, the graveyard of God knows how many ships including the *Flying Dutchman* and its Captain, Van der Decken. You can just spot the foam where the cold Atlantic meets the warm Indian Ocean. Some books say it's the southernmost spot in the country, but it's not. That's Cape Agulhas, a few miles further down but, like Paarl, they didn't have such a good PR man.

East London, out on the east coast, where the first British settlers began arriving in 1820, is a nice, quaint old town that looks as if it's been lovingly preserved. It's full of nineteenth-century buildings in immaculate condition. The city hall with its Anglo-Boer War memorial outside looks almost Italian, even though this was also one of the main landing points for German settlers. But nobody bothers much about it. Anyone who visits East London makes straight for the beach, which stretches for miles and miles and miles and is supposed to out-Bondi Bondi when it comes to surfing. I didn't want to go to the beach. Instead I ended up in a bar in the Garden Park where I picked up another new South African joke:

'What's got four legs and an arm in its mouth? A police rottweiler.'

Further up the coast I called into Durban, which is Africa, India and Miami rolled into one. The most Indian town outside India, it's even more Indian than Bradford. It's also the most touristy beach resort in the country. Its Golden Mile, one big, luxury, palm-fringed hotel after another was, everybody kept telling me, like Rio. It isn't, but if it makes them happy . . .

Apparently at Christmas and the New Year the place is packed. They flock in from all over, from Jo'burg, from the Transvaal, from Cape Town, even from India. But you won't find anybody lying on the beach. There isn't enough room. Everybody is doing their lotus position. In fact, I reckon the lotus position was invented to get as many people as possible on the beach in Durban in the middle of winter.

Marine Parade, which seemed permanently crammed with big, colourful Zulu women selling baubles, bangles and baskets, was, everybody kept telling me, like Copacabana beach. It isn't, but what the hell; it's got palm trees. Nobody told me the back streets, which are crammed with bars, coffee bars, restaurants, discos and everything else anyone could want, not to mention mosques, temples and even the occasional rickshaw, were like Bombay. They didn't have to. I just knew it.

And the atmosphere everywhere is as hot and humid as it is possible to imagine. Not from the weather, but from the millions of curries everybody had the night before. I'm no expert. But to me this is the only beach in the world where people put on their clothes in order to go into the water; where swimming is decidedly not the done thing – instead people simply stand around having their ears dewaxed; where to cool down people buy a curry and rice; and where football, swingball and volleyball can only be played on a tabletop. Providing the tabletop is stood upright, vertically, in the sand and people can get the ball over the top of it.

One evening, forsaking springbok loin and smoked crocodile tail, I ended up in an Indian restaurant somewhere between Victoria Street, the Indian Indian part of town, and Pine Street, near the beach, where you can see every kind of spice and grain, of every different colour and strength. There I sweated, dripped and practically evaporated my way through some fantastic curry served on a plate like a palette. Here right in front of me was what looked like the kind of curry you get back home. But it wasn't. It was softer, sweeter, more succulent. Then arranged around it were a thousand different colours and textures. This one didn't look like coconut, but tasted like it. That one looked like banana, but it sure as hell didn't taste like it. Over there on the edge was this kind of dark red splodge. It tasted fantastic – sweet and peppery at the same time. Next to it was a slice of something that looked like an apricot. I tasted the tiniest portion. Jaraaagh! It was hotter than hell. It must have been liquid dynamite. Don't tell anyone but I tried screaming for iced water. All the waiter wanted to do was talk about the World Cup.

'Are you Welsh, sir?'

I shook my head, gesticulating for something cold.

'The Welsh, sir, very nice people, sir. During the rugby, sir, six of them come into restaurant. The first thing they say is, ten bottles of red wine. Bring ten bottles of red wine. Very, very nice people the Welsh, sir.'

Aaaaaaagh! I began to go woozy.

'The Welsh, sir, they tell me joke. You want to hear joke, sir?' By now I was losing consciousness. 'Wales are playing England at Twickenham. The whistle blows. The Welsh go off immediately. But still it take England twenty minutes before they score their first try. You think that funny, sir?'

'Aaaghhhh.'

'And I've got another joke, sir, a Zulu joke. South Africa has always been run by bothas. Pik Botha, PW Botha. And Botha-lezi. Very funny joke. You think so, sir?'

I also discovered after hours of careful observation that the traditional Zulu dances seem to be based on the simple premise that if you stand still, stamp your feet and scream you won't get anywhere at all. Whether that's significant, I don't know.

If Durban is Bombay comes to Africa, Johannesburg – the largest city in the world not built on a river – is New York comes to the City of Gold. It's full of not exactly huge skyscrapers – even the famous Carlton Centre is only fifty storeys high – but, well, mini-skyscrapers; medium-sized tower blocks; shiny minor tower blocks; concrete tower blocks; desperately boring tower blocks like the ones at home; bank blocks; insurance blocks; mining, gold-trade blocks. It's got more than its fair share of luxury five-star hotels and restaurants for Africa. It's also got that bezazz you get in New York. Everybody rushing around doing things, streets packed with traffic, cars hardly moving; either because there's a protest march blocking the streets, the police have set up an unofficial roadblock in order to earn some holiday money, or there's just too much traffic, you never know. Rubbish is piled almost as high as the Carlton Centre itself. Everywhere; by the side of the street, in shop doorways, by the sides of offices and houses. Cans, boxes, fruit, vegetables, and God knows what else.

But it's also got New York-type problems. It has abject, soul-destroying poverty, which to some people means a sixteen-bedroom mansion on the edge of the mink-and-manure belt with only two Ferraris and a Porsche in the garage, and to others less than a cardboard box on the corner opposite the city hall.

'The only way the streets get cleaned nowadays is if the wind blows,' a civil servant told me. 'There ain't nobody else goin do nothin.'

And, of course, it's dangerous. So dangerous that many hard-nosed, hard-bitten, world-weary guys I know won't think of going anywhere near it. In fact, according to many people it's the most dangerous city on earth, although it's impossible to get hold of statistics to prove it. Because, I was told, they had been stolen. Murder, robbery, kidnapping, rape, you name it, they've got it. They're even developing new methods of murder. In the old days it used to be 'necklacing'. You'd get your guy, throw rubber tyres over him then set fire to the lot. Now, whether there's a shortage of tyres, or they don't want thick black smoke damaging the environment, they've gone a stage further. They pour petrol down the poor guy's throat, stuff a petrol-soaked rag or cigarette in his mouth and set fire to it. The advantage is, it's quick. There's no evidence left behind. And if the police arrive on the scene there's absolutely nothing they can do about it.

In Cape Town an old retired businessman told me Johannesburg was 'an everything-used-to-be city. Everything used to be clean. Everything used to be safe. Everything used to work.' The police used to work. The courts used to work. The high court used to work. Not any more. The only people doing any work nowadays were crooks and gangs and conmen. And they were working every hour God gave them.

Schools, I was told, were now opened to all races. Trouble was one race used them during the day and another race broke through the iron bars and security systems and used them at night in order to learn how to hot-wire the ignition systems of cars as well as to study the local lingo. For the streets of Jo'burg have a language of their own. The crooks or bad guys are majitas. The good guys, or rather the innocent schmucks like you or me who wander around day or night without a bodyguard, are snoories. What the majitas steal or grab from the snoories is called coal. This can either be a de Klerk – a two-rand coin; a cabbage – a green, ten-rand note; a chocolate – the twenty-rand note; a pinkie – the pink, fifty-rand note, or a clipper – a hundred-rand note. Invariably what they use to get their coal is called a 'seven', because that's how long you could spend in gaol if, against all the odds, you are caught, the judge is unimpressed by your smart suit and the invitation to lecture at Harvard on the problems of depriva-tion, and you are actually thrown inside. What you get when you come out is an envelope, or a dolphin. An envelope is a Mercedes. A dolphin is a BMW. You then go down the nearest shebeen, which is an illegal black drinking club, and celebrate your success with all the other majitas in town.

'We've changed dramatically from a country that did noth-ing but throw people into gaol into a country that does nothing but throw people out of gaol,' I was told by a personnel manager who looked like a reject for the so-called élite Vlakplass C10 unit, which was famous, or infamous, for its powers of persuasion.

'If they gave South Africa an enema, they'd stick it into Johannesburg,' I was told by the finance director of a big engineering group based in Durban who refused point blank to go anywhere near the place. 'It's Lagos, New York, Los Angeles, rolled into one. No, sir, if anybody there wants to see me they'll have to come to me.'

When I first arrived there, however, I had no problems. Admittedly I was huddled up inside an armoured personnel carrier. But at least it gave me a chance to see the place as it is.

In Hillbrow, which some people say is the Harlem or even the Bronx of Johannesburg, I wandered around without any hassles. Nobody tried to steal my wallet, beat me up or kill me. Whether it had anything to do with the fact it was a Sunday and the place was practically deserted I don't know. If it had, it can only mean that the crooks and thugs and conmen in Johannesburg are the most Christian crooks and thugs and conmen in the world. They do their worst the rest of the week but on Sunday they rest. Not many people can say that nowadays.

Similarly Yeoville. With its coffee shops, cheap restaurants, clubs and secondhand shops, it's like an early Greenwich Village. But it was safe. Sandton, the leafy suburbs out to the north on the way to Pretoria, is really the out-of-centre business centre. Many small to medium sized companies are based there; lots of smaller banks, many advertising agencies. It's the place for people who don't want to go to Johannesburg. Rosebank, close by, with its rambling old houses and massive shopping centres, looks more like California than Africa.

Alexandra is close by, but a million miles away as well. This is one of the inner-town townships, and consists of long lines of dusty, badly-lit streets of graffiti-covered shacks, all desperately waiting for electricity, running water and the Swish. Flush toilets to you and me.

Parktown, of course, is not part of Johannesburg. It's full of stately homes, many of which used to belong to the gold-mining magnates. Bryanston is the posh part of town with its mock Georgian offices.

During the rest of the week, the streets and pavements of Jo'burg were packed. You couldn't get another person on them. Think twice about leaving your hotel after 8am, and you might as well stay there all day. First, there's no way you'll be able to battle your way across the pavement to your car. Second, there's no way your car could get wherever you wanted to go. Jo'burg is an early-start city. If you want to get anything done you have to leave your hotel at the very latest by Sunday afternoon. If you want to get back don't count on anything earlier than Sunday morning.

People also behave differently than they do in other parts of the country. Nobody – or nobody white – actually walks. When they go shopping they drive to shopping centres. When they go out to a restaurant, they go to a shopping centre. When they want to go clubbing and get bombed out of their minds, they go to shopping centres. Shopping centres with security gates. Shopping centres surrounded by barbed wire and patrolled by a million security guards. Shopping centres with enormous signs saying, 'You're on your own, buddy. Best of luck.'

When they drive they drive their own way. Nobody drives head-to-tail. There is always a big gap between cars. Nobody parks close up to the guy in front. There's always a big gap. Why? Because they are safe drivers? No, because the more space there is between you and the car in front the easier it is to swing out and make a quick get-away. And if you don't drive, you go by train. Except nobody pays the full fare. Instead they call the police, who are paid next to nothing and are, therefore, always prepared to do a deal between you and the railway. One guy told me if he got a cab and the fare came to over R100 he always called a policeman who invariably cut the fare in half. Providing, of course, he got the R50.

'Why not?' he said. It was his own very practical personal contribution to broadening the economic base of the country.

In any restaurant, I couldn't help noticing, no doubt in the interests of goodwill on both sides, whites are only too pleased to let blacks sit with their backs to the door.

It was the same in lifts, although the strangest thing about them was that whenever I got into one, instead of us all standing there in total silence, somebody would always smile and speak to me. 'Good morning, sir,' they would begin. 'How are you today, sir?' Admittedly they would go on to explain that they had just walked over fifty miles to get there, were looking for work, and please could they have some money for the bus fare back home. But it made a nice change from everybody standing staring at each other.

Tell the hotel reception you have to go to a bank or a mining house, even to a bar, and they will not only offer you a minder, they won't charge you for his services. Once, at the Carlton, my minder became so obsessive about my safety I could hardly go to the toilet without him coming with me. Another time at the Sunnyside Park, the former official residence of Lord Milner, the British High Commissioner during the Anglo-Boer War, now a chintzy English country hotel, they wouldn't let me out of the door at night until I saw the lights of the taxi at the steps. One day, however, I had to go to a meeting along Sauer Street near the junction with Prichard Street and not even the bodyguard would come with me. That week, it was the worst area in the city for muggings. As the police cleared up one area, everybody moved on. The Sauer/Prichard/Bree Street area was the current danger spot.

Then, in spite of everything, in the Holiday Inn on Small Street I met a Swedish businessman who told me he loves the place even though he's forgotten how often he's been attacked and robbed and mugged. 'Now I know the tricks,' he told me over a couple or three drinks in the bar, 'I'm not worried. But I used to be.'

The tricks? When you get to your hotel – this Swedish guy always stays at the Holiday Inn on Small Street – open the door of your car or the taxi, grab your briefcase and run straight for the door. Don't whatever you do get out of your car, turn round and get your briefcase out of the car. By the time you do that they've gone: your briefcase, and the car as well.

If you insist on taking your life into your hands, go prepared to be mugged. 'Whenever I go out, I fill my wallet full of tissues. My credit cards I have in a special inside pocket in my trousers. They rob me, they take my wallet, they leave my credit cards behind,' the Swede told me.

'But don't they check? Don't they look in the wallet?'

'Never,' he assured me. 'I've been robbed ten, twenty times.

372

Never they look inside my wallet. They are always in a hurry to get away.'

'What, you mean from the police?'

'No, from other gangs. Everybody is stealing from everybody else.'

The other thing I found was that everybody was always talking about tracking systems, radio links, following and capturing wild animals. By the end of my trip I was as bad as the rest of them. I'd no sooner get into a car than I was asking whether they had a tracking system; if so, which type and where was it fitted. Invariably they had the latest model, fitted inside the petrol tank. One man told me he didn't believe in them. He'd had his registration number painted on the car roof.

It sounded a bit odd. 'So how will that help you track down wild animals?' I wondered.

'Easy,' he said. 'It's the first thing a police helicopter will spot.'

'Oh, you mean those tracking systems. I thought you meant—' Ah, such innocence.

Another guy told me he had the ultimate tracking system. 'If someone points a gun at me, at, say, the traffic lights, I press a button with my foot. This alerts the police. A police helicopter then tracks the car with the gun.'

But in all the time I was in Jo'burg I only met one man who had had his car hijacked. He was in Sandton, the upmarket end of town. He'd been meaning to get a tracking system fitted, but hadn't had time. Driving to the office one morning early he pulled up at the traffic lights by the Holiday Inn. A kid was handing out leaflets about tracking systems. He wound down the window of his car – zap – they were in. From nowhere, a gang appeared, dragged him out of the car and drove off. He was left stretched out on the road surrounded by anti-hijacking leaflets.

I began to sympathise, but he was philosophical. 'What has four legs and an arm?'

'A police rottweiler,' I said.

He looked more disappointed than if I had tried to hijack him.

Will it last? I asked one contact, who looked as though he had just come hotfoot over the koppie and across the veld wearing his brand new tackies. He took a deep breath, put down what was left of his melktert, and brushed the crumbs off his plate.

'I once went fishing with some friends. We came to this stream. It was hot, and, we wanted to cool down. One of my friends saw this native boy standing there.' Native boy! That shows you how much South Africa has changed. 'I said to the native boy, are there sharks in the river? The boy said no, so we all stripped off and had a good swim. When we came out this old chap—' Old chap! See, things really are different. 'This old chap came up to us and said we were very lucky. We asked why. The boy said there were no sharks in the river. Yes, he said. That's because they've all been chased away by the crocodiles.' He grinned. 'The thing is,' he said, 'if you ask the right question you'll get the right answer.'

As far as I'm concerned the right answer is: yes, of course, it will last. First, because Mr Nissan Main Dealer is Mr Nissan Main Dealer. Somehow or other he's magic. Not because of what he has done; in many cases he hasn't done anything. Take his RDP programme, which to the blacks stands for the Reconstruction and Development Programme which is sup-posed to build millions of houses every year for the next five years, and to the whites stands for Revenge of the Dark People. Nothing has happened. 'Please forgive us,' he says. 'The wheels of government grind very slowly and people should not expect miracles. We are ordinary human beings with many limitations.' Can you imagine? A politician says that – and people accept it.

Second, because South Africa has an organisation, a struc-ture, a system for doing things. Sure, some things don't work. But overall it's a million times better than anything else in Africa. It also has a strong economy that is becoming stronger every day. If they hit problems, even big problems like a wild left-wing government, as some people fear, it's not going to destroy the country. It might set things back a couple of percentage points, it won't mean meltdown.

Third, because – and I know this sounds soft – I honestly believe there's this enormous fund of goodwill throughout the country, and that everybody is determined to make it last. At least I honestly, sincerely hope so. Because I just ... I just ... I just love Mr Nissan Main Dealer.

Mbabane

I was looking forward to going to Swaziland. Honest.

Squeezed between South Africa and Mozambique, it is one of the smallest countries in Africa. The books said it was a mountain paradise: hot, dusty, sandy peaks; strips of fields hacked out of the rock; tiny rivers, the occasional stream; long winding roads leading to nowhere. The only absolute monarchy in sub-Sahara Africa, it is ruled by a young king who went to Eton or was in the guards or something. Full of friendly people more interested in burning branches of the lusekhwane tree in homage to the king than in bothering about such frivolous things as democracy, trade unions and constitutional monarchy. They were also, I was told, strong believers in off-the-shoulder leopard-skin fashions. For men. The women could wear more or less what they liked. Most of them, of course, chose to wear less. Although it was touch and go whether the women out in the bush wore less than the women in the clubs, bars and casinos scattered over the country. As for the office, Swaziland was the only country in the world, can you imagine, that actually had the courage to order – not request, but order – women not to wear trousers in the office. Whether they had left it at that, or come up with alternative suggestions I wasn't told.

On top of that – a big plus in my eyes – they were anti-vegetarian. Well, for a few weeks. In other words nobody was allowed to eat the new fruit and vegetables of the season until the king had had a go and passed them fit for human consumption. Then they could tuck in.

I'd been practising how to say Mbahbaney, Mbane, I mean Mbabane, the name of their capital city, all week. I was booked on Royal Swazi Airlines' other plane. They've only got two, and most people reckon they should never have bought the second – though not the guy driving the big new shiny Mercedes around town.

So what happens as soon as we land at Manzini airport? This guy who looks as though he was trained by the baggage handlers at Thiefrow, oops, I mean Heathrow, under some British government technical aid programme, to which I am, of course, a major contributor, is picking up suitcases and throwing them all over the place from the plane to the clapped-out trolley, from the clapped-out trolley onto the concrete strip which is supposed to be the baggage reclaim area. And whose suitcase gets smashed to pieces? You got it in one. Or rather I got it in thirty-seven. Lumps. Twisted bits of metal. Buckled handles. Broken unbreakable locks. In other words, the works.

Did he do anything? Did he try and tell somebody? Did he look even mildly guilty? No way. He's Heathrow-trained. He just carried on grabbing suitcases off the trolley, swinging them round and throwing them – smash – against the concrete. Did any of the others split, break or burst open? Of course not. These kind of things only happen to me. Having piled the suitcases, carrier bags and cardboard boxes in a heap he now started throwing them onto some giant x-ray machine. Zap went the suitcases. Thud went the carrier bags. Plop went the cardboard boxes. And my suitcase? He just left it there, smashed to pieces, the broken handle thrown on top of everything.

'Hey,' I screamed as calmly and as quietly as I could. 'What about my ...'

The guy just looks at me – that Heathrow look! – as if I'm mad.

'What did you do that for?' I sigh the sigh of sighs. He is still just looking at me. 'Do you know how much trouble this is going to cause me?' The weary voice of experience. But like

377

all the other Heathrow graduates who have scratched, broken, buckled, twisted, smashed to smithereens, I forget how many of my suitcases over the years, he's not interested. He just turns and walks away.

'Talk to him,' a man standing by the x-ray machine grunts at me, pointing at some Air Swazi guy with epaulettes on his blue shirt. Then he disappears as well.

'You'll have to talk to the check-in desk,' Epaulettes says. And disappears.

This was turning into a great welcome to Swaziland. By now all the suitcases were through the x-ray machine. Almost everybody was through customs. I scooped up what was left of my poor battered old Delsey, my second favourite travelling companion, and its contents, and staggered to the x-ray machine. Through it everything went and out the other side. Did the security man take the bits of my suitcase of the machine and put them on the floor as he did everybody else's? No way. It was too difficult. I had to do it myself. Then one at a time I had to carry my briefcase, the remnants of my suitcase and everything else across to the customs man. Did he wave me through? Of course he didn't. He wanted everything spread out on the bench in case, he said, I was trying to smuggle in dangerous substances. Like, I suppose, President Mandela's views on democracy, President Mitterrand's speech on 'good governance' in Africa, or a simple guide to picking up suitcases without smashing them to pieces. Airport porters for the attention of.

One-two-three. I slowly unpacked everything that wasn't already unpacked. Four-five-six. I spread everything over the dirty bench. Seven-eight. I let him rifle through everything: books, papers, files, dirty clothes. Nine-ten. I repacked everything and then – eleven-twelve-thirteen – I carried first my briefcase then all thirty-seven pieces of my suitcase along the corridor, out into the tiny arrivals area, through a glass door, down five steps and across to the check-in desk. Again and again and again.

Who was at the check-in desk? Epaulettes. 'So why couldn't

you have sorted everything out back there when I spoke to you?' I said, puffing and panting.

'Because you have to come to the check-in desk.'

'But I've had to carry . . .'

'It's the regulations.' He just stared at me. You know, the stare people give you when you make the most reasonable statement in the world and they're thinking, Who is this nut?

'So are you going to get me another suitcase,' I began, as diplomatically as I felt I could in the circumstances.

'It's nothing to do with me,' he said. 'It's Swazi Airlines.'

'But you're Swazi Airlines.'

'No I'm not. I'm just their agent.'

'You mean Swazi Airlines only have an agent in Swaziland, not a proper office?'

'Yes. We are a small airline.'

Which struck me as stupid. But that, as they say, is Africa. 'So what about my suitcase then?' I returned to the attack.

'You'll have to give it to me. I'll send it back to head office. They'll give you a—'

'How can I give you my suitcase?' I must admit I exploded gently. 'I need it for my stuff.'

'But if I can't show them it's broken, they won't give you—'

'So what am I going to do with my stuff then?' I said, gently simmering. 'You'll have to give me another suitcase while you send this one back to see if they will give me another one.'

'That's the regulations, sir. Where are you going from here?'

'Johannesburg. I'm only here for—'

He grabbed a pad and scribbled furiously on it. 'Sign that,' he said pushing it in front of me.

'So what am I signing?'

'You want your suitcase repaired—'

'I don't want it repaired. How can you repair that? It's smashed to pieces. I want a new—'

'Then you'll have to sign the form.' A pause. 'Sir.'

I signed the form without bothering even to look at it. For all I know I signed away every generation of Biddlecombes for the next two thousand years. He tore the top sheet off the pad and thrust it at me. 'Give it to Swazi airlines in Johannesburg. They'll sort out your suitcase.' In a second, he had turned, dashed into an office behind him and slammed the door. What could I do now? Stand and scream at a slammed door? Or retreat with as little honour and as much suitcase as I had left. I decided to retreat and head for town.

I repeated the same process as before. I picked up my briefcase, walked across the departure area, up the five steps out into arrivals, then outside the airport building. I left it by the side of the road. With a prayer to whoever is the patron saint of protecting luggage left alone in the middle of nowhere in an unknown country, I went back to the check-in desk, picked up thirty-seven pieces of suitcase and stumbled back across the departure area, up the five steps, across the arrivals area and out of the airport. Again and again and again. I dumped everything alongside my briefcase. Then I realised. The whole place was deserted: no people, no cars, no buses and – you got it – no taxis.

Across the road, behind a wire fence, I saw a man in a blue coat. With another little prayer to the patron saint of luggage left in the middle of nowhere, I leapt across the road, skidded down the track to the wire fence and raced up to the blue coat. By now I was hot. The sun was beating down. My blood was boiling. And I had completed a 440-yard dash faster than Linford Christie could dream of.

'Taxis,' I panted. 'A bus into town. Find. Where do I . . .?'

'They've all gone,' he said.

'All gone,' I panted. 'What do you mean, all gone?'

'That was the last flight,' he said. 'They've all gone. There won't be any more until tomorrow.'

'But how can I get a cab?'

'You can't.' He turned towards the hills. 'Not until . . .'

I turned and sped back along the track, across the road, into the airport, across the arrivals area, down the five steps to the . . . 'So where's the guy from Royal Swazi?' I mildly shouted at some poor innocent cleaner. He just stared at me.

'They smash my suitcase, refuse to give me another one,

they make me fill in a form. Now I've missed the bus. All the taxis are gone. How the hell am I—'

He went back to sweeping the floor. Then suddenly the door at the back opened. It was Epaulettes again.

'So how am I going to get into town,' I started again. 'You've broken . . .'

'It's not my fault,' he grunted. 'You should've known it was the last flight and all the taxis would . . .'

'How the hell should I know?' I couldn't help myself. 'It's the first time I've been here. Why the hell didn't you tell me? If you'd told me, I'd have got a cab, got him to wait, sorted . . .' The guy was a million miles away. He was in orbit. '. . . out the problem with the . . .'

In the end, would you believe, the only way I could get into town was by buying an Avis Rent-a-Car. And I mean buying. I couldn't hire one because the Avis desk was closed. The lady who ran it had gone home. The only person I could find in the whole airport was an eager – a very eager – young man who told me he was an Avis driver. Whether he was or not, I don't know. All I know is he seemed to have problems finding any forms to fill in. He didn't know where the keys were kept. He didn't even know where the cars were parked. But he got a car from somewhere, charged me two arms and three legs – but what could I do? I had to get into town – and dropped me outside the big hotel in the middle of Mmbaney, Mboloney, Mbabane, or whatever they call the place. Except it was the wrong hotel. The hotel I wanted was thirteen miles outside Mblarney, Mbarmy, Mbabane, whatever. For some Mblasted reason Mbabane is not just the name of the Mbloody town but the name of the whole Mbloody surrounding area as well. Which in terms of square miles must make it one of the biggest Mdamned cities in the world.

What in any case does Mbabane mean in English? Something sharp and bitter. Sharp as in, sharp enough to smash a suitcase and bitter as in, wait till I get my hands on Royal Swazi Airlines.

The result was, the whole time I was in Mb-Mb I just

couldn't concentrate. I kept cursing the guy who smashed my suitcase. I kept blasting Epaulettes. I kept damning Royal Swazi Airlines to kingdom come. If, of course, they had a plane that could get them there. Then, I couldn't help it, all the other horrors I have suffered at the hands of airlines all over the world came flooding back.

Like the time British Airways bounced me off a plane in Frankfurt in the middle of the night even though I had a valid ticket, had checked in on time and had a proper boarding pass. Like the time in India I thought I was going to need a couple of hundred feet of rope for the final descent. Like the time in Africa flying from Lagos back to Abidjan when I discovered the meaning of fear, as in sit down, make yourself comfortable, enjoy the flight, this could be your last.

We had been in the air about thirty minutes and the hostess had started serving drinks. Everybody was relaxed and chatting. I was sitting next to a Zairois, a member of their human rights commission. I wanted to ask him about his work, but he said we shouldn't talk politics, that was for the office. In that case, I thought, there is only one safe subject: families. When the Africans say, 'You are my brother,' they mean it. But to the African the family is the community, the community is the family.

'How many brothers and sisters have you got?' I asked him.

'Thirty-six, thirty-seven,' he said. 'I can never remember.' His father had many wives, some official, some unofficial. Polygamy is sometimes against the law, sometimes not. 'It all depends. Officially polygamy is wrong, but if you are a Muslim you can have more than one wife. It all depends on money really. If you have the money, you can have more than one wife.'

Other people I have spoken to say polygamy is not as simple as that. The Koran, they claim, says you can marry up to four wives, but if you are afraid of being unfair, of not being able to treat them all on the same basis, then marry only one. Which is something else. Aminata Sow Fall, probably Senegal's leading woman novelist and one of the first women novelists in francophone Africa, maintains that means poly-gamy is out because, she says, 'You can't love two women in the same way. You can love them, but not on an equal basis.' My Zairois neighbour, however, was simply thinking about the cost.

'But if you have two wives, how do you arrange things?'

'You say, one looks after the children, one looks after the cooking, one looks after the house. You arrange everything.'

'Don't they get jealous?'

'Why should they? You are looking after them. They have a home, a family, food. We are all one family.'

And they do it naturally. It might be inconvenient, or more than they can afford, but it's for the family. Their attitude to parents, elderly aunts and uncles, even the brothers and cousins of aunts and uncles, is infused with the same sense of family. Try explaining to an African that we send our parents to old people's homes.

'Why don't you look after them?'

'Well, they prefer to be with other old people.'

'I don't believe you. Every mother and father wants to be with their family.'

'Well, yes but . . . our houses are not big enough . . .'

'In Africa we give up our beds to our parents. If my mother and father want a bed, how can I sleep?'

'Sometimes they need medical help.'

'We think the best thing for the health is to be with the family. If I do not have room for my parents I build a house for them.'

'You can do that in Africa. In England we have to get planning permission . . .'

'But it's for your mother and father.'

The pilot came through the cabin door and recognised the Zairois. They gave each other a big kiss, shook hands and laughed and asked about each other's families. They had met as students in Douala, and had kept bumping into one another in different parts of the world ever since. I was introduced. I practised my Lingala, Mbote mingay, and asked about his wife and children, Mwasi ni-oh, especially the children, N'bana nioh. That earned me a big smile and a kiss on both cheeks. I was part of the family. The hostess pushed past with the drinks trolley from which the captain took a bottle of champagne, and we drank to each other's health, to their wives and, especially, to their children. The ˌchampagne finished, we shook hands again and the captain continued his meet-the-people tour.

We started talking about human rights in Zaire. How many times had the human rights commission met? Did they have a list of political prisoners, if any? Had they visited any prisons? Could anybody go to the commission with a complaint? I was interested, I told him, because I was going to see the UN commission on human rights and wanted some background. The hostess brought us sweet biscuits; being a friend of the captain obviously counted.

Another crew member now came through the cabin door, recognised a passenger, and they had a repeat performance of our ceremony with the captain. At first I thought nothing of it and we continued our chat about torture and how you control the secret police. Then it occurred to me. 'Wait a minute,' I said. 'That's the co-pilot. So who's flying the plane?'

'It's on automatic. They can't sit there all the time. Don't worry,' the Zairois reassured me.

'But shouldn't one of them at least be watching?'

'What's the matter? Haven't you flown before? Are you some kind of bushman?'

We laughed. I ordered another bottle. We were now talking about Amnesty. What right had they to investigate governments? They didn't represent anybody, were not elected by anybody. They relied on rumour and lies. There was no way of assessing their reports objectively. They were only in it for the publicity. They should be accountable—

Then it happened. The plane plunged about 200 metres, levelled out, wobbled a bit and plunged again. Women screamed. Men dropped their glasses and tried to look impassive. I was shaken, I admit. Then it hit me. There was nobody at the controls. We were on automatic pilot – and it was being anything but automatic.

'Get out of the way!' I could hear the pilot racing up the cabin. But the drinks trolley had somehow skewered round and was jammed between two seats. He was trying to free it, but it was stuck tight. Now he was trying to climb over it, bottles and glasses flying, people shouting and screaming. And still we were plunging.

Finally the pilot reached the door. But the door was locked. He couldn't get into the cockpit.

'It must be one of the new anti-hijacking devices,' said my friend. 'Can only be opened from the inside. Stops hijackers.'

And the pilot as well. By now he was tugging and hammering at the door like a madman. The happy, handshaking friend of all had become a demented lunatic. And we were still plunging. Some people were fervently saying their prayers. Women had stopped sobbing and started wailing. The co-pilot at last also negotiated the drinks trolley and they were both kicking and thumping the door and screaming at the tops of their voices.

I'd never been in a plane which had plunged so far. I'd experienced the occasional drop, severe buffeting by storms crossing the Sahara, even been shaken around by helicopters over Burkina Faso. But this looked like the real thing. A lady in front of me was being sick. It was all over the floor and flowing towards me. I didn't know what I dreaded most, being covered by somebody else's vomit or . . .

'Why don't they smash the door down?' I said.

'What with?'

'Don't they have emergency equipment?'

My friend suddenly leapt to his feet. 'Get the emergency equipment,' he screamed. His eyes were bulging, his neck was as thick as a treetrunk. He was white with rage. The pilot and co-pilot stopped immediately. The prayers ceased. The lady even stopped being sick. 'Get the axe!'

Everybody was screaming at once. Pilot and co-pilot ran and fell and scrambled to the back of the plane, practically vaulting the drinks trolley. There and back it must have taken them maybe two seconds, which struck me as odd because I always though time would drag in such circumstances. The axe split into the door like a knife through butter – designed by a locksmith rather than a security expert, I'm glad to say. Then – time started going slowly again – after what seemed like two hours and another ten miles of descent, they were at the controls and I swear, just as I began to see the whites of the eyes of market women on the outskirts of Assinie, the plane began to level out.

My friend was now sobbing gently into a big blue handker-chief. The lady in front was eating chocolates and playing with her headset. It was as if it had all been a dress rehearsal, which I suppose it had, and the performance was over.

We resumed our discussion about human rights, pretending nothing had happened. This was what haute travel was all about.

After a perfect landing at Abidjan, the pilot came on the intercom. 'Thank you for flying with us,' he said. 'We hope to see you again soon. Have a nice day.'

As soon as I had unloaded everything at the right hotel, I went straight back thirteen miles to Mbuyone, Mbane of my life. Mbabane to have a look around. A big modern city it is not. On the other hand, I've been to places in Africa a million times worse. It's got streets and pavements and buildings and office blocks and giant supermarkets and a Chinese embassy which practically dominates the place. And it's got all the legacies you would expect of the British: a fish and chip shop, piles of rubbish all over the place and a Chinese take-away. But for me the highlight was an office called Shylock Services. Now what on earth could they be selling? Or buying? And at what price?

But I didn't enjoy it. All the time I kept thinking of Royal Swazi, my luggage and then, you know what it's like, all the things you have to put up with from airlines.

The things they say to you ... 'Do you have a reservation?'

a broken-down crone at the check-in desk at Uzbechistan Airlines in Beijing said to me once. A reservation? I had a million reservations about flying Uzbechistan Airlines. But how the hell was I to get to Tashkent that night if I didn't fly Uzbechistan Airlines? By bicycle?

In East London, South Africa, we were once very curtly told, 'Will passengers for Johannesburg now kindly take leave of your family and friends and proceed to the departure area.'

Coming in to land at Prague, a voice came over the loudspeakers: 'Captain Honig and the crew would like to say goodbye to all passengers—' Goodbye? What does he mean, goodbye? '. . . and we would like to wish you all—' thud, the plane crashed down, thud, on the runway. The brakes screeched. Smoke came belching out from the wheels '. . . a pleasant stay. Have a nice day.'

And what abut the planes they force you to fly in? Like the fifty-year-old DC3s with their great big balloon tyres, ideal for rough landings, which you still see in parts of South America. Or the equally ancient YAK40s you see in Russia, with net curtains on the windows; not to mention the one-engine YAK18T, so named because you need not one but two sets of nine lives to even think of getting on board. Some planes I've been forced to fly in have been so old they've had outside toilets. Others have been so dangerous I reckon that if there was an emergency, instead of oxygen masks body bags would fall out of the compartments above our heads. That is, if the compartments actually opened.

And the ways they try to save money. Comair, the mini turbo-prop airline which serves many Delta connections in the US, has a wonderful sense of humour. Whenever I've flown with them they start up only one of their propellers to taxi out to the runway. The other one they start up when they are ready for take-off. Which is great fun, because every time I've seen them do it half a dozen people are pressing their call buttons and leaping up and down and making a big fuss because they think one of the engines isn't working. Not as much fun as an old Air Zimbabwe 707, though, which I was told refused to start at Mogadishu Airport one day and all 330 passengers had to get out and give it a push to get it going.

The best moneysavers of all, however, are Romanian Airlines. I once flew out of Bucharest to the Middle East when the pilot switched off three of the four engines to save fuel. Instead of taking three hours the flight took five hours. But, phew, at least we got there.

What they should do, I reckon, is give planes a fly-by date and, instead of all this nonsense about what's for lunch and which film they'll be showing, give you the fly-by date when you make your reservation. As well as the number of engines they plan to be using on your flight. I mean, is that important or is that important?

It's no wonder I feel closer to God on some airlines than on others.

Then the way they board you. Most airlines in Europe and the States board by seat rows. Which is stupid because you still get some fat old lady in row 10 blocking up the aisle for the 327 people sitting behind her. My idea? Board everybody by seat letters. All window seats first, then middle seats, then the aisle seats. Why don't they do it? Because it's sensible – and my idea. Outside Europe and the US, boarding is still pretty much the charge of the flight brigade. When I get back from a trip to the Far East, covered in bites and scratches and bruises, nobody believes me when I say I got them trying to board the plane. They come up with all kinds of exotic suggestions. But, I tell you, it's true.

Then when you get on board there is all this fuss about where you can and cannot put your briefcase. Will somebody please tell me why, if we're flying over nothing but land for fifteen hours, they make this big fuss about not putting your briefcase on the floor behind your legs because it will prevent you getting to your lifejacket. I mean, is that stupid or what?

That's not all. Once, flying into Sofia on British Airways, a stroppy hostess actually insisted that coming in to land I put the *Financial Times* into the pocket of the seat in front of me because reading it I was creating a safety hazard. I ask you!

The *Financial Times* a safety hazard! I guess people may have committed suicide as a result of what they have read in the *FT*, but a safety hazard? On board a plane?

The laugh is, other airlines couldn't care less. I've been on KLM flights in Indonesia where we were still looking for our seats as we were hurtling down the runway. Probably because the pilot couldn't wait to get the hell out of the place.

And the people they sit you next to. I've had them all; fat old ladies, fat old men, kids howling their heads off, nuns, Hare Krishna monks. I once flew out of Tokyo with a Japanese salaryman who ate sour satsumas the whole way back to London in order to, he kept telling me, kleep alake. Whether it worked I don't know. All I know is, when I woke up as we were coming into land the whole plane stank of oranges and I was covered with pips.

In India I was once jammed against a man who spent the flight nursing this enormous cardboard box containing a 21-inch television set. Which was bad enough, but he insisted on having a meal as well. On an overnight flight from Boston I was next to this guy who sat down in a business suit then, before the plane had even begun to move, stripped off and put on pyjamas. In Mexico, on a flight out of Merida, I found myself sitting between an elderly man and woman wearing some kind of traditional costume. The whole flight they spent petting and cuddling and talking to this life-size plastic doll smothered in silks and satin and lace – and passing it to each other in front of me. A million times I offered to change seats. But they said they didn't want to inconvenience me.

Flying out of Buffalo in the States I settled down, got out my papers. This economy-size Harrison Ford complete with hat sits next to me.

'Hi, I'm E seat,' he said.

'Hi,' I said. 'I'm F.'

Trouble was, he called me F for the whole flight. 'Say, F, what do you think of— Tell me, F buddy, what d'ya reckon . . . F, I must tell you, I just love your Australian accent . . .'

My worst experience? I'm on a flight from Dallas to Mexico

City. This long, leggy Texan blonde gets on. She looks as though she's a Jerry Hall clone. She's in the seat next to me. She no sooner sits down then she's all over me. Just bursting to tell me why I should become a Jehovah's Witness.

Then the announcements you get:

'If Bogotá is not your destination now is a good time to leave the aircraft.'

'We're just waiting for a couple of stranglers then we'll be off.'

'Hi, everybody. Just to tell you to settle in, fluff up your little nests and we'll soon have you all home with your loved ones.'

And what about the safety demonstrations? I once flew back tourist class from West Africa on UTA, which an American kept calling 'Hooter'. I was right at the back surrounded by a bunch of camel traders, witchdoctors, and worse still, children. But it was worth it. Somehow one of the French air hostesses, without doing anything different from what French air hostesses do every day of their lives, managed to turn the safety demonstration into the most fantastic cabaret turn I've ever seen. Not, of course, that I've seen many cabaret turns what with doing nothing but work, work, work. Don't ask me what she did. I couldn't tell you. All I know is when she said, 'To inflate the lifevest pull the two toggles downwards,' the whole plane was in uproar. And the whoops and screams and whistles that went on when she showed us how to inflate the lifevest further were unbelievable. I'd willingly surrender a couple of million air miles for a repeat performance – and I didn't see half of it because, you got it, sitting right in front of me was this fat lady with a kid.

The same thing happened all over again when we were coming in to land at Paris. The same girl got on the loudspeakers and promised to have everybody 'on the ground in a few minutes'.

Saturday, I thought I'd make my Royal Swazi Day. No, not Royal Swazi Airlines Day (see how they keep getting in on the act!); Royal Swazi Royal Family Day.

Now I'm not exactly your typical *Hello!* reader and I couldn't care less what Lady Di gets up to with whomever so long as she doesn't jam all the mobile telephone lines in the country, but I thought it might be fun to see the Royal Swazi palace, which is tucked away at the end of a non-Royal Swazi dust track behind a non-Royal Swazi school, the Royal Swazi Memorial Park and the Royal Swazi mausoleum. Especially the Royal Swazi mausoleum. (I wonder if *Hello!* would be interested in a feature on the Royal Swazi mausoleum? With a fixed smile on her lips staring intently ahead of her, Her Royal— No, maybe not. Too much like the real thing.)

But it was not to be. I got as far as the Royal Swazi game reserves. I saw a couple of broken-down Royal Swazi cattle, in a scruffy Royal Swazi field, a dead Royal Swazi pig by the side of the Royal Swazi road and I was off again. I just couldn't concentrate on anything. Not on the royal palace, nor on the royal courtiers, who as far as I could tell were all wandering around in red cloaks and those enormous white plastic trainers. Not on the Royal Swazi king's mother, who apparently is known as the Great She-Elephant of Swaziland and who protects him from everything but women. The poor exhausted man. And not even on any of his six wives. Instead I found myself all the time damning and cursing and swearing at airlines. I just couldn't help it.

First class, Marco Polo, business, club, world traveller (which, incidentally, I often think should be called third world traveller at first world prices). Scum class – that's at the very back next to the toilets. I've done them all. I've been in some first-class compartments so choked with cigarette smoke it almost took away the smell of the stale vomit bags under the seats. On the other hand I've been at the back of the bus where I've had so much space and so much champagne I didn't want to get off.

But wherever I sit I can guarantee you two things. First, the light in the panel above me will be broken, or if it's not, it will be pointing on the seat next to me, or halfway up the aisle, or out of the window – everywhere except down on me. To

391

finish writing my reports for the office I have to balance one foot on the armrest, the other on the headrest three rows in front and my writing pad in the middle of the aisle. You think that's bad. Once I was in row 307, seat M3 between the emergency exit and the toilets. The light, would you believe, was perfect. But could I do any work? No way. The light of the guy three seats in front on the left-hand side was shining right in my eyes.

Second, whatever interactive entertainment is going on will be going on without me, whether it's a movie, a television repeat, Sir David Frost interviewing the person he admires most in the whole world, Sir David Frost, Goon Show repeats, the sound of dolphins scratching themselves at the bottom of the Atlantic, or whatever is happening upstairs in Air France flights in the middle of the night. Somehow, whichever airline I'm on, whichever programme is on, it's never on at whatever seat I'm in. Either the dial has come off or the push buttons don't work or the whole panel is hanging out of the arm rest. Except ... except ... The only things I ever get caught up in are those crazy American inflight aerobic programmes. For some reason, I'm always the one they pick on to lead the pack. And of course, when I pretend I'm from Darkest Mongolia, don't speak English and if they come a step closer I'll open the emergency door, they get irritable and sulk and accuse me of spoiling everyone's fun. Once on a North West flight out of Minneapolis, I refused to join in and nobody spoke to me for the whole flight. It was wonderful.

Then there's the airline magazine. I can guarantee that wherever I sit somebody will have taken the airline magazine out of the seat pocket in front of me, although I'm not so worried now I'm going backwards and forwards to Eastern Europe. On a flight to Tashkent I opened the Uzbechistan Airlines magazine. There in front of me was a big picture and a profile of the Uzbech national football team. Which they proudly proclaimed had been completely wiped out in a plane crash a few years earlier. On another occasion – mid-summer, I forget where – I opened the in-flight magazine to discover the director-general of the airline wishing us all a Happy New Year and telling us that his earnest wish for the next twelve months was that 'the number of take-offs be equal to the number of landings'. Thank you, comrade. I shall certainly make a note to fly with you in future.

One of the biggest in-flight magazine bloomers I've come across was in our very own British Airways organ, *High Life*. 'Two flights on Club World to New York', it waxed, 'could give you and your partner the chance to stroll through the Arab bazaars of Casablanca.' Arab bazaars of Casablanca! Now there's an airline that knows where it's going. I only hope they don't let the pilots read the magazine, otherwise we could be in big trouble.

Oh, yes, I forgot. The dead royal Swazi pig by the side of the road. It was practically fully grown. It looked as though it had been hit by a car and then kicked to the side of the ... Did I ever tell you about the time I got on this plane in Africa? There were live pigs running around all over the place. People were sleeping on the floor. At least I think they were sleeping. Groups of pilgrims on their way back from Mecca were squatting at the back by the toilets around a primus stove brewing their tiny glasses of tea. And nobody said a word.

Which brings me – God help us – to the fare or, I suppose, the unfair necessities of life: those horrible lumps of pathetic plastic nothingness and axle grease. In other words, airline food and drink. I've had so many truly awful airline meals I don't like bringing them up. If you see what I mean. Those small bowls of cherries that taste like ball bearings marinated in jet fuel. That curly sandwich with the fungus on top. That square of white cake that tasted like wallpaper paste. Those tiny little cartons of ... of ... of, well, vomit. I just can't describe it any other way.

Awful they might have been. But at least you could recognise what they were. Well, roughly. The worst thing of all is eating something and then discovering it's not what you think it is. On one flight out of Oslo, I was busy tucking into my fish when an announcement came over the loudspeakers:

'Confession I have to make. When I took the fish out of the ovens to me evident it was, it was not fish. Wish you to change your preferences for wine.' No matter how many times I asked, to this day I have no idea what I was eating. Probably a puffin suffering from foot-and-beak disease.

Air China have a nice idea. Once flying into Shanghai I had a Mongolian fried chicken leg, a whirly bun with tiny lumps of meat scattered around inside it and the thinnest slice of angel cake, all washed down with coffee served by one of the warders, oops, I mean hostesses, straight from an old iron kettle. It was the only plane I've been on where I had to ask for an extension before I could fasten my seatbelt. Which obviously says everything for their standard of cuisine. But for all that they also gave us a tiny little roll which tasted remarkably like the tiny little cardboard box it came in. Inside it – the box, not the roll – was a tiny heart-shaped piece of paper on which was printed the name of the person who prepared it all. In my case it was Sony Dei Tjoh Tjae. Now if every airline did that just think of the correspondence it would generate – from lawyers.

But, now I think about it, the worst thing I reckon I've ever, ever had was on a flight out of Boston. I was given this tiny carton of jam. Not having anything to watch – remember what I said about the movies never working in my seat – I read the label. 'Imitation grape jelly,' it said. 'Artificially flavoured. Low calorie. No sugar added. Low sodium. Fat free. Use of this product may be hazardous to your health. This product contains saccharin which has been determined to cause cancer in laboratory animals.'

Quick, quick, pass the sick bag. I'm going to throw up. Then I'm going to call my lawyer.

The other thing that gets me about airlines – now this is revolutionary stuff – is, why can't they serve the wine at the same time as the food? Not as you're getting off the plane. Not as you're queuing up at passport control. Not as you're climbing into a taxi. I mean, how difficult is it?

I don't think I've yet been on a plane, especially BA Deutsch, when the wine has arrived with the food. I've tried asking for the wine when they serve the watery Coke and stale packets of peanuts; asking for two bottles instead of one on the basis that they only ever get anything half right so I should be all right. Mein Gott, I've even offered to buy the stuff. The only reason I can think is that either the airlines are trying to cut costs, or the hostesses are so busy satisfying their appetites whenever they land, they've never had time to go to a halfway decent restaurant to see how the job should be done properly.

The only time I actually asked for a bottle of wine while I was still eating was on a Lufthansa flight from Vilnius in Lithuania to Frankfurt. The – careful now – hostess gave me a glass of apple juice and when I happened to – I mean, I dared to – point it out she actually shouted back at me, 'Something is wrong mit the brain, ja? You not like German apfel juice?' Honestly, I'm not kidding. That's what she said.

In places like India, parts of the Middle East, the Far East, it's the other way round. I don't mean they serve the wine before the meal. I wish they did. I mean instead of wine they serve water or fruit juice and still it comes after the meal is over.

The only person I've ever come across who mastered the system was a Japanese bank manager I knew years ago in Africa. Wherever he went he took his faithful tea caddy; except inside the tea caddy he had his own booze: wine, whisky, whisky and still more whisky. As soon as he sat down, he was off. If you see what I mean.

The best airline meal I've ever had? It's got to be the one we had flying over Mount Kilimanjaro when for the third time we developed engine trouble. To keep our mind off things, I shall never forget it, they served us great dollops of baked beans – cold – straight from a tin the size of a dustbin, with the help of a dirty great wooden spoon and splodged in the middle of a dirty bit of cardboard. To clean the spoon, after every few helpings the air hostess would ... would ... would ... But at least we landed safely at Nairobi. And ahead of time as well. Because of what the pilot described as 'the strong winds following after us'.

Oops, going on about airlines again. When I came to, I was passing the Chinese Handicraft Mission and a sign pointing to a health and beauty spa called Cuddle Puddle. What happened to the royal Swazi pig I couldn't tell you.

On my last day I had to go to Manzini, the pre-Boer War capital. Which sounds wonderfully Italian, and as if it's full of bars, restaurants, opera houses. But it isn't.

'Don't go there,' everybody kept telling me. 'It's full of robbers.' Which it isn't either. At least not compared to some merchant banks I know.

It's a top-of-the-second-division African city. Or rather town. It's got all the basics, some smart shops and stores, a passable old-fashioned faded English hotel, the new St George, where for breakfast everybody, guests, staff, waiters, even the chef, sits mesmerised in the dining room watching old Hollywood cops-and-robbers films on the television on the shelf in the corner. An average film and you might get a coffee that tastes of axle grease. A good film and you won't get even that until it's over. But I didn't care. All the time I was sitting there plotting the downfall of Royal You-Know-Who Airlines.

I wandered out of the dining room. The waiters were so busy watching television they didn't ask me to pay. The girl on reception was watching the television. She didn't ask me to pay. It was wonderful. Long live old Hollywood movies.

Hollywood, wait a minute, that reminds me. United States ... American Airlines ... American Airlines must have some of the oldest crews in the history of aviation. They're so old I often think AA should be renamed Alzheimers' Airline. I once got a flight from Atlanta. The cabin attendant, as they call them, was so old I reckon he handed out cans of Coke and packets of peanuts to Alcock and Brown. The only way he could make it down the aisle was to be passed from one passenger to the next the length of the aircraft. And in a case of emergency he is going to assume control and tell us all what to do! As for the air hostesses, I'm not saying they were old. It's just that it was a long time since anyone could have wanted to be grounded with them in the middle of nowhere.

American Eagle crews, on the other hand, don't seem to have problems walking. Their problem seems to be with their teeth. Talking to any air hostess on American Eagle is like trying to have a conversation with somebody behind iron bars. Some of them have so much metal around their teeth it would take an airport metal detector a month to cool down after they'd walked through it.

As for Texan Southwest Airlines, all their planes are painted like whales, presumably because they give everyone a whale of a time. On the plane I got not only were all the hostesses wearing hotpants, they also insisted that safety regulations said they had to check the lockers before take-off. This meant, because they couldn't reach the lockers themselves, we had to stand up so they could clamber on to the seats to make certain they were closed. Not one person complained. Probably because it was a whole lot more interesting than flying Japanese Airlines and being served with a glass of Coke and a packet of peanuts by a girl wearing Minnie Mouse ears.

Oops, I'm wandering again. I'm sorry about that. It's just that, well, you know, Royal Swazi somehow keeps chewing me up and I can't concentrate. Now where was I? Oh, yes, Manzini. Which sounds like a bundle of Italian laughs – and isn't. I can remember going down this street and seeing a poster in a window saying 'Happy Birthday Your Majesty'. Obviously put there by one of the 300 royal chiefs or families.

. . . Then there was this girl on South African Airlines who gave me a glass of Chardonnay. 'It's not very cold,' she said. 'Would you like me to put ice in it?' And the girl on British Airways who was pouring out coffee and telling everybody, 'The milk is behind me' until the guy next to me said, 'That's an interesting place to keep it,' and we never saw her again for the rest of the flight.

As for Singapore girls, everyone has their favourite Singapore girl story. Mine is being stuck on a plane at Cape Town while they tried to work out how many meals they wanted to take on for the flight. Tourist was easy. It was full. Business, or whatever they call it, was more difficult.

'We've got seventeen already. We need another five. That's twenty-one,' the head Singapore girl kept saying.

'No, it's twenty,' number two Singapore girl kept saying.

The South African catering guy is standing there waiting to be told how many damn meals they want. Twenty-one, they finally agree. He gives them twenty-one. And, of course, I'm the one who has to go without.

'The trouble is dealing with Africans,' head Singapore girl smiled her Singapore smile at me. 'Why can't they learn to speak English properly?'

Oops, straying off the point again. That's the trouble once I get an idea into my head.

I wandered back to the new St George Hotel. Still everybody was watching television. Still nobody asked me for any money. I decided to get a taxi back to my hotel in Mb – what's the name of the place, Mb – I wrote it down somewhere. Mb – why did you make me lose that bit of paper? The only way the driver could start the engine was by putting the handbrake on, then driving with one hand on the wheel and the other flashing between the gearstick and the handbrake. But it made no difference to me. I don't know why, but as we dawdled past this road to Matsapa, I suddenly thought of the only person I know who has ever got the better of an airline. This was your typical free-wheeling, big-spending, head-office type, who had more platinum cards then I've had lousy airline meals. I'm not saying he's extravagant; but his personal travel and entertainment expenses regularly beat the total travel and entertainment expenses of a string of companies he controls, each employing 100 to 200 people.

He was settling down into his first-class seat on his regular Cathay Pacific flight out of Hong Kong one evening on his way back to London. The flight was full and the crew began their up-grading. This guy had just been given some Cathay Pacific award for being one of their best customers, so the top-dog steward crawled up to him on his hands and knees and did his usual party piece. The flight was full. There was an empty seat next to him. They were going to up-grade somebody from business class. Would it be all right if he sat next to him? Would he like another glass of . . .

'No,' the guy said, it would not be all right. He was a platinum card holder. He had just been given this award for spending enough money with Cathay Pacific to enable them to buy a new fleet of 747s. The last thing he wanted sitting next to him was some grubby up-grade from business class.

'But, but,' the steward spluttered. Please, if he would like another glass of champagne. Please, he was very sorry, he apologised profusely. But, please, the plane was full. He understood his feelings, but it was an up-grade from business class, not, Heaven forbid, from tourist. Was he sure he didn't want another glass of—?

'No,' the guy persisted. He had paid first-class prices for a first-class service. He was damned if he was going to sit next to someone who had not paid first-class prices but would receive first-class service.

By now he was surrounded by the captain, the vice-captain, the purser, the deputy purser and half the crew.

'Ahaaa,' said the captain, in a stroke of genius. Would he object if another first-class passenger sat next to him? He would after all be a fellow first-class passenger, paying first-class prices for first-class services.

'No, of course not,' the guy said. He did not want to be unreasonable. It was just a matter of principle. Naturally he wanted to do anything he could to help. And if it happened to be the slinky blonde in the backless top sitting up front, so much the better.

The crew fell upon every passenger in the first-class cabin. Would they . . .? If they could consider . . .? It would be a great help . . . Show our appreciation . . . I'm sure Head Office will . . .

Everyone said no. Especially the slinky blonde in the backless top. There was no way any of them wanted to be stuck for hours with a troublemaker. In any case, they had all been allocated their seats, and were occupying them. Why the hell should they move?

What did the guy do? Did he swallow his puffed-up pride? Did he back down? Did he hell!

'In that case,' he announced, to the whole crew and the entire first-class cabin, 'I'll catch another plane.' And he promptly collected his briefcases and marched off the plane. Which, you can imagine, created even more of an uproar. All the paperwork had to be re-opened and re-completed. Worse still, they had to open the hold and get his luggage out. In the end, the plane left an hour and ten minutes late.

The guy? He caught a British Airways flight that was about to leave and arrived in London two hours before the Cathay Pacific flight. He had his luggage sent on after him.

My last day in Swaziland. Ever.

When I checked in with Royal Swazi Smash-your-suitcase-to-pieces-and-to-hell-with-it Airlines, there was six inches of ice all over the place. Epaulettes was chill, Chill, CHILL. And when I heaped the thirty-seven items of hand luggage that made up my suitcase on the check-in desk, what did the girl say?

'Next time you fly, we hope you'll choose to fly Royal Swazi Airlines again.'

No way, Royal Swazi Airlines. No way. That's one for each of their two planes.